FAKES

by
OTTO KURZ

Second Revised and Enlarged Edition

DOVER PUBLICATIONS, INC.

NEW YORK

This Dover edition, first published in 1967,
is a revised and enlarged version of the work
originally published in 1948 by Yale University Press.

Library of Congress Catalog Card Number: 67-28921

Manufactured in the United States of America
Dover Publications, Inc.
180 Varick Street
New York, N. Y. 10014

PREFACE TO THE DOVER EDITION

This book was first published in English in 1948 and then translated into Italian in 1961. The present work is a new version and not a mere reprint, as I have corrected a number of textual and typographical errors and have brought the bibliographical notes up to date. In addition, I have added a new Appendix which contains additional information and deals specifically with forgeries which became known after 1948, especially the false Vermeer paintings of Han van Meegeren and the pseudo-medieval German wall paintings. The present edition contains 142 plates, whereas the original had but 95.

It is a pleasant task to thank Mr. Hayward Cirker for his encouragement, kindness and patience, and the editorial staff of Dover Publications for their careful work which helped to improve this book in many ways. I also wish to express my admiration for the anonymous 'magicians' at Dover who are able to produce a photographic facsimile while at the same time allowing the author to correct mistakes which were overlooked many years ago.

London
August, 1966

OTTO KURZ

PREFACE TO THE FIRST EDITION

Throughout this book the word 'fake' is used in a wider sense than usual. Besides outright forgeries, it has been made to cover works of art which have been tampered with in various ways: spurious alterations, the signature of a famous artist added fraudulently or—the reverse procedure—the signature of a minor master removed in order to pass off a picture as the work of some famous painter—all deceits of this sort surely had to be included in a survey of forgeries.

A good deal of the existing literature on fakes is disappointing. Eudel's well-known book is a collection of highly entertaining and wittily told stories, but they bear, for the most part, little or no relation to facts. Other writers confine themselves to warnings which are wise but trite: they tell us that collectors should buy at reliable dealers, ask for a guarantee of authenticity, avoid the small curio-shops of fashionable resorts and so forth.

There are no general rules for the detection of fakes. Each case has to be studied on its own merits. A book on forgeries must necessarily be an enumeration of single instances. There is, however, one comfort for the student and collector: each detected forgery is apt to betray a whole group. Fakes hunt in packs, they are rarely made as unique specimens, and the fabrications of the same workshop wear a distinct family likeness. Once one has seen several works by the same hand the individual style of the forger is revealed, and after that it is comparatively easy to assign their proper place to fresh specimens of the same group as they turn up.

Works of art—including forgeries—cannot be described in words. They have to be seen, if not in the original then at least in reproduction. This book is confined to forgeries of which a reproduction is on record. As the illustrations are perforce limited in number, I have endeavoured to give copious references to reproductions, one or other of which should be accessible in any large art library.

The question will be asked: Can a forgery be distinguished from an original in a photograph? The answer is that though photographs of the original and the imitation may in many cases look deceptively alike, especially where the main difference lies in colour or surface texture, the essential marks of the forgery frequently show up even in a black-and-white illustration. I have tried to keep my illustrations to examples of this kind.

The selection of forgeries has been restricted by yet another consideration. In a book of this type the forgeries taken as typical had to be acknowledged forgeries, i.e. forgeries not only in the author's opinion but by general consent. The fakes discussed here have been declared spurious, in practically all cases in print, by some competent and eminent authority. There are no new 'revelations' but the reader will, I hope, be compensated by the fact that the opinions offered are more than personal opinions.[1]

Although I have long been interested in forgeries and have been collecting notes for a number of years, I could not have written this book without much help and advice generously given by many people. My chief debt is to Dr. Leo Planiscig who, with the greatest liberality, put his photographic archive at my disposal. Dr. Ernst Kris did the same with his unique collection of photographs of goldsmiths' work. In 1937 Dr. Planiscig and Dr. Kris arranged an exhibition of forgeries at the Kunsthistorisches Museum of Vienna. This exhibition stimulated and helped me in my own enquiries and I offer them both my heartiest thanks.

I also wish to thank all those who have helped me in various ways, advised on special problems, allowed me to examine forgeries or have given permission for the illustration of pieces from their own collections; particularly Professor Tancred Borenius, Mr. Wolfgang Burchard, Sir Kenneth Clark, Professor William Cohn, Sir Percival David, Mr. E. P. Goldschmidt, Dr. E. H. Gombrich, Mr. Basil Gray, Dr. Hans D. Gronau, Dr. F. Grossmann, Dr. Jacob Hess, Mr. W. B. Honey, Dr. Paul Jacobsthal, Dr. Betty Kurth, Mr. Denis Mahon, Professor L. A. Mayer, Dr. E. G. Millar, Mr. Charles Mitchell, Dr. Ludwig Münz, Dr.

1. To avoid misunderstandings it should be noted that the names of authors quoted in the footnotes refer to the scholars who exposed the fakes in question, not to those who published them as originals.

Carl Nordenfalk, Dr. Otto Pächt, Mr. A. E. Popham, Mr. Bernard Rackham, Dr. Grete Ring, Mr. Albrecht Rosenthal, Mr. Helmut Ruhemann, Professor F. Saxl, Dr. Alfred Scharf, Dr. Hanns Swarzenski, Professor Daniel V. Thompson, Mr. Ellis K. Waterhouse and Mr. Francis Wormald.

I owe a special debt which I can never discharge to Elizabeth Senior and Dr. Hermann Burg. Elizabeth Senior, whose early death in the blitz was so grave a loss to scholarship, encouraged and helped me from the day I started on this book, read and corrected the first draft and drew my attention to many interesting forgeries. Dr. Burg gave me all the advantage of his learning and wide practical experience. Always on the look-out for forgeries, he drew my attention to everything of interest which turned up in the art market or in the sale room.

Finally, I have to thank the Trustees of the British Museum, the Director of the Victoria and Albert Museum and the Curator and Trustees of the Lady Lever Art Gallery for permission to reproduce objects from their collections.

CONTENTS

ILLUSTRATIONS

PART ONE

PAINTING

PART ONE

PAINTING

Painting was not only the first of the graphic arts to receive systematic study, it also enjoys by far the largest place in public and private collections, as well as in literature. The turnover of the picture market is about as great if not greater than that of all other arts and crafts taken together. This would lead one to expect that the number of faked pictures would at least equal that of all other kinds of fakes. But surprisingly enough there exist comparatively fewer fakes of pictures than of sculptures, not to mention products of craftsmanship.

This state of things becomes explicable if we consider the enormous supply of pictures, which is almost as large as the demand. For though the countless old pictures that turn up from all sides hardly correspond to the kind of picture which is really sought for, such small defects can easily be remedied. Touching up of various kinds, and above all the simple method of affixing a famous name—complete with an expert's certificate—to some obscure picture, are much easier to achieve than complete forgeries. These old pictures, without quality, frequently little more than wretched ruins, and covered by over-zealous restorations, flood the picture market.

SCIENTIFIC METHODS OF EXAMINING PICTURES

For many years attempts have been made to emancipate the examination of pictures from aesthetic standards. Accordingly several scientific methods have been developed. They offer most valuable help to the student, and have become indispensable to the restorer by rendering the structure of paintings visible to a degree far beyond the power of the unaided eye. But though the spuriousness of a picture may occasionally be proved by an X-ray photograph or by the chemical analysis of pigments, there is no scientific test by which to establish its genuineness. Many false pictures can pass all scientific tests. No available method of scientific analysis allows us to dispense with sound and unprejudiced judgment, based on comparison and experience and above all on the correct assessment of the artistic qualities of the picture in question.

Microchemical Analysis of Colours.

Already in the early nineteenth century laboratories had taken up the analysis of colours scratched off old or allegedly old pictures. But comparatively large particles were needed to enable the scientist to make an analysis. The advantages of such a proceeding were therefore rather dubious, as the removal of a sufficient amount of colour entailed serious damages to the painting under examination. Nowadays this drawback has been disposed of by the microscope. The prick of a hypodermic needle provides all that microchemistry requires. Care must be taken, however, to avoid getting the samples from restored parts of the picture.

The usefulness of the analysis of colours is based on our knowledge of the various pigments used by the painters of different periods.[1] Thus neither Prussian blue nor zinc white were used before the eighteenth century. Synthetic ultramarine, cobalt blue and cadmium yellow are inventions of the nineteenth century. About twenty years ago a 'Laughing Cavalier' allegedly by Frans Hals gave rise to a dispute in the Dutch law courts.[2] Although one of the most famous authorities on Dutch painting attested its authenticity, the modern origin of the picture could be proved beyond doubt by the chemical analysis of the colours. Synthetic

1. A. M. De Wild, *The Scientific Examination of Pictures* (1929), gives a useful 'chronological chart of pigments'. D. V. Thompson, *The Materials of Medieval Painting* (1936), is the standard work on the subject. For a complete bibliography see *Gentsche Bijdragen tot de Kunstgeschiedenis*, vol. 8 (1942), pp. 37 sqq.
2. See p. 59.

ultramarine, cobalt blue and zinc white, all unknown in the time of Frans Hals, were found. This settled the dispute.

In certain circumstances chemical analysis may prove the spuriousness of a picture but it can never establish its authenticity and age. There exists no pigment which could not easily be procured today even if it is no longer in general use. A famous instance is the presence of archil, a dye prepared from certain lichens, in the 'Flora' bust. This coloured wax bust was acquired in 1909 for the Berlin Museum as a unique work of Leonardo da Vinci.[3] While the newspapers of the world were still praising Bode's incomparable flair, a letter published in *The Times* caused general stupefaction. The writer pointed out that he knew the bust to be the work of a half-forgotten English sculptor Richard Cockle Lucas (1800–83). His son, Albert Dürer Lucas, confirmed this, adding that as a young man he helped his father to make the wax bust. A London dealer had brought a Leonardesque painting of Flora to Lucas and had asked him to copy it in wax. This was the true origin of 'The Flora of Leonardo'. This should have settled the question but Bode and many others remained unconvinced. They no longer regarded Leonardo as the author of the bust but insisted that it must be a work of the sixteenth century, and as such it remained on exhibition in the Kaiser Friedrich Museum. One of the arguments advanced in its favour was the presence of archil, said to have been completely unknown after the sixteenth century. In 1937 an ardent defender of the 'Flora' regarded this still as conclusive proof of the genuineness of the bust.[4] He ignored that T. von Frimmel discussing the 'Flora' in 1911 had proved that archil was easily obtainable then and must have been available in London around 1846.[5]

X-ray Photographs.

X-rays are absorbed in varying degrees by the different pigments composing the paint-layer of a picture. The shadows

3. The literature is extensive; the best accounts of the history of the 'Flora' are found in S. Reinach, *Amalthée*, vol. 2 (1930), pp. 426 sqq., and G. Pauli, *Belvedere*, 10. Jg. (1931), pp. 1 sqq.

4. A. Donath, *Wie die Kunstfälscher arbeiten* (1937), p. 43.

5. Frimmel, *Blätter für Gemäldekunde,* vol. 6 (1911), p. 20.

appearing on the negative exposed to the rays directly behind the picture help in the study of certain aspects of its structure, and the varying degrees to which the priming and pigments absorb the X-rays give hints regarding the chemical composition of the picture; e.g. colours containing lead offer considerable resistance to the rays.

More important is the fact that pigments concealed under the surface of a painting may reveal themselves on the X-ray photograph, and shapes and outlines that remain invisible to the naked eye can be detected in this way.[6] Consequently the shadowgraph may help in the detection of fakes, in cases where spurious pictures have been painted over badly preserved or less pleasing genuine ones.

Thus a portrait of Edward VI (1537–53) was painted over the portrait of a Dutch girl, painted in the seventeenth century (*Plate* 1).[7] The girl's face was used for the sterner features of the young king, but it was painted over and extended by a domed Tudor forehead. Her large starched collar was altered into a smaller one of more fanciful cut. The carnation she held in her hand became a dagger. Her full skirt was narrowed and cut off below the knees to make place for the princely legs. Sixteenth-century ornaments, a feathered beret, and the royal coat of arms completed the change. To make these extensive alterations the picture had to be entirely repainted. Its quality did not improve in the process. The picture of the girl was probably no masterpiece, but it was a genuine and competent piece of painting. Edward VI is stiff and disproportionate, and would look nicer if his misshapen legs were hidden beneath the skirts of the little girl he obliterates.

6. A Burroughs, *Art Criticism from a Laboratory* (1938). J. Rawlins, *From the National Gallery Laboratory* (1940).

7. The painting is in the Victoria and Albert Museum. The Edward VI trick was performed twice over. The second time a Dutch portrait of a lady was used, face and hands were taken over almost unchanged, while her bodice was enlarged to form the royal waistcoat, and her chain and cuffs were also incorporated in Edward's costume. Cf. C. H. Collins Baker, 'Faking a King', in *The Connoisseur*, vol. 92 (1933), pp. 161 sqq. On the perpetrators of these forgeries—E. Holder and P. E. Zincke—see below, p. 73.

Occasionally the shadowgraph may help us to recognise spurious alterations in pictures. Professor Puyvelde describes an interesting case from the Museum of Brussels.[8] A flower garland by Daniel Seghers had an all too pretty portrait of Hélène Fourment as its centre-piece. It was suspicious because flower wreaths usually surround religious scenes. X-ray photographs confirmed the doubt: they revealed the outlines of the Virgin and the white linen of the cradle. Neither the adoring angels nor Saint Joseph were missing from the composition. Consequently the picture was cleaned, a process which removed the features of Rubens's second wife with lightning rapidity and revealed the original composition in a complete state of preservation. It had been covered by a more alluring subject.

Ultra-violet Light.

The mercury-vapour lamp is unable to detect fakes but it shows up patchings and repaints by differences in fluorescence. Thus the actual state of preservation may be ascertained; but this does not apply if the whole surface of the picture has been repainted. Some varnishes render this examination impossible, as they become fluorescent in ultra-violet light. On the other hand, illegible signatures may frequently be read under the mercury lamp.[9]

Photomicrographs.

The use of greatly enlarged photographs of small portions of pictures in order to render visible the minute details of an artist's brushwork was invented by Mr. A. P. Laurie.[10] To be able to see how the single strokes of the brush follow upon one another is a near approach to seeing the artist at work in his studio. Certainly the brushwork of some painters is highly personal and may help

8. 'L'Application de la radiographie aux tableaux', in *Journal de la Radiographie et d'Electrologie,* vol. 17 (1933), pp. 83 sqq. *Apollo,* vol. 21 (1935), p. 19.

9. J. J. Rorimer, *Ultra-violet Rays and Their Use in the Examination of Works of Art* (1931), pp. 46 sqq.

10. A. P. Laurie, *The Brushwork of Rembrandt and His School* (1932); *New Light on Old Masters* (1935), pp. 139 sqq. M. L. Hairs, *Revue belge d'archéologie et d'histoire de l'art,* vol. 26 (1957), p. 162.

to distinguish an original from a copy which perfectly resembles it. But though it may be characteristic, an artist's way of painting is not constant. His brushwork changes with his evolution— the design, expression, and colouring of a whole picture remain a safer guide than a few strokes of paint.

The measuring of the refractory index of the oil film is another invention by Mr. Laurie.[11] It is intended to determine the age of the medium employed in painting, but no definite results have been obtained up to now by this method.

The study of the imprint of the artist's fingers on pictures has been much advertised as a means of identification, but nothing has ever come of it.

MECHANICAL TESTS AND THEIR CIRCUMVENTION

Hardening of Colours.

One of the most common tests made to ascertain a picture's age is to prick its surface with a pin. If the paint is new the pin will stick in its soft surface, if it is old it will slip on its glassy hardness. But by heating the oil film may be considerably hardened, and moreover many fakes are now well over a hundred years old and have acquired a sufficient degree of solidity to resist the pin.

The second method is the spirit-test. Old colours are difficult to dissolve in alcohol, while fresh colours come off with a moistened swab. This method is as dangerous as all 'hard' cleaning, in case the dubious picture may turn out to be an original after all. Many artists mixed their glazes with varnish or other resinous substances which rapidly dissolve in alcohol, leaving the picture in a sadly denuded state.[12] Forgers, moreover, have found a means to defy this test. They lay a thin coating of size over their picture between colour and varnish. As this is invisible as well as insoluble in alcohol it may well deceive, unless the size is discovered by chemical reaction.[13] Notwithstanding these

11. A. P. Laurie, *New Light on Old Masters* (1935), p. 134.

12. M. Doerner, *The Materials of the Artist* (1935), p. 377.

13. A. P. Laurie, *New Light on Old Masters* (1935), pp. 148, 160. See also below, pp. 56 and 60, and on the method of H. van Meegeren, p. 329.

drawbacks and dangers, an oil-painting of which a large part comes off at the first contact with a weak alcoholic solvent may be regarded as modern.

Cracks.

Cracks are a frequent and disagreeable defect of pictures damaging both to their aesthetic appearance and to their state of preservation. Yet many of those who feel attracted by old pictures tend to forget that the crackling of their surface does not endow them with any of that added charm which patina gives to bronzes or the intentional crackling of the glaze to Chinese porcelain. Cracks occur when a picture is subjected to bad treatment or when the layer of paint and priming becomes too stiff to follow the distension and contraction of panel or canvas.

According to chemical composition and the varying influence of atmosphere and temperature, the varnish alone may crackle so that the damage may be removed with it, or the paint itself may have been affected, or lastly the priming may break up and produce cracks which tear through painting and varnish.[14]

The width of cracks is by no means a measure of their age. The deepest furrows appear on some eighteenth- and nineteenth-century pictures which were painted with unsuitable material. Worse cracks may be caused by strong heat than by centuries free from accidents or ill treatment. Notwithstanding these considerations, cracks are widely regarded as the supreme indication of a picture's genuineness, and therefore forgers have devised various means of producing genuine and impeccable specimens.[14a]

Some advise the baking of the pictures: the finished picture is first heated and then exposed to a low temperature, so that the paint cannot follow the swift contraction of panel or canvas. Others prefer to use 'antique' varnish, a patent device guaranteed to crackle the surface of every picture on which it is applied by its abnormal faculty of contracting while drying. A still simpler means consists of covering the picture with a coating of glue before the varnish has had time to dry. The stiffening of the glue breaks up the surface of the paint, and it is removed after it is dry

14. T. v. Frimmel, *Handbuch der Gemäldekunde* (1920), pp. 115 sqq. A. P. Laurie, *New Light on Old Masters* (1935), pp. 120 sqq.

14a. On the old and still used method of rolling the canvas see p. 37.

and has done its duty. As fresh cracks are almost invisible they are filled with soot or grey colour.

Icilio Federico Joni, the Italian painter, restorer, and forger, who has enriched literature by an amusing and elucidating autobiography, recommends various methods probably not used by him alone. I quote some of his technical hints. Though no one could expect a craftsman to divulge his major secrets, he seems to be fairly straightforward in what he says, and even where he tries to conceal his meaning, it may easily be read between the lines. 'On a piece of linen-canvas, not too coarse (in fact muslin was the best for the purpose), you applied several layers of gesso for gilding, thick enough to make it of the same consistency as the early painters used in preparing their panels, and to allow the gold to be burnished where it has to appear as background or decoration. The canvas is then wrapped round a roller, and rolled this way and that, until the proper crackle is obtained. When the painting itself had been done already, the following was found an even better method. We first damped the painting, and then with a pointed instrument indicated all the cracks as we wished them to appear, not on the front, but on the back of the canvas; and then by rolling the canvas backwards, we made the cracks open up on the front, just where we wanted them. After that the canvas was stuck on to an old panel with strong glue, and the illusion was almost perfect.'[15]

To distinguish all these different kinds of artificial cracks from their natural prototypes is not easy. It is true that paint on panels cracks parallel to the fibre of the wood, while canvas cracks usually issue from a central point, with outlines resembling the tissue of a spider's web; but forgers know this at least as well as anybody else. If one wishes to be sure about a picture one should find safer ways than to rely on the examination of the pattern formed by its cracks. Though they are often very cleverly made, the patterns of cracks effected by attacking the picture's surface with a pointed instrument may be recognised more easily by their uniformity. Cracks painted on a picture cannot escape the magnifying glass, though they may well be so cleverly made that they defy the naked eye. These two methods are employed by restorers who

15. Joni, *The Affairs of a Painter* (1936), p. 297.

wish to give their work unity with the unrestored parts of a picture. Painted or incised craquelure covering only single portions of a picture may usually be ascribed to their activities.

Other Damages.

The damaging of their own work to destroy its revealing freshness is very usual with forgers who specialise in the production of 'primitives'. Sometimes whole portions of the painting and gilding are scratched off, including the gesso, but even if the forger inflicts large-scale damage on his work, he never ventures to destroy any essential parts of it. He would never for instance touch a face. As time and the elements are liable to be less considerate, this psychological symptom may occasionally be conclusive.

Particularly clever forgers damage the 'primitives' they have just painted and proceed then to 'restore' their own work, in order to put it above suspicion. For a visibly restored picture is to-day what a cracked picture was some years ago. The restorations are accepted as a certificate. Joni mentions a simple way of achieving the desired effect of wear and tear: 'After applying the spirit varnish, and letting it dry well, I gave it the additional patina, which had to lie on the surface like a thin film of dust; I then dipped a small wad of cotton wool in spirit and lightly wiped it over the surface of the painting, so as to destroy its uniformity. In certain parts the spirit worked more strongly than in others, and the effect was rather deceptive.'[16]

Fly-spots are another sign of age which is readily produced by forgers, as it seems to have a favourable effect on some of their dupes. Joni, whose customers appear to have been particularly keen on the fly-blown touch, gives two recipes: 'I tried my hand for the first time at imitating the fly-blown effect of the original surface. I mixed some colour of about the right tone, and taking a brush with a rather stiff bristle dipped in this, I sprinkled it over the surface by tapping the brush with my finger,' and he adds: 'the illusion, if not perfect, was quite good enough for those days.' Later on he developed a more refined method: 'We got the fly-

16. Joni, *The Affairs of a Painter*, p. 180.

blown effect with a pointed stick, dipped in fairly solid paint of the right colour, which produced a most lifelike result.'[17]

EARLY FORGERIES

To the End of the Seventeenth Century.

The beginnings of picture-faking go back to the fifteenth century but in these early stages the borderline dividing imitations and fakes is not yet clearly defined.

Pietro Summonte records in 1524[18] that Colantonio, the Neapolitan painter who flourished in the middle of the fifteenth century, was a pastmaster in the imitation of Flemish painting which stood in high esteem in the time of King René of Anjou. Among the examples of deceptive imitation achieved by Colantonio quoted by Pietro Summonte, the affair of the portrait of Charles, Duke of Burgundy is the most revealing: 'It so happened that a very well done portrait of Charles, Duke of Burgundy, was brought from Flanders. Colantonio managed to borrow this portrait from the merchant to whom it belonged. He copied it with such exactitude that one picture could not be distinguished from the other, and returned to the owner not the original but his own version. The merchant did not doubt that he had his own Flemish picture till Colantonio revealed his successful trick.'

There is no evidence that Colantonio, who was a great painter, ever went beyond this practical joke, but by the middle of the sixteenth century we hear that, at least in Spain, the practice of faking pictures was already fully developed. A Spanish connoisseur of the sixteenth century, Don Felipe de Guevara (died 1563), writes in his *Treatise on Painting*:[19] 'What Hieronymus Bosch did with discernment and decorum, others did—and they are still doing it—without either discretion or judgment. As they saw how much favour this kind of painting had found in Flanders, they decided to imitate it, and painted monsters and weird visions, as they thought that the imitation of Bosch consisted only of these things. Countless pictures of this kind were signed with

17. Joni, *The Affairs of a Painter*, pp. 161, 297.
18. F. Nicolini, *L'Arte napoletana del Rinascimento* (1925), p. 161.
19. F. de Guevara, *Comentarios de la pintura*, ed. R. Benet (1938), p. 126.

the name of Hieronymus Bosch, fraudulently inscribed. They had been smoked in the chimney to give them a genuine and antique appearance.' These remarks are by no means unfounded, as is shown by the large number of copies and imitations of Bosch's pictures.

By the beginning of the seventeenth century the collecting of old pictures had become so widespread a hobby that the traffic in pictures was almost totally commercialised. Art-dealers soon began to have difficulties in satisfying their customers' growing demand for genuine old pictures, and simultaneously painters felt tempted to imitate the style of the great masters of the Renaissance.

Both these tendencies are proved by eloquent documents as well as by pictures. The texts show that the art of faking pictures was as perfect in its tender youth as it is in our day. Baglione's biography of the painter Terenzio da Urbino, which was published in 1642, about twenty years after this artist's death, reads like a modern essay on a faker: 'Terenzio, who was born at Urbino, was one of those painters who want their new pictures to be taken for old ones. He hunted for worm-eaten and dirty old pictures and frames which showed some painting, however badly done. He repainted these, inspiring himself by some old drawing, and mixed his colours in such a way that the old things began to look like something worth while. The painting being finished, he blackened his work by smoke and made it look a hundred years old with the help of some coloured varnishes. . . . Once Terenzio got hold of a fine antique frame, carved and gilded. This he used for a Madonna and other figures copied after an old drawing, and he took so much pains and so mixed the colours that he succeeded in turning out an object looking like a genuine antique. Everybody who was not a professional of high standing would have taken it for an old picture. Terenzio felt tempted to pass it off as a Raphael to his patron, Cardinal Montalto, though it was ungrateful of him to play such a trick on the man who employed him. The cardinal showed the picture to some experts, who recognised the swindle and told him that it was a pasticcio. To which the cardinal replied that he was in the habit of ordering pasticcios from his cook, if he wanted any, for this worthy man was excellent at such mixtures.

He was deeply disgusted, and gave Terenzio the sack, without seeing him again.'[20] Unfortunately none of Terenzio's fakes have been identified so far.

Albrecht Dürer shared Raphael's fate. Towards the end of the sixteenth and the beginning of the seventeenth century quite a number of artists painted not only in his style but excelled in copying him, and above all in composing new pictures compiled from his works. We do not know how many of these pictures and water-colours were painted with fraudulent intentions. Some of them are above suspicion, as they were signed by their authors. For instance, the altar-piece by J. G. Fischer (1580–1643) at Schleissheim is certainly no fake.[21] But the artist felt sure that Dürer had found the supreme versions for the representation of the apostles. Therefore he assembled Dürer's four apostles, together with the central figure from the Heller altar-piece, in the foreground of his picture. He apparently lacked models for the six heads of the background. They make one feel that J. G. Fischer did well to copy as much as he could from Dürer.

Imitations of this kind exist in large numbers. Occasionally drawings were copied in painting, not to speak of the pictures derived from Dürer's woodcuts and engravings. This posthumous cult of Dürer would be of little importance for our subject, if art-dealers had not exploited it to satisfy their patrons. Dürer's popular monogram was freely employed to stamp as an original by his hand any work which was supposed to represent his style. Nowadays we still find his initials on all kinds of pictures and drawings, whether they are German, Italian, or Flemish, copies, pasticcios, or original creations by other artists. This degradation of a signature to a trade-mark is an unimaginative fraud, but it acquires interest through a document of unparalleled candour which lets us trace a still fashionable practice to its very source.

This document is the diary of Hans Hieronymus Imhoff,[22] a

20. G. Baglione, *Le Vite* (1642), p. 157. Dr. Jacob Hess, who is preparing a critical edition of Baglione, kindly directed my attention to this passage. G. Mancini, *Considerazioni sulla pittura* (1956), p. 257.

21. F. Burger, *Die deutsche Malerei*, vol. 1 (1913), p. 102, fig. 107.

22. Published by E. Rosenthal in *Jahrbuch der preuss. Kunstsammlungen*, vol. 49 (1929), Beiheft, pp. 41 sqq.

grandson of Willibald Pirckheimer, the famous humanist, who was a close friend and patron of Dürer. The bulk of the important collection of Dürer's works had been sold at the death of the father of Hans Hieronymus to the Emperor Rudolph II, but there remained numerous works of minor value. Fifty years later, the Imhoff family being impoverished by the Thirty Years War, Hans Hieronymus decided to part with the most valuable books and the remains of the art collection. He was helped in his design by the great reputation his collection enjoyed on account of its provenance. Moreover, he did not refrain from enhancing its charms by numerous attributions to great masters and spurious signatures.

On the occasion of the sale concluded through the painter Abraham Bloemaert in 1633, Imhoff wrote in his diary:

'Thank God we were able to conclude a much better deal than we ever could have hoped for, as there was not a single piece of importance among the things we sold, which were for the larger part small water-colours. Moreover, it may well be doubted of many among them whether they were actually painted by Dürer....'

A year later Imhoff sold another lot to M. van Overbeck, an art-dealer of Leyden. Among the things contained in his list appear:

'II. Our Lady with the child, painted on parchment ... It was painted for my ancestor Hanns Imhoff at Antwerp: I described it to Overbeck as a work by Lucas van Leyden; an sit, dubitatur a multis; estimated at thaler 100.

'III. Our Lady painted on wood in oil-colours, small. My father of blessed memory caused Dürer's signature to be put under this piece, but there were not sufficient grounds to believe that Dürer had painted it. For 50 thaler.

'IV. A fine lion on parchment; though A. Dürer's sign appears on this sheet, it is generally believed that it had been painted by Hanns Hoffmann; for 40 thaler.'

After these two satisfactory sales, Imhoff attempted to sell such remains of his collection as had been refused by his foreign customers. He sent them to Ratisbon and Prague, but was much less lucky here than he had been with his patrons from the Netherlands. This is an item from this lot: 'St. Sebastian, small wood-carving, said to be by Dürer but no expert was willing to declare it as an original; for 8 thaler.'

Copies, attributions, false signatures—hardly any of the practices common in the modern picture-trade are absent from this document.

It is interesting to note that the Archduke Leopold Wilhelm, one of the greatest collectors of pictures, who was one of the most prominent buyers at the sale of Charles I's art-treasures, was arduously collecting Dürers at the very time of the Imhoff sales. He was bent on acquiring important panels, but as far as his purchases can still be identified they were of a kind all too similar to the Imhoff Collection. The fifteen 'Dürers' quoted in the inventory of 1659 are almost exclusively works by Dürer's followers, as for instance Kulmbach's 'Coronation of the Virgin'. This picture had been embellished to this end by Dürer's signature, suitably placed, where one of the little angels seems to be pointing to it. This was done without regard for Kulmbach's own signature, modestly concealed in the hem of the Virgin's cloak. Other items from the inventory are pasticcios after Dürer manufactured by Hans Hoffmann or similar artists, which likewise boast the inevitable A.D. Lastly the dealers did not refrain from affixing this magic sign on Flemish paintings of the sixteenth century, as for instance on Joos van Cleve's 'Virgin with the Coral Beads', the background of which was obliterated for the purpose. One may see from these examples that frauds of this kind were not limited to the Imhoff family.[23]

Luca Giordano (1632–1705), whose skill in counterfeiting was proverbial, is said to have issued victorious from a lawsuit in which he was accused of swindling over a picture representing Christ healing the cripples. This had been bought by one of his patrons as a certified Dürer. He proudly showed it to Luca, who uncovered his own signature concealed on the picture. The angry patron had recourse to the law, but the verdict of the court was that nobody could blame Luca for painting as well as the famous Dürer. This affair is no mere anecdote, for the *corpus delicti* turned up some years ago. This picture represents 'Christ healing

23. G. Glück in *Jahrbuch der kunsthist. Sammlungen,* vol. 28 (1909), pp. 1 sqq.

the lame man'; it is partly composed of motives derived from Dürer's prints, but is executed in a style plainly betraying the Italian Baroque. On the top of the central arch of its architecture appears Dürer's signature, while Luca Giordano's name is written in small letters along the left edge of the picture, so that they could be hidden by the frame (*Plate* 2).[24]

In Venice there lived Pietro della Vecchia (1605–78), 'the ape of Giorgione'. His imitations of the great Venetians, Giorgione, Titian, Palma Vecchio, Pordenone, were regarded as most deceptive. Sandrart relates in his *Academia* how he once detected one of these faked Giorgiones.[25] After extolling the deceptive excellence of Pietro's Giorgiones, he says: 'I myself had a narrow escape from committing this error. At Nuremberg in 1650 the Count Palatine Charles Gustav who later became King of Sweden, showed me a picture representing a warrior who draws his dagger in a fury, and asked me by whom I thought it to be. I contemplated the picture for a long time but only by examining its back was I able to recognise that the canvas was of recent origin and that the picture could therefore not be by Giorgione whose style it mirrored with such perfect fidelity. Pietro likewise painted a young warrior who carries a standard, a picture so well done that the Count Palatine Rupert reproduced it in mezzotint . . .' This picture used to be in the Schönborn Collection. The mezzotint, dated 1658, is inscribed with the name of Giorgione.[26] There are numerous replicas of the warrior drawing his dagger: one of them is in the Dresden Gallery.[27]

24. W. R. Valentiner in *Art in America*, vol. 1 (1913), pp. 195 sqq. Valentiner's deductions are somewhat confused by the fact that he used only De Dominici's earlier biography of Luca Giordano (G. P. Bellori, *Le Vite* (1728), p. 380) and not the final corrected one (B. de Dominici, *Vite de Pittori* (1763), vol. 3, pp. 438 sq.). Cf. also E. Petraccone, *Luca Giordano* (1919), p. 156. Nemes Sale, Munich, November 2, 1933, no. 118. On Giordano's forgeries, see now: A. Griseri, *Arte antica e moderna*, vol. 13–16 (1961), pp. 417–438.

25. J. V. Sandrart, *Akademie* (ed. Peltzer, 1925), p. 373.

26. F. Saxl, in *Mitteilungen der Gesellsch. f. vervielf. Kunst* 1908, p. 57; 1909, p. 28. A. M. Hind, in *The Connoisseur*, vol. 92 (1933), p. 390.

27. M. Boschini, *Carta del navegar pittoresco* (1660), p. 503. G. Fiocco, *Venetian Painting of the Seicento* (1929), pl. 33.

Though apparently an intentional faker, Pietro della Vecchia tried to recreate the romantic atmosphere of Giorgione's paintings by works of his own inventions. Sébastien Bourdon (1616–71) and Jean Michelin (1623–96) had a bad reputation in France for their dangerously deceptive copies. Louis Henri Loménie, Comte de Brienne, one of the great collectors of the period, kept a note-book which contains instructive details regarding these two *dangereux copistes*.[28] 'I have seen a copy by Bourdon of the small Madonna by Annibale Carracci which Jabach sold for 1500 livres.' Michelin specialised in faked Le Nains but once at least the count scored over this *fourbe achevé en fait de copies*. In his notebook he says: 'I made Forest paint me a copy of my little Hagar by Mola for 100 livres and sold it to the botcher Michelin for 400 livres as an original by Mola.'

Regarding the methods used by the French fakers to make their pictures look old, William Sanderson wrote in 1658:[29] 'It is said that Laniere in Paris, by a cunning way of tempering his Colours with Chimney Soote, the Painting becoms duskish, and seems ancient; which done, he roules up and thereby it crackls, and so mistaken for an old Principall, it being well copied from a good hand.' This shows that Joni's method of producing cracks in pictures (see p. 29) is far from being a modern invention.

To close this chapter showing how deeply involved seven-teenth-century artists were with the darker side of contemporary trade, mention should be made of a more harmless incident show-ing how Rubens himself became involved in an imposture by a chain of coincidences. Though it seems to have taken him by surprise, he mastered the situation as a man of the world and had occasion to exercise his diplomatic skill.

In 1603 the Duke of Mantua entrusted Rubens with a diplo-matic mission at the Spanish Court.[30] One of its objects was to present to the Duke of Lerma a series of fine copies of the most excellent paintings in Rome. There was no intention of passing

28. *Gazette des Beaux-Arts*, 3 ser., vol. 33 (1905), pp. 332 sq. On Michelin see P. Jamot, in *Revue de l'art*, vol. 63 (1933), pp. 207 sqq., and V. N. Lazarev, *Les frères Le Nain* (1936), p. 70.

29. W. Sanderson, *Graphice* (1658), p. 16.

30. C. Ruelens, *Correspondence de Rubens*, vol. 1 (1887), pp. 181, 195. E. Harris, *The Prado* (1940), p. 27.

them off as anything but copies. But when the mission arrived at Madrid the pictures were found to have been so badly damaged by dampness that it was feared at first that the present could not be delivered at all. After they had been dried Rubens retouched them and also painted two additional canvases to complete the series. Then the pictures were solemnly presented to the Duke. 'When I came to the Duke with the other ambassadors', Rubens wrote, 'he showed himself highly satisfied with the excellent quality and the large number of the pictures which had certainly (with the help of my clever retouches) gained in authority and apparent age by the damage they had suffered. Thus the majority of the pictures were regarded as originals, without any doubt and without any attempt by us to pass them off as such. The King and Queen, their courtiers and some painters also saw and admired the pictures.' A fortnight later Annibale Iberti, Rubens' co-ambassador, says in a letter to the Duke of Mantova: 'The Duke of Lerma showed the pictures to the Florentine Carduccio, the old court painter. We prepared Carduccio beforehand for what he was going to see, so that his verdict on the pictures should be in harmony with the delight felt by the Duke!'

Dutch Forgers of the Eighteenth Century.*

Once the practice had been launched, the tradition of faking became continuous, though its objects changed with taste, place, and period. More or less intentional imitations of the Dutch masters of the previous century are the most widely spread of eighteenth-century fakes.

Though the great inspiration which sustained this school had already flagged before the end of the seventeenth century, the production of pictures continued to be large. Genre-painters, and above all landscape painters, followed in the footsteps of their famous ancestors. The number of eighteenth-century Dutch pictures of second-class or third-class quality which are sold as masterpieces of the seventeenth century is considerable.

This practice may be partly excused by the fact that the painters of this period tried to make their paintings as similar as possible to those of their ancestors. The painter Jacob van Stry (1756–1815), for instance, succeeded in turning out fairly good eighteenth-century

* See also below, p. 324.

versions of Aelbert Cuyp's sunny placidity. They may occasionally still be offered as authentic works of Stry's greater forerunner.

The irresistible attraction Vermeer van Delft has for modern forgers was foreshadowed in the late eighteenth and early nineteenth centuries. But then he was imitated, not faked. Dirk Jan van der Laen (1759–1829) frequently signed his pictures, even when they happened to represent motives derived from Vermeer. This is proved by a picture at Aken which is a variant of the 'Little Street' in the Rijksmuseum. But in the second half of the nineteenth century two of his pictures were declared as Vermeers. One of them bears Vermeer's signature, but there is no means of knowing when it was thus adorned. Van der Laen is a painter of undeniable charm, but he has a lightness of touch plainly betraying the late origin of his pictures. His works were accepted all too easily as the 'early manner' of the older master.[31]

Romanticist Fakes.

The Dutch imitators did their best to continue an uninterrupted tradition. They made a not altogether unsuccessful attempt to put back the clock. But meanwhile a new spirit began to animate fakers in other countries. The imitation of a familiar pictorial ideal was superseded by a growing tendency to evoke far away periods. The romanticist predilection for mystifications prepared a fertile ground for frauds of every kind. The early fakes of 'primitives' were the result of more or less sound stylistic and technical studies, and in general the impression of sweet primitiveness was so well achieved that they still occasionally appear among genuine pictures, enhanced as they are by the genuine ageing they have undergone during the century of their existence.

Among the forgers of early German masters Franz Wolfgang Rohrich (1782–1834) was the most successful.[32] His 'Lucas

31. Bredius in *Kunstchronik*, vol. 18 (1883), p. 68. J. Six in *Oude Kunst*, vol. 4 (1918–19), p. 33. A. B. de Vries, *Jan Vermeer van Delft* (1945), p. 75, fig. 28.

32. A. Rasczynsky, *Histoire de l'art moderne en Allemagne* (1839), vol. 2, p. 500. T. v. Frimmel, *Handbuch der Gemäldekunde* (1920), p. 258. N. v. Holst in *Zeitschrift für Kunstgeschichte*, vol. 3 (1934), p. 43. *Katalog der Gemäldegalerie zu Schleissheim* (1914), p. 200. Sir Robert Witt, in *The Graphic*, February 25, 1928, p. 307.

Cranach' (*Plate* 4), pretending to represent the Duchess Sophie of Saxony with the little John Frederick, exists in about thirty identical versions. No wonder Rohrich is said to have saved 1500 florins while a student at the Academy of Munich.

Rohrich was not at all bad at catching the general impression of Cranach's later portraits. But on closer examination some shortcomings become evident. His lady's complicated mushroom hat, hung with strands of pearls, jewels and finger-rings, and the over-sumptuous jewellery which covers her neck and shoulders, make Cranach's most extravagant fashion pictures look sober. Compared with these, the bad draughtsmanship (see especially the eyes) and the complete lack of modelling become evident. The signature placed on the jewel on Sophie's hat is perhaps the greatest of these absurdities. It carries two names, Cranach and Muler. This is a tribute to a theory that Lukas Cranach was really called Lukas Muler and derived his current name from his birth-place, Kronach. Rohrich wanted to be on the safe side and put down both names.

The predilection for literary and historical subjects, so charac-teristic of nineteenth-century painting, is clearly reflected in this group of forgeries. The life of the German mercenaries, the *landsknechte,* in their picturesque and strange attire, was a parti-cularly favourite subject. The small panel shown in *Plate* 3 belongs to this category. The source of the composition is a large painted table-top in the Museum of Art and Industry in Vienna.[33] While on this table the groups of soldiers occur as part of a larger decora-tion of religious and ornamental scenes, a *genre* picture of this type is utterly impossible at the alleged time of origin. But the forger's confidence in the irresistible appeal such a fine military costume piece would have for medieval-minded Germans was fully justi-fied, as a prominent museum acquired and exhibited his work.

THE METHODS OF THE FORGER

Alterations.

Even this short survey of the early history of picture-faking demonstrates that we have not only the fabrication of new 'old

33. *Anzeiger des Germanischen Nationalmuseums* (1936–39), p. 19.

pictures' to consider. Over-painting and every kind of alteration and embellishment are a much more frequent method of fraud. Frequently such portions of pictures as were liable to offend either the eye or the sense of propriety of their owners were concealed or repainted. The 'clothing' of naked figures is more common, even in our day, than one would think. There are many other kinds of improvement. A sweet Madonna with an ugly Joseph looking over her shoulder would look sweeter without him, and therefore he is compelled to hide under the black background. Salome with the head of Saint John, displaying his bleeding neck, can hardly be hung in a drawing-room. But let the severed head be exchanged for a tray, heavy with golden ornaments and precious stones, and she becomes 'the Jeweller's Daughter'.[34]

The young Misses Payne at the harpsichord are accompanied by their matronly mother (*Plate 6*). Somebody evidently thought that Reynolds' way of painting sweet youth would look more alluring without the elderly chaperon. Some shrubs, a cloud and a piece of sky, and the two young girls were alone (*Plate 5*). The curator of the Lady Lever Art Gallery saved the poor obliterated mother and restored one of Reynolds' most individual compositions to its original state.[35]

What some pictures have too much, others have too little. A charming Dutch interior, famous as 'The Slippers', has only recently been restored to its original condition, as a still-life without figures.[36] On an old reproduction can still be seen a little girl with a dog in her lap, sitting on the doorstep, a weak copy in re-

34. Picture by Lucas Cranach: Blakeslee Sale, New York, 21 April, 1915, no. 66. Friedländer-Rosenberg, *Lucas Cranach* (1932), p. 82. A similar case is a 'Salome' attributed to Giuseppe Maria Crespi: *La Critica d'Arte*, vol. 1 (1936), p. 181, fig. 2. *The Art News*, June 11, 1938.

35. Port Sunlight, Lady Lever Gallery. *Museums Journal*, vol. 35 (1935), p. 280. R. R. Tatlock, *English Painting in the Lady Lever Gallery* (1928), p. 61. E. K. Waterhouse, *Reynolds* (1941), p. 122, pl. 115. T. Bodkin, *Dismembered Masterpieces* (1945), p. 32, pl. 58.

36. The picture, probably by Samuel van Hoogstraaten, is now in the Louvre. *Gazette des Beaux Arts*, 1933, Premier semestre, p. 232. In 1842 (Smith Supplement 20) it was still in its original state.

verse of a child in one of Pieter de Hooch's *Courtyards*.[37] Only now, after the removal of this figure, can the somewhat rigid charm of the composition with its sequence of unbroken verticals be fully appreciated.

The borderline between extensive restoration and forgery is difficult to draw. There can be no doubt that the most common type of forgery is not the newly painted picture, but the wreck which has to serve as foundation for a new painting. The advantages of this method are obvious. The panel or the canvas shows at the back all the symptoms of age and authenticity, and of the picture itself smaller or greater parts are ancient, and help to dispel any doubts which may be caused by the modern portions. Moreover, by following the outlines of the original, the forger need not bother about the composition, and is almost safe from lapses into treacherous modernisms.

One such 'restoration' of which Joni was very proud, may serve as an example for countless similar cases. At Joni's suggestion, as he relates in his autobiography,[38] a certain Signor Angeli bought an old painting at a sale in Siena. 'Singor Angeli brought it straight to me; he told me that he had paid a high price for it although it seemed to him to be much repainted, and he was afraid he had made a bad bargain. To avoid all responsibility I cleaned it in his presence, and we found that, apart from a nice gold background, and the original frame, there was nothing left but the pale ghost of a fine picture by Bernardino Fungai. Signor Angeli was rather depressed at the sight of the wreck; and I felt uncomfortable myself. I thought it my duty to restore it carefully, seeing that I had advised him to buy it, and I did not want him to lose his money. My work was most successful and Signor Angeli was really pleased with it . . . A foreigner, who saw the picture, was enthusiastic about it, and especially satisfied with the restoration. He found a buyer for it, worked up quite a reputation for the picture, and published it together with another Fungai in the Rassegna d'Arte.' Indeed, the picture now resembles closely the other Madonnas

37. Wrotham Park, Earl of Strafford Collection. W. R. Valentiner, *Pieter de Hooch* (1929), p. 54. A replica of this picture is mentioned by Smith (Supplement 15). It belonged for some time to the same owner as 'The Slippers'.

38. I. F. Joni, *Le memorie di un pittore di quadri antichi* (1932), p. 234. *Affairs of a Painter* (1936), p. 287. *Rassegna d'Arte,* vol. 13 (1913), p. 126.

attributed to Fungai.

The heads of the Virgin, the Child, and Saint Joseph are to be seen on a picture attributed to Dürer. In its present state the Madonna and the Child are rather faithful replicas of Dürer's 'Madonna with the pear'. This resemblance was not quite as apparent when the picture first turned up in Portugal. Then portions amounting to about half of the picture's surface were missing. And as the panel is literally filled with faces the missing portions were vital ones. Since it travelled east this picture has been twice restored, each subsequent restoration bringing it closer to Dürer's style, and it proudly shows his name warranted by an unauthentic signature.[39]

A few words should be said regarding a particularly revolting type of vandalism which is at present assuming large proportions, namely the carving up of pictures in order to create 'interesting' and easily saleable fragments. Outsiders hardly realise how many masterpieces of old painting are thus being sacrificed and sold piecemeal every year. The reasons for this barbarism are obvious. It is almost impossible to find buyers for the mythological canvases of the late Renaissance and the Baroque, which are too large for the average modern room. But such a canvas may contain figures of elegant Venetian ladies which, when cut out, fit into modern rooms and satisfy the taste of the modern collector. Single portraits find a readier market than large portrait groups which, however, lend themselves easily for cutting up. It is only by rare good luck that the two halves of a large Dutch family portrait both landed finally in the National Gallery and could be reunited.[40] Usually single heads or figures are cut out and the rest of the picture, having become unusable, is then destroyed. In the same fashion religious compositions which are thought unsuitable for the drawing-room, have to provide unobjectionable and attractive fragments.[41]

39. H. Tietze, in *Wiener Jahrbuch für Kunstgeschichte*, vol. 7 (1930), p. 238. On a similar case, a landscape by Altdorfer (London), see H. Tietze, *Kunst und Künstler*, vol. 26 (1928), p. 340.

40. T. Bodkin, *Dismembered Masterpieces* (1945), p. 31.

41. L. Venturi, 'Reconstruction of a Painting by Andrea del Castagno', in *The Art Quarterly*, vol. 7 (1944), p. 23. Since the publication of Professor Venturi's paper, the fragment shown on fig. 4 has been mutilated again See also L. Venturi, *The Rabinowitz Collection* (1945), p. 21.

Spurious Signatures.

A signature is one of the most obvious and simplest additions calculated to enhance a picture's value. The practice of affixing false signatures is widespread and started early. Dutch pictures are foremost among the victims as Dutch painters very frequently signed their pictures, and the collector expected therefore to purchase a signed work. Thus the correct name has in numerous cases been spuriously added to perfectly genuine pictures. More often, however, famous names are used as trade labels. If cleverly faked, such a signature may be hard to distinguish from its genuine models, particularly if some time has passed since it has been added to the picture. If of comparatively recent date it may be betrayed by its freshness and the weak adherence of its pigment to the picture.

Reference has already been made to some early cases of faked signatures. These examples could easily be multiplied. There is, for instance, the large series of apocryphal names and dates on early Venetian paintings in the Museo Correr and the Academy of Venice which are apparently the work of an over-zealous Venetian patriot of the Romantic period.[42] Patriots of Bologna must have felt an invincible desire to discover the works of Franco Bolognese, all of whose paintings are lost but who has been immortalised in Dante's *Divine Comedy*:[43]

'Brother', said he, 'the leaves more smiling shine
By Franco of Bologna's brush made fair'.

Abbate Lanzi, the historian of Italian painting, knew several works by this founder of the Bolognese School. The chief piece of evidence was a panel representing the Madonna enthroned. This showed the proud and very visible signature, 'Franco Bol: Fece 1312'. Lanzi wrote in 1795, but as early as 1839 grave doubts regarding the authenticity of the panel were expressed. The picture, which is now in Rumania, seems genuine, although heavily repainted; the signature was invented and painted by some ardent patriot of Bologna, probably not long before 1795.[44]

42. L. Testi, *La storia della pittura Veneziana* (1909), vol. 1, pp. 123, 180 sqq.

43. Purgatory, canto 11, lines 82–3 (M. B. Anderson's translation).

44. L. Lanzi, *Storia Pittorica*, vol. 2, part 2 (1795–6), p. 10. G. Rosini, *Storia della Pittura Italiana* (1839), vol. 1, p. 249, pl. 11. A. Busuioceanu, in the Memorial Volume *In memoriam Vasile Parvan* (1934), p. 68, fig. 2.

Many of the early forged signatures are no longer deceptive. Some, however, are not without interest as indication of changing tastes. It is surprising to find that Vermeer's masterpiece, 'The Painter in His Studio' (Picture Gallery, Vienna), still bears the false signature 'Peter de Hoogh' whose work was in the first half of the ninteenth century more highly valued than Vermeer's.[45] The name Mantegna frequently occurs on Italian pictures. He was one of the very few early masters whose works were valued and collected long before the rediscovery of Italian painting before Raphael. His works were rare, the works of his contemporaries plentiful and cheap, and connoisseurship rudimentary. Thus we find Mantegna's name on works as heterogeneous as Francesco Cossa's 'Annunciation' (Dresden), Giambono's 'Dead Christ' (Padua), Giovanni di Paolo's 'Saint John Preaching in the Desert' (Tours), and Carpaccio's 'Meditation on the Passion' (New York) and 'Dead Christ' (Berlin).[46] This last picture showed Mantegna's name already in 1627, not without some justification as it comes very close to Mantegna's style and spirit.

The removal of genuine signatures is a not uncommon practice. Unscrupulous dealers scratch out the signatures of little-known masters to enable them to pass off their pictures as the work of a famous and highly priced painter. Already in the eighteenth century a connoisseur observed that the signature of Elsheimer's pupil, Johann König, had been removed from one of his pictures which was then sold under Elsheimer's name.[47] This particularly vicious practice is still rife. A picture by the Bolognese painter Antonio Pirri might be quoted as an example, the signature of which disappeared in recent years.[48]

In some cases a name has been changed into a more famous one by altering part of the original signature. The German painter Hans Schäuffelein signed H.S. The curve of the S rising above the H was erased and the vertical bar of a second H added to the first.

45. K. Wilczek, *Katalog* (1936), p. 94. *Het Parool*, 6. 8. 1947, p. 1.

46. R. van Marle, *Italian Schools of Painting*, vol. 7, p. 365; vol. 18, p. 260. *The Burlington Magazine*, vol. 6 (1904), p. 306. N. Pease, in *Bulletin of the Metropolitan Museum of Art*, N.S., vol. 4 (1945), pp. 1 sqq.

47. H. S. Huesgen, *Nachrichten von Frankfurter Künstlern* (1780), p. 25.

48. R. Longhi, *Officina ferrarese* (1934), p. 114, pl. 156.

Thus Hans Schäuffelein became Hans Holbein.[49] A Venetian 'Madonna and Child' in the Cook Collection had an inscription with the obviously false name Antonello da Messina. A recent cleaning of the picture brought out the genuine signature of Giovanni Mansueti. The forger had retained as much as he could of the original lettering. The discovery of the old signature corroborated Professor Borenius' attribution of the picture to Mansueti, published many years before the cleaning of the picture.[50] In the same way the signature of Rembrandt's pupil Reynier van Gherwen was replaced on one of his pictures by his master's name.[51] In the course of time the original signature became partly visible under the forgery and the signature has thus become a curious mixture of the two names (Fig. 1).

FIGURE 1

The practice of false signatures on old pictures became so widely spread, that they lost credit and are consequently used to a lesser degree nowadays.

The signature of modern pictures is imitated more easily. In a letter to the *New Statesman*[52] Lucien Pissarro complained that he saw one of his own pictures offered for sale in London, adorned by a spurious imitation of his father's signature. He tried to have it removed through legal intervention, but there does not seem to exist any law by which the owner could be compelled to remove the forgery, and the picture was sold as a work by Camille Pissarro.

49. 'The Wheel of Fortune' in the Duke of Devonshire Collection. Burlington Fine Arts Club, *Exhibition of Early German Art*, 1906, no. 57, pl. 34.

50. *Burlington Magazine*, vol. 23 (1913), p. 26; vol. 85 (1944), p. 206.

51. Vienna Picture Gallery, no. 1275. *Führer* (1906), vol. 2, p. 184. G. Tsarlov, 'Rembrandt et son entourage', in *La Renaissance*, vol. 19 (1936), p. 46.

52. 20 August 1938.

Fraudulent Copies.

The masterpieces of painting have been copied in every period, either for the edification of the copyist himself or for the benefit of patrons, desiring to enjoy the company of some picture they could not acquire in the original. Consequently there exist copies of all kinds of pictures, and their quality ranges from personal interpretations of great artistic value to very inefficient and blurred versions of the original. Although these facts are well known, copies of pictures have been confused with their prototypes ever since they were first made. Insufficient knowledge of the original, some mistake as to its present whereabouts, and a dim notion that painters occasionally repeat their own works, help to increase the confusion. Though the great majority of copies are perfectly innocent, there is no denying the fact that some were ordered with the intention to cheat.

As early as the seventeenth century collectors tried to safeguard against attempts at exchanging their purchases for valueless copies. In 1691 Duke John Adam Andrew of Liechtenstein instructed the painter Franceschini, who acted as buyer for the duke's collection, to impress a special seal on the back of every canvas before it was dispatched. For the duke feared that his bankers, who were in charge of the transport, might exchange the original pictures for cheap copies ordered by them specially for this purpose.[53] But even the marking of the reverse of pictures occasionally failed to prevent their being exchanged for copies. Towards the end of the eighteenth century a painter obtained permission from the town councillors to copy Dürer's famous self-portrait in the town hall of Nuremberg. As a precautionary measure the original was sealed and marked on the back. Whereupon the copyist sawed off the front of the panel with Dürer's painting, used the thinned board for his copy, and left his work with the seals at the back with the councillors of Nuremberg, carrying off the original, which eventually landed in Munich.[54]

Another practice which can be traced back to the seventeenth

53. *Jahrbuch der K. K. Zentralkommission,* vol. 5 (1911), Beiblatt, cols. 91 sqq.

54. M. Thausing, *Albert Dürer* (1882), vol. 2, p. 95. *Dürer-Ausstellung im Germanischen Museum, Nürnberg* (3rd edition, 1928), p. 50, no. 51.

century is the duplicating of an original which has been bought once only but sold twice. This is what happened to Holbein's 'Madonna with the Burgomaster Meyer.' Le Blond of Amsterdam bought this picture in the first half of the seventeenth century and resold it locally. It reappeared in 1709, was bought by Prince Wilhelm of Prussia in 1822, and came to Darmstadt, through his daughter the Grand-Duchess Karl of Hesse. Simultaneously the picture developed a second pedigree. It was pawned from Amsterdam to a Venetian banker in 1690 and was bought in Italy for the royal collection of Saxony in 1743. Till the confrontation of the two pictures in 1871 nobody knew which of them was the original and which duplicate. Now the picture at Darmstadt is generally recognised as Holbein's work, and thus we know that the Venetian firm of bankers were cheated.[55]

Copies of heads and other details from famous pictures are frequently accepted as studies by the master's own hand. Sir Anthony van Dyck is celebrated for the beautiful hands by which he ennobled the appearance of the persons he portrayed. Therefore it was a pleasant surprise to find a whole canvas filled with hands betraying unmistakably Van Dyck's style. However, the general enthusiasm was considerably cooled when it was proved that these hands belonged to portraits painted at different periods of Van Dyck's career but which had been assembled in the Liechtenstein collection since the eighteenth century.[56]

GROUPS OF MODERN FORGERIES

A survey of modern 'old masters' is made easier by the fact that not all styles, schools, and masters are being forged in equal proportions. Forgery on a large scale need only be feared where the demand considerably exceeds the supply and where it is impossible to provide enough suitable specimens by cheap copies or obscure old pictures with or without over-painting. Foremost among faked pictures are Italian 'primitives', most of all portraits in Quattrocento style, Frans Hals and Vermeer van Delft of the

55. P. Ganz, *Hans Holbein* (1911), p. 251.
56. *Trésor de l'art belge au XVIIe siècle* (1910), pl. 55; F. M. Haberditzl, in *Kunstgeschichtliche Anzeigen* (1911), p. 107.

1. Portrait of King Edward VI painted over a seventeenth-century Dutch picture representing a little girl. (By courtesy of the Director of the Victoria and Albert Museum.)

2. 'Christ Healing the Lame Man'. Painted by Luca Giordano in imitation of Dürer.

3. False German picture in fifteenth-century style. (By courtesy of the Director of the Bayerisches Nationalmuseum, München.)

4. F. W. Rohrich. Imitation of Lucas Cranach. (By courtesy of Kunstverlag Wolfrum.)

5. 'The Misses Payne' by Sir Joshua Reynolds, as the picture was before it was cleaned. (By courtesy of the Trustees of the Lady Lever Collection, Port Sunlight, Cheshire.)

6. 'Mrs. Payne and her two daughters'—the overpainting removed. (By courtesy of the Trustees of the Lady Lever Collection, Port Sunlight, Cheshire.)

7. Madonna. Forgery in the style of Lippo Vanni. (By courtesy of
Mr. H. Ruhemann.)

8. Madonna. Forgery in the style of Bartolo di Fredi.

9. Triptych in the style of the Siennese School of the fifteenth century. Modern forgery. (By courtesy of the Courtauld Institute of Art.)

10. X-ray photograph of the top of the triptych shown in Plate 9. (By courtesy of the Courtauld Institute of Art.)

11. Portrait of a lady. Forgery after Gentile Bellini.

Dutch, Greco of the Spanish masters, and the great French painters of the nineteenth century. In these fields the number of fakes accepted as originals is indeed appalling. The Flemish primitives follow only at a distance, and other schools have escaped the plague almost entirely—up to now.

Italian Primitives.

'Mio figlio vende quadri con fondo d'oro a ricchi Inglesi ed Americani.' (From a letter).

The magic attraction of the mellow shine of golden backgrounds for well-to-do tourists could not fail to catch the attention of their hosts. Their eagerness to help their guests was genuine, and they felt that the main thing was to satisfy them.

The forgers who did and do their utmost to keep pace with the demand fully avail themselves of the great advantages offered to them. Every early picture of the Italian School, and be it of the lowest artistic quality, is eagerly sought for, and commands a high price. There is no need to produce masterpieces. We hardly ever find spurious Giottos or Duccios, while the number of dubious works by the 'minor masters' is constantly increased. The task of distinguishing between genuine and spurious pictures is particularly difficult. Genuine Trecentist or Quattrocentist Madonnas of fifth-rate quality may possess nearly all the unattractive features characterising their counterfeits. Their colour-scheme may be unrefined, faces and hands badly drawn, facial expression and gestures may be pettish and affected. The sad thing is that objects of so poor artistic quality should be such favourites with collectors.

A panel (*Plate* 7) from the collection of counterfeits assembled by Mr. Ruhemann allows us a fairly good insight into the wiles of high-class faking.[57] Though quite a good piece of work, this picture is given away by various symptoms. The holes made by woodworms, visible at its sides, prove that the panel was carved after the worms had attacked it. The painting is executed on

57. I am most grateful to Mr. H. Ruhemann, who kindly permitted me to reproduce this picture, though he intends to publish it himself with a technical commentary. Reproduced in colour in H. Tietze, *Genuine and False* (1948), pl. 38.

muslin, which was rolled after it was finished to produce the cracks, and then only fixed on the panel. The head of the child is the most successful part of the picture, but the good impression it produces is undone by the painting of the Virgin's blue cloak, which is done in broad uneven strokes and is manifestly new. The panel was launched as a Lippo Vanni. Many of its peculiarities we find again on a picture attributed to this master which is in the Pinacoteca of Perugia.[58] The face of the child is almost exactly the same on both pictures, and so are the curls surrounding it. Also the Madonna's hair is arranged in the same way, and her curiously drawn ear, which has only a double contour, with no inside drawing, has been minutely copied from the panel at Perugia. The Madonna's eyes, nose, and lips reappear on Mr. Ruhemann's panel, but the single features seem to have slipped out of place. This is no mere sign of inferior quality, but has a special reason: the acknowledged characteristics of Lippo Vanni's personal style had to be incorporated into a composition derived from another artist.

For the forger had previously copied the Madonna from a polyptych attributed to Bartolo di Fredi.[59] This copy (*Plate 8*) was subjected to much cracking and scratching. Otherwise it is perfectly literal, except for the clumsy angular outline that destroys the rhythm of the whole design. When the painter of this copy later on ventured on a work by Lippo Vanni he repeated this composition, down to the smallest fold of the garments, but he had to change the 'stylistic characteristics' of faces, ears, and hair.[60]

The boards of the triptych shown in *Plate* 9 are coarse and uneven, and certainly such faulty pieces of wood would never have been used by an old master.[61] The unevenness of the central

58. Van Marle, vol. 2, p. 461, fig. 301.

59. Van Marle, vol. 2, p. 493, fig. 319.

60. Dr. A. Scharf was the first to recognise the individual style of this 'artist'.

61. The triptych forms part of the collection of fakes belonging to the Courtauld Institute (Department of the History of the Technology of Art). Professor Thompson very kindly put this triptych and the X-ray at my disposal and imparted to me most valuable information on the subject.

panel causes a very visible cut through one figure. But irregularity is easily mistaken for antiquity, and anyhow the forger was above all anxious to employ old wood. Yet the wood is his undoing. The shadowgraph (*Plate* 10) reveals the worm-holes which were stopped up and then covered with the priming. Of course, fifteenth-century painters had no reason to paint on worm-eaten wood. The long, machine-made nails which are hidden from view, but which are clearly shown by the X-rays, are another piece of evidence. But apart from the dubious quality of the wood and the revelations of the shadowgraph, the modern origin of this triptych may be gathered from its style. The child is not primitive, but a badly drawn modern baby. Another striking thing about the triptych is the prevailing uncertainty as to the identity of the saints. None of the four saints represented has been given a really distinctive attribute. This would be most unusual on a genuine picture. The figure of the knight with the sword is copied from Matteo di Giovanni's 'Madonna with Saints' in the Gallery of Sienna. This youthful saint was one of Joni's favourites. He appears on a painting which he reproduced in the Italian edition of his memoirs as well as on one of his painted book-covers.[62]

Quattrocento Portraits.

'He ordered a very large number of fifteenth century portraits, which went like hot cakes.' (Joni, *Affairs*, p. 188.)

False portraits considerably outnumber religious subjects. Genuine portraits of this period are very rare. But they are highly in demand as they evoke the heroes and the famous beauties of Renaissance society. In this particular field it would be comparatively easy to distinguish originals from counterfeits but so far no serious attempt has been made to weed out the numerous forgeries. The excessive rarity of genuine portraits ought to caution everyone against being too ready to accept newcomers. However, the extraordinarily high quality of the originals is still far more important than their small number. In fifteenth-century Italy the painting of a portrait was no everyday matter. Only persons of high social standing had their portraits painted, and in every case

62. Joni, *Memorie*, pl. facing p. 240. The false Siennese book-cover is illustrated in *Kunstgewerbeblatt*, N.S. XIV, 1903, p. 229 (see below, p. 299).

the artist did his utmost to render the character and individuality of the men or the beauty and charm of the ladies. There exist no second-rate portraits to which the imitators could have confined their attention as they did with religious subjects. They certainly never succeeded in catching even a shred of the gracefully undulating silhouette of fifteenth-century beauties or of the medal-like sharpness attained in the genuine male portraits. Notwithstanding their shortcomings, the forgers did not despair of their task. They bravely set out to create a new type of picture: the fifth-rate fifteenth-century portrait.

No task is as delicate as the drawing of a female head and bust in profile. Many imitators have tried their hands at it. None of them has been successful but their attempts are legion. The less sophisticated type of imitation is exemplified by the portrait shown on *Plate* 11. It goes under the name of Gentile Bellini. With its crude outline and clumsy modelling the picture shows so little of Quattrocento spirit that we are surprised to discover that it really has some connection with Gentile. The lady has been copied from the female donor of Gentile's 'Madonna' in the Berlin Gallery—with some alterations that cannot be said to enhance her charms. The forger moreover concentrated on the superficial signs of age; he covered the whole panel with a network of minute cracks and sprinkled it liberally with fly-spots.

Variations of famous portraits are not uncommon. In a nineteenth-century copy after the enchanting female portrait in the Poldi-Pezzoli Museum of Milan, hardly more than the gown and jewel of the lady has been changed.[63] When this portrait appeared on the art market some years ago it was hailed as a discovery 'as meaningful as would be the discovery of a new Beethoven sonata or even a symphony'. One female portrait turned up— less poetically—with a certificate of authenticity issued by the Paris Préfecture de Police.[64] In spite of this police protection it is but a feeble imitation of Piero della Francesca's famous portrait of the Duchess of Urbino (Florence). However, Piero's monumental simplification has been turned into emptiness, and his grandiose landscape background into a jumble of molehills.

63. A. Sabatini, *Antonio e Piero del Pollaiolo* (1944), p. 78.
64. *The Burlington Magazine*, vol. 56 (1930), pp. 218, 280.

Blatant modernisms are no drawback; on the contrary, the most successful forgeries usually offer a judicious blend of the old and the new. We are always eager to discover our own ideals in the art of the past. Hence the success of a group of portraits of Renaissance women seen through the eyes of Hollywood. The rigid features, the shaved foreheads and the long necks of the originals are grotesquely exaggerated, one might almost say caricatured, but they show the Renaissance lady as our popular historical fiction imagines her: cool, inscrutable, and of ravishing beauty.

Faked male portraits are somewhat rarer than female ones. Here again we meet free copies of famous pictures, like a false Jacopo Bellini, a portrait of Lionello d'Este, to which Roberto Longhi drew attention.[65] It is derived from a particularly fine model, the portrait by Giovanni Oriolo in the National Gallery; however, the copyist blunted the sharp outlines of the silhouette and thus the brilliant characterisation of the original was lost. Languishing youths with landscape background are a frequent type of forgery: often but not exclusively they affect the style of the Umbrian School.[66]

Family portraits seem to be extremely rare. I know of not more than two. One forgery, in the stores of the Dresden Gallery, shows the profiles of husband and wife, without the slightest attempt to make a group of the two stiff figures.[67] The so-called Montefeltre family stands on quite a different level: it even found brief access to the National Gallery (*Plate* 12).[68] This panel shows a man and two children, all seen in profile, as they look out through an open window on a landscape with a fortress on a hill. The picture's title is derived from the badge with the Montefeltre arms stamped into the gesso in the right-hand top corner of the picture but it proved impossible to identify the portrayed from the genealogical tree of the Montefeltres. The scholar who published this picture for the first time,

65. *Catalogo della Esposizione della Pittura Ferrarese*, Ferrara (1933), p. 29. R. Longhi, *Officina ferrarese* (1934), p. 19.

66. An example is a spurious Crivelli portrait mentioned as a fake by Van Marle, vol. 18, p. 62, note 1 (*La Coleccion Lazaro de Madrid* vol. 1, 1926, p. 364).

67. *Die Staatliche Gemäldegalerie zu Dresden* (1929), p. 143, no. 300.

68. *The Burlington Magazine*, vol. 44 (1924), p. 195. M. Davies, *National Gallery Catalogue, The Earlier Italian Schools* (1961), p. 256.

was aware of its many unusual features. 'It has no pedigree,' he wrote, 'and as it is somewhat unusual it deserves to be described carefully, if only for the benefit of the gentlemen whose motto is *omne ignotum pro falsifico.*' Alas, the gentlemen were right with their motto in somewhat dubious Latin. The picture is a forgery, although it is one of the best that have been made. It is the work of a gifted painter, able to express himself in the language of the fifteenth century without being forced to follow a model slavishly. The careful description just mentioned should, however, have been a warning against too ready acceptance. 'The wormholes', we are told, 'had penetrated the gesso and paint in more than a dozen places, and had to be stopped before the picture was exhibited.' This fact alone is sufficient to condemn the picture. Real worm-holes are rarely found in the upper layers of a painting. Neither gesso nor paint are palatable to the worms who live on an exclusive diet of wood. The holes must therefore have been produced artificially. This is only a minor technical point. The idea of showing a family enjoying a view through a window betrays a note of modern sentimentality quite foreign to the spirit of the age to which the Montefeltre family pretends to belong.

Early Flemish Painters.

As we had occasion to say at the beginning of this chapter, forgeries of the early Flemish masters are comparatively rare. After such promising beginnings as Colantonio's deceptive imitations of his Flemish contemporaries (see p. 31) and the Spanish Bosch imitations of the sixteenth century, the industry faded out. There was little interest in the early masters among the collectors of the seventeenth and eighteenth century. As in the case of early Italian paintings (see p. 44) the demand could easily be satisfied by putting famous signatures on genuine old pictures. 'Joannes de Eyck fecit Anno MCCCC21. 30.Octobris' was inscribed on a painting of 'The Enthronement of St. Romold, Archbishop of Dublin' (Chatsworth).[69] It was painted almost a

69. H. Walpole, *Anecdotes of Painting* (1871 ed.), p. 22, note 1. A. Marks, in *The Burlington Magazine*, vol. 10 (1906–7), p. 383. Sir M. Conway and T. Borenius, *Catalogue of the Loan Exhibition of Flemish and Belgian Art* (1927), no. 129, pl. 59.

century after its alleged date, but until 1906 it was believed to be Jan van Eyck's earliest dated work. Jan van Eyck was one of the artists whose fame remained undiminished through the changing fashions. The same applies to Lucas van Leyden whose monogram can be discerned on a fantastic 'Temptation of St. Anthony' in the Vienna Gallery.[70] The picture, which has been in the Imperial Collections since the eighteenth century, is the work of one of the painters who worked in the style of Hieronymus Bosch in the second half of the sixteenth century.

The accomplished technique of the early masters seems to deter most forgers. Almost the only forgeries which turn up from time to time, are portraits in the style of Roger or Bouts, usually of very poor quality.[71] However, there flourished at least one workshop in Brussels which specialised in Flemish primitives. A fair example of its work was included in the Flemish Exhibition, held at Burlington House in 1927.[72] 'The Madonna with two female Saints' is no invention of the forger, not even a new combination of different figures from genuine pictures. The forger himself has revealed that this painting is copied from a badly damaged small panel by a Bruges master of about 1480. The copy, considerably enlarged and rather disagreeable in effect, is however very efficiently done, and shows how the best results can indeed be obtained by the forger if he chooses his model among the third-rate. As to the forger's pitfalls, Friedlaender mentions an amusing trait: 'St. Catherine receiving the ring was depicted; the ring was, however, no longer recognizable in the poorly preserved original. In the copy, the Infant Christ busies himself quite unaccountably with the finger of the saint, since he has no ring to bestow.' The

70. *Jahrbuch der kunsthistorischen Sammlungen*, vol. 2 (1884), p. 159. G. Glück, *Pieter Bruegels des Älteren Gemälde* (1910), p. 16.

71. Burlington Fine Arts Club, *Catalogue of a Collection of Counterfeits* (1924), no. 60, pl. 6.

72. *Exhibition of Flemish and Belgian Art, Illustrated Souvenir* (1927), p. 33, no. 86. R. Fry, in *The Burlington Magazine*, vol. 50 (1927), p. 261. C. Hulin de Loo, in *Académie Royale de Belgique, Bulletins de la Classe des Beaux-Arts*, vol. 9 (1927), p. 46. F. Winkler, in *Kunst und Künstler*, vol. 28 (1930), p. 364. M. J. Friedländer, *On Art and Connoisseurship* (1942), p. 271, pls. 38, 39.

history of this forgery is quite interesting. It may serve as a warning against too great confidence in mechanical tests of genuineness. Usually the hardness of the colours is regarded as the surest proof of age (see p. 27). 'The Marriage of St. Catherine' withstood all alcohol tests and was declared genuine by the technical experts.

El Greco.

Greco kept a large workshop, mainly occupied with repetitions of the more successful of his pictures. In the inventories of his studio, drawn up by his son after Greco's death, some compositions are represented by as many as four or five repetitions of various dimensions. That a distinction was made between originals entirely by the master's hand and studio copies becomes evident from an entry in the inventory which lists four versions of the 'Purification of the Temple', one of which is distinguished by the words 'this is the original'.[73] The Greco vogue of our century drew all these replicas out of their obscure dwellings, and some works appeared on the market in series of twenty and more versions.

Apart from these authentic replicas it should not be overlooked that Greco was never quite as forgotten as his discoverers of the twentieth century would have it. Long before his revival his name was famous enough to be occasionally attached to works of a very different style, as is proved by an Italo-Flemish sixteenth-century portrait in the Vienna Museum.[74] This picture shows the misspelt inscription: '. . . toscopoli f.anno MDC', which seems to have been added in the eighteenth century. This forger was very ignorant, for not only did he misspell the artist's name, but he apparently did not know that Domenico Theotocopoli invariably signed his pictures with Greek characters.

Though Greco himself provided so well for the collectors, the supply is evidently insufficient in one part of his *œuvre*: portraits were not multiplied like devotional pictures, and this shortcoming was eagerly remedied by his forgers. The easiest way to

73. *Archivo Español de Arte y Arqueología*, vol. 3 (1927), p. 289.

74. *Führer durch die Gemälde-Galerie, Wien* (1908), no. 596. M. B. Cossio, *El Greco* (1908), pp. 27, 551, pl. 106. J. Camón Aznar, *Greco* (1950), pp. 74, 1391, fig. 47.

effect this was to use portraits by other painters, preferably Spanish ones. But modern copies and imitations had to be added as well. The 'Portrait of an Elderly Man' in the Prado has been used several times for this purpose, sometimes even including the signature (*Plate* 13).[75] The copyists did not strive for quality in their work. A long face, large eyes and a pointed beard are all that is usually expected of a Greco. All these features appear on a fraudulent copy of the so-called self-portrait in New York which, incidentally, is no self-portrait.[76] The copy looks like a caricature of Greco's style. The head is of a grotesque egg-shape, the face extremely elongated. The Star of Santiago on the sitter's coat has been added by the copyist to make it perfectly clear that the portrait represents a Spaniard.

Vermeer.

When speaking of the retrospective style of Dutch painters of the eighteenth and early nineteenth centuries (see above p. 39) I mentioned Dirck Jan van der Laen (1759–1829) who painted landscapes in the manner of Vermeer. However, this was rather an exception, the day for Vermeer had not come yet. It is symptomatic that the value of his pictures could be enhanced by the addition of faked signatures of minor masters. Thus the 'Painter in his Studio' (Vienna) still shows the fraudulently added signature of Pieter de Hooch,[77] and the 'Diana' (Mauritshuis) even bore the name of Nicolaes Maes.[78]

The Impressionists raised Vermeer to the rank of one of the world's greatest painters. Now his works, which were always very rare, are coveted like those of no other artist and have become the dream of every collector. The forgeries are, for a large part, old pictures into which Vermeer's famous colour scheme of yellow and blue has been introduced. Thus his two views of Delft were, in recent years, joined by a third one which was exhibited at the

75. F. Rutter, *El Greco* (1930), frontispiece and pl. 35; review by A. L. Mayer, in *Pantheon*, vol. 8 (1931), p. xxxvii.

76. A. L. Mayer, in *Belvedere*, vol. 5 (1924), *Forum* p. 139, fig. 2.

77. See above, p. 45.

78. A. B. de Vries, *Jan Vermeer van Delft* (1939), p. 77.

Munich Gallery with the Thyssen Collection.[79] The picture, hailed as the 'greatest surprise' of the exhibition, was in reality an ordinary Dutch landscape of the eighteenth century, with fields in the foreground and a small village in the distance. One day the modest houses of this village were ennobled by the addition of the steeple of the New Church of Delft. Together with a few other architectural details copied from Vermeer's painting, this was regarded as a sufficient transformation. Thanks to a vigorous protest by Dr. Bredius, the famous Dutch connoisseur, the 'View of Delft' disappeared as suddenly as it had turned up.

In other cases Dr. Bredius' criticism was of no avail. The head of a girl with a coquettish smile still occupies a place of honour in a great gallery.[80] It is a combination of two of Vermeer's paintings: the face is copied from the picture at Brunswick, while the general arrangement and the pearl shining in the girl's ear are an imitation of the 'Head of a Girl' in the Mauritshuis. Some other female heads are painted in a broad, impressionistic technique for which it would be difficult to find any parallels in the work of Vermeer or of his contemporaries. An imaginary late style was put forward as an explanation of this strange phenomenon.

There exist some fraudulent copies, but no imitation can bear the test of being compared with the natural grace of pose and expression of the exquisite originals. It is no mere chance that concerts were one of Vermeer's favourite subjects. He endowed his figures with a rhythm evocative of music. The guitar-player at Ken Wood swings with the tune she is playing. Her ear is bent towards the instrument, her lips are humming the tune, and her eyes and the light playing on her face fall in with the rhythm. Even her curls have been caught by the movement, and it proves the failure of the copyist to understand the picture that he left them out on his version.[81] His girl does not think of her guitar,

79. (Heinemann-Fleischmann:), *Sammlung Schloss Rohoncz, Gemälde* (1930), no. 338, pl. 68. *Der Cicerone*, vol. 22 (1930), p. 364. A. Bredius, in *The Burlington Magazine*, vol. 61 (1932), p. 145.

80. A. Bredius, in *The Burlington Magazine*, vol. 61 (1932), p. 145. A. B. de Vries, *Vermeer* (1948), p. 64.

81. *Burlington Magazine*, vol. 52 (1928), p. 43. *Kunst und Künstler*, vol. 26 (1928), pp. 246, 322 sq.

12. The 'Montefeltre Family'. Modern forgery, once attributed to Melozzo da Forlì. (By courtesy of the Trustees of the National Gallery, London.)

13. Fraudulent copy of a portrait
by El Greco.

14. 'Merry Cavalier'. Forgery of a Frans Hals.

but looks coquettishly at the spectator. She is evidently not musical. Compared with this profound misunderstanding of its model's main theme, the other shortcomings of this copy, which was long taken for the original, appear almost negligible. But it cannot be overlooked that the brilliant light has gone flaccid, the folds of skirt and carpet have stiffened, and the landscape hung on the wall has had to forgo all its life and charm.

Vermeer is just now the centre of all discussions on forgeries. It is still too early to speak of the Van Meegeren affair, as up to now only insufficient reports in newspapers are available.[82] But this spectacular case tends to obscure the fact that long before the emergence of Van Meegeren, Vermeer belonged to the most ill-used of old masters. There is perhaps no other painter with so large a percentage of forgeries among his officially recognised *œuvre*.

Frans Hals.

The misrepresentation Frans Hals had to endure is almost as bad as that suffered by his younger compatriot Vermeer. His main advantage is that he has more authentic works to back him up. Since his own lifetime his sketches have been the target of copyists and imitators. In modern times not even his more formal portrait style has escaped imitation. But it remains doubtful whether one may speak of imitation when the sitter in such a 'Frans Hals' portrait shows an anxious expression instead of the boldness typical of the master. This portrait shows a man in a broad-brimmed black hat who holds a wine-glass clumsily between his fingers. Apart from the initials F.H. and the thick impasto in the face there is not much to recall Frans Hals, and one wonders how such a wretched performance could ever have been accepted as genuine.[83]

This is not the usual type of unauthentic Hals. What is most admired is the broad brushwork of his studies and of his late pictures. In consequence laughing children and fisher-people were multiplied until one tends to forget the limited number of such pictures painted by the artist himself. Neither is there a lack of merry drinkers and laughing cavaliers. The famous canvas at

82. * See below, p. 329.
83. W. R. Valentiner, *Frans Hals* (1923), p. 300.

the Rijksmuseum appears to have been the model for a much
coarser version which kept the Dutch Law Courts busy in the
much discussed case Muller & Co. versus de Haas (*Plate* 14).[84]

This picture had been sold to a firm of art dealers together with
a certificate of authenticity issued by one of the greatest authorities
on Dutch painting, the late Dr. Hofstede de Groot. Later the
genuineness of the picture was suspected, and in the ensuing lawsuit experts were called to give their opinion. Sir Charles Holmes,
then Director of the National Gallery in London, Professor W.
Martin, Director of the Mauritshuis, and Dr. J. E. C. Scheffer, Professor of Inorganic Chemistry in Delft, were unanimous in condemning the picture as a modern forgery. The results of the chemical analysis were particularly illuminating:

(1) The picture is painted with a gummous medium which is
soluble in water. The colours are of remarkable softness.

(2) The coat of the 'Merry Cavalier' is painted with artificial
ultramarine, a colour first produced in 1826.

(3) In the background Thénard's blue was found, a pigment
consisting of cobalt oxide and alumina, first produced by Thénard
in 1820.

(4) The white of the man's collar is zinc white, a pigment for
the first time manufactured in 1781.

The painter of the 'Merry Cavalier' did not bother which
colours were used in Hals' lifetime; he was, however, aware that his
picture would be submitted to the usual alcohol test. By attempting
to dupe the experts he was too clever by half. The colour film
of an oil painting hardens in the course of time to such a degree
that it does no longer, or not easily, yield to alcohol. In order not
to be given away by the alcohol test, the forger used a gummous
medium which is soluble in water, but withstands alcohol.

The presence of three modern colours in the work of a painter
who died in 1666 should have sealed the fate of the 'Merry
Cavalier'. But Dr. Hofstede de Groot, with a stubbornness worthy
of a better cause, stuck to his opinion. He settled the law case
before judgment was given by buying the picture for his own

84. I quote from the account of the dispute given by C. Veth in *Maandblad
voor beeldende kunsten*, vol. 2 (1925), pp. 334 sqq. See also *The Burlington
Magazine*, vol. 46 (1925), p. 192.

collection for 50,000 guilder. Then he went to attack the evidence of the chemical analysis. His counter-arguments were:

(1) The soft colours of the 'Merry Cavalier' are no proof of its modern origin. A Dutch restorer found a method to soften the colours of old oil paintings.

(2) Natural ultramarine is distinguished from artificial by the inclusion of minute white or colourless impurities. Of course, Frans Hals used natural ultramarine, the only one known in his time; but he knew of some method to purify it.

(3) In regard to Thénard's blue, Dr. Hofstede has not come to a final opinion, but 'as I am firmly convinced of the authenticity and antiquity of the picture, I feel confident that a solution for this problem will be found.'

(4) The manufacture of zinc white is so simple that every painter could have done it himself.

Moreover, for Dr. Hofstede the results of the scientific examination are not only inconclusive, they are also irrelevant. Under the slogan 'Eye or Chemistry', stylistic or chemical analysis, he declared that the only competent judge of works of art is the trained eye of the connoisseur. It is unnecessary to stress the fact that this antithesis does not exist, and that the evidence of style and science, if correct, will always agree. A glance at the photograph of the 'Merry Cavalier' will be sufficient to convince every unprejudiced observer that the picture is nothing but a crude and superficial imitation which, inexplicably, deceived a very great connoisseur.

With Frans Hals it should be observed that, broad though the strokes of his brush may be, every single one of them sits exactly in the right place and is highly expressive of light, shape, or character. The mere lavish use of broad impasto, combined with one of Hals' familiar subjects, does not yet constitute an original by his hand.

The fact that the majority of the pictures by Frans Hals are in private, and often inaccessible, collections offers golden opportunities to the forger. A comparison between original and copy is in many cases impossible, and it is thus easy to sell fraudulent doubles which boast the pedigree of the originals. Prince Demidoff in San Donato was the owner of two splendid portraits by Hals. When his collection was broken up, the two pictures were separated, a deplorable act of vandalism as the artist conceived the portraits of husband and wife as one composition. The portrait of Stephanus Geraerdts, alderman of Haarlem, was acquired by the Antwerp Museum, while the portrait of Isabella Coymans, his wife, landed eventually in the collection of Baron R. de Rothschild, where it remained unknown and inaccessible. Meanwhile a fraudulent copy had made its appearance on the art market in Paris. Everybody regarded it as the original, and it was acquired for one of the choicest and most select of America private collections.[85] When, some years later, students had an opportunity to see the original in the Rothschild Collection, the swindle became clear. Even in a black-and-white reproduction the defects of the impostor are obvious. The intense expression of the features which Frans Hals imparted to his portraits, proved, as always, inimitable. All the details of the dress look dull when one compares their pedantic execution with the spirited brush strokes of the original. From the moment a comparison was possible, the decision between original and forgery was not difficult. But were it not for the reappearance of the authentic Demidoff portrait, the copy would most likely still occupy the place of honour. Still another factor contributed to its temporary success: in front of a work of art, which we believe to be a famous and well-established masterpiece, our critical faculties lie usually dormant.

Corot and the Impressionists.

While Corot was still alive quite a number of minor French painters endeavoured to follow in his footsteps. Those who knew him personally used to borrow his sketches in order to copy them. The good-natured master never refused this favour; occasionally he even found time to touch up their copies with a few brush strokes.[86] To-day these pupils and

85. W. R. Valentiner and C. Hofstede de Groot, *Pictures in the Collection of P. A. B. Widener* (1913), pl. 15. N. S. Trivas, *The Paintings of Frans Hals* (1941), p. 58.

86. E. Moreau-Nelaton, in A. Robaut, *L'œuvre de Corot*, vol. 1 (1905), p. 333. A fraudulent old copy after Corot has been studied in an instructive paper by D. Rosen and H. Marceau, in *Technical Studies in the Field of the Fine Arts*, vol. 6 (1937), pp. 37 sqq.

imitators of Corot are forgotten, with one exception: Paul Desiré Trouillebert (1829–1900), a gifted painter who came very close to Corot's manner. He became famous when in 1883 Alexandre Dumas Fils bought one of his landscapes as an original by Corot.[87]

This gives a fair idea of the possible fate awaiting such imitations if they did not find a safe refuge in some provincial museum. Apart from these followers, the international fame of Corot's silvery manner created many deliberate fakes. The grey tone and blurred outlines, which were considered the chief characteristics of a Corot, were easy enough to imitate. The thousands of false Corots on the other side of the Atlantic are a standard joke among European collectors, but it remains doubtful whether European collectors have any reason to crack jokes about the credulity of their American colleagues. Corot pictures of this kind can and ought to be ousted by a careful comparison of every piece with Robaut's catalogue of Corot's authentic pictures, for this painter knew certainly more of Corot's true *œuvre* than anybody else.[88]

The uncomfortable evidence of Robaut's catalogue was circumvented by a trick which was originally devised only to deceive an eccentric old man who developed a mania for buying Corots by the hundred, on the condition that no single sheet or picture should cost more than 100 francs. Thus the paralytic Dr. Jousseaume spent the end of his life buying cheap Corots that some persons with a lively sense of business never ceased to supply. After having collected 2,414 Dr. Jousseaume died in 1923. Had he lived longer Corot's *œuvre secrète* might have reached an even more spectacular figure. This collection was picked up by the doctor in single pieces and small lots from what he describes as dealers in a small way. This did not hinder those who published it after his death from pretending that the whole collection formed the contents of an *armoire mystérieuse* which Corot was supposed to have left in the house of some friends. But even the finest examples of this surprising *œuvre* do not call for any romantic explanation. The great majority would be a horrible calumny to

87. P. Eudel, *Le truquage* (1887), pp. 128 sqq.
88. A. Robaut, *L'œuvre de Corot* (1905).

any good painter. It is useless to pretend that a real artist could become a mere scribbler in private, as it has been done by the advocates of the mysterious cupboard. To the eye of the unprejudiced this fabulous collection consists of a number of oil paintings ranging in subject from 'Robbers' to a 'Joan of Arc'. Probably not one of these pictures is a fake. They are merely trash as it can be picked up in Paris by the hundred. However, the bulk of the collection does not consist of paintings, but of sketches. The great majority of these are done in a plain and simple technique similar to gouache, which is called *détrempe*. Corot never used this very rough way of making a coloured sketch. But Dr. Jousseaume possessed 1,000 *détrempes*. The swindle was crowned by the inscriptions, which appear to have formed the main attraction of these sheets. They are scribbled in various handwritings bearing at the best a very vague resemblance to Corot's own hand. Their contents are not very inspiring. They pretend that the artist was engaged in a perpetual soliloquy of which he jotted down the most insignificant remarks. 'Shall I turn to the right or to the left?' is one of the more frequent notes. The language is banal, and the comments are frequently coarse.

'Near the village of Lignières, I just completed two sketches which are very similar to one another; this happens to me often enough.' That is just what the authors of the swindle would have wished Corot to say of himself.

Or another: 'Valley near Gallardon, I am asking myself what will become of all my sketches after my death, well here I am giving way to my melancholy ideas, I shall be happy if somebody profits by them.' Somebody did profit.[89]

Among nineteenth-century French painters Corot holds easily the record for forgeries. Daumier follows at a distance. The position might, however, be reversed were we to take into account the ratio between genuine and spurious works. Daumier's not very numerous oil paintings have been vastly increased in num-

89. R. Huyghe, 'Simple histoire de 2,414 faux Corots', in *L'Amour de l'Art*, vol. 17 (1936), pp. 73 sqq., 146 sqq.

bers by spurious repetitions and by oil copies of his water-colours and book illustrations.[90]

Of the Impressionists it may be said that the moment of their general recognition coincided with the appearance of the first forgeries. The recently published letters of Camille Pissarro (1830–1903) to his son Lucien give us some insight into the depths of misery and contempt through which the Impressionists had to live for many years. It was only during the last ten years of his life that Pissarro found buyers for his pictures. In 1893 the first forgery turned up. Two years later Pissarro wrote: 'I am conducting a campaign here against forgers who are peddling fake paintings and gouaches, among others a large gouache by Piette, signed with my name, forged of course, and misspelt.'[91]

Paintings by the early imitators and contemporaries of the Impressionists, all provided with false signatures, constitute the majority of forgeries. Copies and pasticcios are still the exception. *Plate* 15 shows a curious concoction. It is a large pastel on cardboard, which appeared some time ago on the art market under the name of Degas. The composition is copied from Manet's 'Intérieur du Café' (in the Burrell Collection), the figure of the old gentleman with the silk hat is lifted from another Manet, the 'Café-Concert' (in Baltimore).[92] This transplantation accounts for his dwarfish proportions. The forger made up by industry for the talent he lacked: he adorned the back of the cardboard with a large and clumsy copy after one of Degas's nudes (*Plate* 16).

In 1944 the discovery of some false Manets in a loan exhibition which then toured England, was widely discussed in the daily

90. Cp. a fraudulent copy after the water-colour 'L'Attente' (the original is in the Victoria and Albert Museum) discussed in *The Journal of the Walters Art Gallery*, vol. 3 (1940), p. 37; and a copy after a woodcut: *Exhibition of Paintings, Bomford Collection* (1945), pl. 10; T. Bodkin, in *The Times*, November 27, 1944; *The Times Literary Supplement*, September 8, 1945.

91. C. Pissaro, *Letters to his son Lucien*, edited by J. Rewald (1943), pp. 213, 277.

92. Manet's originals are nos. 303 and 443 in the catalogue compiled by Jamot and Wildenstein. The original of the Degas on the back is the drawing of the Vente Degas (1919), III, no. 314.

papers. One of the pictures, the authenticity of which was disputed, was a portrait of Madame Manet, an almost literal repetition of a painting in the Museum in Oslo. It would perhaps be rash to condemn the disputed version as a mere copy, as has been done by most experts.[93] The hands and the dress are the work of a great painter, and are, in every respect, worthy of Manet himself. The rest of the picture, especially the face, betrays an inferior and clumsy hand, and the unfinished background is hardly more than a jumble of meaningless brush strokes. The most likely explanation of this striking difference in quality seems to be that this is a canvas which Manet abandoned at an early stage and which was later touched up and made saleable by another hand. This procedure is not uncommon and, it is reported, was used more than once on Manet's and Cézanne's unfinished works.[94]

An account of forgeries in this field would be incomplete without a reference to the Duret pedigree swindle. The name of Théodore Duret is intimately connected with the history of the Impressionist movement. He was one of the first admirers of the Impressionist painters, he bought their works at a time when they were generally laughed at, and he defended them courageously in the press. His first collection was sold in 1894 and a pedigree 'from the Duret Collection' came to be regarded as the best guarantee of a picture. In later years, when his mental faculties and his memory were no longer strong, a gang of swindlers made use of his name. They used Duret as a kind of agent, and he bought, sold, and certified their products. When he died, his collection consisted for the most part of forgeries. His executors tried to weed out the doubtful pieces before the sale of his pictures,

93. *Exhibition of Paintings, Bomford Collection* (1945), no. 17; see also the review in *The Times Literary Supplement,* September 8, 1945. Letters in *The Times,* 1944, December 8 (T. Bodkin), December 9 (H. J. P. Bomford), December 12 (P. Oppé).

94. See the remarks of J.-E. Blanche (*More Portraits of a Lifetime,* 1939, p. 147) on the fate of Manet's unfinished *Baigneuses* (I owe this reference to Dr. F. Grossmann). Two different aspects of this ever-changing picture can be seen in the reproductions in (1) T. Duret, *Histoire d'E. Manet* (1902), p. 94, and in (2) Jamot-Wildenstein, *Manet* (1932), fig. 63.

15. 'Intérieur du Café'. Pastel. A pastiche from two paintings by
É. Manet.

16. Nude in the style of Degas. On the reverse of the false Manet (Plate 15).

but the harm was already done and true and false sail now under the flag 'certified by Duret'.[95]

Vincent Van Gogh.

More than thirty hitherto unknown Van Goghs appeared on the art market between 1925 and 1928. They were painted in the artist's characteristic style and represented his favourite motives. Among them there were four self-portraits (*Plate* 17) and as many groups of tall flame-like cypresses. The sunflowers, the sower in full sunlight, the Zouave, they were all present. The leading experts certified their authenticity, collectors bought them eagerly and all thirty-three were duly incorporated in de la Faille's authoritative catalogue of Van Gogh's *œuvre*, published in 1927. In 1928 a large and comprehensive Van Gogh exhibition was held in Berlin. During the preparations for this exhibition, when they were seen side by side with fully authenticated works, serious doubts in the newly found pictures were uttered for the first time. Investigation showed that all thirty-three pictures could be traced back to the Berlin dancer and art dealer Otto Wacker. Interrogated, Wacker asserted that he had bought the pictures from a Russian residing sometimes in Switzerland, sometimes in Egypt, whose identity he had pledged his word not to reveal. In the ensuing lawsuit a number of experts appeared in the witness-box. They contradicted each other and themselves, and though the trial ended with Wacker's condemnation, the general impression was one of confusion.[96]

How was it possible that some thirty new versions of well-known pictures could turn up without arousing suspicion? It was greatly in their favour that Van Gogh himself occasionally repeated his compositions. Thus Otto Wacker (or rather the painter

95. *Kunst und Künstler*, vol. 26 (1928), p. 296. J.-B. de la Faille, *Les faux Van Gogh* (1930), p. 16.

96. C. Glaser, in *Kunst und Künstler*, vol. 27 (1929), pp. 131 sqq. J.-B. de la Faille, *Les faux Van Gogh* (1930). G. Ring in *Kunst und Künstler*, vol. 31 (1932), pp. 153 sqq. H. Ruhemann, 'Les méthodes d'expertise scientifique au procès des Van Gogh', in *Mouseion*, vol. 6 (1932), pp. 132 sqq. J.-B. de la Faille, *Vincent Van Gogh* (1939), p. 553.

in the back room who worked for him) did not have to create new
and plausible Vincents: all he had to do was to copy existing
pictures. In general the Wacker pictures give of Van Gogh all that
copies can give. Seen by themselves, they reflect a good deal of the
impression of the originals, and reveal their inferiority only when
confronted with their prototypes. They are plausible, not because
they are conceived in the spirit of Van Gogh but because they
are, for the larger part, faithful copies. The two versions
of the Zouave's head are nothing but a detail copied from
the famous painting. In most cases some minor alterations were
made or the background was changed but still they are copies
which may, at least from memory, easily be confused with the
originals. Where the forger tries to invent, his work becomes at
once unconvincing.

An attempt to out-Van Gogh Van Gogh characterises all the
Wacker forgeries. The originals look sober, compared with the
restless, nervous brush strokes of the imitations. What the forger
had got hold of was Van Gogh's habit of modelling the surface of
his pictures with bold strokes, applied with thick paint. These
powerful strokes of the brush give his pictures their rhythm and
their true meaning. Though the forger aped this technique he
neither caught the one nor the other. Neither did he succeed in
copying Van Gogh's way of painting, where the final modelling is
usually applied on top of a thick impasto, while the imitator, content to imitate the superficial aspect of his models, painted in Van
Gogh strokes, without the Van Gogh foundation. The difference
between the two methods has been studied with the help of X-ray
photographs.[97]

After the trial Wacker disappeared from the stage but the confusion created by the contradictory statements of the witnesses
allowed some of the forgeries to be infiltrated again into Van
Gogh's *œuvre*. Thus a Dutch art dealer acquired some of the
Wacker pictures as a promising investment. To provide them
with the much-needed authentication, he managed to prove by

97. A few of the X-ray photographs are reproduced in a paper by K.
Wehlte in *Kunst und Künstler*, vol. 31 (1932), pp. 177 sqq., and in A. Donath,
Wie die Kunstfälscher arbeiten (1937), figs. 32–3.

some heavy editing, that Vincent himself had referred to them in his letters.[98]

PORTRAIT SWINDLE

'Odi falsas inscriptiones statuarum alienarum.' (Cicero to Atticus).

The portraits of famous personalities of all countries and periods are sufficiently in favour to produce an artificial increase of their numbers. The more modest the artistic value of such a portrait, so much the easier does the forger's task become.

False portraits fall into two main categories:

(1) Imaginary portraits, usually book illustrations, either engraved or cut in wood,

(2) Old but uninteresting portraits touched up to resemble some celebrity.

The first group hardly comes under the heading 'forgery'; it is swindle, pure and simple. It is not always easy to differentiate between credulity, indifference, cynical fraud and the other motives which may have brought these 'portraits' into the world. In old times publishers thought that one face would do as well as another for a public that had no means of checking them, and similar methods are said to be still in use with some modern illustrated papers. Others merely counted on their readers' indifference. Schedel's *Nuremberg Chronicle* (1493), where the same block is used more than a dozen times to represent as many different persons, is a frequently quoted example. One woodblock showing the half-figure of a young man holding an open book, had in turn to serve for Azariah, the son of Odad, for the prophet Zephaniah, for Aesop, Valerius, Corvinus, the philosopher Krates, Philo Judaeus, Aulus Gellius, Donatus, Priscian, and finally for John Wycliffe.[99] An old man in profile, likewise

98. L. Justi, 'Philologia Wackeriana', in *Museum der Gegenwart,* vol. 3 (1932–3), pp. 120 sqq. An analogous case are the two versions of the *Jardin de Daubigny*. Cf. A. Hentzen, in *Zeitschrift für Kunstgeschichte,* vol. 4 (1935), p. 325; vol. 5 (1936), p. 252.

99. H. Schedel, *Liber Chronicarum* (1493), fol. 49v, 55, 70, 79, 82v, 97, 114, 132v, 143v, 238.

with a book, was printed as the likeness of Solon, Demetrius of Phalerum, the Stoic philosopher Panaitios, and Suetonius. In the chapters on medieval history the same block appears again as the Venerable Bede, Hugh of Saint Victor, Bernardus Compostellanus, Alexander of Hales, Johannes de Monte Villa and, for the last time, as the chancellor Jean Gerson.[100] We have no reason to smile at the credulity of a former age. A modern scholar accepted these woodcuts as portraits and included them in his iconography of the Byzantine Emperors.[101]

A similar case, quoted by M. H. Spielmann, is amusing but quite typical: 'In 1644 the *Mercurius Civicus* (the first English illustrated paper) gave a portrait in four successive weekly numbers, of Prince Maurice, Prince Rupert, the Marquess of Newcastle, and Sir Thomas Fairfax—and it was the same portrait each time, and nothing changed but the name.'[102]

Examples could be multiplied *ad libitum*.[103] One is perhaps worth quoting. In 1536 a report of the execution of Sir Thomas More was published on the Continent. No portrait of the Lord Chancellor was at hand but the publisher had a woodblock on which was represented the death of St. James the Greater. St. James as well as Thomas More was beheaded: for this reason Hans Weiditz's woodcut of the martyrdom of the Apostle appeared as frontispiece of the *Faithful Report of the Death of Sir Thomas More*.[104]

More honest were the engravers of 'altered portraits'. At any rate they took the trouble to alter the faces of their engravings before affixing a new name. The practice was common among the

100. Ibid., fol. 59, 80v, 82v, 111, 200, 213v, 214v, 227, 240.

101. S. P. Lampros, *Leukoma byzantinon autokratoron* (1930), pl. 11 sqq.

102. M. H. Spielmann, *The Title-Page of the First Folio of Shakespeare's Plays* (1924), p. 17.

103. See the illustrations in Holinshed's *Chronicle* (1577) and in Powell's *Historie of Cambria, now called Wales* (1584) studied by J. E. Lloyd and V. Scholderer in *The National Library of Wales Journal*, vol. 3 (1943), pp. 15 sqq., or the series of fictitious portraits published by François Langlois which form the subject of a fascinating book by R. Payer von Thurn (*Faust im Bilde*, 1919).

104. C. Dodgson, in *Maso Finiguerra*, vol. 1 (1936), p. 44.

engravers of the eighteenth and nineteenth centuries who used their engraved copper plates, for the sake of economy, for new portraits, changing the head only and leaving all the rest unaltered. It happened occasionally that the first portrait regained its interest and was therefore reinstated in its original place. An English seventeenth-century engraving of a man on horseback, based on Van Dyck's equestrian portrait of Charles I, served in five successive states as portrait of Oliver Cromwell, Louis XIV, Cromwell for a second time, Charles I, and again Cromwell.[105]

The same economical method was practised by Sir Thomas Lawrence when he had to paint the portrait of Wilhelm von Humboldt for the Waterloo Gallery in Windsor Castle. Lawrence is said to have painted the features of the German statesman on top of a portrait of Lord Liverpool which was no longer wanted. When she came to Windsor, Humboldt's daughter was amused to find her slightly-built father's head on the shoulders of an unusually tall gentleman.[106]

The case of the false Prince Rhodocanakis is unique. He actually published his own photograph as the portrait of an ancestor by Sir Peter Lely (1618–80). 'His Imperial Highness, the Prince' Demetrius Rhodocanakis, the author of this imposture was probably the most successful swindler of the nineteenth century. This Greek merchant who lived in London conceived one day the idea to declare himself a descendant of the last Emperor of Byzantium, and spent the rest of his life fabricating documents, genealogical trees and even tomb inscriptions proving his imperial descent. By some clever manoeuvre he got the British Foreign Office and the Papal Court to accept his titles.[107] He dedicated a large *de luxe* publication (1872) to his namesake and alleged ancestor Constantine Rhodocanakis, physician to Charles II. It has a frontispiece showing the features of Demetrius himself,

105. G. S. Layard and H. M. Latham, *Catalogue Raisonné of Engraved British Portraits from Altered Plates* (1927). The collection described in the catalogue is now in the British Museum.

106. A. von Sydow, *Gabriele von Bülow* (1929), pp. 222, 225.

107. The entertaining life-story of this famous swindler has been told in *Zeitschrift für Bücherfreunde*, vol. 12, part 1 (1908–9), pp. 173 sqq.; ibid. p. 190 on the Lely portrait.

taken, as the text tells, from a portrait 'painted by Sir Peter Lely, engraved by Robert Nanteuil'. Neither painting nor engraving ever existed; the portrait of the Honorary Physician to the King is in reality the re-drawn photograph of the impostor. On a visit to Vienna, Rhodocanakis selected a Van Dyck in the Imperial Gallery (No. 1032) and declared it to be a portrait of one of his ancestors. This suggestion was gratefully received by the Keepers, and, until a different identification was proposed, the picture was duly catalogued as 'Portrait of Prince Rhodocanakis'.[108] To this day, however, nobody seems to have realised that the Prince Rhodocanakis who suggested the name was the notorious swindler.

In 1845 *The Art Union,* the leading English art periodical of the time, led a campaign against various abuses in the art trade. Among these portrait swindle played an important part. 'There is another class of fraudulent pictures', we are told, 'which have no pretensions to be considered works of art, but may rather be included in the category of curiosities. We allude to portraits of eminent persons, such as Shakspere, Milton, O. Cromwell, Queen Elizabeth, and others—but these are among the favourites. The way of proceeding is to find among worthless, old, unknown portraits, such as in period and costume bear some resemblance or arrangement of feature that may, by means of engravings of the above eminent persons, be readily altered into the generally received likeness of them. The cavaliers of Elizabeth's reign, with their frills and oval-shaped heads, make passable Shakspere; a priest of Charles I's reign will do for a Milton; any obscure general in armour, with a tolerable nose, can be converted into an Oliver Cromwell; and a red-haired, long-faced lady, with plenty of ruff, makes a Queen Elizabeth: but if it happens to be a pretty face, it is transformed into a Mary, Queen of Scots.'[109]

Nowadays, with the help of X-rays penetrating the surface, most of these transformed portraits had to reveal the secrets of their previous identity, like the portrait of the little Dutch girl

108. *Burlington Magazine,* vol. 69 (1936), p. 153. To the Dresden Gallery he even sent a whole batch of forged documents successfully claiming another Van Dyck portrait (No. 1035) as Prince Rhodocanakis-Giustiniani.

109. *The Art-Union,* vol. 7 (1845), p. 344.

17. Self-portrait by Van Gogh. Forgery.

18. Self-portrait by Leonardo da Vinci. Eighteenth-century forgery.

19. The Duke of Wellington. Attributed to Sir Thomas Lawrence. Forgery after a daguerreotype.

who was changed into King Edward VI. (See above p. 25.)[110] Even more spectacular was the transformation of a female saint into a self-portrait of Leonardo da Vinci, which was done in the early eighteenth century.[111] This picture enjoyed great popularity for a long time and was regarded as one of the treasures of the Uffizi Gallery. In the seventeenth century Cardinal Leopoldo de Medici started the collection of artists' self-portraits in the Florentine Gallery. He and his successors tried to assemble portraits of all outstanding artists and, as no painted self-portrait of Leonardo existed, one had to be fabricated to gratify the Grand Duke's desire for a complete series (*Plate* 18).

The portrait shown on *Plate* 19 was hawked on the Continent a number of years ago. The head is not badly painted but the rest is extremely poor, particularly the arms which are of a ridiculous shape. The picture was offered as a portrait of the Duke of Wellington painted by Sir Thomas Lawrence. It is no portrait forgery for it actually represents the Iron Duke. It is copied from a daguerreotype taken in 1844, fourteen years after the death of Lawrence.[112]

110. Many of these altered portraits are the work of Edward Holder and P. F. Zincke who were active in the first half of the nineteenth century. A. Wivell, *An Inquiry into the History, Authenticity, & Characteristics of the Shakspeare Portraits* (1827), pp. 169 sqq. M. H. Spielmann, in *The Connoisseur*, vol. 22 (1908), pp. 93 sqq.

111. R. Sanpaolesi, in *Bollettino d'arte*, vol. 31 (1937), p. 495. Cf. also E. Möller, in *Belvedere*, vol. 9–10 (1926), p. 34.

112. For an engraving after this daguerreotype see Lord G. Wellesley and J. Steegman, *The Iconography of the First Duke of Wellington* (1935), p. 53, pl. 38.

PART TWO

CLASSICAL PAINTINGS AND MOSAICS

PART TWO

CLASSICAL PAINTINGS AND MOSAICS

CLASSICAL PAINTINGS

With the excavation of Herculaneum, around the middle of the eighteenth century classical painting became the centre of interest and forgeries began to make their appearance.[1] The most famous of these early forgeries was a 'Jupiter and Ganymede' painted by Mengs which deceived even the great Winckelmann (*Plate* 20).[2]

Among the few surviving specimens are two strange 'encaustic' paintings executed on slabs of slate. This classical technique of painting with heated wax as a medium was, in the eighteenth century, only known from the classical authors and therefore particularly occupied the minds. Both encaustics can hardly be taken seriously but enjoyed a wide publicity.

The 'Muse of Cortona' first appeared in 1744 (*Plate* 21).[3] She has been endowed with a romantic story. According to one of several versions, she was dug up by a farmer together with some

1. F. G. Consoli, in *Napoli Nobilissima*, N.S. vol. 2 (1921), pp. 84 sqq. These forgeries show unmistakably the late-baroque style of their period. Engravings after some of them can be found in A. Ambrogi's edition of Vergil (1763–5; vol. 2, p. 93; vol. 3, p. 191; etc.).

2. Goethe, *Italienische Reise*, 18 November 1786. C. Robert, *Archaeoogische Hermeneutik* (1919), p. 332, fig. 256. A. M. Morghen Tronti, *Commentari*, vol. I (1950), pp. 109–111.

3. *Saggi di dissertazioni accademiche pubblicamente lette nella nobile Accademia Etrusca di Cortona*, vol. 9 (1791), pp. 221 sqq. *Gazette Archéologique* (1877), p. 41. O. Donner von Richter, in *Jahrbuch des Freien Deutschen Hochstifts* (1902), pp. 161 sqq. E. Berger, *Die Wachsmalerei des Apelles* (1917), p. 62, fig. 1. C. Albizzati, in *La Critica d'Arte*, vol. 2 (1937), pp. 22 sqq.

20. 'Jupiter and Ganymede'. Imitation of a Roman fresco by Anton
Raphael Mengs. (By courtesy of the Gabinetto Fotografico Nazionale.)

21. The Muse of Cortona. Eighteenth-century imitation of a classical fresco.

antique bronzes which none ever saw. Though the picture represents a naked girl, the farmer mistook her for the Madonna and
worshipped her. When he found out that the image was profane
he used the slate to stop a window near his furnace. There his
landlord discovered it after some years. The picture stayed in the
squire's family until it was presented to the local museum. Nobody ever ascertained whether the medium of the painting actually
is wax, but the coy downward glance of the girl is sufficient evidence of the picture's modern origin. Nobody will ever know
whether the squire was fooled or whether he fooled the Academy
of Cortona.

An attempt to outdo the Muse was made with a portrait of
Cleopatra, Queen of Egypt.[4] It claimed a marsh near Rome as its
site of discovery, and was declared to be a contemporary portrait
of Cleopatra by the painter Timomachos. From 1822 onwards
the picture was boosted by every available means of publicity.
However, it was sold only once, and then only to another Italian
who hoped to resell it at a profit. While in good condition,
Cleopatra seems to have been a horrible picture. The doll's face
with lips parted and eyes turned to simulate agony, the trim
hairdress and the affected gestures of a provincial actress, all make
her unworthy of the attention she once aroused. The owner got
two scientists to analyse this masterpiece. Their certificates are
full of eulogy, and both fervidly asserted that the painting was
ancient as well as encaustic, though no signs of wax were found.
Notwithstanding these efforts, the picture found no buyer in
Italy. Therefore the story and the certificates were reprinted in
various languages to advertise the encaustic abroad. These papers
appeared all over the world, their authors calling themselves sometimes Count Orloff and sometimes Michael Iwanoff. In England
the boosting was done by the Italian poet Ugo Foscolo, who published an article on the 'encaustic' in the *London Magazine* of May
1826.[5] In a letter written a little earlier Foscolo's secretary told the
owner that there would be little chance of selling the picture in
England without any hints at a suitable provenance, however
discreet. Later on the picture was offered to the Louvre, but was

4. E. Berger, *Die Wachsmalerei des Apelles* (1917), pp. 11 sqq. figs. 2–4.
5. Reprinted in *La Bibliofilia*, vol. 15 (1913–14), pp. 70 sqq.

eventually returned to Sorrento. After her journeys across Europe poor Cleopatra was much the worse for wear. The swindle had failed.

Many ancient frescoes are in a sadly mutilated condition. Over-zealous restorations have done them great harm. Nowadays little attention is paid to fragments which can be found in older collections of antiques, as they are frequently retouched to such a degree that hardly anything can be discerned of the original surface.

Examination under the quartz-lamp will show the restored portions with the greatest distinctness. A good example for this is the figure of a winged Victory in the British Museum belonging to a series of detached frescoes from the Tomb of the Nasonii, all of which have been rather heavily restored. Of this Victory Mr. Hinks has published two photographs, one taken in normal light, the other in the ultra-violet fluorescent cabinet. In the latter all restored parts appear as dark patches, showing that, among other portions, the head of the figure is entirely modern.[6]

Of the 'Flute Player' (*Plate* 22) it has been said: 'For purity of pose and outline, and simplicity and breadth of colouring (in spite of heavy modern retouches), nothing from the antique surpasses the lovely head, in the British Museum, of a shepherd playing on the pipes, with its almost Giorgionesque fancy and feeling.'[7] In this case heavy modern retouches seem to be an under-statement; the entire surface of the painting is modern.[8] The lavish praise bestowed on the 'Flute Player' seems exaggerated, though the figure has a certain romantic charm. The fresco is said to have turned up in 1823 which would make it a contemporary of the 'Cleopatra'.

Completely undisguised is the nineteenth-century character of a fresco with a female nude in a coquettish pose, described as 'precariously but gracefully reclining on a slender branch against a black background.' Modelled with a naturalism quite foreign to

6. R. P. Hinks, *Catalogue of the Paintings in the British Museum* (1933), fig. 59, pl. 23.

7. E. Strong, *Art in Ancient Rome*, vol. 2 (1929), p. 23.

8. R. P. Hinks, *Catalogue of the Paintings in the British Museum* (1933), no. 92.

ancient art, this nude looks as if it had come out of the pages of
Le Nu au Salon or some similar publication. This fresco was
acquired for the archaeological museum of a great American
university, to give the students an opportunity of getting intimately
acquainted with a masterpiece of ancient art.[9]

CLASSICAL MOSAICS

Mosaics did not escape the fate of paintings. This may easily be
understood from the prominent part mosaics played in the interior decoration of classicism. Moreover, one marble cube looks
very much like another, and genuine Roman mosaics certainly
look very fresh and new, so that the forgers had nothing to fear in
that respect.

The frescoes in the Pyramid of Cestius were still visible in the
eighteenth century, but have disappeared since. We know them
from engravings. They incited an eighteenth-century artist to
compose a 'Roman' mosaic. He copied two of the ladies represented
on the walls of the pyramid and let them approach a small tripod.
But he thoroughly sentimentalised his ancient models. Their
heads have sunk down on their shoulders and their glance has
assumed a pathetic appeal, unable to make up for the lack of grace
of their pose. On the wall-painting one of the ladies carried a wine-
jug and a plate with some object on it. By some misunderstanding
the forger interpreted this object as a locust. It stands up like a
live animal, but the problem how a live locust could be carried on
an open plate remains unsolved. Perhaps the artist thought the
lady might pour wine on it from her jug.[10]

A mosaic representing the death of Archimedes belonged to
Jerome Bonaparte, King of Westphalia (*Plate* 23). It was published
in 1924 with a treatise intended to prove its antiquity from the very
oddness of its iconography. Archimedes is not drawing circles in
the sand on the floor of his room, as the scene is described by the
classical authors, but he is sitting in a comfortable chair by a table,
on which lies a slate. This he is trying to protect from the on-

9. *Art and Archaeology,* vol. 20 (1925), p. 126. P. Wolters, in *Archaeologischer Anzeiger* (1925), p. 282.

10. R. Herbig, in *Römische Mitteilungen,* vol. 48 (1933), pp. 312 sqq.

slaught of the soldier. The author of the pamphlet is at great pains to prove the identity of this tablet with the sand-covered abacus of antiquity, and the necessity of the table on which it rests. He might have saved his pains had he thought of looking at one of the most famous representations of Archimedes. In Raphael's 'School of Athens' the great mathematician bends down to draw figures on a slate looking exactly like the object on the table of the mosaic. This motif is the prototype of the purely Roman work, but the artist thought the posture somewhat inconvenient for a mathematician at home. Therefore he furnished his room with a comfortable chair and a convenient table, both of a design utterly impossible on an ancient monument. Of this mosaic S. Reinach said very aptly that it was probably executed by some zealous French artist who may have been among the competitors for the 'prix de Rome' in the time of Napoleon.[11]

During the classicistic period the descriptions of the famous paintings of antiquity as given by Pausanias were a favourite object of speculation and reconstruction. Such an attempt was made by the two brothers Riepenhausen, who published a series of drawings representing the underworld as painted by Polygnotus on the walls of the Lesche of Delphi. These drawings were reproduced in Rome in 1829. Long after this experiment had lost all interest for archaeologists some crafty forger availed himself of the opportunity it offered. He copied some of the drawings as a mosaic of red porphyry standing out against white ground, gave his works a suitably fragmentary contour and succeeded in passing off his 'Scenes from the Underworld' as genuine, until their prototypes were unearthed.[12] For the portraits from Centuripe see appendix p. 335.

11. F. Winter, *Der Tod des Archimedes* (1924). S. Reinach, in *Revue Archéologique*, vol. 22 (1925), p. 169. H. T. Bossert and W. Zschietzschmann, *Hellas and Rome* (1936), pp. il and 274. F. W. Goethert, *Zur Kunst der römischen Republik* (1931), pp. 56 sqq. B. Pace, *Arte e civilita della Sicilia antica*, vol. 3 (1945), p. 215. F. M. Feldhaus, *Geschichte des technischen Zeichnens* (1953), p. 7. W. Treue, *Kulturgeschichte der Schraube* (1955), p. 18. E. J. Dijksterhuis, *Archimedes* (1956), p. 32.

12. P. Wolters, in *Archaeologischer Anzeiger* (1925), p. 279.

22. Flute player. Imitation of a Roman fresco. (By courtesy of the Director of the Victoria and Albert Museum.)

23. The Death of Archimedes. Forgery of a classical mosaic.

PART THREE

ILLUMINATED MANUSCRIPTS

PART THREE

ILLUMINATED MANUSCRIPTS

EUROPEAN

The faking of whole manuscripts was attempted but rarely. Nevertheless illuminations are dangerous ground for connoisseurs and collectors. For every manuscript, however genuine, may contain spurious parts, ranging from whole pages to inserted initials. It is difficult to manufacture whole manuscripts, but it is comparatively easy to effect minor changes which, if taken at face value, may increase not inconsiderably the interest of a manuscript.

The art collector's interest in illuminations is of comparatively recent date. Old catalogues hardly take any notice of the decoration of manuscripts. Manuscripts in general were valued by the interest of the texts they contained, consequently prayer-books of the later Middle Ages were valueless. For this reason we find hardly any forgeries made before the beginning of the nineteenth century. Such few ones as there are owe their existence to bibliophile interests.

Thus a seventeenth-century librarian at Vienna added the missing title-page to the Calendar of Filocalus, a Renaissance copy of a late antique manuscript, copying for this purpose the corresponding page of another codex with the same text. This was known to him from an engraving published in 1634. But to the simple composition of the dedicatory page which, in the original, shows nothing but two children holding a tablet, the engraver had added a pompous archway in contemporary style. As the Vienna manuscript was written and illustrated by a German artist around 1500 the addition is easily discovered. It can be dated between 1634 and 1671, as the Vienna title-page was engraved in this year.[1]

Till far into the nineteenth century forgeries were not made or introduced into manuscripts for mercenary reasons. On the contrary, fakers were patriots who strove to establish the local history of literature and art on a broader basis. As to literary fakes, there is no need of quoting Macpherson.

One of his followers on the Continent was Vaclav Hanka (1791–1861), who forged a codex of early Czech poetry. At the same time he was a prolific forger of signatures in illuminated manuscripts.[2] In 1818 Hanka became librarian of the National Museum of Prague. This position afforded ample opportunities for his patriotic ambitions. He invented a whole school of Czech painters, whose names he inserted into the manuscripts wherever it occurred to him. He did not waste many thoughts on the likelihood of his inventions. The *Jaromirsch Bible,* one of the manuscripts he enriched after his own fashion, contains initials with prophets. Every prophet holds an empty scroll. Hanka adorned these handy scrolls with signatures, as for instance, ' Bohussus Lutomericensis pinxi'. In this case he even added a date: 'anno MCCLVIII'. This proved fatal to the ' School of Bohemian Painting ' as the *Jaromirsch Bible* is a fourteenth-century manuscript. Moreover in no period did artists make use of the first person in their signatures.

The amount of work achieved by Hanka's imaginary artists varies at his will. Some apparently never made more than a single initial. But his favourite was Sbisco de Trotina. He inserted the name of this fictitious artist into two famous manuscripts, the

1. J. Strzygowski, *Die Calenderbilder des Chronographen vom Jahre* 354 (1888), p. 24. The engraving is published in A. Bucherius, *De Doctrina Temporum* (1634), p. 275. The title-page from the Vienna MS. 3416 is reproduced in H. J. Hermann, *Beschreibendes Verzeichnis d. illuminierten Hss. in Österreich,* N. F. vol. 1 (1923), fig. 1. Its prototype from Brussels, MS. 7548, in P. Clemen, *Belgische Kunstdenkmäler,* vol. 1 (1923) fig. 1.

2. The first to doubt the authenticity of the inscriptions was the great Slavonic scholar Kopitar. M. Vasmer, *B. Kopitar's Briefwechsel mit Jakob Grimm* (1937), p. 82. A. Woltmann, *Repertorium f. Kunstwissenschaft,* vol. 2 (1879), pp. 2 sqq., 138 sqq. J. Neuwirth, *Mitteilungen d. Vereins f. Geschichte d. Deutschen in Böhmen,* vol. 29 (1890–1), pp. 297 sqq.

'Liber Viaticus' (Prague XIII, A.12) and the 'Mariale Arnesti' (Prague XVI, D.13). The latter manuscript contains a characteristic example of Hanka's work. In the scene of the Annunciation the angel displays his message on a scroll. It reads: 'Hoc Sbisco de Trotina p(inxit).'

Hanka's inventiveness was outdone by a patriotic painter of Verona, who produced a whole manuscript containing what purports to be the foundation of the painters' guild of Verona. This large-scale forgery goes beyond any of the earlier attempts to vie with Florence in being the cradle of Italian painting, though such attempts had been made ever since the seventeenth century. But they had never gone beyond false signatures or literary fakes of a far more modest character.

In Battistella's 'Memories and Stories' we are confronted with a manuscript consisting of two parts containing between them thirty-seven written pages and eleven sheets with drawings. It enjoyed the unexpected honour of being published a few years ago by a scholar of international reputation in a luxurious bilingual edition enriched by a learned commentary and first-rate reproductions.[3] The accounts of the painters' lives and works and of the foundation of their guild of Verona in 1303 are embedded in a tangle of love stories clumsily modelled on Boccaccio. Style and spelling are a caricature of medieval Italian. Battistella, the alleged author of the book, is described as a notary of Verona, but in the complete list of the members of this profession preserved from the thirteenth century onwards no similar name appears. Among the leading characters of the manuscript are a painter Altichiterio and his son Altichierino. Altichiero is the most famous medieval painter of Verona. His work in Padua still exists and documents referring to him are dated from 1369 to 1384. These dates were ignored till far into the nineteenth century, and Altichiero was assumed to be a contemporary of Giotto and Duccio. In choosing the dates for Battistella's stories around the end of the thirteenth and the beginning of the fourteenth century the faker was directed by this hypothesis. J. P. Richter writing in 1935 had to reconcile these dates with the progress of art history by creating a new ancestor to the well-known Altichiero.

3. Jean Paul Richter, *Altichiero* (1935).

As to its outward appearance, it was prudently written on sheets of paper showing almost no watermarks. The nineteenth-century hand of its author is disguised by long shafts and a somewhat shaky attempt to imitate fifteenth-century lettering. The illustrations, pen-and-ink drawings touched up with water-colour, consist of a series of portraits representing members of the 'guild' which are plainly romanticist in character, but which Richter accepted as fifteenth-century copies of originals a hundred years older (*Plate* 24). 'They give access to a strange world, nearer, so it seems, to early Japanese woodcuts and to other oriental curios than to our traditional ideas of Italian art. I feel sure that the latter produced similar works but this is not easily proved.'[4]

Numerous drawings by the same hand and with the same provenance are in the Museo Civico of Verona. One of them bears an inscription similar to the handwriting of the manuscript, and a fourteenth-century date.[5] It is assumed that the whole lot comes from the pen of the painter Pietro Nanin, who was for many years Director of the Academy of Verona (b. 1808, d. 1889).

The manuscripts fabricated by another forger, are so ludicrous that they make even "Altichiero" look correct in comparison. Henri Fabre, of Lausanne (1829–91), indulged in manuscripts of special interest for French collectors. He usually copied his texts from old books. Among his best titles are: 'Chronique de la Pucelle', 'Joinville's Voyage de St. Louis', and 'Chronique de France'. The vellum he used is thick as boards and just as hard. The lettering and decoration are so unlike all genuine manuscripts that nobody can be deceived by them who ever saw a medieval manuscript from afar. The alternating blue, red, and black script, as well as the coarse ornaments, look like a caricature of nineteenth-century book-decoration.[6]

With the progress of the nineteenth century the growing in-

4. J. P. Richter, *Altichiero* (1935), p. 8.

5. G. B. Cervellini, 'La Cronaca su Altichiero recentemente pubblicata è falsa' in *Atti del R. Istituto Veneto di Scienze, Lettere ed Arti*, vol. 95, 2 (1935–6), fig. 3.

6. British Museum, Add. MS. 30042. L. Delisle, in *Bibliothèque de l'Ecole des Chartes*, vol. 50 (1889), p. 439. S. de Ricci, *Census of Medieval and Renaissance Manuscripts*, vol. 2 (1937), p. 1374, no. 49.

terest for everything medieval led to the investigation of the old techniques of painting and illumination. Several old technical treatises were published, and inspired artists as well as forgers. Though whole manuscripts are occasionally faked, they appear not too often. There are too many pitfalls threatening the faker: the wording of the text, spelling and grammar, the writing materials, the lettering, and last and not least the illuminations.

A small prayer-book with illuminations which recently appeared in the auction-room has escaped hardly any of the defects enumerated here. The texts are confused and were evidently copied and compiled at random, without any knowledge of the contents and order of a Book of Hours .The Latin is faulty, brown ink was used to convey the impression of faded script, and the lettering is an anachronism. Medieval penmanship was the fruit of a laborious training such as a forger would rarely have an opportunity to undergo. Apart from this, the general sense of form has changed so fundamentally that a modern hand can hardly be disguised in lettering, which must be penned with unhalting fluency to look convincing. In this particular case the writing could hardly be mistaken for old script. But compared with false manuscripts of earlier origin, even this is a considerable step forward. So are the illuminations, which are better than most spurious pieces, though they look rather neo-Gothic.

Up to now such experiments have been rare. The average modern fakes of medieval illuminations may be divided into two main groups:

(1) Touched-up and embellished manuscripts.

(2) Fakes purporting to be fragments of manuscripts.

(1) *Touching-up.*

The work done by Mrs. Wing on some manuscripts of the collection of John Boykett Jarman which had been damaged by floodwater from the Thames may serve as a good example for touched-up miniatures. Part of the Jarmann Collection is now in the British Museum.[7] Mrs. Wing's restorations can be recognised by a disagreeably penetrating shade of blue, which she occasion-

7. The Jarman Collection was sold 13th June 1864; S. de Ricci, *English Collectors of Books and Manuscripts* (1930), p. 170, note 1.

Explicit Lib. V. Incipit Lib. VI.

Onus quidem Virgilius sexta plenus est, in qua hic liber

25. Theseus. Pen drawing copied from a Pompeian fresco and inserted in a manuscript dated A.D. 1467.

24. Portrait of Altichiero from the 'Cronaca su Altichiero'.

26. Ornamental border from a genuine 15th-century manuscript. (By courtesy of the Warburg Institute.)

27. Ornamental border. Modern work in 15th-century style.

ally mixes with red to get a violet tone of similar unattractiveness. Faces touched up by her are powdery pink, and their features have become of a uniformity unusual even for the poorer kind of fifteenth-century miniatures.

Among single leaves of a Flemish Book of Hours (Brit. Mus. MS. Add. 25698), all showing these symptoms, a landscape appears. It is enclosed by a genuine early fifteenth-century border, but must be a work of Mrs. Wing, as no landscape was ever included among the subjects illustrated in a Book of Hours. Though landscapes may appear as pictures of the months, they would have to include representations of the constellations and of the 'monthly occupations' of man. The connection of Mrs. Wing with the Jarman Collection is established by one of her own works (in the collection of Dr. E. G. Millar).[8] It is a 'Flight into Egypt', the background being an exact copy of a genuine illumination in a manuscript of the Jarman Collection.[9] Here one also notices that her whole technique is perceptibly coarser than that of her fifteenth-century prototypes.

This is intentionally honest restoring, but only a small step leads to fraudulent changes in old illuminations. A few strokes of the brush are sufficient to add, for instance, a coat of arms. One of the coats of arms most coveted by collectors is that of the famous bibliophile Matthias Corvinus, King of Hungary (1443–90). His coat of arms has been spuriously inserted into more than one manuscript which has no connection with his library.

Manuscripts and incunabula frequently contain bare spaces where the writer or the printer left blanks either for illuminated initials or for miniatures. Such empty spaces offer welcome opportunities for spurious ornamentation (*Plate* 25).[10]

8. Mrs. Wing's connection with the Jarman Collection was discovered by Dr. E. G. Millar, Keeper of the Department of Manuscripts at the British Museum who kindly communicated to me the facts underlying, this passage.

9. Now in the British Museum, Add. MS. 25695; a French Book of Hours from the second half of the fifteenth century.

10. A good example is a pen-drawing representing 'Theseus on Crete', which is inserted in a genuine Servius Manuscript of A.D. 1467. The drawing

Heinrich Klemm, a German collector of the last century, is responsible for outstanding examples of this practice. He brought together an important collection of early books, which became the foundation of the Deutsches Museum für Buch und Schrift at Leipzig. The value of this collection is seriously impaired by Klemm's desire to see the objects of his collection embellished. He caused missing initials to be illuminated and had many miniatures and ornamental borders added. A copy of the famous forty-two line Gutenberg Bible is an important example of these activities.[11] The copy was an exceptionally rich one, the printed text having been adorned by 136 genuine miniatures and two ornamental borders. Some of the miniatures and one of the two borders were cut out by a previous owner. To make up for this damage a subsequent proprietor in the seventies of the last century had the Bible restored by Pilinski in Paris, who mended the parchment, repainted the cut-out border, and added some smaller ornaments at the beginnings of several chapters. But this was not sufficient for H. Klemm. Not only did he complete Pilinski's border, but he also added numerous others and provided 143 new miniatures in addition to the 136 genuine ones, which did not escape touching-up. His borders may be recognised from the pointless and aimless distribution of the small sprigs between the leaves as compared with the beautiful precision of· a genuine ornament of corresponding style and period.[12] (*Plates* 26, 27.)

Another way of augmenting the value of a genuine manuscript is to erase parts of the text and substitute illuminations. This fraud cannot well deceive anybody who takes the precaution of reading the text, for then the absence of whole passages cannot escape notice.

has been published with a learned commentary. But it is a modern copy after a well-known fresco from Pompeii. The motive of this insertion was not fraud, but sheer delight in mystification. Cf. *Archäologischer Anzeiger* (1919), pp. 118 sqq.; (1923), p. 24.

11. Cf. J. Schinnerer, *Zeitschrift für Bücherfreunde*, N. F., vol. 5, 1 (1913), pp. 97 sqq.; see also P. Schwenke, *Gutenbergs zweiundvierzigzeilige Bibel* (1923), p. 9. H. Klemm, *Beschreibender Katalog des Bibliographischen Museums* (1884), p. 11.

12. From Brussels MS. 9026, fol. 485. Cf. V. Leroquais, *Le Bréviaire de Philippe le Bon* (1929), pl. IX.

28. Walter von der Vogelweide. From the Manesse Codex. Early fourteenth century. (By courtesy of the Warburg Institute.)

29. Portrait of Abélard. Modern forgery.

(2) *Fragments*.

The cutting out of illuminated portions from manuscripts is a regrettable but widely spread practice. Such cuttings were not made entirely at random. These vandalous methods were employed almost exclusively on manuscripts which were thought to be of little or no value as a whole. This affects above all liturgical manuscripts and prayer-books, and among these primarily such manuscripts which contained only a few initials or miniatures in a comparatively large bulk of written pages. Damaged or fragmentary manuscripts were of course frequently stripped of their illuminations, but this hardly applies to interesting texts. Rare texts of historical or literary value were not dismantled as a rule. In fact genuine fragments with initials or miniatures represent in the vast majority ecclesiastical subjects. Therefore any profane and above all any alluring historical subject appearing on a fragment should be viewed with a certain degree of suspicion.

It is comparatively easy to fabricate spurious fragments. A page of an old manuscript may be used for this purpose. The script can be erased on one side, while the genuine writing on the reverse of the 'miniature' enhances its value. But there are also examples without script on the back, and those in which the text has been faked along with the miniature.

Illustrated on *Plate* 29 is one of three false miniatures which have been derived from a famous model, the celebrated fourteenth-century collection of German minnesingers known as the 'Manessische Liederhandschrift'.[13] 'Abélard dreaming of Héloise' was taken for the French prototype of the Swiss miniature representing Walter von der Vogelweide (*Plate* 28); but it is nothing but a tracing of Walter's figure, with some minor alterations, as for instance the omission of the sword and the lengthening of the beard. The scroll has been inscribed with a letter from Héloise.

One of the two other miniatures is derived from the Manesse illustration showing a lady weaving, in front of whom a poet kneels. The other is a cunning combination of this same lady with Walter von der Vogelweide. The artist enhanced these composi-

13. E. Stange, *Die Miniaturen der Manessischen Liederhandschrift und ihr Kunstkreis* (1909), pls. 1–4. R. Stettiner, *Das Webebild in der Manesse-handschrift und seine angebliche Vorlage* (1911), pls. 1–8.

tions by giving them an erotic turn and adroitly adorned them with a background of chequers, as it is typical for French illuminations of the fourteenth century. On the back of the two other fragments passages from the *Roman de la Rose* are inscribed. They have no relation whatever to the illustrations, and it is significant that both have been chosen from the first canto.

Here I want to introduce the work of a faker, who, to judge from the number of examples known to me, must be quite prolific.[14] He apparently reckons with a widely-spread conception of mildly sweet and lyrically flirtatious Middle Ages. He is fond of representing young minstrels and damsels, preferably with musical instruments and with a sugary expression on their faces. It is hard not to recognise the young man wearing the stage costume of a page if one has seen him once. The stereotype formula employed for the ladies' *decolleté* is noteworthy (*Plates* 30, 31). His predilection for concerts may be explained by the fragments of old vellum he frequently used. They come from choir-books of various description, and it is particularly apposite that bars of church music should be illustrated by scenes of musical wooing. Less easy to explain is the fragment of a Graduale with an illumination representing a hunting-scene which was shown at an exhibition in Amsterdam in 1935.

Like many fakers of miniatures, this artist thought that he was putting himself on the safe side if he provided a nice net of cracks

---

14. The *œuvre* of this faker is considerable. It ranges from 'fragments' to entire manuscripts, e.g. an illustrated Juvenal. (C. G. Boerner, *Katalog XXV* (1913), pls. 4–5; *Bibliothèque de l'Ecole des Chartes*, vol. 75 (1914), pp. 229 sq.) Another of his more ambitious creations is illustrated in M. J. Friedlaender, *On Art and Connoisseurship* (1942), pl. 37. There exists also the painted outside of an ivory polyptych by the same hand (The G. A. Hearn Collection of Carved Ivories (1908), pl. 65). Some of his works go under the name of the Anglo-Spanish painter Jorge Ingles; cf. C. R. Post, *A History of Spanish Painting*, vol. 4, 1 (1933), p. 70 note. Dr. C. Nordenfalk kindly refers me to two publications in which characteristic works are illustrated: K. Luthmer, *Sammlung Thomee* (1931), pl. 55, and *Italiaansche Kunst in Nederlandsch Bezit* (1934), no. 430. Recently, the activities of the 'Spanish Forger' have been studied by M. Soria in an illustrated note in *The Connoisseur* (June 1946), p. 126.

30 and 31. Modern miniatures in fifteenth-century style.

32. Joan of Arc. Miniature in fifteenth-century style.

to cover his works. This was, of course, only possible with a layer of paint much thicker than that on genuine illuminations.

Another group of fakes is destined to pander to the historical tastes of collectors. Mr. F. Wormald kindly called my attention to two miniatures at the British Museum. One represents Henry VIII and Charles V before the throne of Pope Leo X.[15] The dragon of heresy lies at their feet, transfixed by a broken lance. This proves that it must be copied from some representation of Saint George. The style of the nineteenth century is written plainly over the whole thing from the folds of the garments to the ludicrous appearance of Henry VIII. The three names are inscribed on the green canopy, the colour of which is utterly impossible for the throne of a pope. But apart from all these apparent lapses, the technique alone would reveal this fake. Instead of the fine and thin painting of genuine miniatures a thick layer of colour covers the parchment.

'Hernando Cortez landing on the shore of Mexico' is another suspiciously alluring subject.[16] At first sight this miniature looks slightly more deceptive. The composition might be copied from some old book illustration, but the artist inadvertently adorned the foreground of his work with some tropical plants in a style which is unmistakably of the nineteenth century. Again the greasiness of the colours betrays a technique alien even to the latest period of genuine book-illumination. On the back of the parchment is outlined a very neat map of the western hemisphere which would never stand a comparison with genuine sixteenth-century maps.

Some initials with pictures of Jeanne d'Arc form a worthy counterpart to 'the Defenders of the Faith' and to 'the Conqueror of Mexico'. But even as fakes these miniatures are of an infinitely poorer quality.[17] The success of these forgeries can only be understood if we consider that they were not destined to deceive con-

15. Additional MS. 35, 254 S.   16. Additional MS. 37, 177.

17. Andrew Lang, *The Maid of France* (1908), frontispiece and plate facing p. 108. Cf. S. Reinach in *Burlington Magazine*, vol. 14 (1908–9), p. 356; vol. 15 (1909), p. 51. Anatole France, *Vie de Jeanne D'Arc* (1908), vol. 2, p. 480. *Jeanne d'Arc et son temps. Musée des Beaux-Arts, Rouen* (1956), no. 193.

noisseurs. Though the subject in itself gives more ground for
suspicion than all the other symptoms, it seems difficult to resist
an effigy of Saint Joan in full armour and carrying her historical
sword and standard (*Plate* 32). On one of the two miniatures her
face looks as if it had been drawn by some fashion designer of the
eighties or nineties of the last century; on the other the armour
she wears is adorned by circular and heart-shaped plates the
appearance of which excludes every hope of authenticity.

ORIENTAL

In Europe the charms of Eastern miniatures were not discovered before the beginning of the twentieth century. The
dangerous fakes were made for oriental collectors, particularly
for the important Indian collections. But here again outright fakes
are perhaps not quite as frequent as forged signatures. Foremost
among these range the alleged signatures of Behzad, the painter
most popular in Eastern and Western literature.

There is, however, no lack of modern fakes. On the whole the
forgers of fifteenth- and sixteenth-century Persian miniatures are
much more skilful than their European colleagues who try to
imitate Western illuminations. The design of the more efficient
oriental forgeries is so closely modelled on genuine illuminations
that it might be difficult, in black-and-white reproductions, to recognise them for what they are. As a rule heavy colours without
lustre have superseded the jewel-like brilliance of old illuminations. This is probably due to the use of a different medium. Anyhow, reds look brownish and all other colours have a grey tinge.

The great majority of such miniatures pose as fragments, or
rather as stray leaves from the albums of oriental collectors. But
the enhancing of genuine manuscripts by inserted illuminations
is not limited to forgeries of European miniatures only. The
forgers apparently did not always reckon with customers initiated
into Persian literature, for occasionally they even illustrated
mystical texts, such as the 'Masnawi' of Rumi.[18] This is as little
fitted for the insertion of numerous court-scenes, concerts, and

18. British Museum. MS. Or. 7693. Mr. Basil Gray was kind enough to
draw my attention to this manuscript, as well as to the following examples.

dances as any purely mystical text could be. But an ambitious forger of the nineteenth century adorned such a manuscript with quite a large number of miniatures. He was not content to fill the white pages preceding each book and the more limited space at the end of chapters, but erased many passages in order to gain room for his fabrications. In one case some fragments of letters are peeping out above the edge of a miniature. Many of the patterns used for the backgrounds of these miniatures are quite geometrical and visibly modern. However, stylistical evidence is quite unnecessary where the presence of so many lords, ladies, and musicians so manifestly establishes the iconographical impossibility, as happens in this particular case. But the author of this confusion, who barbarically ruined a carefully written book, was not ashamed of further raising the pretentiousness of this pasticcio by faking a colophon with the date A.H. 695 (A.D. 1295), while the original manuscript is of a much later date.

As they are comparatively easy to fabricate, the pen drawings of the Riza Abbasi type are favourites with the fakers. The style of the early seventeenth century is aped quite well by some of their works. However a spurious pen-and-ink copy made after a plate in a modern book (*Plates* 33 and 34), clearly demonstrates the poor draughtsmanship of the modern imitator. Even the limp pencil outlines on which he tried to improve with his pen are still visible. The expression of this old man has gone as insipid on the copy as the facial expressions on any modern fake of a European painting or drawing. To judge by its source this forgery seems to be an exception from the rule, and to be of European origin. It is, at any rate, poor enough to make it plausible.[19]

Plate 35 is a forgery meant to imitate a primitive Persian miniature.[20] This rather large figure of a bearded man is squatting on its ugly green background in a posture of almost dreadful symmetry, which is, moreover, stressed by the bulky shape of the instrument he is playing. Most amusing are the faker's attempts at mutilating his masterpiece. He applied his colours rather thickly

19. British Museum, Persian drawings, 1930–6–7–013. The drawing is copied after pl. 148 of P. W. Schultz, *Die persisch-islamische Miniaturmalerei* (1914).

20. British Museum, Persian drawings, 1937–7–10–0329.

on a dark brown ground and then rubbed off about half of what he had put on. So the brown shines through the green background, and this again through the red and brown of the figure. The face alone has been spared, but it got a nice crackling instead. All these symptoms occur, of course, as little on oriental miniatures as on European ones, but they are common to European and oriental counterfeits. I am at a loss to decide at which period this miniature is aimed, but so, perhaps, was the faker.

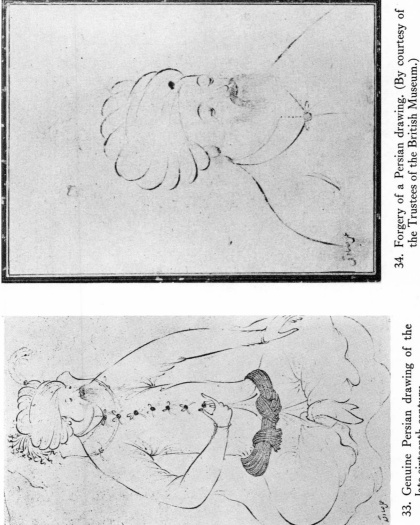

34. Forgery of a Persian drawing. (By courtesy of the Trustees of the British Museum.)

33. Genuine Persian drawing of the late sixteenth century.

35. Forgery of a Persian miniature. (By courtesy of the Trustees of the British Museum.)

PART FOUR

DRAWINGS

PART FOUR

DRAWINGS

The following anecdote is recorded by Condivi:[1] As a boy Michelangelo worked in the studio of Domenico Ghirlandaio. 'There he was given a drawing of a head to copy, which he did with such exactitude that his master took for the original the copy which Michelangelo returned to him, until he found the boy rejoicing over his success with one of his companions. Afterwards many people compared the two sheets, without finding any difference between them. For in addition to the perfect rendering of the original design, Michelangelo had been careful to smoke the paper of his copy, in order to make it look as old as its model. He got quite famous by this incident.'

Michelangelo's successful trick anticipates two essential qualities of faked drawings: the exact copying of the original and the artificial ageing of the paper. But above all this passage from Condivi explains the origin of most of those sheets which are regarded as fakes nowadays: every apprentice in the workshop of a painter or sculptor was given drawings or prints to copy, as part of his education. This was the initial stage, before he was allowed to draw motives from pictures or sculptures, while studies after the living model formed the most advanced stage. Of course the pupils tried to come as close as possible to the originals without any fraudulent intentions. Some of these copies were probably soon mixed up with the collection of originals available in every workshop. Thus James Northcote describes in his *Memoirs of Sir Joshua Reynolds* (1813) p. 13, how Hudson, Reynolds' first master,

1. A. Condivi, *Michelangelo* (1553, ed. d'Ancona, 1928), p. 37. Similar but less detailed is the account in Vasari (*Le Vite*, ed. A. M. Ciaranfi, vol. 6, p. 386).

set him to copy drawings. It is amusing to note Northcote's classicistic bias against Guercino: 'It appears that Hudson's instructions were evidently not of the first rate, nor his advice to his young pupil very judicious, when we find that, probably from pure ignorance, instead of directing him to study from the antique models, he recommended to him the careful copying of Guercino's drawings, thus trifling his time away; this instance serves to show the deplorable state of the arts at that time in this country: however, the youthful and tractable pupil executed his task with such skill, that many of those early productions are now preserved in the cabinets of the curious in this kingdom; most of which are actually considered as originals by that master.'

The accumulated number of such exercises is large, though of course only a small proportion of the copies made for the sake of study have been preserved. These innocent attempts form the majority of what are generally regarded as faked drawings. It may often be difficult to distinguish efficient workshop copies from original drawings by the master they emulate—particularly if the originals are lost. The same applies to the work of early professional copyists. I have spoken above (p. 33) of the imitators of Dürer who were so numerous during the later sixteenth and early seventeenth century. Drawings and water-colours, for which Dürer was rightly famous, naturally formed a large percentage of their output. Hans Hoffmann was the most diligent and most efficient of these copyists. Most of his water-colours after Dürer are carefully and proudly signed and dated, but, as H. Imhoff's diary tells us, the idea of introducing Dürer's monogram on such sheets arose early. Though highly efficient, a variation of a Dürer subject like the 'Blue Jay', signed and dated by Hoffmann, could never be seriously deceptive, even without the signature. He dispensed with many of Dürer's delightful details in the rendering of the feathers, and moreover he simplified the design by turning the bird into an almost frontal position. Thus the vigorous outline of the original was lost.[2]

It is easy to enumerate the shortcomings of a copy of this kind

2. London, British Museum. Cf. F. Winkler, *Die Zeichnungen A. Dürers,* vol. 3 (1938), p. 60. H. S. Francis, in *Bulletin of the Cleveland Museum of Art,* vol. 34 (1947), p. 13.

if its prototype is available. But we ignore how often we fail to make the right diagnosis if this is not the case.

Sir Peter Lely was accused, a few years after his death, by Constantijn Huyghens of having replaced originals from the Royal Collections by copies.[3] It is not known whether there is any truth behind this allegation, but it shows that the same practices, as they were occasionally applied to paintings, were at least feared in the more modest realm of drawings, even at such an early date.

In the eighteenth century the professional skill of copyists rose high, not only because of the steadily growing interest in drawings as works of art but chiefly in the service of the many facsimiles of drawings which were published at that time. It is only natural that collectors should have felt misgivings at the growing skill of imitators. The excellent copyist Ploos van Amstel (1726–98), for instance, has frequently been called a forger, but no proof of his alleged activities has been found.[4]

From these few remarks on the early history of the imitation of drawings one may gather that the number of deliberate fakes is small compared to the innumerable copies and imitations of style made for no fraudulent purpose. However, enough drawings exist which may be mixed up very easily with originals, as the techniques of drawing are comparatively simple and very deceptive effects may be reached by a skilful hand. Only rarely a clue is given by the drawing materials. Graphite, for instance, was not known before the second half of the sixteenth century, therefore a pencil drawing by Dürer must necessarily be posthumous.[5] Watermarks are rarely of any help, as the fakers either avoided them or found no difficulty in providing genuine old paper for their purpose. The only symptom that may arouse suspicion is the overzealous damaging of spurious sheets. Here the forgers are inclined to outdo nature. It is astonishing how many drawings were saved out of fires with more or less conspicuous signs of the ordeal.

3. *Burlington Magazine*, vol. 69 (1936), p. 135.

4. B.F.A.C. Exhibition 1924, no. 111, pl. 8. A. E. Bye, 'Ploos van Amstel' in *The Print Collector's Quarterly*, vol. 13 (1926), pp. 305 sqq. F. Lugt in *Jahrbuch der preuss. Kunstsammlungen*, vol. 52 (1931), p. 55.

5. J. Meder, *Die Handzeichnung* (second edition, 1923), p. 5.

One of the earliest forgers of drawings was the Bolognese painter Denys Calvaert (1540–1619). He copied figures from Michelangelo's and Raphael's frescoes, introducing some small variations so that his copies could pass as original sketches. These drawings were ordered by a certain Pomponio who smoked them and sold them to collectors. When the Cardinal d'Este showed Calvaert his collection, the artist had the pleasure of recognising a nude from the 'Last Judgment' and two figures from the 'School of Athens' as his own works.[6]

It is natural that Raphael, who in the eighteenth and nineteenth centuries was regarded as the greatest of all painters, should also range foremost among those who were faked. The great majority of these spurious sheets are copies after original sketches. They are usually well done and follow their models line by line, even in the cross-hatchings. However, their lack of freshness and character and the copyist's halting strokes become visible when such a copy is confronted with its prototype. In the Louvre drawing for the 'Belle Jardinière', for instance, the Child plays hide and seek with Saint John. In the act of peeping round at his playmate Jesus leans his face against his mother's knee, a delightful idea which Raphael expressed by the confluence of the two perfectly matched curves of leg and cheek. The copyist did not adopt this daring invention. He kept the cheek well apart from the knee. By this subtle alteration he spoiled not only the children's game but also the serene intimacy of the scene. The forger was also unable to render the light lines by which the landscape was hinted at on his model. But he conscientiously imitated the net of ruled squares covering Raphael's sketch as a mechanical help for the enlargement into the full-size cartoon. But the copy lacks the firm contours that are indispensable for such an enlargement.[7] Other copies are of an even better quality, though Raphael's sweeping rhythm and unity of form and movement was never caught by an

6. C. C. Malvasia, *Felsina Pittrice* (1841), vol. 1, p. 197. A. E. Popp, in *Zeitschrift für bildende Kunst,* vol. 62 (1928–9), p. 60.

7. T. Borenius and R. Wittkower, *Catalogue of the Collection of Drawings formed by Sir Robert Mond* (1937), no. 193, pl. 32. For the original see O. Fischel, *Raphaels Zeichnungen,* vol. 3 (1922), pl. 120.

imitator.[8] The fraudulent intentions of imitations of this kind are proved by numerous restored corners and other artificial damages.

Spurious inventions of Raphael drawings, or rather pasticcios after his works, are much less successful. O. Fischel illustrated such a sheet which fully reveals the dispirited monotony of a draughtsman who is no artist. The reiteration of the same figure without the experimental variations which are characteristic of such repetitions on an artist's sketch is alone condemning. Some lines added in 'Renaissance' script and the date 1503 show that this drawing is a deliberate fake.[9]

Raphael's popularity is said to have diminished in our time, but his fakers remain unabashed. The very recent forgery illustrated in *Plate* 37 is a partial copy of an original sheet (*Plate* 36). Presumably it was not executed after the drawing itself, but after a reproduction contained in a sale catalogue.[10] The head of the child is copied with great efficiency and exactitude, but the forger omitted almost all the other figures represented on the original sketch. He included only one of the sketches of children. On the original these figures obviously represent the Christ Child, and the sketch is destined for one of Raphael's Madonnas, but the forger was unaware of this and added a winged Cupid to the figure of Christ. This figure, for which he lacked a model, is completely different in style. The same applies to the child drawn in the left corner and emphatically crossed out to give the impression of Raphael trying out and rejecting several ideas. The drawing is adorned with several blotches and three 'restored' corners. In addition to this it boasts no less than three collectors' marks, all of them false. The two to the left refer to the collections of J. F. Gigoux and Carlo Praver,[11] while the third one is a copy of Lugt No. 1916, but the forger endowed it with a crown. He evidently belonged to that thorough class of people who think of everything. His model bears the number 74; this he did not copy, but he put '75' in the corresponding corner of his imitation.

8. J. Meder, *Die Handzeichnung*, (second edition, 1923), pp. 660 sqq.

9. O. Fischel, 'A Forger of Raphael Drawings', in *Burlington Magazine*, vol. 51 (1927), pp. 26 sqq.

10. Sale C. G. Boerner and P. Graupe, Berlin, 12 May 1930, no. 121.

11.. F. Lugt, *Les Marques des collections* (1921), nos. 1164 and 2044.

36. Drawing by Raphael (Genuine).

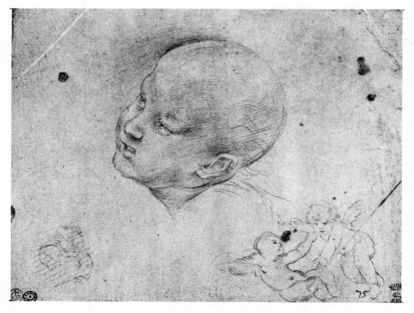

37. Drawing by Raphael (False).

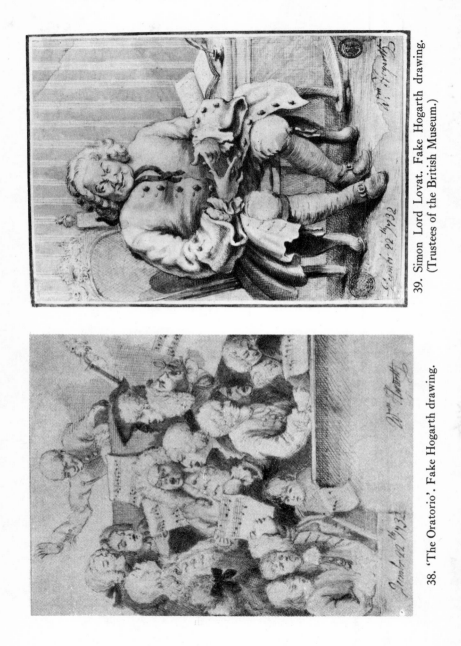

39. Simon Lord Lovat. Fake Hogarth drawing.
(Trustees of the British Museum.)

38. 'The Oratorio'. Fake Hogarth drawing.

The works and the method of this forger were found out by D. A. Scharf.[12] The collector's mark with the crown is a kind of signature tune; it occurs e.g. on a drawing in the style of Guardi which was copied from a plate in the same catalogue as the Raphael. Illustrations in sale catalogues seem to have been the forger's main source of inspiration.

In the nineteenth century early German drawings were faked along with early paintings. Two drawings of *landsknechte* in full garb are characteristic for this type of forgery.[13] By their richness of detail these drawings were meant to pander to the strong historical interest of this period. But to make them more valuable they had been enhanced by signatures reading 'L. 1522'. This is aimed at Lucas van Leyden, but this ambitious denomination is not warranted by the style of the drawings, which show no relation to this artist. Their models appear to have been Swiss drawings of the sixteenth century, but their smooth and academic technique differentiates them clearly from their prototypes.

False Guercino drawings have been produced since the late eighteenth century. E. Hoffmann has proved that a group of drawings at Budapest are copied from engravings after Guercino.[14] The fraudulent character of these copies is revealed by the fact that the draughtsman was careful to copy in reverse, in order to pass his works off as the original sketches for the engravings. He is given away by small but significant misunderstandings.[15]

It is astonishing that Hogarth should have been made the object of forgeries in Italy. This faker worked on rather simple lines. All his drawings are copied from engravings, and show the same date which he found inscribed on the

12. I owe the photographs here reproduced to the kindness of Dr. Scharf.

13. H. Tietze and E. Tietze-Conrat, *Die Zeichnungen der deutschen Schulen* (1933), p. 44, no. 350, pl. 122.

14. E. Hoffmann in *Jahrbücher des Museums der Bildenden Künste in Budapest*, vol. 6 (1929–30), 268, figs. 62–71.

15. A forgery of Guercino drawings on an unusually large scale has been discovered by Mr. Denis Mahon who kindly communicated to me his as yet unpublished results. When these are published, it will be seen that few collections of drawings have kept aloof from these forgeries.

subscription ticket for 'A Midnight Modern Conversation'. 'Decembr 22th 1732' is the date which he copied with 'The Oratorio' (*Plate* 38). We find the same date also on a copy after Hogarth's engraved portrait of Lord Lovat (*Plate* 39) though this engraving bears the date 1746 in the original. Though these copies are rather exact, they lack Hogarth's power, and especially the drawing of the faces and hands is very weak. The Lord Lovat drawing was turned out in several samples, coloured in varying degrees. One of the greatest difficulties the forger had to contend with in his series was the background. At first he apparently tried to cover this inconveniently empty space with a shadow, but on the example illustrated here he ventured on a blue and yellow wall-paper.[16]

There are two methods of reproduction which lend themselves to forgery: counterproofing and squeezing from drawings and paintings. By adequate damping and pressing counterproofs can be produced from any chalk drawing. Even if such a counter-proof has been retouched, it can usually be found out. The out-lines have a peculiar irregularity and raggedness, not similar to any kind of line drawn by hand. Most of the counterproofs in existence belong to the same class as most old copies of drawings: they are not fakes, but reproductions.[17] It is the same with squeezes or offprints in oily pigment made from paintings. To produce them the outlines of some part of a picture are gone over with oil-colour, and this is transferred by rubbing to a sheet of damp paper, after which the picture is cleaned, and the squeeze embellished with chalk or water-colours. On these large-scale sheets the mechanical character of the copy is still more visible than on the counterproofs of drawings.[18]

Silhouettes of famous personalities may be produced without much difficulty, as a profile cut out of black paper, or merely painted with ink, will serve the purpose, provided that the right

16. A different kind of Hogarth imitation are the drawings illustrated by M. H. Spielmann in *The Magazine of Art*, N.S., vol. 1 (1903), p. 554.

17. J. Meder, *Die Handzeichnung* (1923), p. 538.

18. J. Meder, *Die Handzeichnung* (1923), p. 540. Burlington Fine Arts Club, *Catalogue of a Collection of Counterfeits* (1924), no. 321, pl. 10. K. T. Parker, *The Drawings of Antoine Watteau* (1931), p. 14.

kind of name is affixed to it. Thus somebody conceived the idea of launching silhouettes of famous composers. The first to appear was a Schubert (*Plate* 40), who, but for the eyeglasses, bears no resemblance whatever to the well-known features of the composer. But a rather blotchy wreath surrounds this effigy, which is completed by a suitable inscription. Schubert's friend, the writer Bäuerle, dedicates this priceless treasure to a friend: 'Der Compositeur Franz Schubert, meinem lieben Freunde gewidmet. Bäuerle'.[19]

In 1927 the Beethoven centenary produced an unexpected counterpart to this masterpiece (*Plate* 41).[20] Beethoven looks, if possible, still less like himself than Schubert, but the wreath is evidently a close relation to the one adorning the other silhouette. The same applies to the forger's predilection for white collars and to the beginning of the inscription, 'Der Compositeur Beethoven'; it goes on 'meiner lieben Gräfin Guiccardi. Comtesse Therese Brunsvik.' What a lucky coincidence! For a century these ladies have been competing for the honour of being Beethoven's 'immortal love'. The forger did not want to miss the right one, so he let one 'immortal love' dedicate the silhouette to the other.

19. Österreichische Galerie, Wien, *VI. Ausstellung, Fälschungen*, no. 112.

20. *Der Tag*, Vienna, 20 March 1927. The activities of this very industrious forger have been studied in a fascinating paper by O. E. Deutsch, 'Der Schwarzkünstler Kuderna', *Österreichische Musikzeitschrift*, vol. 19 (1964), pp. 1–9.

PART FIVE

PRINTS

PART FIVE

PRINTS

Collectors fear above all to be cheated by old copies of prints 'exactly like the originals'. These deceptive copies do not belong to the category of forgeries. Their right place would be in a history of plagiarism. It is often asserted that none of the deft copyists conceived this theft as an act of piracy in the modern sense. It would be more correct to say that there existed no law to protect the artists. Privileges against pirated editions, which were occasionally granted, were of little use.

Dürer wrote at the end of his woodcut series 'The Life of the Virgin': 'Woe to you! you thieves and imitators of other people's labour and talents. Beware of laying your audacious hand on this our work.' Plagiarists were not to be deterred by mere words, and Dürer was their favourite victim. Once one of them even dared to sell fraudulent copies of Dürer's engravings in Nuremberg under the artist's own eyes. The town council decreed under the 3rd of January 1512: 'A stranger who has sold prints in front of the Town Hall, among which are some bearing the mark of Albrecht Dürer, copied fraudulently, must engage on oath to remove all these marks and to sell no work of the kind here. In case of contravention all these prints shall be seized and confiscated as spurious.'[1] Plagiarising was permitted: only the artist's signature found legal protection. Thus artists were continually cheated of the fruits of their labour. William Hogarth was so annoyed by this practice that he introduced into Parliament, with the help of some friends,

1. M. Thausing, *Albert Dürer* (1882), vol. 1, p. 336. T. Hampe, *Nürnberger Ratsverlässe* (1904), vol. 1, p. 139.

a Bill for the protection of prints.[2] This Bill became the foundation of the modern copyright law.

There exist no rules which could be generally applied in the detection of fraudulent copies of this type. Many of them are inexact and of visibly poorer quality than their prototypes, but others were executed with the most efficient exactitude. In these cases the differences may become so subtle that the connoisseur can hardly rely on his own judgment. Luckily this work was done by the scholars who built up the first comprehensive collections of prints. They established the various 'states' of the plate, and also listed and distinguished the existing copies.

Not by fraudulent copies alone was the demand for prints with famous signatures satisfied. Printsellers had an even simpler and speedier method. They took a copperplate or woodblock by some minor artist, added a famous signature and published a new and 'improved' edition. Here again Dürer was the chief victim; woodcuts and engravings fraudulently adorned with his famous initials are not less frequent than paintings with the false monogram. (See *supra*, p. 33.)

A woodcut representing the Madonna and Child, the Child sitting on the globe and holding a crown with stars above his mother's head, is inscribed with the monogram M.G. and the date 1510. This points to Matthias Grünewald, the painter of the Isenheim altarpiece. However it has been proved beyond any doubt that the composition is an exact copy in reverse of a drawing by Francesco Vanni, dating from about 1600—ninety years later than the date on the woodcut.[3] Hermann Voss who discovered the relation between drawing and woodcut, regarded the latter as a forgery perpetrated in the seventeenth century. Such an early fraud is, however, most unlikely. The style of the Madonna is typical of Italian devotional woodcuts of the seventeenth century.[4] It seems that in the nineteenth century someone got hold of the

2. F. G. Stephens, 'Hogarth and the Pirates', in *The Portfolio*, 1884, pp. 2 sqq. A. Dobson, *William Hogarth* (1902), p. 48.

3. G. K. Nagler, *Die Monogrammisten*, vol. 4 (1864), p. 572, no. 18. H. W. Singer, *Sammlung Lanna* (1895), no. 5672. H. Voss, in *Der Cicerone*, vol. 3 (1911), p. 917. O. Kurz, *Falsi e falsari* (1961), p. 123.

4. Cf. G. Nicodemi, *I legni incisi dei Musei Bresciani* (1921), pl. 32 and 33.

block, cut out the hatchings in the left bottom corner and inserted the monogram which was intended for Matthias Gerung. Later a kind of second edition was produced with the addition of the date 1510.

In other cases the signature of a less well-known artist had to make room for a name of higher market value. There exists a series of ornamental engravings signed by Léonard Thiry, an artist belonging to the School of Fontainebleau. When his name had been forgotten, the signature was erased from the copper-plates and replaced by the name of his master Rosso, who had retained his popularity.[5]

Hieronymus Bosch's fantastic creations were the delight of sixteenth-century collectors. A posthumous school of Bosch followers kept his style alive up to the end of the sixteenth century and, as we have seen (see *supra* p. 31), false Bosch panels painted for the Spanish market rank among the earliest art forgeries. While the Bosch fashion was at its height, Hieronymus Cock, the great print publisher of Antwerp, calculated that a hitherto unknown composition by the master would find a ready market. He took a drawing by Pieter Brueghel, 'Big Fishes Eat Little Ones', had it engraved and published it under Bosch's name in 1557.[6] Though the fraud must have been perpetrated under Brueghel's very eyes he was apparently no party to it. Brueghel's original drawing, still in existence, is honestly signed: '1556. brueghel'. 'Big Fishes Eat Little Ones' was evidently a great success so that a copy was made. By then Pieter Brueghel, 'novus Hieronymus Boschius' as a contemporary called him, had become an artist of world fame; the engraver therefore put Brueghel's name under his copy.

Cock's swindle seems modest compared with the effrontery of his contemporary, the Parisian publisher Richard Breton. Breton owned a set of 125 woodblocks of grotesque figures drawn by a French imitator of Hieronymus Bosch. Other publishers would have been content to publish them as the work of Bosch. Breton had a better idea; he published them as the only drawings ever

5. P. Jessen, *Der Ornamentstich* (1920), p. 72. R. Berliner, *Ornamentale Vorlageblätter* (1925), pl. 130.

6. R. van Bastelaer, *Les estampes de Peter Bruegel* (1908), p. 48. O. Benesch, *Die Zeichnungen der niederländischen Schulen* (1928), p. 12.

40. Silhouette portrait of Franz Schubert. Modern forgery.

41. Silhouette portrait of Beethoven. Modern forgery.

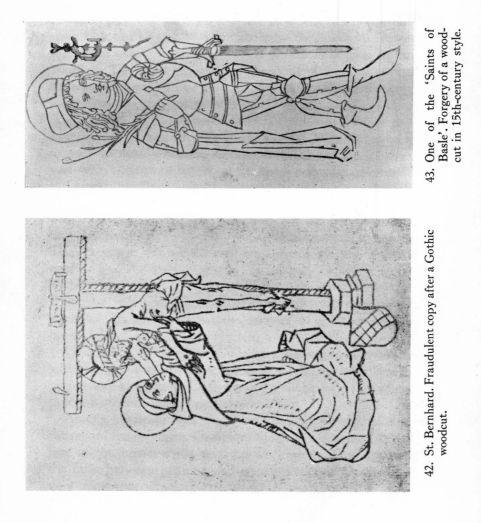

43. One of the 'Saints of Basle'. Forgery of a woodcut in 15th-century style.

42. St. Bernhard. Fraudulent copy after a Gothic woodcut.

made by François Rabelais. In 1565, twelve years after the poet's death, the woodcuts appeared as Rabelais' last work under the title *Les Songes Drolatiques de Pantagruel,* and were long regarded as a kind of pictorial supplement to *Gargantua.*[7]

Modern reprints from the original blocks or plates are deeply despised by collectors. However they are originals in the best sense of the word. Woodblocks and copperplates may have suffered to a certain degree and may show some blanks or indistinct portions, or in the case of wood, wormholes. But they always give a faithful version of the original. Etchings and dry-points suffer more severely by time and printing, and the details of the design show a definite inclination to vanish. Therefore they are often subjected to more or less extensive reworking, which has effects similar to the repainting of old pictures. As with paintings, the damage done to the original may be but slight, but often becomes grave enough to make such reprints no better than copies and worse than photographic reproductions of the originals.

The different states of a block or plate, as revealed by the prints, may offer most interesting sidelights on the artist's way of working. But more often than not the differences between two states are almost imperceptible and quite insignificant. They are, however, a hobby of the collectors, and were therefore eagerly taken up by their obedient servants, the forgers.

In the eighteenth century Anton de Peters produced a unique first state of Rembrandt's 'Petite Tombe' by erasing the toy of a child in the foreground.[8] The alteration was so cleverly done that it deceived the greatest connoisseur of the time, Adam Bartsch, a fact the more remarkable as Bartsch was aware that the Rembrandts in the Peters Collection had been tampered with.[9] A clever use of the pen may likewise create a valuable new state. Claude's etching of the 'Flight into Egypt' was given a 'first state' by the addition of three letters to the signature: Claude signed 'CLAV'

7. W. Fraenger, *Die Trollatischen Träume des Pantagruel* (1922). Bibliothèque Nationale, *Exposition Rabelais* (1933), p. 181, J. Porcher, in *Les songes drolatiques de Pantagruel* (1959).

8. H. Bouchot, in *Gazette des Beaux-Arts,* 3rd ser., vol. 22 (1899), p. 385.

9. *Festschrift für M. J. Friedländer* (1927), p. 317.

and the forger added 'DIO' with the pen. He did it well enough to deceive, at least temporarily, the learned author of the catalogue of Claude's *œuvre*.[10]

Very convincing copies of prints of all kinds can be produced by hand. Even elaborate engravings, with abundant cross-hatchings, were sometimes copied with utmost efficiency. This kind of make-believe was brought to its highest degree of perfection by seventeenth- and eighteenth-century draughtsmen.[11] Some of their sheets were acquired as rarities by every large collection. It must have cost hard work to make them, and their price can hardly have been much below that of the print they copy. A 'Jacopo de Barbari' in the Print Room of the British Museum might almost be called a miracle of neat and patient penmanship.[12] This kind of copy of an elaborate engraving is rarely meant to be deceptive. Matters become more serious if the copy is made after an original in a more simple technique. Fifteenth-century woodcuts, for instance, have comparatively plain outlines which can easily be reproduced by a tracing. A fifteenth-century woodcut representing Christ bending down from the cross to embrace Saint Bernhard was made the object of such a tracing (*Plate* 42). Though one might think that a design composed of comparatively few outlines could be traced with complete exactitude, the copyist committed a sufficient number of blunders to give himself away. He omitted to consider that the ridges of a block can never produce lines crossing each other like the lines of a drawing. The place where the top of the cross cuts through the halo of Christ is clearly visible. Apart from this, the tracing is full of misunderstandings: the margin of the original woodcut cut across one arm of the crucifix. As the tracing is not surrounded by a line, there is no plausible reason why one of the arms of the cross should be shorter than the other. The soutane of Saint Bernhard was cut off in a similar way. In the original his feet are supposed to be outside

10. A. P. F. Robert-Dumesnil, *Le Peintre-graveur français*, vol. 11 (1871), p. 164. *Catalogue of the Exhibition of Seventeenth-Century Art, London*, 1938, p. 205, no. 644.

11. A. Weixlgärtner in *Jahrbuch der kunsthist. Sammlungen*, vol. 29 (1910–11), pp. 357 sqq. J. Meder, *Handzeichnung* (second edition, 1923), p. 44.

12. Copy after the engraving Kristeller, no. 28.

the frame. In the tracing the poor saint breaks off without feet. The copyist tried to make up for these shortcomings by adding a few rather primitive attempts at hatchings and by altering the drawing of the faces; the head of Jesus particularly is none the better for the process. Moreover, a small protrusion appears under the right arm of Christ. This is the outline of one of the stones that form the wall of the saint's cell on the original woodcut. By thorough cleaning all the ink that had not been absorbed by the fibre of the paper has been washed away, so that the drawing looks as flat and impersonal as a print and no trace of the pen can be made out any longer. Therefore this drawing was for a long time regarded as a print.[13]

Drawing by hand becomes most dangerous to the collector of prints if damaged sheets are restored by the addition of hand-made portions. Smaller or larger parts of an engraving may be drawn so skilfully and the paper with which the remains of the original are patched up can be glued on with such mastery that it becomes difficult to distinguish old and new parts, even with the help of a magnifying-glass. The examination becomes much easier, of course, if the print is not mounted. In most cases these restorations affect only small and insignificant portions of the print, but occasionally more than half of a sheet may be new. Thus the lower half of a print of Schongauer's 'Virgin with the Parrot', has been completed.[14] From the breast of the Child upwards everything is new and drawn by hand. The general effect is quite convincing, the patching up of the paper is hardly notice-able, and the Virgin's hair, for instance, is copied with complete exactitude. Only in the darker shades do the hatchings become suspiciously blurred. However, in this particular case a com-parison with the original shows that the restorer failed to catch the outline of the Madonna's cheek, so that she looks as if she had a toothache. But on the whole the work is done well.

Photomechanic reproductions of prints are passed off more often as originals than one would think. Though ordinary prints

13. Recognised by J. Meder in *Mitteilungen der Gesellschaft für verviel-fältigende Kunst* (1909), pp. 45 sqq. *Enciclopedia Italiana*, vol. 32 (1936), pl. 71.

14. M. Lehrs, *Geschichte und kritischer Katalog*, vol. 5 (1925), p. 189, no. 4.

of photographic negatives and some types of reproduction, like the half-tone plate, have little chance of deceiving anybody, some proceedings come dangerously near the appearance of original prints. Zincographs can hardly be distinguished from woodcuts, as the way the design is rendered by lines in relief is the same with both techniques. Only occasionally some line of the zincograph betrays the etching, while woodcuts sometimes show the structure of the wood.

This process is dangerous mainly as regards woodcuts. The collotype is given away by the peculiar shape of the tiny dots of which it is composed. They are not points but minute crooked lines looking like maggots. Besides, the collotype shows a distinct lack of depth and relief which may distinguish it from original prints. Most dangerous of all proceedings is the photogravure. For it is printed from a copper plate such as is used for most art prints. In particular the velvety surface of a mezzotint may be well imitated by photogravure. Without the help of an original for comparison it is often impossible to make sure whether what we see is an original print or a photomechanical reproduction.

It would be a mistake to assume that reproductions produced in the pre-photographic era are no longer dangerous. Even where the technique of original and reproduction differs as widely as a dotted print from its lithographed copy, the result may still be deceptive. In the British Museum there is a famous dotted print, a half-figure of the Madonna, inscribed 'Bernardinus Milnet,' probably the name of the artist.[15] When the print was discovered in the early nineteenth century, its owner, Mr. Nathan Hill of Manchester, wanted others to share his pleasure. He had forty lithographic facsimiles made for distribution among various collections, including the Bibliothèque Nationale of Paris. In due course the original dotted print passed into another private collection and was lost sight of, and in its absence the lithograph copy in the Bibliothèque Nationale was promoted to the position of a fifteenth-century original.

The study of the watermarks only helps occasionally as there exists enough old paper of every description which can be used for forgeries. Neither do the measurements give a safe lead.

15. C. Dodgson, *Prints in the Dotted Manner* (1937), p. 22, pl. 24.

Prints are washed and dried, stretched and pressed, and the paper may distend or shrink till differences of more than half an inch can be observed between undoubted originals printed from the same plate. We have to admit that in certain cases prints can be reproduced with so high a degree of exactitude that it is pure snobbery if collectors prefer a bad impression of the original but worn-out plate to a reproduction which faithfully renders the original in its pristine splendour.

In the field of prints new and bold inventions are not welcomed with the same enthusiasm as in other fields. On the contrary, works that are not included in the great catalogues are looked upon with justified suspicion. Therefore spurious inventions are rare and were mostly perpetrated at a comparatively early date. One of the earliest of these seems to be the 'Virgin at the Gate', an engraving which was for a long time regarded as Dürer's work.[16] It looks convincing enough at first sight and one can well understand that it deceived many connoisseurs. Even when it came to be recognised that the engraving could not be by Dürer, one scholar still believed it to be a genuine composition by Dürer, but engraved by another hand. It is in fact quite a remarkably intricate pastiche. The forger carefully consulted Dürer's works even for the smallest detail. The Virgin is a copy of the beautiful title-page of 'The Life of the Virgin'; Dürer's 'woe to thieves and imitators' did not deter this forger from plundering three other woodcuts of this series for the figure of God the Father, the angels and the landscape, while the plant in the foreground has been copied from Dürer's early engraving, 'The Promenade'. The fraudulent intention is proved by Dürer's monogram and the date 1522 on a tablet in the foreground. The forger copied Dürer's prints straight on to the copperplate so that everything on his engraving appears in reverse. This method had a double advantage: he did not have to resort to the troublesome use of a mirror, and it made his multiple plagiarisms less obvious.

The Rembrandt imitations of Benjamin Wilson were more in

16. Bartsch no. 45, who regarded the engraving as a copy. G. W. Reid, in *The Fine Arts Quarterly Review*, N.S., vol. 1 (1866), pp. 401 sqq. M. Thausing, *Albert Dürer* (1882), vol. 2, p. 78. V. Scherer, *Dürer, Klassiker der Kunst* (third edition), p. 343.

the nature of a hoax than real forgeries.[17] In 1751 Wilson etched a landscape in Rembrandt's style in order to deceive the master of Reynolds, Thomas Hudson, who had declared himself an infallible connoisseur of Rembrandt. Hudson fell promptly into the trap.

Romanticist German forgers turned to primitive woodcuts. But as their main aim was to be primitive, they were inclined to sacrifice everything else to it. Thus the figure of a saint illustrated here (*Plate* 43), one of a series called 'The Saints of Basle', shows deplorably weak draughtsmanship though he is copied from an early woodcut in the State Library of Munich, where the forger is said to have worked.[18] He continually improved upon and added to his series, so that three different editions of 'The Saints of Basle' are known. The title-page shows the date 1414, impossibly early for woodcuts of this type. By two methods did the forger attempt to give his works the desired antique appearance: bad drawing and a very thorough washing of the sheet till the lines became grey, to suggest bleaching by time.

17. F. Davis, in *The Illustrated London News*, 25 November 1933, p. 866.

18. J. D. Passavant, *Le Peintre-Graveur*, vol. 1 (1860), p. 186. W. L. Schreiber, *Handbuch*, vol. 6 (1928), no. 2077. For the original see *Mitteilungen der Gesellschaft für vervielf. Kunst*, 1930, p. 74.

PART SIX

STONE SCULPTURE

PART SIX

STONE SCULPTURE

ARTISTS OF THE RENAISSANCE AS FORGERS OF CLASSICAL SCULPTURE

Ut quidam artifices nostro faciunt saeculo,
Qui pretium operibus maius inveniunt, novo
Si marmori adscripserunt Praxitelen suo,
Trito Myronem argento . . .

(Phaedrus, Lib. V.)

Phaedrus' verses are one of the earliest references to forgeries of works of art. In the time of Augustus works of art were being collected in a way not materially different from that of our own time. The predilection for works of earlier periods, sculptures, silver, and paintings, caused the manufacture of copies, imitations and outright forgeries, wherever the demand exceeded the supply. Our time is in this respect much nearer to the Roman Empire than to the Middle Ages. It must be understood that this is not a question of greater honesty. The Middle Ages knew in abundance fakes which pandered to their peculiarities. They abound in false relics of saints and martyrs, in fraudulent imitations of precious stones and in faked documents. Works of art, however, were collected like curios, for the sake of some appeal in their subject, provenance or supposed date. These might well be fictitious but as style and personal artistic authorship were unknown criteria, faking, in our sense, was out of the question.

In the Renaissance things changed fundamentally. With the new appreciation of classical antiquity and with the recognition of artistic individuality, classical sculpture became the prototype and goal of all artists. They strove to imitate it and to reach its perfection. Hence the contrast between contemporary judgment on Renaissance fakes of pictures and of sculpture. A successfully faked Raphael, if discovered, was regarded as a common fraud:[1] deceptive forging of classical sculpture was hailed as a supreme and enviable achievement.

Thus the young Michelangelo acquired early fame by making a statue of 'Cupid Asleep' to which he gave an antique appearance by burying it and which was sold in Rome as a classical sculpture in 1496.[2] Even a specialist in 'counterfeited antique heads in marble, which have been sold as antiques'—Tomaso della Porta (d. 1567) —was not despised but praised by Vasari who had a mask by his hand on his mantelpiece 'which everyone takes for an antique'. There is no shadow of blame in Vasari's account of Tomaso. He 'worked marble exceedingly well', and 'masks he made so well that no one equalled him'; 'not one of our imitators was superior to this Tommaso, of whom it seemed to me right that record should be made'.[3]

A Venetian relief in the Este Collection is a counterpart to Michelangelo's 'Cupid' (*Plate* 44). This forgery of a Greek funeral stele contains two motives derived from Michelangelo.[4] His David may be recognised in the background of the relief, which is a notably clever imitation of antique sculpture. The draperies floating so strangely above the heads of David and the youth on the left would be more suitable for some nymph or marine goddess, but to the artist they evidently represented a characteristic feature of ancient statuary in general. The posture of

1. See p.32.
2. A. Condivi, *Michelangelo* (ed. d'Ancona, 1928), pp. 59 sqq. G. Vasari, *Le Vite* (ed. A. M. Ciaranfi, 1932), vol. 6, p. 392. G. B. Gelli, *Le Vite* (ed. G. Mancini, *Archivio Storico Italiano,* ser. 5, vol. 17, 1896, p. 36). C. de Tolnay, *The Youth of Michelangelo* (1943), p. 201.
3. Vasari, *Lives* (transl. by G. du C. de Vere), vol. 9 (1912), p. 238. The figures from the tomb of Pope Paul IV (*Der Cicerone,* vol. 3, 1911, p. 170) show Tomaso's classicist style.
4. L. Planiscig, *Venezianische Bildhauer der Renaissance* (1921), p. 340, fig. 347. E. Panofsky, *Hercules am Scheidewege* (1930), p. 32, fig. 26. W. Born, in *Apollo,* vol. 32 (1940), p. 9.

the man on the left is the second derivation from Michelangelo that has been incorporated in this antique relief. It is a variation on the statue of Christ in Santa Maria Sopra Minerva. As this statue was finished in 1521, we gain a *terminus post quem* for our relief. The motif of the standing youth who is taking leave from the deceased, has been well understood by the sixteenth-century artist. He resembles the main figure on a Greek votive relief which in the sixteenth century formed part of the Grimani Collection.[5] Part of the top of the stele and the shoulder of the youth on the right were left unfinished, probably to give the impression that the original surface was worn away. Moreover, the artist ventured on damaging his relief: he hewed off part of the leg and foot of the seated man, but was careful not to destroy the outline of his calf.

As Planiscig has shown, the imitation of classical sculpture flourished in sixteenth-century Venice. A relief, roughly contemporary with the stele described, shows the scene of a *Conclamatio* (*Plate* 45).[6] A sarcophagus, now in the British Museum, seems to have served as model for the composition.[7] There we see the parents and mourners gathered around the body of a dead child. The forger was apparently attracted by a genre trait of the London relief: the child's shoes and lapdog can be seen under the bed. Instead of the dead child the forger represented a young woman in a strange costume, leaving her breasts bare, and in a pose surprising in a corpse: her head is propped on her raised arm like that of the sleeping Ariadne. The forger gave free scope to his archaeological knowledge by adding a number of classical figures from different contexts to the traditional *Conclamatio*. Three solemn gentlemen wearing the toga and crowned by laurel wreaths approach the couch, musicians play the tube and the curved horn, and a winged genius holds what are presumably meant to be the remains of an inverted torch. His legs are missing. They can

5. C. Anti, *Il R. Museo Archeologico di Venezia* (1930), p. 55.

6. G. E. Lessing, *Wie die Alten den Tod gebildet* (1769; *Werke,* ed. G. Witkowski, vol. 6, pp. 131, 423). S. Reinach, *Répertoire de la statuaire,* vol. 1 (1897), p. 49. *Jahrbuch des Deutschen Archäol. Instituts,* vol. 3 (1889), pp. 152, 370. L. Planiscig, *Andrea Riccio* (1927), p. 388, fig. 490. G. Sanarelli, *L'igiene nella vita pubblica e privata dell'antica Roma* (1940), pl. 6.

7. No. 2315. S. Reinach, *Répertoire de reliefs,* vol. 2, p. 496.

44. Sixteenth-century imitation of a classical relief.

45. *Conclamatio.* Renaissance forgery of a Roman relief.

never have existed as the place allotted to him is much too low down on the slab to allow the necessary space between his torso and the lower edge. Although the Renaissance origin of this relief became a recognised fact in the nineteenth century, it is still occasionally being reproduced as a Roman rendering of the scene. Its latest appearance was, I think, in 1940, in an Italian book on hygiene in Roman times.

Michelangelo was apparently not the first artist who let his work be buried in order to have it excavated as a classical sculpture. The prestige of ancient sculpture in porphyry was such that the first modern artist who rediscovered the method of working in porphyry, used his skill for forging. Marc' Anton Michiel, the great Venetian connoisseur of the sixteenth century, noticed in the collection of Francesco Zio:[8] 'The porphyry cup, with three handles and a spout, was made by Pietro Maria (da Pescia) an engraver of precious stones from Florence, who buried it, together with many other of his works, in Rome, at the time of King Charles' invasion (1495), so that it was cracked a little, and it was necessary to put a copper band around it. This cup has been sold several times as an antique at very high prices.' This forgery was perpetrated in 1495, thus preceding even Michelangelo's 'Cupid.'

The suggestiveness of burial is so potent that the mere fact that an object has lain in the earth and has been excavated, is sufficient to establish its antiquity. There need not be any intentional fraud: objects may have been hidden in the earth or may have sunk into the soil accidentally. Whatever the circumstances, if they are found, they are regarded as antiques of proven genuineness.

Garden sculptures disappear rather quickly in the soil once they are forgotten and neglected. The statue of a prince or hero in classical armour, now in the Klagenfurt Museum, was dug up on a Roman site in Carinthia (*Plate* 46).[9] The legs and right arm are

8. Marc'Anton Michiel, *The Anonimo* (ed. Frimmel, 1896), p. 96; (ed. Williamson, 1903), p. 111. E. Kris, *Meister und Meisterwerke der Steinschneidekunst* (1929), p. 39.

9. S. Reinach, *Répertoire de la statuaire*, vol. 1 (1897), p. 604. R. Egger, *Führer durch die Antikensammlung in Klagenfurt* (1921), p. 62. S. Ferri, *Arte romana sul Danubio* (1933), pp. 89 sq., figs. 62–4. R. Wagner–Reiger, *Das Schloss zu Spittal* (1962), pp. 111–114.

missing, the left arm is damaged. Because of the circumstances of the find it was generally accepted as a Roman statue. Archaeologists found fault with some details but the suggestive power was so strong, that they explained away everything unsuitable by a supposed modern reworking of the surface of the statue. However, the most telling detail, the richly decorated *laminae* of the cuirass (*Plate* 47) are in such high relief that the possibility of reworking is excluded. The statue is a typical work of North Italian art of the middle of the sixteenth century when the classical cuirass was the fashion for the portrayal of princes. All the details of the cuirass, from the shoulder straps and the gorgon's head to the richly decorated kilt, correspond exactly to these adaptations of classical armour. The excessively elongated proportions are one of the outstanding characteristics of Mannerist art. The 'Deeds of Hercules' on the base of the statue which was found simultaneously, form one series with the bases of some pilasters in the nearby Renaissance castle of Porcia, with the decoration of which the supposed Roman statue presumably stood in some direct connection.

In conclusion I should like to mention a small but pleasurable forgery, though it was made at a later date. Three very small reliefs are among the treasures of classical art that came into the Museo Nazionale of Naples with the Borgia Collection. Two of these marble slabs represent camels, strangely floating on waves issuing from the mouths of male heads, but the third, which is slightly larger, shows a rhinoceros. This animal is a precise relief copy of Dürer's woodcut, dated A.D. 1515. Thus one of the quaintest works from Dürer's *œuvre* has found admittance to classical imagery through the whim of some sculptor of the eighteenth century.[10]

MODERN FORGERIES OF GREEK AND ROMAN SCULPTURE

Since the end of the fifteenth century generations of forgers have worked to supply the world with spurious antiquities. Technique and archaeological exactitude have been improved con-

10. *Bollettino d'Arte*, vol. 7 (1913), p. 143. M. Sperlich, *Archäologischer Anzeiger* (1961), p. 137. On early forgeries of classical sculptures see also below, p. 336.

stantly and the horizon has widened, so that it includes now even the earliest epochs of Greek art.[11]

The standard types of Cretan art, as they are generally accepted all over the world, are largely due to the remarkable zest and inspiration with which the excavators of ancient Crete set about the reconstruction of its remains. The interest and novelty of their finds induced them to embark on reconstructions of unparalleled comprehensiveness. They were not content to restore monumental wall-paintings and terra-cotta reliefs of which nothing was left but minor fragments of what is supposed to have been a human figure or an animal. They even rebuilt part of the palaces and created a new style of sculpture from modest fragments. Casts and photographs of these reconstructions were spread through the museums and in current literature until these archaeological experiments became universally accepted as Cretan art. It has been forgotten that they are reconstructions and they are now widely quoted and reproduced as originals.

Soon some of these pieces served as prototypes for deliberate forgeries. The declared favourites were certain faience statuettes of snake goddesses which had been built up from scanty remains. Their chief exponent, which is well known to every schoolboy, was composed with the help of a·few badly fractured fragments.

This faience figure became the prototype of a marble figure, for some parts of which a second reconstruction was used, which was built up from a few small fragments of the skirt and one of the hair. However, the marble offspring of these two faience figures is fairly complete; only one of her hands has been damaged to avoid suspicion.[12] Her skirt boasts many flounces and is protected by a neat embroidered apron. As has been pointed out by Mr. Casson, the vertical grooves of the single pleats of the skirt were cut with a steel or iron gouge. The forger forgot that his statue

11. Cf. the chapter on fakes in G. M. A. Richter, *The Sculpture and Sculptors of the Greeks* (1950), pp. 183 sqq.

12. A. J. B. Wace, *A Cretan Statuette* (1927). S. Reinach, in *Revue archéologique*, série 5, vol. 23 (1926), p. 350. Sir J. Forsdyke, in *Journal of Hellenic Studies*, vol. 47 (1927), p. 299. G. Lippold, in *Gnomon*, vol. 5 (1929), p. 289. S. Casson, *The Technique of Early Greek Sculpture* (1930), pp. 5 sqq., 236.

should be a goddess of the Bronze Age. Under her pointed carnival-hat this figure looks rather girlish, particularly in profile. So do her sisters, the goddess with a snake, and the lady with arms akimbo. The chryselephantine snake goddess looks rather more gloomy.[13] The industry and the success of the modern Cretan forgers are remarkable. Among their victims was the excavator of Knossos. Statuettes in gold and ivory, bronze figures, gold rings and engraved seal stones, often with startling subjects, are the main products of their workshops.[14] Few students of ancient art realise to what an extent our idea of Cretan art is based on fanciful archaeological reconstructions and modern forgeries. As Salomon Reinach aptly quoted: 'Cretenses semper mendaces.'

The collectors of ancient Rome already had a marked predilection for the severe style of archaic Greek sculpture and were supplied with imitations by the so-called neo-Attic School of Athenian sculptors. After having been forgotten, early Greek sculpture was rediscovered in the early nineteenth century when Thorwaldsen restored the sculptures from the Aegina pediments. Nowadays archaic sculpture has become one of the most highly appreciated periods of Greek art and the best forgers try their hand on Greek sculptures of the sixth century B.C. Hence the general struggle to capture the celebrated archaic smile. Hard as one may try to catch it, the facial expression of archaic sculptures remains elusive. It is impossible to reproduce the appearance of something the meaning of which is not known. The archaic smile is neither a real smile nor a grimace, but its counterfeits are invariably either or both. Notwithstanding this, the contraction of the muscles and the general appearance of such faces is often rendered sufficiently well to cause dangerous mistakes.

13. G. Glotz, *The Aegean Civilisation* (1925), p. 397. G. Lippold, in *Gnomon*, vol. 5 (1929), p. 289. C. Praschniker, in *Wiener Jahrbuch für Kunstgeschichte*, vol. 10 (1935), p. 93. For a similar forgery see D. K. Mill in *American Journal of Archaeology*, vol. 46 (1942), pp. 254 sqq.

14. Lefebvre des Noettes, in *Aréthuse*, vol. 3 (1926), pp. 63 sqq. P. Couissin, in *Revue Archéologique*, série 5, vol. 24 (1926), p. 81. *Gnomon*, vol. 4 (1928), p. 170 (B. Schweitzer); vol. 5 (1929), p. 289 (G. Lippold). C. Praschniker, in *Wiener Jahrbuch für Kunstgeschichte*, vol. 10 (1935), p. 93. L. Banti, *Studi e materiali di storia delle religioni*, vol. 17 (1941), p. 18.

46. Torso of an emperor. Sixteenth century. Erroneously believed to be antique. (By courtesy of the Landesmuseum, Klagenfurt.)

47. Detail from Plate 46. (By courtesy of the Landesmuseum, Klagenfurt.)

48. Athena. Forgery of an archaic Greek statue. By Alceo Dossena.

49. Forgery of an archaic Greek group. By Alceo Dossena.

Alceo Dossena, the famous forger of monumental statues, tried his hand on the problematic smile. His 'Fighting Athena' smiles with a slightly irregular face (*Plate* 48). She has, moreover, been disfigured by a definitely hooked nose.[15] Every genuine Greek sculpture, even of a far later date, invariably shows a straight line from brow to nose-tip. This Athena was alleged to come from the same pediment as the fragmentary group of 'A Hero Abducting a Woman' (*Plate* 49), where Dossena avoided this danger by breaking off the woman's nose, but nevertheless the smile shines out from a curved mouth and rounded features that are an insult to all archaic sculpture. The young man, though evidently copied from one of the wounded men from the Aegina pediments, restored by Thorwaldsen, has the same weak and fleshy roundness of face as the woman. His features are cunningly disposed, so that he seems to break into a grin when fore-shortened, though he looks serious enough when faced by the spectator.[16] The Standing Goddess in Berlin tries to circumvent the problem by the extreme stiffness of her features.[17] But why are her lips so curved and full in such a frozen face?

The real pitfall is the modelling. Hair and draperies are easiest to copy. However, the rendering of the hair tends to become a little too soft in the hands of the forgers, and mistakes are occasionally made in the design of the draperies. Here the Standing Goddess at Berlin again avoids the issue, by displaying a rigid stylisation of her garments that goes beyond the severest archaic style. Unfortunately her creator conceived the strange idea of relieving her stiffness by letting her slide her left thumb under the shawl covering what is supposed to be her breast. This gesture was familiar to Napoleon, but one would hardly expect to find it in archaic sculpture.

The shape and outline of such figures is often judged with less severity than it ought to be done. The straight slim body of the

15. *Jahrbuch des Deutschen Archäol. Instituts,* vol. 43 (1928), p. 162, fig. 14.

16. *Jahrbuch des Deutschen Archäol. Instituts,* vol. 43 (1928), p. 221, figs. 67–70.

17. *Revue des études anciennes,* vol. 32, (1930), pp. 105 sqq. *Antike Denkmäler,* vol. 4 (1931). *Revue archéologique,* 5 ser., vol. 36 (1932), p. 102. C. Picard, *Manuel d'archéologie grecque,* vol. 1 (1935), pp. 278, 591.

ephebe was the ideal of Greece. The Greek conception of female beauty was governed by this ideal. This has not always been sufficiently appreciated by the forgers and their female statues frequently show curves alien to their ancient prototypes. It seems very difficult to abnegate the modern conception of the human body, and where it has been done, as for instance in the Standing Goddess of Berlin, the artist had to model a dummy with less resemblance to a human being than is shown by early archaic Greek figures. Even such an exceptionally good forgery as the torso of an Athenian Kore which was made with expert archaeological advice, looks almost unimpeachable when seen from the front, but viewed in profile the sculptor's deeply rooted belief in female rotundities becomes evident.[18] This forgery was only detected when the head turned up; that is, to be quite correct, when its two heads were offered simultaneously to the owner of the torso, and he was faced with a dilemma, as both were made of the same marble and fitted equally well on the Kore's neck. This situation was due to a little intrigue. While the torso was sold to a foreign museum, the head remained in Italy. When the dealer who had sold the headless Kore finally yielded to his customer's insistence and promised to procure the head as well, he did not feel inclined to let the colleague, who was looking after this piece, have a fair share of his profit. He preferred to order another head from the sculptor who had made the first and was in the possession of the model. Meanwhile, his competitor offered the first head to the customer, who had not expected to get two heads for one figure. Dossena almost succeeded in concealing the saliences of the female body in his Kore. This self-denial was crowned with success, as this statuette was the only one of his works that actually deceived the Metropolitan Museum of New York, though only for a very short time.[19] But Dossena's large sculptures, the 'Athena' as well as the 'Abduction of a Woman', show the unrestrained expression of the artist's appreciation of the female body. Even the two sitting

18. *Jahrbuch des Deutschen Archäol. Instituts,* vol. 43 (1928), p. 146, figs. 5, 6. C. Albizzati in *Historia,* vol. 3 (1929), pp. 652 sqq.

19. *Bulletin of the Metropolitan Museum of Art,* vol. 24 (1929), pp. 4, 145, figs. 9, 11.

women on the throne at Boston[20] show the same heaviness of form, though their model was the slim rising goddess from the 'Ludovisian Throne'. Some of these differences of proportion might be confirmed by measurements, but the essential difference lies in the fact that genuine archaic sculptures are neither unnatural nor thin, but the peculiarly graceful and discreet rendering of their charms has not been matched by any modern imitator.

The iconography of forgeries is usually simple. They are in most cases variations of existing types. If any inventions are made they either correspond to the most common conceptions of early art, like certain archaic goddesses, or they are devised with a view to augmenting the interest of a forgery by endowing it with an enigmatic touch.

Dossena's 'Abducted Woman' (Plate 49) is a fine example for such a simple enigma. The group has evidently been derived from the well-known archaic group representing 'Theseus carrying off Antiope'.[21] In the original, the head of Theseus is pressed against the breast of Antiope whom he carries, and his left arm encircles her body, so that his hand becomes visible under her left shoulder. Dossena altered this composition. He displayed the body of the woman, unhampered by her abductor, and dressed her in the garb of an Athenian Kore. He did not even venture on representing the torso of the youth, therefore he placed his bent head at the bottom of his group, near the hips of the woman. But he copied the left hand appearing under the girl's left shoulder, without regard for the fact that it can belong to neither of the two figures, given the postures he assigned to them. All Dossena did to explain this part

20. Jahrbuch des Deutschen Archäol. Instituts, vol. 26 (1911), pp. 50 sqq. E. A. Gardner, in Journal of Hellenic Studies, vol. 33 (1913), pp. 73 sqq. W. Klein, in Jahrbuch des Deutschen Archäol. Instituts, vol. 31 (1916), pp. 231 sqq. A. v. Gerkan, in Jahreshefte des Österreichischen Archäol. Instituts, vol. 25 (1929), pp. 125 sqq. Ch. Picard, Manuel d'archéologie grecque, vol. 2 (1939), p. 142; review by G. M. A. Richter, in American Journal of Archaeology, vol. 49 (1945), p. 387. F. Baroni, Osservazioni sul Trono di Boston (1961). L. Byvanck, Bulletin Antike Beschaving, vol. 36 (1961), pp. 60–63.

21. From the frontal of the temple at Eretria, Chalkis, Museum, F. Studniczka in Jahrbuch des Deutschen Archäol. Instituts, vol. 43 (1928), pp. 171 sqq. C. Albizzati in Historia, vol. 3 (1929), p. 656.

of his sculpture was to add the remains of a right hand on the woman's right shoulder. And there he let the matter rest. If one compares the group with its Eretrian prototype these two hands offer no problem at all, but taken seriously they lead to the complicated reconstruction of a group of three persons, one of which is a goddess, standing behind the girl and helping the youth to abduct her.[22]

Though naturally a little more complicated, the iconography of the throne at Boston may be explained by a similar proceeding. It is generally agreed that these reliefs have been conceived as counterparts to the 'Ludovisian Throne'. As the 'Ludovisian Throne' has Aphrodite as main subject, Eros was chosen as the centre of its counterpart. The two bending women were matched by two seated ones, the breast and chiton of one of which was copied from the Aphrodite of its prototype. Hardly more imagination was needed to carve a youth playing the lyre, after the model of the Ludovisian girl with the flute. The other wing seems to have been slightly more problematic for the sculptor. Also the marble slab at his disposal was a little smaller. He crammed in a figure with an old man's wrinkled face but with a woman's peplos. The object in the hand of this person is probably meant to replace the incense vessel of the veiled woman in the Ludovisi relief. The large relief centres in a balance, of which nothing is to be seen but the holes in which the beams are supposed to have been fastened and the two scales. Each scale carries a version of the skinned Marsyas, one *en face* and the other in profile. The relief is none the worse for the absence of the beam, which would cut nastily across the arms of Eros and the knees of the two ladies. This whole conbination is sufficiently enigmatic to arouse grave doubts whether so intricate a composition could be a modern invention. But that may just be what the artist intended.

The state of preservation of the marble and the kind and extent of damages it had to endure forms the centre of the examination of every sculpture. As to the marble itself almost every variety is available, either from the original sites or from blocks or sculptures hewn and carved in antiquity. The marble can be subjected

22. *Jahrbuch des Deutschen Archäol. Instituts,* vol. 43 (1928), p. 196, figs. 44, 45.

to high temperatures or damaged by acids, and the effects of these practices seem to look so very nearly genuine that experts are unable to see any difference. However, certain kinds of damages are suspicious in themselves. The smaller wing of the Boston throne, for instance, has been broken in two with a sharp instrument. It is supposed that this might have happened during the excavation, but the ugly scar remains suspicious, particularly as the other wing shows two cracks crossing the leg and thigh of the youth in almost the same place as two much slighter cracks on the Ludovisian flute-player. Faces are damaged very effectively by the removal of flat portions of their finished surface. The rough patches gained by this method hardly impair the general impression of the face, though they give a convincing impression of decay. Dossena was a master in this delicate art. The head of his Athena,[23] his most effective specimen, bears—damages and all—a close resemblance to the Seated Goddess at Berlin.[24] No wonder Athena was rumoured to have been found on the same mysterious site.[25]

Forgeries are frequently in splendid condition. Damages are usually confined to less essential parts of the statues. Apparently their makers could not bring themselves to destroy their own creations. The existing spurious fragments were made as fragments. In Dossena's abduction group it has been observed that one of the long locks of the youth has been carried over the break, thus proving that the break was there when the sculptor started his work.[26]

Though they are rather numerous, the fakes of no other period of ancient art have reached in number or in ambitiousness the archaic forgeries. The undisguisably modern ideas that every artist must betray in the bodies and faces he models remain the best guides throughout. As to motives, almost all these sculptures copy frequent types, instead of trying to create new ones.

Fakes in Praxitelian and Hellenistic style are betrayed by their soft sensuousness and by the sentimentality of their expression.

23. *Jahrbuch des Deutschen Archäol. Instituts*, vol. 43 (1928), p. 164, fig. 16.

24. *Antike Denkmäler*, vol. 3 (1924), pl. 38. Ch. Picard, *Manuel d'archéologie grecque*, vol. 2 (1939), p. 110.

25. *Bulletin of the Metropolitan Museum of Art*, vol. 24 (1929), p. 3.

26. B. Ashmole, in *Journal of Hellenic Studies*, vol. 50 (1930), p. 101, fig. 4.

Small, usually badly damaged female heads are most frequent and may be misleading. Less dangerous are statuettes like a Venus, which comes from a collection notorious for its forgeries.[27] It is comforting to know that this nice little woman was not created alone. A twin sister was published by the witty critic of Monsieur de Grüneisen.[28] To make a change this second edition was cut off a little higher up.

Roman portraits achieved general popularity long before Greek sculpture began to be more than the delight and study of the initiated. A series of heads representing Roman emperors and Greek and Roman philosophers and poets formed an almost indispensable part of every self-respecting library or art gallery since the Renaissance. Of course, only a small number of these sculptures were genuine; copies and new sculptures had to fill the ranks. When these collections were assembled more attention was paid to the denomination of the portraits and to the relative completeness of each series than to the artistic quality of the single busts. A large number of them were probably always considered as copies after genuine portraits. When the iconographical interest in these portraits began to wane and they had in many cases been removed from their original settings, where their main task was to fulfil a decorative function, a number of them wandered into the collections of classical sculpture. Among the Roman portraits now assembled there many such specimens may still be found.

The imposing head of Julius Caesar, which was acquired as a Roman original by the British Museum in 1818 (*Plate* 50), can hardly have been made much more than thirty years before that date.[29] It shows marks of artificial corrosion and may be regarded as a classicist fake. The forger was inspired by the popular portrait busts which are generally regarded as likenesses of Caesar. But as

27. W. de Grüneisen, *Art classique, Exposition Galerie M. Bing, Paris,* 1925.

28. C. Albizzati, in *Historia*, vol. 1 (1927), pp. 34 sqq., figs. 6, 7.

29. A. Furtwaengler, *Neuere Fälschungen* (1899), p. 14. F. J. Scott, *Portraitures of Julius Caesar* (1903), pp. 164 sqq., fig. 46, pl. 33. C. R. Beard in *The Connoisseur*, vol. 90 (1933), p. 73. E. Boehringer, *Der Caesar von Acireale* (1933), pp. 16, 24, pls. 39–40. B. Ashmale, *Forgeries of Ancient Sculpture* (1962).

50. Portrait bust of Julius Caesar. Eighteenth-century imitation after the antique. (By courtesy of the Trustees of the British Museum.)

51. Modern copy after a relief in the funeral
chamber of Ti at Sakkara.

realism was thought to be the foremost virtue of Roman portrait-ure, he exaggerated the features of his prototype to get a stronger effect. The cheeks are more hollow, the nose is sharper, and the lines of his face have been deepened. Thus the lofty nobility of Caesar's portraits has been changed to an expression of some severity. Iris and pupil have been indicated, a practice unknown in stone sculpture before the time of Hadrian, which disposes of the bust as a contemporary portrait. Nevertheless it used to be one of the most popular effigies of Caesar. It has been repro-duced in numerous historical works as his authentic likeness. Caesar has, however, been banished from the Roman Gallery of the British Museum and is now on guard at the entrance to the Reading-Room. I do not think that many of the readers stop to look at him there or are at all aware of his presence, but he is, after all, a fine example of classicist sculpture, and deserves some consideration.

Nowadays Roman portraits are not sufficiently coveted to be a very tempting subject to forgers. To make them worth while they have to use rare materials like porphyry. This Egyptian stone enjoys, moreover, an almost mythical reputation regarding the difficulties caused to the sculptor by its exceptional hardness. These difficulties are somewhat exaggerated, but they were ex-ploited by some Roman forgers of the nineteenth century, who turned out a number of heads in porphyry which have nothing antique about them but occasional vestiges of Roman costume. These figures are characterised by their abundant and unruly growth of hair, by the soft oval of their faces, and by their typically modern 'beauty'.[30]

Roman and early Christian sarcophagi frequently need such extensive and skilful restorations that it is only natural if those who execute them occasionally embark on a sarcophagus of their own. J. Wilpert has revealed an early Christian sarcophagus at the Museo Torlonia as a fake.[31] It is covered with strigils, which are neat, crisp, and sharp-edged, as if they were made of metal. The

30. G. M. A. Richter in *Bulletin of the Metropolitan Museum of Art*, vol. 24 (1929), p. 145, fig. 10. C. Albizzati, in *Historia*, vol. 3 (1929), p. 671. R. Delbrueck, *Antike Porphyrwerke* (1932), p. 133, pl. 56.

31. *Art Bulletin*, vol. 9 (1926–7), p. 108, fig. 21.

sculptor evidently was delighted by their curve, and made it as full as possible and more rounded than any of its Roman prototypes. These strigils are interrupted by two rather sharply carved figures in suspiciously high relief. A Good Shepherd with an ironical sidelong glance is followed by Saint Peter who carries two headless lambs in his satchel and two pigeons in his hand. The general conception of this figure is derived from a relief representing Saint Peter carrying the stray lamb. It is interesting to note that both the figures on the false sarcophagus display not only identical clumsy shoes and leggings, but also identical feet and knees. With the exception of the missing heads of Peter's lambs, which never existed, nothing was done to damage this sarcophagus. It was evidently thought to look convincing enough without such petty devices.

EGYPTIAN SCULPTURE

While the mass of spurious Egyptian antiquities consists of cheap unpretentious souvenirs made for tourists, a group of native stone masons produced in recent years a series of pseudo-antique sculptures of remarkable workmanship. Keeping rather faithfully to genuine models, their works are highly deceptive and deceived a number of experts. The forgers specialised in the severe monumentality of the Pyramid Period and in the realistic portraiture of the Tel-el-Amarna epoch, the two most valued periods of Egyptian art. The limestone relief of a girl carrying a pitcher and a cage with two geese is a characteristic example of the forgeries in the earlier style.[32] (*Plate* 51) The modelling of the figure seems genuine enough. This mastery of the means of artistic expression of the third millennium B.C. would be most remarkable were it not for the fact that a famous model has been slavishly copied. Among the reliefs covering the walls of the funeral chamber of Ti, near the Sakkara Pyramid, is a procession of female servants carrying provisions on their heads and pitchers in their hands.[33] The forger chose one of these girls as his model. He

32. L. Borchardt in *Zeitschrift für ägyptische Sprache und Altertumskunde*, Beilage zu Heft 66 (1930), fig. 5.

33. Illustrated in H. Ranke, *The Art of Ancient Egypt* (1936), fig. 202.

slightly changed her features, making them rather negroid, and he misunderstood the Egyptian convention of showing the forms of the human body through the thin linen garment. He faithfully copied the slight line between the girl's legs by which the Egyptian artist indicated the hem of the short narrow skirt above her ankles, but he omitted to continue the line across the legs so that they must be regarded as bare and the dress begins at the girl's shoulders but ends nowhere.

The forger shows his failure to understand ancient art more by the whole conception of his relief than by its single features. The relief does not pretend to be a fragment but a complete composition. Here the modern conception of 'art for art's sake' comes in, an idea completely alien to ancient Egypt. The servants of Ti had a magical function, they provided the owner of the tomb with food and drink in after-life. A 'Woman Going to Market' as a work of art is a characteristically modern idea.

MEDIEVAL AND RENAISSANCE SCULPTURE

The statuary decoration of the Romanesque and Gothic cathedrals has been renovated. without any fraudulent intention. The reason for these extensive renovations was mainly the reviving interest in the Middle Ages and the desire to restore the original splendour of the churches. What Viollet-le-Duc did to the French cathedrals was nothing but applied archaeology. He did it so thoroughly and on the whole so well, that it is hard to make out what he left untouched, what are slight retouches, and what has been completely renewed. With the passing years the renovations assume more and more the weathered surface of the originals.

Viollet-le-Duc was probably the most efficient restorer, but much the same happened to all cathedral sculptures. Not always, however, are the restorations as hard to distinguish from the genuine parts as Viollet-le-Duc's best works. If, for instance, the body of a statue shows every imaginable sign of decay and is left without any vestige of its original surface, it cannot be expected that its head and shoulders should be in a perfect state of preservation. Nevertheless a whole series of such trunks fitted with new heads and shoulders in the nineteenth century were acclaimed by prominent German scholars as corner-stones of medieval German sculpture.[34] The damaged statues were cut off just below the shoulders and the new busts were fastened on the trunks. Their hollow cheeks, sunken eyes, and strong noses look very impressive indeed. This restoration of the monumental sculptures in the Church of the Holy Cross at Gmünd was certainly not intentionally fraudulent, but they were received with as much enthusiasm as many successful fakes. Restorations are to the art historian what forgeries are to the collector.

Romanesque sculpture is renowned for its austerity, just as archaic sculpture is renowned for its smile. Therefore one should not be astonished to find an angry frown on the brow of a neo-Romanesque Madonna and a glare of rage in the face of the Child Christ on her lap (*Plate* 52). It seems to be even more difficult to catch the serious but strictly neutral expression of Romanesque sculpture than the celebrated smile of archaic art. But even apart from her expression this particular Madonna offers many weak points to criticism. Her drapery is just as impossible for the twelfth as for any other century, but as she is seated in a folding armchair of the Renaissance that matters little. Plain interlacing evidently was the only medieval ornament the forger knew. Therefore the Virgin's cloak, the chair, and the base all show the same pattern.

Though Alceo Dossena (1878–1937) was not successful with his archaic smile, he avoided the worst mistakes made by his less gifted colleagues when counterfeiting medieval sculpture. His Pisano Madonnas look quite dignified, whether they be made of wood or stone. Dossena's performance as Giovanni Pisano is remarkable. It is one of the rare cases in which a forger actually succeeded in catching the fundamental facts of an artist's personal style, together with an almost correct expression. If Dossena had limited his activities to this sculptor he would probably never have been found out. But his astounding faculty of assimilating the characteristics of different periods and artists led him to try his

34. W. Pinder, *Die deutsche Plastik des vierzehnten Jahrhunderts* (1925), p. 54. H. Beenken, *Bildhauer des vierzehnten Jahrhunderts* (1927), frontispiece. Review by J. Müller in *Zeitschrift für bildende Kunst,* vol. 62 (1928–9), Kunstchronik, p. 94. F. Kieslinger in *Belvedere,* vol. 13 (1928), pp. 84 sqq.

hand at widely different tasks, and that was his undoing. Once suspicion had been aroused it was not too difficult to trace his personality through the different styles he imitated. Anyhow, the catastrophe happened late enough to make him the most famous of all forgers. He emerged from the scandal as an artist of renown, which was more than he deserved.

It would be wrong to suppose that his whole *œuvre* was included in the travelling exhibition arranged on his behalf after his discovery. Some of his works may easily have escaped detection. Even dead, Dossena will thus remain an active danger to all those who expect historical sculptures to be very grand, but just the least bit stiff, a little boring, slightly empty, and above all not too outmoded.

Dossena's Pisano Madonna (*Plate* 53) is a very spirited combination of the Madonna from the Camposanto and the one standing above the entry to the Baptistry of Pisa.[35] The Virgin's head and the beautiful sweep of her veil towards the Child, as well as the Child itself and the hand of the Virgin supporting it, are derived from the Camposanto Madonna. So is the rare and beautiful idea of letting the glances of Mother and Child meet. But the statue in the Camposanto is only a half-figure, consequently Dossena combined it with the lower portion of the Madonna from the Baptistry. To make this possible he shifted the Child, which sits on the right arm of the Camposanto statue, to the left arm of his Madonna. The right hand holding the draperies he derived from the Baptistry statue, from which he copied the folds, but not without rearranging them, in order to strengthen the verticalism of his figure, which looks more 'Gothic' than its prototypes. Dossena, moreover, accentuated the sweeping movement of his sculpture by letting its draperies trail on the floor, while they spread only slightly and end rather abruptly on the base of the original statue. Yet the Gothic S-line of the figure was exaggerated only little, and the overdose of softness and sentimentality administered to the two faces is but slight.

However, Dossena could not escape the perils threatening all fakers of Quattrocentist art, whether they specialised in painting

35. H. Tietze, in *Metropolitan Museum Studies*, vol. 5 (1934–6), p. 14, figs. 23–5. *Kunst und Künstler*, vol. 27 (1929), p. 157.

or in sculpture. Their general tendency to become sentimental could rarely be kept within the bounds of their prototypes. But it must be owned that Dossena's tomb of Maria Catherine de Sabello is much more beautiful than average Quattrocentist forgeries (*Plate* 54).[36] It is inspired by Bernardo Rossellino's tomb of the Blessed Villana.[37] Dossena deemed it unnecessary to imitate the delicate play of the folds on Villana's body. His model for the background was Mino da Fiesole's tomb of Cecco Tornabuoni in Santa Maria sopra Minerva. The inscription on the tomb is a howler. It starts with the words: 'Obiit enim praefata Maria Catharina de Sabello anno Christi MCCCCXXX' ('But the aforesaid Maria Catharina de Sabello died in the year of the Lord 1430'). Dossena had apparently little Latin. He copied part of some inscription out of its context, and naively took *praefata* for some kind of title. Beside such defects slight omissions become negligible. But the lack of sandals, which makes the straps surrounding 'Praefata's' bare feet look rather out of place, is amusing.

As artists the modern sculptors were, on the whole, more efficient than the painters. The damaging of marble is not difficult, and besides most of the genuine sculptures of the Renaissance are not damaged at all. Therefore the forgers rarely ventured to inflict artificial damages on their marbles. Thus they are above the care for pigments, cracks, and ageing. This rendered their success easy. Apart from the discovery of the Dossena swindle, only an insignificant number of such forgeries have been exposed up to now. This is not much better with paintings. But while only comparatively few of the flood of imitated pictures could hold their own beside the fine originals of the great museums, their sculptured counterparts are everywhere. They intermingle with the genuine pieces until true looks false and false looks true.

The true spirit of early Renaissance sculpture was hardly ever grasped by the forgers, though its outward appearance is often rendered well enough. A fair estimate of the damage done to the art of this period may be gained if one compares the bust of Saint

36. D. B. Graves in *Parnassus*, vol. 1 (1929), no. 2, p. 18. F. Baumgart in *Kunstchronik und Kunstliteratur*, April 1929, pp. 1 sqq. Cf. also *Bulletin of the Museum of Fine Arts*, Boston, vol. 35 (1937), pp. 83 sqq.

37. Florence, Santa Maria Novella.

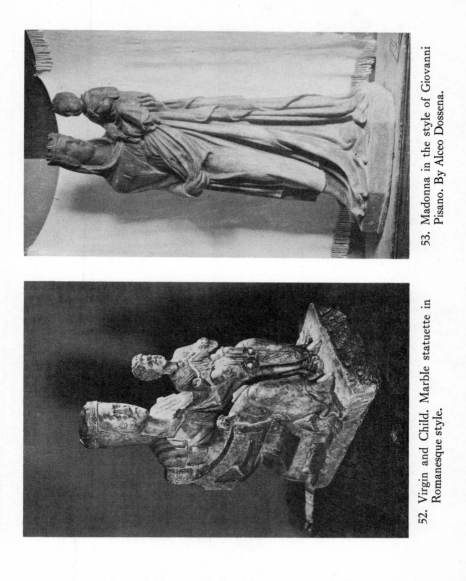

52. Virgin and Child. Marble statuette in Romanesque style.

53. Madonna in the style of Giovanni Pisano. By Alceo Dossena.

54. Tomb in Quattrocento style. By Alceo Dossena.

55. Bust of Saint John after Antonio Rossellino.

John (*Plate* 55) with its original, a full-figure statue of the boy
Saint John by Antonio Rossellino.[38] The face of the original is
handsome and even sweet, but its forms are severe and its expression is serious. The copy, though on the whole exact, has
softly blurred features and an affected smile. The hexagonal shape
of the bust is impossible in Rossellino's time. To see this bust
without its model would lead one to think that it never had one,
but is an invention of the nineteenth century.

This bust of Saint John the Baptist is but one example of
an army of children's heads and busts which have been added
to the genuine representations of the 'Giovannino' and the Child
Christ.

Children's busts are among the subjects which turn out comparatively well in the hands of mediocre artists. The result is an
inundation of art history and the collections with usually quite
competent-looking busts and heads of children, and these may
sometimes be the work of real artists, but rarely date from the
Quattrocento. Some of these children laugh outright, while
others are content with a sly smile, two fleeting expressions which
were first rendered by Frans Hals in the seventeenth century.
Others are made with more feeling for Quattrocento sculpture,
but are less lifelike and not as sensitively carved.

This invasion of impostors is the cause of the difficulties art
history has to face when trying to distinguish the Florentine
sculptors from one another. Mino da Fiesole, Desiderio da
Settignano, Antonio Rossellino, and Benedetto da Maiano never
come closer to each other than in their posthumous works, many
of which have already been attributed to two or three of them in
succession.

But for their greater success and more widely spread fame,
which made them spring forth in comparatively large numbers,
modern marble Madonnas and portrait busts and reliefs in Quattrocento style are rather similar in kind to their pictorial counterparts.
The Madonnas largely conform to the tradition of picture forgery
and keep to the lowest possible artistic quality. The Relief illustrated here (*Plate* 56) belongs to this class of undeserving poor.

38. W. v. Bode, *Denkmäler der Renaissanceskulptur*, pl. 333. A Venturi,
Storia dell'arte italiana, vol. 6, p. 624.

From the huge ear of the Madonna to the tips of her flattened fingers, from the insignificant lines which are supposed to represent the folds of her dress to the ornamentation of the niche, and from the Child's deformed head to his square toes, this relief is the work of a modern stonemason. The inscription shows the date 1443, the primitive outlines of some tools, and the syllables *To Da Do o*, obviously chosen to evoke the name of Donatello. The character of this puerile mystification indicates that the relief must be of comparatively early origin.

Among false marble portraits—the rank and file is of terra-cotta —false princesses in the style of Francesco Laurana or Mino da Fiesole form one of the most prominent groups.[39] The bust of Lucrezia Donati, the mistress of Lorenzo il Magnifico (*Plate* 58) is a work of Giovanni Bastianini, the master forger (see p. 148).[40] The delicately modelled head is inspired by Laurana's so-called 'Marietta Strozzi' (now in Berlin, but until 1877 in Florence), perhaps also by one of Luca della Robbia's relief portraits (Bargello); but her features correspond less to Quattrocento ideals than to the '*Femme fatale* of the Renaissance' as she was imagined by late Romantic writers and artists. The bust is, however, of undeniable charm and deserves its place of honour in the Victoria and Albert Museum as an outstanding example of Italian art of the nineteenth century. The National Gallery in Washington possesses a similar, but less fine work by Bastianini, a bust modelled in gesso over a wooden core. According to the inscription the bust is a portrait of Giovanna Albizzi modelled in 1460, a date surprisingly early as this lady was born in 1468.[41] Most of the forgers contented themselves with a superficial imitation of their models. The high foreheads and long necks and noses, the downcast eyes, were easy enough to imitate. The difficulties began with the delicate touch of

39. H. Tietze, in *Metropolitan Museum Studies,* vol. 5 (1934–6), p. 12, fig. 22. *Das Kunstblatt,* vol. 14 (1930), pp. 195 sqq.; vol. 15 (1931), p. 63.

40. E. Maclagan and M. H. Longhurst, *Catalogue of Italian Sculpture* (1932), p. 168, pl. 119e.

41. A. Foresi, *Tour de Babel* (1868), p. 40. G. Swarzenski, *Gazette des Beaux-Arts* (1943), p. 289. S. Keck, *Magazine of Art,* vol. 41 (1948), p. 320. G. Galassi, *La scultura fiorentina* (1949), p. 171. I. Cardellini, *Desiderio da Settignano* (1962), p. 81.

56. Madonna. Marble relief dated 1443. Modern forgery.

57. Portrait relief in Quattrocento style.

58. Lucrezia Donati. Marble bust in Quattrocento style. By Giovanni Bastianini. (By courtesy of the Director of the Victoria and Albert Museum.)

vibrating life which is the charm of the originals. Some forgers wanting to keep on the safe side omitted it, others were less well advised and drove modern realism too far, but this did not lead to their detection. One of the very few modern pieces of this kind that were actually returned to the dealer by a museum is a rather supercilious looking young woman. Though unmistakably modern in type and costume, this young lady was accepted as a work by Mino da Fiesole. But it was refused on second thoughts.[42]

Portrait reliefs are of course favourites. They may easily and unobtrusively be derived from medals, as well as from portrait reliefs on epitaphs and monuments. The peculiar low relief, standing out against a plain background, always looks in style, however modern· its expression. Speaking of this type of relief, one of the most popular of Quattrocentist sculptures should not be passed unmentioned: the so-called 'Saint Cecily' ascribed to Donatello. Though frequently apostrophised as a modern imitation, this relief is still popular as an original. It was perhaps not created as a forgery. The delicacy of modelling, coupled with the slight tinge of bitterness in the saint's expression, suggest that it must have been conceived by an artist of some distinction. But the sober classicism of its contours and particularly the hairdress and diadem exclude the Quattrocento as a possible date of origin.[43]

The relief illustrated in *Plate* 57 is a sculptured counterpart to the 'Montefeltre family' (see p. 53). Nobody will ever know why a small monk was placed behind a much larger lady. Also her hairdress is beyond explanation. Like the picture, this relief is a fair example of the more florid conception the later nineteenth century had of the early Renaissance.

The figure of a crouching woman in *Plate* 59 was made by the Venetian sculptor Antonio dal Zotto, and was later 'discovered' as a Michelangelo. But this was not the fault of the worthy artist, who made, among other things, the popular statue of Goldoni

42. *Bulletin of the Detroit Institute of Arts,* vol. 7 (1925), pp. 15 sqq. *The Art News,* 23 May 1931, p. 13.

43. P. Schubring, *Donatello, Klassiker der Kunst,* p. 177. A. Venturi, *Storia dell'arte italiana,* vol 6 (1908), p. 424, note 5. I. Cardellini, *Desiderio da Settignano* (1902), p. 81.

erected at Venice. The unfinished figure of a woman was in dal Zotto's studio when he died. That was in 1918; by 1929 the sculpture had migrated to a German collection and was published as a Michelangelo in a leading periodical.[44] It is a pity that its creator did not live to witness the triumph of his modest study in Michelangelo's celebrated technique. Dal Zotto attempted to imitate Michelangelo's way of approaching the block from the main front, working his way gradually to the depth of the figure, by disengaging limb after limb from the marble, and finishing the back only after the rest had been finished. He also did his best to copy Michelangelo's way of using the dented chisel. For his experiment he invented a contrapposto figure, which is no heroic creature in Michelangelo's line, but a crouching nymph. Notwithstanding this motif, he visibly strove to approach his ideal by the abrupt turn of the head of the girl and by the load of rough marble on her back, weighing her down. But here the parallel ends. He did not even attempt to imitate Michelangelo's real way of working. Dal Zotto hewed his nymph out of the block with the help of the usual pointing process (one of the *puntelli* is clearly visible on the knee), a method despised by Michelangelo.

Forgeries of German stone sculptures are rare with the exception of the delicately carved reliefs and roundels of Kehlheim stone which were collected and forged since the seventeenth century. We had already occasion to mention the early imitators of Dürer, painters like Hoffmann and Fischer, who compiled single figures from the master's works to new compositions, and the anonymous engraver who compiled the 'Virgin at the Gate' from five different woodcuts and engravings.[45] They were all surpassed by Georg Schweigger (1613–90) who was more than a simple *pasticheur*. Had he been born a hundred years earlier, he would rank with the best sculptors of the German Renaissance. Most of his delightful miniature reliefs are in the style of the early sixteenth century. They are usually signed with the artist's name or with his initials. Once Schweigger composed a series of reliefs with scenes from the life of Saint John the Baptist which he dated 1510 and

44. *Jahrbuch der preussischen Kunstsammlungen,* vol. 49 (1928), pp. 50 sqq. *Das Kunstblatt,* vol. 14 (1930), p. 200.

45. See above p. 113.

59. Antonio dal Zotto. Imitation of Michelangelo.

60. Georg Schweigger. Naming of Saint John the Baptist. The monogram
and the date 1510 are spurious.

1511 and signed with Dürer's monogram.[46] The 'Visitation' is a free and clever interpretation of the woodcut in Dürer's 'Life of the Virgin'. In the 'Naming of Saint John' in the British Museum many but not all details are copied from woodcuts of Dürer (*Plate* 60). He even dared to copy parts of figures, investing them with new heads or bodies. His imitative power is shown by the fact that these composite figures do not look ridiculous or out of style. Of the last of the series, 'Saint John Preaching' (Brunswick), Schweigger carved a second version (Vienna), which he honestly signed with his name and the date 1645.

CHINESE STONE SCULPTURE

Before the beginning of this century Europeans were practically unaware of the existence of Chinese sculpture, and the Chinese themselves never valued sculpture as highly as painting or pottery. By Chavannes' publication only was general interest in this hitherto unknown art aroused,[47] and European collectors began to be on the look-out for suitable objects. The Chinese forgers appear to have been very quick to avail themselves of this opportunity. As soon as the first collectors arrived in China their hosts must have begun to fabricate spurious pieces, for which there would have been hardly any use before that time. Their task was rendered easy by the comparatively simple technique and design of the originals they imitated.

Given a rubbing of the original, it is not difficult to reproduce a Han relief. This was done to part of the lower portion of a slab from the funeral chamber of pseudo-Wu Liang. The rubbing is reproduced in *Plate* XLIV of Chavannes' atlas. The copy looks fairly convincing, though the forger did not feel very sure about

46. M. Thausing, *Dürer* (1884), vol. 2, p. 46. G. W. Reid, in *The Portfolio* (1884), pp. 70 sqq. *Zeitschrift für Kunst- und Antiquitäten-Sammler*, vol. 2 (1885), pp. 1 sqq. J. von Schlosser, *Werke der Kleinplastik* (1910), vol. 1, p. 20. H. Kohlhausen, in *Der Cicerone*, vol. 18 (1926), p. 86. M. Sauerlandt, *Kleinplastik der deutschen Renaissance* (1927), pl. 108 sq.

47. E. Chavannes, *Mission archéologique dans la Chine septentrionale*, 1909–15.

the correct inside drawing of his figures (*Plate* 61).[48] He drew ugly masks with almond-shaped eyes, instead of the typically Chinese faces with pin-head pupils under arched eyebrows, Several of the horses, admirably drawn in the original, have visibly deteriorated in the copy. The inscriptions, as has been pointed out by Paul Pelliot, are faulty copies of those on the original slab. Moreover, in one of the two scenes represented in the upper portion one of the main figures has been omitted for lack of space, so that the representation is no longer complete. But the shield bearing the name of the missing person has been included by the negligent forger. The scene represents Duke Huan of Ch'i who is prevented by a general from forcing a terrible peace treaty on his beaten adversary, Duke Chuang of Lu. The figure omitted is that of the wise counsellor who settled this incident to the satisfaction of all parties.[49]

The imitation of Chinese Buddhist sculpture is considerably facilitated for those who produce and sell the ware by the poor quality of a large percentage of the genuine pieces. Though there are many works of high quality among the Buddhist statues, steles and cave sculptures, the huge production necessitated by a religion demanding the largest possible number of images kept the average production on a low level. This fact was fully exploited by the forgers. Adolf Fischer, for instance, who assembled the Chinese collections of the Museum of Far Eastern Art at Cologne, first went to China in 1901. By the time he had made his last journey in 1912 he had been sold quite a respectable number of fakes, which were probably made specially to suit him.

The results of Professor Pelliot's examination of the inscriptions on the Buddhist monuments of the Cologne Museum of Far Eastern Art are as amusing as they are elucidating. One stele full of flat figures, of complete and mechanical symmetry, bears an inscription indicating the year 501 A.D. But the date it gives, is the

48. K. With, *Bildwerke Ost-und Südasiens* (1924), pl. 4. P. Pelliot in *Artibus Asiae* (1925), p. 153.

49. Most of the forgeries of Han reliefs seem to be free copies of the Wu Liang slabs; for characteristic examples see *T'oung Pao*, vol. 14 (1913), pp. 809 sqq.; vol. 28 (1931), p. 457. O. Fischer, *Die chinesische Malerei der Han-Dynastie* (1931), p. 139.

thirtieth day of the third month of the second year of the period
ching-ming. It is the forger's bad luck that this particular month had
only twenty-nine days. Like several others, this inscription is derived from a genuine one published by Chavannes, but the slight
alteration of the date proved fatal. It is not easy, even for a Chinese
forger, to pick his way among the intricacies of Chinese chronology.[50]

Another case is represented by the statue of a seated monk,
with an inscription pointing to the year 1027. But the Sung emperor said in this inscription to be in the fifth year of his reign is
called by his posthumous name Jên Tsung, which was given to
him after his death in 1063.[51] In these cases there can be no question of apocryphal inscriptions engraved on genuine monuments.
The quality of this rough and square sculpture of a monk is such
that one feels relieved at being spared the necessity of regarding it
as ancient. The same applies to a large number of the monuments
assembled at the Cologne museum. It is a course for scholars who
want to know what to beware of.

Steles and reliefs of this type are not confined to the Cologne
museum. They may be found in many places. An example from
Cleveland, Ohio, is inscribed with a particularly early date corresponding to A.D. 440. Its back view is characteristic. It has been left
without decoration, except for an engraved floral ornament in a
style half Greek, half modern, but completely unknown in ancient
China.[52]

50. A. Salmony, *Die chinesische Steinplastik* (1922), pls. 32, 33. P. Pelliot
in *Artibus Asiae* (1925), p. 56.

51. A. Salmony, *Die chinesische Steinplastik* (1922), pl. 62. P. Pelliot in
Artibus Asiae (1925), p. 57.

52. *Artibus Asiae* (1925), p. 136.

PART SEVEN

TERRA-COTTA

PART SEVEN

TERRA-COTTA

GREEK AND ETRUSCAN

No other material is as easy to handle as clay, and none is cheaper. How lucky for the forgers and their patrons that much sought for works of art were shaped in this convenient medium. It allowed the fakers to embark on large-scale production once some suitable types had been firmly established, and they fully availed themselves of the opportunity. Their output of Greek statuettes, as well as of busts and reliefs of the Renaissance, was so prodigious that it can only be compared with that of Corot forgeries. Like Corot's *œuvre secrète,* these forgeries turned up in crowds, and though particularly the Greek variety has been detected and exposed, the number of such fabrications is so large that they will be popping up among originals for a long time to come.

The genuine Tanagra statuettes were excavated in the early 'seventies of the last century. They were received with enthusiasm by archaeologists and collectors. Apart from their genuine charm, they owed their success to the general propensity to collect decorative figurines and trinkets. Greek terra-cottas were regarded as forerunners of china figurines. The forgers were very quick to exploit this vogue. By 1880 they had produced an astonishing number and variety of fakes. They faked every kind of classical terra-cotta, but were unable to match the graceful pose of the best Tanagra statuettes. One workshop, the seat of which seems to have been Athens, specialised in terra-cotta groups of two and more figures. Their success was so great that they almost ousted the interest in the more modest genuine excavations from Tanagra. As

61. Forgery of a Chinese relief in the style of the Han period.

62. 'Eternel Printemps'. Terra-cotta group.

63. 'Love in the Graveyard'.
Terra-cotta group.

64. False Etruscan sarcophagus.

they are of a rather different style, these groups purported to come from a special site. Sometimes it was pretended to be Ephesus and sometimes Myrina in Asia Minor. It was not difficult to expose the spurious character of these provenances, as the few terra-cottas which were actually excavated on these sites are of a very different type. Therefore the statuettes sailed henceforth under the more general label of 'Asia Minor', to migrate later to Corinth and even to Boeotia, the site of the genuine Tanagra statuettes.

S. Reinach has given a concise survey of the long-drawn battle that raged between those who exposed the fraud and its very spirited defenders.[1] They refuted the charges over and over again, for not only had large collections been formed, consisting exclusively of false terra-cottas, but their sweet and predominantly amorous character was decidedly endearing. Once one has begun to regard as antique the group of 'l'Eternel Printemps' (*Plate 62*) it must be difficult to clear one's notion of classical art from such an entrancing conception. The lady—a variation of Canova's statue of Pauline Bonaparte as Venus (Rome, Villa Borghese)— graciously listens to the declaration of a fervent youth who kneels in front of her *guéridon*. A girl weeping on the steps of her dead lover's stele, attended by Cupid, is a subject that must appeal to sentimentalists (*Plate 63*). What does it matter if the stele is adorned by rosettes or if the folds of the girl's garments fall in ripples never seen in antiquity? The sentimentality of the faces, their vivid expression of mirth or tearfulness, was just what the collectors of these antiquities appreciated. They did not want to notice that the figures were far too long and too softly modelled, and they were blind to the ridiculous puerility of all the details. Apart from simple love scenes, subjects from classical literature were selected for this manufacture. Charon's barge was a predominant favourite, but many other scenes, like Ulysses

1. A. Cartault, *Sur l'authenticité des groupes en terre cuite d'Asie-mineure* (1887). S. Reinach in *The Classical Review* (1888), pp. 119 sqq., 153 sqq.; reprinted in his *Chroniques d'Orient* (1891), pp. 586 sqq. A. Cartault, *Terres cuites grecques* (1891). A. Furtwaengler, *Neuere Fälschungen von Antiken* (1899), pp. 15 sqq. O. Théatés in *Le Musée*, vol. 5 (1908), pp. 171 sqq. G. M. Richter, *The Sculpture and the Sculptors of the Greeks* (1950), pp. 186 sqq. C. Albizzati in *Enciclopedia Italiana*, vol. 14 (1932), p. 757, figs. 4, 6.

tempted by the sirens, Priam and Helen, or Oedipus and Antigone, competed for the choice of eager collectors. Genuine terra-cottas unfortunately never represent such alluring subjects.

As to the appearance of their surface, these groups were sub-jected to arduous ageing. Here again clay is most convenient and offers great advantages to an adroit forger. All the figures were broken into rather small pieces and fixed up again. Only the heads were spared this ordeal. Though patched up, all these groups are complete, down to the fingertips. Intense application of mud and dirt on the surface, as well as inside the hollow sculptures, presented no difficulties. However, their freshness was never subdued, to the unending delight of many passionate collectors.

This is only a very cursory description of what has been de-scribed as the 'demi-monde des terres cuites', but once warned one may frequently recognise the peculiar soft formation of the figures, the nervous ripple of the draperies, and the over-elaborate hair-dress of these beauties and their suitors.[2]

Some terra-cotta plaques with reduced copies of portions of the Parthenon frieze were introduced into archaeology as Phidias' original sketches.[3] This must have come to them as a rather un-expected honour; these plaques are simply fragments from current reproductions. They were broken up into fragments, small enough to make their origin escape the notice of archaeologists. They actually got into several collections, but their relation to the Parthenon could not remain concealed. They were either regarded as preliminary studies for the celebrated frieze or—more modestly —as Roman copies from the time of Augustus. However their modern origin was finally established when it could be proved from certain details that they were formed from the same moulds as the reduced nineteenth-century reproductions.

A large archaic sarcophagus which was purchased by the British

2. Particularly instructive is a plate in the *Encyclopaedia Britannica* (14th edition, vol. 21, p. 956, pl. 2) where a faked terra-cotta is illustrated for com-parison amid a number of genuine ones. I owe the photographs reproduced in pls. 43 and 44 to the kindness of Dr. O. Pächt.

3. C. Waldstein, *Essays on the Art of Phidias* (1885), pp. 212 sqq., 258 sqq.; pls. 9, 11, 13. A. H. Smith in *Journal of Hellenic Studies*, vol. 14 (1894), pp. 264 sqq. *B.F.A.C. Exhibition* 1924, no. 218.

Museum in 1873 quickly became the most popular Etruscan sculpture. Though it was withdrawn from exhibition in 1936, it will probably occupy this position for some time to come. No single part of the structure of this sarcophagus corresponds exactly to genuine Etruscan art of the archaic period. Notwithstanding this, its general appearance is so convincing that one fully understands the reluctance of the museum authorities to believe that it was made by the brothers Pietro and Enrico Penelli (*Plate* 64).[4]

The British Museum acquired the sarcophagus in 1873 from Alessandro Castellani who had bought it from Pietro Penelli. Ten years after the acquisition, Enrico Penelli who had meanwhile become restorer at the Louvre, told Salomon Reinach, the French archaeologist, that the sarcophagus was his own work, made with the help of his brother Pietro. They buried their masterpiece in Cervetri and excavated it. At that time only one sarcophagus of the same type was known. Now in the Louvre, it had originally formed part of the Campana Collection where Penelli held the office of restorer. He had—extensively—restored the Campana sarcophagus and had had every opportunity of studying it. What he produced was no mere copy. The portraits of the deceased couple show a touch of humour completely alien to Etruscan sepulchral art. Husband and wife are gesticulating with animation and seem to be grinning at some joke. The realistically modelled body of the man is completely nude, a case unique in Etruscan tomb sculpture. The woman, on the other hand, wears a most extraordinary dress, including a pair of trousers reaching below the knee. The reliefs on the sarcophagus are remarkable imitations of archaic art. The inscription is copied from an Etruscan brooch in the Louvre, a fact thinly disguised by the omission of part of the letters. But notwithstanding the woman's breeches and the untimely facetiousness of the couple, the whole monument is so impressive that misgivings are easily overruled. After it has been illustrated for sixty years as the most important monument of Etruscan art, it is hard to part with what has become an inveterate habit.

The Louvre sarcophagus from the Campana Collection was used a second time as a model for forgeries, showing the same

4. S. Reinach in *Revue archéologique*, 4th series, vol. 4 (1904), p. 188. H. Sauer, *Die archaischen etruskischen Terracottasarkophage* (1930).

bold, imaginative treatment as the British Museum sarcophagus. The two masks of *bucchero* ware which were presented to the British Museum in 1866, are probably another masterpiece of the brothers Penelli.[5] The faces of the couple on the Campana sarcophagus have been copied as masks. They have, however, been covered by an engraved tattoo of a design strangely anticipating surrealism. The male mask is adorned with 'witches who are snake-charming; in the middle a woman seated on a camp-stool, and beneath her a symbol of lightning; on the cheeks wild geese'. In order to avoid boring symmetry, one snake has five feet, the other only four. The female mask is tattooed even more richly: a warrior on each cheek, charging his opponent across the upper lip, a goddess lion-tamer on the bridge of the nose, with two lions poised on the eyebrows. On the tiara an unidentified animal in relief strides between two gracefully reclining ladies. Every bit of empty space is filled with rosettes, stars and birds.

RENAISSANCE

Giovanni Bastianini (1830–68) is the true genius among forgers.[6] His follower, Dossena, was a skilful sculptor with a gift of imitation, but Bastianini was an artist. In his short life he created his own version of the great men of the Renaissance, and it appears that the 'Bastianini Renaissance' was admired with almost more fervour by his contemporaries, than the genuine Quattrocento.

In fulfilment of his contract with Giovanni Freppa, a Florentine dealer, he was obliged to fabricate numerous Madonnas to be sold

5. G. Karo, in *Athen. Mitteilungen,* vol. 45 (1920), p. 156. *Corpus Vasorum Antiquorum,* British Museum, fasc. 7, IV B.a., pl. 7. O. Vessberg, *Studien zur Kunstgeschichte der römischen Republik* (1941), p. 99. L. Goldscheider, *Etruscan Sculpture* (1941), p. 32, pl. 93. J. D. Beazley, in *The Journal of Roman Studies,* vol. 34 (1944), p. 148. On false Etruscan terra-cotta figures, see also below, p. 337.

6. A. Foresi, *Tour de Babel* (1868). N. Barstow, 'The Romance of Art. The Forgeries of Bastianini' in *The Magazine of Art* (1886), pp. 503 sqq. D. Brunori, *Giovanni Bastianini* (1906). C. G. E. Bunt, in *The Connoisseur,* vol. 110 (1943), pp. 134 sqq. (with illustrations of Bastianini's principal works).

as Mino or Desiderio. They look quite nice if he allowed them to smile, but are inclined to look bored if they are serious. He also had to model or carve female busts in which he tried to imitate the style of Francesco Laurana (see above p. 136).

Male portrait busts were his true vocation: here he developed a style of his own, modelled in a general way on the more realistic portraits of the Renaissance. But he was far more realistic and knew how to impress his public by the lively expression of his heads. Moreover, he had a highly developed sense of plastic unity and was, as I have said, a real artist.

Bastianini's bust of Savonarola follows closely contemporary portraits.[7] The features have, however, become rather like those of an old woman and the monk's cowl has been misunderstood completely. The appeal of the bust lies in the new motif: Savonarola's inspired glance towards heaven, an expression completely foreign to the old portrait (*Plate* 65).

The bust of Savonarola's friend and follower Girolamo Benivieni (1453–1542) created an enormous commotion after it had been acquired by the Louvre in 1866.[8] Now we know that it is a portrait of a Florentine workman. But even without knowing this, it may, after eighty years, easily be recognised as a typical nineteenth-century study from the model. The sixties of the last century saw the struggle of modern realistic art for official recognition. In this fight the Benivieni bust was enthusiastically greeted as a partisan, a classical witness, combining the authority of the Renaissance with complete realism. The doors of the Louvre which remained closed to the modern realistic school for so many years, were wide open to a work of the abhorred style in suitable historical disguise. Nobody would, at the time, have suspected the truth, had not the dealer Freppa suddenly insisted on making it known.

7. The bust stands now in the cell of Savonarola in the Convent of San Marco at Florence. The Victoria and Albert Museum possesses a replica. E. Maclagan and M. H. Longhurst, *Catalogue of Italian Sculpture* (1932), p. 168. *The Connoisseur*, vol. 110 (1943), p. 134, figs. 2–3.

8. R. Becker, *Die Benivieni-Büste des G. Bastianini* (1889). A. Michel, in *Les Arts*, May 1903, pp. 14 sqq. E. Maclagan and M. H. Longhurst, *Catalogue of Italian Sculpture* (1932), p. 168, pl. 118. *The Connoisseur*, vol. 110 (1943), p. 134, figs. 4–5.

The bust of Marsilio Ficino (*Plate* 66) is derived from the half-figure by Andrea di Piero Ferrucci in the Duomo of Florence.[9] It is on the whole a faithful but somewhat desiccated version of its model. The fine expression of thoughtfulness has been lost and an oppressive mass of realistic detail has taken its place.

Nobody seemed to care for the fact that this kind of realism was completely unknown in the Renaissance, when artists believed in a more general characterisation of the individual. Quite on the contrary, people evidently wished that Renaissance artists had been more like Bastianini. Had the truth not leaked out nobody would have found it, and there may still be numerous works by Bastianini which are taken for genuine, as they escaped the lime-light of the Benivieni scandal.

'La Chanteuse Florentine' is a somewhat exceptional work in Bastianini's *œuvre* (*Plate* 67). He seems to have been inspired by Ghirlandaio's elegant ladies who come to visit Saint Ann and Saint Elizabeth on the frescoes in Santa Maria Novella. The statuette's upturned face has the sentimental glance, turned heaven-wards, so characteristic of Bastianini's work. This statuette aroused as much admiration as Bastianini's other works.[10] A letter addressed in 1866 to Freppa by a French collector, shows that such an enchanting subject was favoured even more highly than the dramatised portraits of famous men. 'I should like to inquire, dear Sir, whether you might indicate to me an interesting terra-cotta bust in Florence, resembling in style the Benivieni bust. However, I should prefer a bust of a young man or a young lady, in short a pleasing subject. I need not stress that I am looking for something beautiful by the hand of an artist of the Quattrocento. I should be most grateful if you could give me details of any such bust you may know of, together with its price. A terra-cotta statuette in the style of the figure brought to Paris by M. Castellani ('La Chanteuse Florentine'), about 40 cm. high, would also be most acceptable,

9. E. Maclagan and M. H. Longhurst, *Catalogue of Italian Sculpture* (1932), p. 168, pl. 119a. For a reproduction of the tomb of Ficino see *Enciclopedia Italiana*, vol. 15, p. 221.

10. A. Foresi, *Tour de Babel* (1868), pp. 30 sqq., 104 sqq. *Musée Jacquemart-André, Catalogue itinéraire* (7th ed.), p. 96, no. 678.

66. Terra-cotta bust of Marsilio Ficino. By Giovanni Bastianini. (By courtesy of the Director of the Victoria and Albert Museum.)

65. Terra-cotta bust of Savonarola. By Giovanni Bastianini. (By courtesy of the Director of the Victoria and Albert Museum.)

67. 'La Chanteuse Florentine'. By Giovanni Bastianini.

provided the subject were interesting and the statuette in a fine state of preservation.'[11]

With the 'Chanteuse Florentine' an autograph letter by the composer Rossini to his friend Castellani used to be exhibited at the Musée Jaquemart André. It was designed to enhance the romantic appearance of the girl: 'Il me plaît de déclarer que cette adorable statuette en terre cuite (qui fait part de la collection de mon ami Castellani) ne chante pas ma cavatine "Di tanti palpiti", qui fit le bonheur des Vénitiens en 1813; elle fredonne une chansonette du célèbre compositeur Ludrone, qui naquit à Padoue en 1500; cela veut dire (Dieu merci) qu'elle ne chante pas la séduisante musique de l'avenir. G. Rossini. Paris ce 2 Avril 1866.' Very appropriately this letter was written in French, though both writer and recipient were Italians. It is dated two days before the Castellani sale when the 'Chanteuse' was successfully sold as a work of the fifteenth century to the great French collector Edouard André.

Bastianini's biography is one of the most interesting documents for the attitude of the world towards fakes and their authors. It was no secret that Bastianini worked by contract for an art dealer, and many people saw his works in his studio and knew that it was their supreme aim to conquer the world as sculptures of the Renaissance. Yet everybody seemed to think that this was no swindle, but something to be proud of. G. Freppa said that he did not tell his patrons that these sculptures were antique. But as they followed the current conception of Renaissance style and were moreover covered with convincingly damaged paint and dirt, he must have been well aware that nobody would regard them as the one-man show of a modern sculptor.

Though he was the only one to acquire fame and to be found out, Bastianini was by no means the only forger of Quattrocentist terra-cottas working in Florence round the middle of the last century. Quite on the contrary, it is far more likely that many of the Florentine dealers of the period employed sculptors who had the duty of providing them with antiques, and above all with Virgins in relief and with busts of men, girls, and saints.

11. Letter by M. Edmond Bonnaffé to Freppa, Bastianini's employer, 11th January 1866.

When in 1903 a bill forbidding the export of antiques was passed by the Italian Senate the Florentine dealers protested against these restrictions of their liberties. Their arguments were very enlightening:[12] 'The advocates of the Bill ignore the fact that everything [sold by the dealers of Florence] is not the product of the art of the past, that innumerable objects have lain for years, for centuries indeed, despised, dust-bitten, and worm-eaten, until he [the dealer] discovered them thus half destroyed, and restored them with his enlightened patience, supplying missing parts, polishing them up, completing them with fragments of other objects, and recomposing the whole in fashion so pleasing and artistic as to excite the fancy of the foreigner, who pays for such work with chinking gold. And they do not consider that behind the shop of the dealer, in his back room, no unskilled workmen but real artists attend to the delicate task of reconstruction and restoration. Nor do they consider that these fifty and more dealers give work to over a thousand such artists, and are a source of gain which percolates through the whole city.'

These manufacturers did such thorough work and their products were absorbed so whole-heartedly by the collectors and museums that the effect on the historical appreciation of Renaissance sculpture was almost disastrous. Some of these back-room artists were masters of sentimentalised realism, preferring the curly head of Saint John as an adolescent to other subjects. There were those who strove to attain the grand manner of Bastianini by modelling their male busts on death-masks, recognisable by their sunken eyes and cheeks and by their lipless mouths. Others concentrated on the exaggerated realism of the 'Benivieni' kind. Their favourites were Saint Jerome and Saint Magdalen with excited and emaciated faces and terrible sinewy necks. As to the Madonnas, they are not intrinsically different from their more expensive marble sisters.

Even terra-cottas may be subjected to embellishments other than cleaning or repainting. This is proved by the bust of a young woman which was thoroughly trimmed during its journey from

12. I quote a passage from their petition as translated in *The Magazine of Art*, N.S., vol. 2 (1904), p. 80.

Paris to Washington.[13] The loose curls of this rather severe-looking lady have been pressed closer to her head and her skin and dress were smoothed and restored. The base in the shape of a cherub's head, which had been left in the rough by its maker, has been 'finished' smoothly. If possible the portrait looks still more conceited and ill-tempered than in its previous state, but it fails to look more convincing. Apart from the modern modelling of the head and the bust, the way it ends in a cherub's head was unknown in the fifteenth and early sixteenth century. When emblems as bases of busts became usual in the later sixteenth century they were arranged in a very different manner.

13. *Les Arts*, Décembre 1907, p. 25. R. Wittkower in *Apollo*, vol. 26 (1937), p. 84, fig. 9.

PART EIGHT

SCULPTURE IN WOOD

PART EIGHT

SCULPTURE IN WOOD

In this field the forger encounters few technical difficulties. A block of wood, a knife, and the will to cheat are all that is needed. And the two latter elements are sufficient if an old piece of wood-carving has the bad luck to fall into the forgers' hands. The tricks brought into play are frequently of such surprising simplicity that they might arouse the envy of many a music-hall cartoonist.

Long narrow heads seem to be the most popular feature of El Greco. A male head, dating apparently from the seventeenth century, possessed the proportions required for the creation of a genuine Greco sculpture. A few cuts of the knife and the saint had become thin enough, and a little clever carving provided a certain dose of Greco's 'personal' style. The dose is very modest, but it seemed sufficient, particularly for a painter's excursion into the field of sculpture. Only the nose did not lend itself to the transformation, and therefore a new one had to be carved, which fitted Greco's rare sculptural masterpiece 'to measure' and would do even more honour to a monument to Cyrano de Bergerac.[1]

Late Gothic artists represented God the Father with the traditional attributes of an emperor. He wears a crown on his head and sits on a throne with the globe in his hand. These figures of God the Father are common enough, but secular portraits are scarce in Gothic sculpture, therefore the figure of God had to become the likeness of an emperor. All the attributes could remain unchanged, but the beard had to be shaved. And after this

---

1. *Sammlung Schloss Rohoncz, Plastik und Kunstgewerbe, Ausstellung München* 1930, pl. 6. R. Berliner in *Belvedere,* vol. 10 (1931), p. 24. For the original state cf. *Pantheon,* vol. 5 (1930), p. 219.

slight manipulation, Rudolf of Hapsburg emerged with a smooth chin.[2]

The fakers of wooden figures seem to have a predilection for German art. Not that the art of other countries went entirely unharassed. Even Dossena did not disdain the cheaper material for his Madonnas in the style of Giovanni Pisano,[3] and the last years brought us a number of Chinese figures made of wood, which, however, look more exotic than aesthetic or ancient.[4] But by far the largest output of wooden fakes is devoted to German Gothic and Renaissance sculpture. Quite a number of them date back to the first half of the nineteenth century, a period which one imagines to have been rich enough in good and cheap originals. The minute carvings of the sixteenth century, particularly profane subjects and portraits of small dimensions, were the favourites of these early collectors. Especially among models for medals forgeries are numerous, and we shall have occasion to meet some of them in the section on medals.[5] Characteristic of this early antiquarian taste are portraits in Renaissance dress. A boxwood statuette of a lady in the rich court dress of the early sixteenth century conforms to this ideal. This figure, which is now in the Czartoryski Museum in Cracow, is a very competent imitation of German Renaissance sculptures, and especially the head is very well done. That some scholars still believe the figure to be genuine is probably caused by the fact that it is a slightly altered copy after the portrait of the Archduchess Margareta from the tomb of Maximilian I in Innsbruck. The modern origin of the figure becomes patent as soon as one looks at the folds of the dress. With the old artist the graceful disposition of the drapery was almost an article of faith; the imitator contented himself with indicating a few meaningless folds.[6]

2. *Oertel Collection, Sale Lepke,* Berlin, 6 May 1913, p. 16, no. 27, pls. 11–12. H. Tietze, in *Metropolitan Museum Studies,* vol. 5 (1934–6), p. 8, fig. 6.

3. *The Bulletin of the Cleveland Museum of Art,* vol. 12 (1925), pp. 39 sqq. F. A. Whiting in *Art and Archaeology,* vol. 27 (1929), p. 279.

4. O. Sirén in *Artibus Asiae* (1925), pp. 140 sqq.

5. See below, p. 192.

6. G. Troescher, *Conrad Meit* (1927), p. 62, fig. 7. For the statue in Innsbruck, see V. Oberhammer, *Die Bronzestandbilder des Maximiliangrabmales* (1935), fig. 251.

A small wood relief showing a knight on horseback, which is a copy of Burgkmair's Emperor Maximilian, belongs to the same class of forgeries. This relief was endowed with the miraculous virtue of showing the coat of arms of every prospective buyer. A German aristocrat could not resist the temptation to acquire it as the portrait of one of his ancestors, complete with arms, initials, and the date 1536. He discovered too late that this particular coat of arms was granted to the family only in 1540. The dealer had to refund the price paid for the 'ancestor', but he tried to come into his own by equipping the relief with another coat of arms and the date 1528.[7]

The peculiar features of the Hapsburgs seem to exercise considerable attraction. Rudolf, the clean-shaven founder of the dynasty, Maximilian in his various disguises, and numerous others, share the company of this bust (*Plate* 68), which was handed around as a portrait of a member of the Hapsburg family, leaving its identification to specialised research. In spite of its deterring ugliness, its modern expression and its comical hat, it was almost acquired by the director of a famous museum.

Gothic figures invented from end to end by the fakers seem to be rare. The danger of tell-tale modernisms is after all considerable. But when the forger copies or varies genuine models he is on safe ground and free from most of the pitfalls threatening his own inventions. Already around the middle of the nineteenth century a workshop, probably in the Tyrol, specialised in the figure of an armoured Saint George, of which quite a number of specimens exist, which are apparently copies after an original now lost.[8]

It is amusing to meet one of the famous Dinanderie ladies from the Rijksmuseum, this time in wood. The model provided the copy with an unimpeachable costume. But compared with the well-preserved original, the copy looks almost heartbreaking in its poor condition. The forger who put it into this state was ruthless enough to cut off the nose and one hand of his lady.[9]

7. J. Brinckmann in *Kunstgewerbeblatt*, N.F., vol. 14 (1903), p. 232.

8. W. Pinder, *Die deutsche Plastik des fünfzehnten Jahrhunderts* (1924) pl. 58. G. Lill in *Belvedere*, vol. 6 (1924), *Forum*, pp. 33 sqq. W. Pinder, *Die deutsche Plastik*, vol. 2 (1929), p. 381.

9. Burlington Fine Arts Club, *Catalogue of a Collection of Counterfeits* (1924), no. 221, pl. 52.

68. Forgery of a German portrait bust. Wood.

69. 'The Beautiful Virgin of Salzburg'. Detail.

70. Christ enthroned. Ivory relief in Byzantine Style. (By courtesy of the Museo Civico, Bologna.)

At Salzburg a Gothic Madonna (*Plate* 69) enjoyed for years a popularity which almost equalled the fame of the festivals. It was managed with a masterliness worthy of Reinhardt. Tourists will perhaps remember having seen her photograph, postcards of which were on show in almost every shop window of the town. They bear the polyglot legend: 'Die schöne Madonna von Salzburg; The beautiful Virgin of Salzburg; La belle Vierge de Salzburg.' Her producer inspired himself on Michael Pacher's altar of Saint Wolfgang, near Salzburg,[10] adding a highly successful dose of modern sentimentalism. Her dress is also modern, for the low-cut circular neck line is quite impossible in the period to which she is supposed to belong, while it is very similar to the local costume of our day which has won such wide popularity in recent years. As the model is kneeling and the ambitious forger was resolved to turn out a standing figure, he was at a loss what to do about her drapery below the knees. And the result fully reveals his uncertainty; he therefore preferred to circulate photographs ending above the danger line.[11]

10. W. Pinder, *Die deutsche Plastik des fünfzehnten Jahrhunderts* (1924), pl. 80

11. For a full-size illustration see *Moderne Welt*, vol. 6 (1924), Heft 14.

PART NINE

IVORY CARVINGS

PART NINE

IVORY CARVINGS

In the nineteenth century the fabrication of pseudo-Gothic ivories assumed such vast proportions that a kind of nihilism began to reign among collectors and connoisseurs. The task was no longer to single out fakes, but to find those pieces which are certainly genuine. Raymond Koechlin, the greatest authority on Gothic ivories, thought it necessary to compile a list of those French Gothic ivories the provenance of which may be traced backwards beyond the beginning of the nineteenth century, the time when forgeries made their first appearance.

He wanted to supply a safe basis for students by including only pieces which had either been reproduced in early publications or which were at least authenticated by circumstantial descriptions.[1]

Provenances, particularly those of medieval French ivories, are frequently deceptive. Some of the French cathedral treasures were assembled only in the nineteenth century, and some dubious pieces appear among the gifts composing them. On the other hand, convents occasionally decided to part with their valuable ivories, which wandered into private collections overseas. But this fact is concealed and an exact copy is shown to the visitors, who are told that this is the original, which has never left the premises.[2]

1. R. Koechlin, 'Quelques ivoires gothiques français connus antérieurement au XIX*e* siècle' in *Revue de l'art chrétien*, vol. 61 (1911), pp. 281 sqq., 387 sqq. *Les Ivoires gothiques français*, vol. 1 (1924), pp. 36 sqq., 541. For an addition to Koechlin's list see M. C. Ross, 'A Gothic Ivory Mirror-Case', in *Journal of the Walters Art Gallery*, vol. 2 (1939), pp. 109 sqq.

2. e.g. an Ottonian ivory in the Monastery of Seitenstetten (A. Gold-schmidt, *Elfenbeinskulpturen*, vol. 2, no. 16); the original was sold to America some years ago.

As soon as interest in medieval ivories began to awaken the forgers began to insinuate their products among the genuine pieces.

One of the most successful of these early forgers may be called the Trivulzio forger as he copied several pieces fiom the Trivulzio Collection in Milan. Only in recent years were his activities exposed by Sir Eric Maclagan.[3] The date of his work is roughly indicated by the history of the Trivulzio Collection which was assembled towards the end of the eighteenth century and by the acquisition of some of the forgeries by a Hungarian collector in the second quarter of the nineteenth century.

The forger copied the consular diptych of Areobindus (A.D. 506) no less than three times. One of his versions is an exact copy of the original in the Trivulzio Collection. In the two others he omitted the monogram of Areobindus, replacing it by a rosette copied from a similar diptych in Novara.[4]

Another of these forgeries copies a wing from the diptych of Philoxenus, which was also in the Trivulzio Collection. Here the forger copied everything, including the inscription, and added only one of the foliated motifs from the Trivulzio-Novara series. But he was not successful in his attempt at completing the missing portion of his panel: only half of the medallion that contained the name Philoxenus still exists on the original, and he failed to guess the name from the subsisting letters $\Phi I \ldots \Xi EN \ldots$ and timidly inserted an X, so that his inscription reads: '$\Phi IX\Xi EN$', which fails to make sense. Though the design of the Philoxenus diptych is very simple, the copy lacks the neat angulaity of the carving peculiar to the original.[5]

What is perhaps the most conspicuous of the Trivulzio forgeries is known in two specimens. It is a copy after another Trivulzio ivory representing Christ enthroned. The model is encased in a

3. Sir Eric Maclagan, 'Ivoires faux, fabriqués à Milan au début du XIXe siècle' in *Aréthuse,* vol. 1 (1923), pp. 41 sqq.

4. Maclagan, *Aréthuse,* vol. 1, pl. 5, 1. R. Delbrueck, *Die Consulardiptychen* (1929), pls. 14, 42; text pl. 5, fig. 1 a, b, c.

5. Maclagan, *Aréthuse,* vol. 1 (1923), pl. 5, 2. R. Delbrueck, *Die Consulardiptychen* (1929), pl. 30; text pl. 5, 3. A. Maskell, *Ivories,* pl. 8, 3.

neo-Renaissance book-cover.[6] The forger copied the shell pattern forming the frame of this book-cover on to one of his ivories.[7] For the second specimen (*Plate* 70) he designed an acanthus ornament, which is hardly more convincing.[8] Neither is the idea of placing Christ's footstool on acanthus leaves a fortunate one. The notions of the forger regarding the rendering of perspective in Byzantine art, may well be described as dim. On the Trivulzio relief all four legs of the throne were represented, while the forger was content with the front legs. But he forgot to omit the bar, which is fastened between the back legs of the throne on his prototype. On his relief this bar hangs in the void.

Without altering anything in the posture of Christ or in the arrangement of the draperies, the forger yet missed the style of his model. He wanted to stress the rigidity which is regarded as an outstanding characteristic of Byzantine art, therefore he made the throne and the halo too straight and too symmetrical. Christ's face has become flat and stiff in an effort to mimic Byzantine conventions. In less prominent parts, particularly in the hands and feet, we catch him off his guard. Here the fine stylised design of the original has been replaced by the naturalism of the forger's own epoch.

The chances of copies have been somewhat diminished by the comprehensive publications of old ivory carvings. Duplicates of known originals are received with misgivings. Only copies of little-known pieces have a fair chance of success. Here the plaster casts which were in vogue during the last century offer some opportunities. For occasionally casts of unpublished and inaccessible objects were made, which could be utilised for very promising forgeries.

This happened to an eleventh-century ivory relief belonging to

6. A. Goldschmidt and K. Weitzmann, *Die byzantinischen Elfenbeinskulpturen*, vol. 2 (1934), p. 41, no. 54, pl. 22 (Trivulzio ivory, now at Basle). H. Peirce and R. Tyler, *Three Byzantine Works of Art* (1941), pl. 12.

7. *Aréthuse*, vol. 1 (1923), p. 42, pl. 6.

8. Bologna, Museo Civico. H. Graeven, *Frühchristliche und mittelalterliche Elfenbeinwerke* (1900), no. 10. *Bollettino d'Arte*, 2nd series, vol. 2 (1922–3), p. 192.

the Prince of Öttingen-Wallerstein.[9] Casts of this small relief were on sale before the original was published. Before their true origin was found out copies of this reproduction had got into the treasure of a Bavarian convent and the Victoria and Albert Museum. When the original eventually became known its authenticity was doubted. But though ivory reliefs are particularly well adapted for casting, the cast had some faulty portions, which the forger had to complete in his versions of the piece, and all his additions are blunders. The relief represents Christ under an arch, which is crowned by the dove of the Holy Ghost, while the symbols of the Evangelists appear in the four corners of the panel. Owing to some technical defect of the cast, Saint Mark's lion is rather indistinct, and was misunderstood by the forger, who took it for an eagle. Therefore Saint John's symbol appears twice on each copy, while Saint Mark remains unrepresented. But two eagles were not enough for the forger. He also changed the dove of the Holy Ghost into an eagle.

These forgers kept to models of ivory. A Venetian forger tried his luck with the copy of a mosaic in the Baptistry of Saint Mark's. 'The Beheading of Saint John' occupies a whole arch of this chapel while the forger had to accommodate the composition to a narrow panel; but he was not disturbed by this change of proportion. He placed the throne at the head of a flight of steps, thus filling the height of his piece of ivory, and put the figures and groups as close together as possible. He had to omit not only one of the servants lowering the body of Saint John, swathed in bandages, into the grave but also cut off this body above the feet, leaving what looks like a strange bandaged parcel, hardly to be recognised without knowledge of the mosaic. On the mosaic two priests and a deacon officiate at the funeral. On the ivory one priest has been omitted and the deacon's vestment was misunderstood and rendered as the frock of a Franciscan. The back part of the Gothic throne of the mosaic has been strangely merged into the dress of the lady standing by its side, so that the seat of the throne has become a

9. At Castle Maihingen. R. Berliner in *Münchner Jahrbuch der bildenden Kunst*, vol. 12 (1921–2), p. 44, fig. 4. O. Pelka, *Elfenbein* (2nd edition, 1923), p. 378, fig. 293. M. H. Longhurst, *Catalogue of Carvings in Ivory*, vol. 2 (1929), p. 126.

kind of patch on her skirt. On the whole the merging of Byzantine art with fourteenth century Gothic, which gives the mosaic its peculiar charm, has not been rendered in any way by the forger. In fact, the ivory has no style whatever. The relief was acquired in the early nineteenth century for the Royal Collection of Berlin. In 1900 it was withdrawn from exhibition as a forgery. It would, however, be rash to presume that ivories of this type are naive forgeries which can deceive no longer. As late as 1927 one of the foremost authorities on Byzantine art tried to prove its genuineness in a learned paper.[10]

Some of the makers of false ivories are particularly resourceful in the choice of their prototypes. Their models range from the sculptures of Notre Dame to Raphael's 'Transfiguration'. The catalogue of the Hearn Collection gives a good survey of the more fanciful of these combinations.[11] The 'artist' who seems to have provided the great majority of the numerous ivories acquired by this collector was rather careless in his adaptations. He changed the group of the coronation of the Virgin from the Virgin's portal of Notre Dame of Paris to a group of two bearded men, and even one of the attending angels had to grow a beard on the ivory. Two of the scenes from this 'Notre Dame triptych' are derived from the reliefs in the choir, which are of a later date than the portal. One of the original reliefs represents Christ appearing to the three Marys. The forger omitted two of them, leaving Jesus alone with one, to whom he seems to be giving a coin.

The elements composing a diptych from the same collection are still more varied. The neo-Gothic subdivision of its arches contains three scenes on either side. On top of the right wing a bishop raises his hand to bless a *Noli me tangere*, placed in the portion below, which is, moreover, adorned with the dove of the Holy Ghost, which makes no sense. The other scene, placed under the protection of the bishop, consists of three figures from

10. *Münchner Jahrbuch der bildenden Kunst*, N.F., vol. 4 (1927), pp. 366 sqq., fig. 2. Review by A. Heisenberg, in *Byzantinische Zeitschrift*, vol. 29 (1929–30), p. 146.

11. *The G. A. Hearn Collection of Carved Ivories* (1908). C. R. Morey, 'Pseudo-Gothic Ivories in the Hearn Collection' in *American Journal of Archaeology*, vol. 23 (1919), pp. 50 sqq.

Raphael's 'Transfiguration', namely Christ, the kneeling woman, and one of the apostles. Even though the carving is very clumsy, it is nice to find Raphael's last picture on a 'Gothic' ivory.

Nothing was sacred to this ivory specialist, who roamed through art history from end to end and copied whatever struck his fancy. Neither the famous statue of the Virgin from the Chartreuse de Champmol near Dijon, nor Bernini's sculptures in the Casino Borghese escaped imitation in ivory, after the ivory statuettes of the Louvre had been exhausted all too quickly. To procure suitable Baroque pieces for an all-round collector Rubens was drawn in. His Ildefonso triptych and even the Medici cycle became ivory reliefs. But less popular pictures, like a triptych by Joos van Cleve, had to serve the same purpose. Nothing escaped this relentless carver's knife.

Beside these works of a roving copyist, an ivory statuette of Judith (*Plate* 71) looks comparatively sensible, for it is a copy of an alabaster statuette by Conrad Meit of Worms (*c.* 1520).[12] But it belongs, nevertheless, to the group of ivories of the Hearn type, which are still being fabricated and sold on a large scale. The copyist substituted a long plain face for the genuine Judith's soft oval. He thought her legs and waist too plump but by his attempt at improving the figure of his Renaissance model he spoiled its harmony. The upper and lower part of the ivory lady's body look as if they would belong to two different persons. The severed head of Holofernes has on the ivory been given the characteristic appearance of the head of Saint John.

A more 'scientific' class of forgers is more considerate in the choice of models and their 'transpositions' are therefore much more deceptive. Medieval enamels, for instance, are a better prototype for 'Carolingian' ivories than Raphael's works for Gothic diptychs. Therefore enamels were used with good success by a forger some of whose works were bought by German collectors, mainly in the 'fifties of the last century. Ornamental scrolls with the Virgin in their centre, as they occur on early Limoges work, were copied in ivory to form the centre of a triptych, the wings of which are genuine enamels. This scheme was repeated, with ivory

12. In the National Museum at Munich. G. Troescher, *Conrad Meit* (1927), pls. 5, 6.

wings copied from a Carolingian book-cover. The Adoration of
the Kings as it appears on Limoges caskets was another welcome
model. A composition frequently used for this particular group
of forgeries represents Jacob blessing his grandsons. This is a
rather queer choice for the gable of triptychs, but the forger
thought it convenient. He copied it from an enamel (now in the
Victoria and Albert Museum) which he found in an illustrated
sale catalogue.[13]

More imaginative forgers chose objects with a greater appeal
to the fancy of their prospective patrons. They faked such iconographical curiosities as had been devised by the scurrilous spirit of
the later Middle Ages. It is no wonder that these inventions, which
have not lost their lure up to our day, should have been revived in
France, the classical country of ivory carving.

The 'Vanity groups' are attractive as well as weird and above
all moralising. The genuine renderings of this theme date from
the late Middle Ages. They are well known as pendants, on which
only the heads of the living and the dead were represented, and
there also exist groups where either a young woman or a young
couple are seen standing back to back, with a skeleton or an old
hag as an unattractive and warning counterpart. The romanticist
editions usually consist of an almost naked woman with a skeleton
at her back. The skeleton also wears a scarf, for the sake of
decency, and worms crawl all over its bones. Why 'Voluptuous-
ness' has to wear wooden shoes on her bare feet is a problem
that can hardly be solved. The sculptor of one of these groups
invented a neo-Romanesque socle, which he inscribed: 'Mors
omniom terribilissimom.' But the un-Christian meaning of this
inscription is as unsuitable for the fifteenth century as its spelling
is faulty.[14]

The 'Vierges ouvrantes' are the religious counterpart of the
Vanity groups. A hollow statuette of the Virgin and Child can be
opened in front, like a triptych, to reveal the Passion of Christ.
This disagreeable invention is not new. *Vierges ouvrantes* occur in

13. H. Graeven in *Jahrbuch der preussischen Kunstsammlungen*, vol. 21
(1900), pp. 75 sqq. O. Pelka, *Elfenbein* (1923), pp. 380 sqq.

14. R. Berliner in *Belvedere*, vol. 9 (July to December 1930), p. 102,
pl. 71.

old inventories and some genuine specimens subsist.[15] There are
at least three forgeries of such figures, apparently carved in the
early nineteenth century. They resemble each other and seem to
be derived from one model, which has not been traced up to now.
The arrangement of the numerous scenes inside the statuettes is so
intricate that one is inclined to believe that such a scheme could
not have been invented by a forger. But on the other hand, the
arrangement of the scenes in trefoils and rhomboids is more
strange than Gothic, and the modelling of the little figures shows
the weak rotundity of other archaistic ivories of the early nineteenth century.[16]

Anyhow, the appeal of the general idea was so irresistible that
the forgers did not stop at such images of the Virgin. They were
joined in due course by ivory kings, knights, monks and nuns,
all with highly interesting insides.[17] Apparently this special art
has not died out. In the shopping centres of art-loving cities
there are windows full of ivories 'in style', among which these
'figures ouvrantes' play a prominent part.

Some ivory weapons deserve a place beside these ivory curios.
A Renaissance shield carved in ivory is a truly preposterous forgery. Its central relief is a copy of Antonio Leoni's 'Conversion
of Saint Paul'. On the shield a winged angel replaces Christ;
possibly the forger wanted to pass off the composition as a battle
scene. He did his best to compose a decorative border and spared
neither victories nor gods, neither prisoners nor trophies, crown-
ing his work, which may be called baroque in the original, derogatory sense of the word, with a Tudor coat of arms. This 'objet
d'art' was sold in 1905 in an Italian holiday resort.[18]

15. e.g. a much restored ivory figure in the Cathedral Treasury at Evora
(Portugal). Cf. Biblioteca Nacional de Lisboa, *Guia de Portugal,* vol. 2 (1927),
plate facing p. 59.

16. *Les Arts,* May 1903, p. 15. A. Maskell, *Ivories* (1905), pp. 171 sqq.,
383, pls. 38, 84. R. Koechlin, *Les ivoires gothiques français* (1924), vol. 1,
p. 51; vol. 2, p. 3, no. 9; vol. 3, pl. 4.

17. *The G. A. Hearn Collection of Carved Ivories* (1908), pl. 39. M. H.
Longhurst, *Catalogue of Carvings in Ivory,* vol. 2 (1929), p. 129.

18. A. Maskell in *The Art Journal,* 1906, p. 293. O. Pelka, *Elfenbein*
(1923), pp. 402 sqq., fig. 416.

The ivory handle and sheath of the 'Dagger of the Malatestas' is a forgery of similar pretentiousness. The sheath is richly carved with the portraits and emblems of Sigismondo and Isotta. Francesco Siepi is the artist who achieved this masterpiece of modern carving.[19]

We have surveyed the rich opportunities open to anyone who desires to produce spurious ivories without wanting to exert his creative vein. The number of inventive fakes is comparatively low. Such inventions as there are, are mainly neo-Gothic, as the graceful carvings of the Gothic period are most ardently sought by collectors.

The style of Gothic ivories has been imitated with considerable efficiency. The diptych illustrated here (*Plate* 72) gives a fair idea of the skill and technical routine of the forger who outreached his models in the easy flow of all curves, the sugary sweetness of facial expression and the horribly smooth finish, luckily never achieved in the fourteenth century. But apart from its style the diptych is given away by its iconography. On the right wing Christ with the spade, carried in a strange, upright position, seems to belong to the *Noli me tangere*. The Saint kneeling at his side is, however, not Magdalene but a nun. Above this scene, Christ, identifiable by the halo with the Cross, reappears, the horribly long fingers raised in blessing. On the left wing Saint John the Baptist addresses a donor kneeling at his side with a strange gesture of his exaggeratedly lengthened hand. The forger evidently did not study medieval iconography, even in its simplest aspects.

The Madonna on *Plate* 73 is an ivory specimen of the Marcy group (see below p. 219). She looks like her silver sisters; her smile is a little overdone, and her figure is too shapeless. Her draperies are neither Gothic nor convincing in any other way. The whole figure looks bulky. The elegant snake, which seems to be very much at ease under the Virgin's feet, has wings, which is rather queer. Moreover, the Child throws its head, so far back that one may well fear that it will break off. The carving of the throne is a fair example of Marcy's meticulous Gothic architectures.[20]

19. C. Ricci, *Il Tempio Malatestiano* (1924), p. 407, fig. 480.

20. E. Molinier and F. Marcou, *Exposition retrospective de l'art français* (1900), p. 7, pl. 3. O. v. Falke in *Belvedere*, vol. 1 (1922), p. 12.

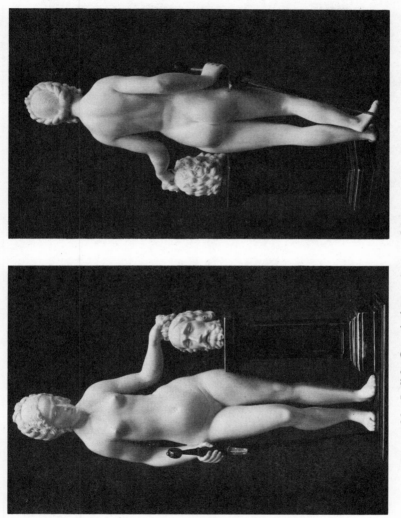

71a and b. Judith. Copy in ivory after an alabaster original by Conrad Meit.

72. Forgery of a Gothic ivory diptych.

The smooth consistence of ivory makes it particularly inviting for the carver's knife. Therefore restorers occasionally see fit to indulge in extensive beauty treatments which are much more damaging to the pieces subjected to it than the patina, damages, and cracks they may have acquired in the course of time. The genuine charm vanishes in the same degree as the unfortunate ivory is 'restored' to smooth correctness. Sir Eric Maclagan demonstrated this to the Society of Antiquaries. He had become interested in an ivory group representing the finding of Christ in the Temple, and consulted M. Koechlin, who produced a photograph of the same group, previous to its treatment in a beauty parlour for ivories. The comparison of the two states is indeed discouraging. While the original group was somewhat battered, its high quality was perfectly visible and could be appreciated fully. With the scraping of the surface and recarving of the figures every vestige of artistic character and style has been destroyed.[21]

The completing of damaged pieces is far more tempting and even more dangerous to the collector. Tricks of this kind can be countered by examination with ultra-violet rays. The fluorescence of the surface of new and old ivory is different: old ivory looks mottled and yellow under the quartz lamp, new ivory bright purple. Artificial ageing of new ivory by colouring does not affect its fluorescence.[22] This test is of particular importance for the examination of restored pieces, which are often so cunningly composed of new and old parts that they appear to the naked eye to be made all of one piece.

A Gothic casket in the Metropolitan Museum is a revealing example of this kind. It is genuine, with the exception of the front, a corner of the lid, some undecorated portions, and most or all of the metal mountings. But the lid was very efficiently restored and the front was copied from a similar casket, with which it had been united for a time in the same private collection. Baron Spitzer had acquired one incomplete and one intact casket, but he sold two complete specimens, the one having been restored fol-

21. *The Antiquaries' Journal*, vol. 2 (1922), p. 199, figs. 4, 5.

22. J. J. Rorimer, *Ultra-violet Rays and Their Use in the Examination of Works of Art* (1931), pp. 28 sqq., frontispiece and figs. 18–21.

lowing the corresponding parts of the other. The copy is so well done that its true history would still be undiscovered had not the mounting of the Metropolitan Museum casket aroused suspicion.[23]

This is not a unique case. Old and new parts can be combined so cleverly that it is impossible to distinguish them. Thus, once suspicion has been aroused, the whole piece is regarded as a forgery. This happened to a fine Gothic casket in Leningrad, with scenes from the romance of Tristan and Isolde. It has the same provenance as the New York casket. We know from old descriptions that, up to 1871, the Tristan casket had no lid. Seven years later the casket was shown at a Paris exhibition in perfect condition, with the lid.[24]

Even the art of the Ancients had to suffer occasional intrusions of false ivories. Apart from some chryselephantine Cretan goddesses (see p. 122), these forgeries are on a modest scale. An Etruscan ivory mask has been illustrated by C. Albizzati in a very instructive paper on forgeries of classical art.[25] It is a female head with wide open eyes and an awe-inspiring gorgonian stare. Pedantically carved spirals frame the face. This ivory lady looks rather intriguing, but Albizzati succeeded in finding the model from which she was copied: an Etruscan terra-cotta head of the fourth century B.C. in the Museum in Orvieto.[26] Although the copy is on the whole quite faithful, the expression of the two works is totally different. Unconscious reminiscences of modern decorations and of African masks crept in, and it was certainly this admixture of the modern and the exotic which assured the success of this forgery.

An ivory case for surgical instruments was made to be passed off as the instrument case of a Greek doctor. The profile of Hippokrates is carved in the centre of its lid, with four snakes in the four corners, the whole being framed by a Greek *cyma*. This forgery panders to the widespread interest in the history of science.

23. Th. T. Hoopes in *Art Bulletin,* vol. 8 (1926), pp. 127 sqq.

24. O. v. Falke, in *Pantheon,* vol. 1 (1928), p. 75. R. S. Loomis, *Arthurian Legends in Medieval Art* (1938), p. 55.

25. *Historia,* vol. 3 (1929), p. 668, fig. 15. Cf. Detroit Institute of Art, *Small in Size, Great in Art* (1946), pl. 8.

26. P. Ducati, *Storia dell'Arte Etrusca* (1927), pl. 204.

Hippokrates looks like a nineteenth-century professor. However, the severely simple design and the very bad condition of the ivory make it look antique enough to be deceptive.[27]

Muhammedan ivories were the speciality of the Spanish master forger D. Francisco Pallás y Puig (1859–1926).[23] This imitator appears to have led a life not dissimilar to those of his prominent colleagues in other countries. His activities are described as the attempts of a gifted but honest imitator who desired to equal famous prototypes. The rest was done by his exploiters, while he was content with declaring from time to time some object as his work, thus delightedly scandalizing all but the owners of his works. Here, as in other cases, it may be assumed that the artist knew well enough what was expected of him, and his successful attempts at 'smoking' his ivories show his undisguised ambition to produce genuine antiquities. Moreover, he used the help of a learned adviser for the Arabic inscriptions.

Hispano-Moresque ivories were the speciality of Pallás. His works look remarkably genuine and could be identified only with the greatest difficulty had he not deigned to lift his incognito himself, at least in a few cases. Since some of his works were thus identified and even drawings from his hand became known, it is now easier to identify his personal style. His ornamental motifs are, as a rule, quite correct, and though they are closely modelled on genuine carvings they are hardly ever slavishly copied. As usual with forgers, he failed in the proper understanding of the things of the past. An ivory box in New York which seems to be his work, shows a prince in an impossible squatting attitude.[29] The representation of a figure sitting cross-legged was a matter of course to the Oriental artist but proved the stumbling block to the modern Westerner. Typically modern and very abstruse was also the idea of carving two servants who present the prince with

27. Th. Meyer-Steinegg and K. Sudhoff, *Geschichte der Medizin* (3rd edition, 1928), p. 69, fig. 47.

28. M. Gómez-Moreno in *Archivo Español de arte y arqueología,* vol. 3 (1927), pp. 233 sqq. with numerous illustrations. Cf. also A. Goldschmidt, 'Pseudo-Gothic Spanish Ivory Triptychs of the Nineteenth Century', *The Journal of the Walters Art Gallery,* vol. 6 (1943), pp. 49 sqq.

29. *Archivo Español de arte y arqueología,* vol. 3 (1927), p. 241, figs. 37–38.

flower-pots. The favourite objects of Pallás were pyxes and caskets, but occasionally he also ventured on a couple of chessmen.

The forgers of Chinese ivories specialised in works of the earliest period. They took their inspiration from the greatest find in the field of Chinese archaeology, the discovery of the archives of oracle bones in Honan. Chance excavations on the site of the capital of the Shang-Yin dynasty brought to light thousands of oracle inscriptions from the second millennium B.C. which opened a new chapter of Chinese history. The number of inscriptions was quickly augmented by spurious additions. One forger thought the oracles would look nicer on ivory dragons than on the usual shapeless pieces of bone or tortoiseshell.[30] He carved a number of alligator-like crocodiles which show a rather comic blend of modern naturalism with the stylised angularity of archaic Chinese art. He covered the backs of his animals with long inscriptions which are a clumsy imitation of early Chinese characters, and he got his dates completely muddled (*Plate* 74).

30. *Journal of the R. Asiatic Society* (1913), pp. 545 sqq. Burlington Fine Arts Club, *Exhibition of Chinese Art* (1915), pl. 55. P. Pelliot, in *T'oung Pao* vol. 22 (1923), p. 7, note 1.

PART TEN

BRONZE SCULPTURE

PART TEN

BRONZE SCULPTURE

PATINA

It is a widely accepted assumption that the patina of bronzes is the most important proof of their authenticity. Not enough consideration is given to the fact that fine coatings of patina may easily be fabricated with the aid of chemicals. Even a thick layer of actual verdigris may be produced in comparatively short time.

Though it is by no means difficult to cultivate real copper-rust, simpler methods have occasionally been employed by forgers. Thus an after-cast from a Fatimid bronze lion would be given away by its coating of spurious verdigris, even if its genuine model were unknown.[1] The whole body of this ewer is engraved with ornaments consisting of thin lines, which are, of course, faithfully reproduced by the cast. In some places they have been touched up with green colour, meant to simulate copper-rust. The whole is highly polished, and the lines of the engraved pattern can be seen with perfect clearness through the 'verdigris'. This would be impossible with real rust.

On the whole the importance of the patina is much overrated. The patina of genuine pieces may have been removed; many Greek and Roman bronzes in old collections were stripped in this way. Even more frequently they were covered with a black varnish imitating patina. Renaissance artists disliked the shining surface of polished bronze. Vasari enumerates the various methods

1. Victoria and Albert Museum, Salting Bequest (M. 708–1910). The original is in the Louvre; reproduced in G. Migeon, *Manuel d'art musulman, Arts plastiques* (1927), pp. 382 sqq., fig. 191. *Les Arts* (1903), p. 13.

by which they tried to anticipate the effects of time:[2] 'Some apply oil to blacken the bronze, some use vinegar to make it green, some make it black by giving it a coating of varnish.' The patina of many modern forgeries looks convincing enough. Attention should therefore be concentrated on the work itself, on its style and quality and on the sculptural details of its surface.

AFTER-CASTS

Though a cast is the mechanically exact reproduction of its model, it can never do full justice to the artistic qualities of its prototype. The whole surface of an old bronze was chased after casting. Much of the charm of old bronzes consists of these details wrought by chasing which fail to appear in an after-cast, left either in the rough or finished off with a smooth surface which is at once lifeless and uninteresting.

This becomes evident when original and copy are examined side by side. Andrea Riccio's firedogs in the shape of sphinxes, which now form part of the Salting Bequest, were stolen by the forger Weininger from the Este Collection of Vienna. They were confided to him for restoration, but he replaced them by casts and sold the originals. As the originals are covered with a coating of black lacquer there was no essential difficulty about the patina. But all the small irregularities which gave the surface its life and charm have disappeared. The hair of the sphinxes and particularly their wings have lost all the minute details of their single curls and feathers. Though no essential part has been altered, the sphinxes look more like works of the nineteenth century than like Renaissance bronzes.[3]

An after-cast of Riccio's 'Arion' fully reveals the contrast between the original and its mechanical copy. For not only has the

2. G. Vasari, *Le Vite* (ed. Ciaranfi, 1927), vol. 1, p. 142. Similar methods were used by the sixteenth-century imitators of classical coins; cf. E. Vico, *Discorsi sopra le medaglie de gli antichi* (1558), p. 66.

3. L. Planiscig, *Andrea Riccio* (1927), figs. 279, 280. Even before Weininger's theft became known the Vienna sphinxes were recognised by Dr. Planiscig as late after-casts; see his *Die Estensische Kunstsammlung* (1919), p. 123.

vividly moved and unruly hair on the musician's head become a tangle, but his parted lips, which were suggestive of the sounds he utters in the original, have been degraded to a stupid grimace.[4]

While these casts were meant to be deceptive, another class of mechanical reproductions of old bronzes were made without fraudulent intention. During the Gothic revival of the nineteenth century medieval bronze implements, in particular candlesticks and ewers, were reproduced on a large scale. These after-casts were originally destined to serve in churches, but it was inevitable that they should soon be mistaken for old pieces or fraudulently sold as such.

Falke and Meyer energetically fought this evil by the publication of a fully illustrated catalogue of all the medieval bronze and brass candlesticks and ewers they recognised as genuine, adding to every original such casts and copies as had come to their knowledge.[5] The fact that plaster-casts of a certain original exist renders a piece closely resembling it doubly suspicious.

Spurious combinations of different bronzes are particularly dangerous. Occasionally faked bronze candlesticks were composed of parts derived from different originals or supplemented by additional parts. In some cases imitations of medieval enamel were stuck on to spurious pieces as a further enhancement. The forger's own additions are almost always telling. In considering them it should above all be borne in mind that these bronze objects are implements destined for use. It should, for instance, be reckoned as a fatal verdict if a candlestick has a thorn too thick and blunt for its purpose. The spout of ewers ought to be narrow. Wide funnels were neither usual in the Middle Ages nor would they have been practical for the purpose of sprinkling a thin ray of water over the hands of the priest celebrating mass. The handles of genuine pieces always fit the hand comfortably, while they are often extravagantly uncomfortable on spurious pieces.

Another means of detecting imitations of this kind is a close examination of the technique of casting. The bodies of genuine

4. Original in the Louvre: L. Planiscig, *Piccoli Bronzi* (1930), pl. 50. After-cast in Vienna: J. v. Schlosser, *Werke der Kleinplastik*, vol. 1 (1910), pl. 5.

5. O. v. Falke and E. Meyer, *Bronzegeräte des Mittelalters* (1935).

73. Madonna. Ivory. By L. Marcy.

74. Forgery of an antique Chinese ivory
carving.

75. The Granvella Venus. Bronze and silver. (By courtesy of
Kunsthistorisches, Vienna.)

ewers are invariably cast in one piece. Consequently the white line of soldering metal along the spine or on the legs of a figure betrays its modern make, for imitations of the simpler kind were often cast in halves. If the faked ewer has been cast in one piece, the lines of the file may often be observed where the thin ridges, caused by the edges of the single sections of the modern mould, have been filed off. With the *cire perdue* technique such ridges were, of course, out of the question.

But on the whole such details, helpful though they may be, can be hidden by the forger, or may be absent altogether. What may be observed in every case is the handling of the whole surface and the chasing of portions like manes and paws. The work of the modern craftsman is often betrayed by a certain routine mannerism. In general all features of a spurious piece will be smoother and more indistinct than their prototype.

There is something else that should not be overlooked: two genuine candlesticks may form a pair, but otherwise no two pieces are exactly alike. Imitations, on the other hand, have a natural inclination to hunt in packs, and if two or more pieces coming from the same mould are known one may be sure that there is something fishy about the matter.

CASTS AFTER ORIGINALS OF DIFFERENT MATERIAL

Spurious after-casts in bronze were not made exclusively after bronze originals. If the model is of another material than its counterfeit, identification may become more difficult. On the other hand, the model may have some technical peculiarity which is unlikely on a bronze and may be the clue for the detection of the forgery. A hallmark visible on a bronze relief may be reckoned as such a peculiarity. It is visible on a number of copies cast after two silver reliefs by Moderno, one of which represents the Flagellation and the other the Madonna surrounded by saints. These sixteenth-century reliefs form part of the former Imperial Collections of Vienna. They got the hallmarks between 1805 and 1807, when a law ordering the re-marking of all silver had been issued in Austria. In 1860 galvanoplastic copies of these reliefs were shown at an exhibition. These casts initiated a long series of bronze fakes the spurious character of which may be gathered without difficulty from the nineteenth-century hallmark.[6]

In other cases the poor and rough character of the casts is so manifest that they could be recognised as forgeries even if their original model were unknown. An Etruscan bronze mirror with a relief representing Apollo, Zeus, and Hermes on its back was sold to the Museum of Geneva by 'a travelling craftsman from Italy'. In order to endow it with a sufficiently primitive appearance the cast had been left as it was when the mould was broken. The outlines of the figures and particularly their faces can barely be made out. The engraved ornament surrounding the relief is likewise of the poorest quality. It is nothing but a very bad cast after a silver mirror in the Museo Archeologico at Florence. As Etruscan mirrors with reliefs on the back are rare, the same piece had already been used as a model for the manufacture of fakes in the 'eighties of the last century. The earlier faker was more ambitious than his follower. He chose silver for his material and gave a highly polished finish to his relief, so that the dry precision of his work betrays him, just as the later piece is given away by its crudeness. The success of his forgeries must have outreached his boldest expectations. One of his mirrors got into the Metropolitan Museum in New York, the other into the National Museum of Athens.[7]

So far we have dealt with casts which did not pretend to represent something essentially different from their models. But it has happened more than once that an after-cast was accepted as a masterpiece of very different origin from its prototype. This is what happened to a Roman head of the second century A.D. The original marble, which represents a boy with charmingly rounded features, forms part of the sculptures adorning the corridors of the Uffizi. One is inclined to think that the mere vicinity should have prevented a bronze after-cast of this head from being accepted by the Bargello as a work by Desiderio da Settignano. Yet this is

6. L. Planiscig, *Die Bronzeplastiken* (1924), p. 247. Thieme-Becker, *Künstlerlexikon,* vol. 24, p. 605. Cf. *Aréthuse,* vol. 4 (1927), p. 183, pl. 29.

7. *Jahreshefte des Österreichischen Archäologischen Instituts,* vol. 27 (1932), p. 160; vol. 29 (1935), Beiblatt p. 203.

precisely what happened, though the cast is exactly like its model, with the only exception of the curls, which were too deeply cut into the marble to be reproduced in bronze. The forger attempted to improve their blurred and flattened surface by engraved lines which resemble neither Roman nor Renaissance sculpture. Notwithstanding this, nobody seemed to notice that the bronze by no means resembled the style of Desiderio, whose name it carried, till its prototype was recognised by a mere chance.[8]

Early medieval and Romanesque ivories have been widely circulated in plaster-casts which have been occasionally used by forgers for the fabrication of spurious medieval bronzes. A particularly fine Carolingian book cover, representing Saint Gregory, was cast in bronze for this purpose.[9] The deeply undercut relief suits the original material but it is out of style in a bronze relief. As all ivories of the Middle Ages have been published in excellent reproductions, such forgeries are not very dangerous.

SPURIOUS ALTERATIONS OF BRONZES

With bronzes, as with sculptures in stone and terra-cotta, there is little danger of subsequent alterations. Bronze does not easily lend itself to spurious changes. An exchanged head is perhaps a unique occurrence. A full-length bronze statuette by the Austrian sculptor Anton Fernkorn represented the Viennese banker Sina. The attitude of the banker has a strong resemblance to that of Rauch's famous statuette of Goethe. This similarity induced a forger to saw off the head of the unsaleable banker and to substitute for it Goethe's well-known features.[10] More common is the engraving of genuine but plain bronze objects with figure scenes. Thus undecorated Etruscan mirrors were frequently embellished

8. W. v. Bode, *Denkmäler d. Renaissance-Sculptur Toscanas* (1892–1905), pl. 312c. P. Herrmann, in *Mitteilungen aus d. sächsischen Kunstsammlungen,* vol. 5 (1914), pp. 1 sqq.

9. The original is in the Museum in Vienna.

10. *Österreichische Galerie, 6. Ausstellung,* no. 31. H. Tietze, in *Metropolitan Museum Studies,* vol. 5 (1934–6), p. 4, fig. 5.

by mythological scenes and a fine Greek bronze vessel was spoilt by a 'Triumph of Poseidon'.[11]

Rarer are inscriptions added in modern times. A thirteenth-century ewer in the shape of a cock has on its tail an inscription giving the date A.D. 1155 and the name of the artist, Burcart Rufus. Although the lettering is not in the style of the twelfth century, the inscription was regarded as genuine for a long time.[12]

Occasionally we meet with the opposite practice, the removal of a genuine signature, well known to us from picture forgeries. (Above p. 45.) On Bertoldo's signed Bellerophon, one of the most famous bronzes of the fifteenth century, the artist's signature had to disappear under a thick coating of wax, obviously for the purpose of selling the bronze as a work of classical antiquity.[13]

FORGERIES BY ARTISTS OF THE RENAISSANCE

The fate of Bertoldo's 'Bellerophon' is typical for a whole class of Renaissance bronzes, the statuettes, mostly of classical subjects, made for the studio of the connoisseur and humanist. Made in emulation of the Graeco-Roman bronzes, their modern origin and the names of their creators were soon forgotten and a large number landed in collections of classical antiquities. Many were rediscovered there in comparatively recent times, like the 'Bellerophon', others are still disguised as Roman bronzes.

It is often not easy to draw the border-line between ancient and Renaissance bronzes. A few cases have as yet not been finally decided. There is no doubt that a number of Renaissance bronzes were intended as forgeries from the beginning. This is clear in the case of bronzes which were cast as fragments with the intention of imitating damaged antique sculptures.

In the Vienna Museum is a slender Venus, whose oval face, with downcast eyes, recalls Giorgione. The statuette, one of the love-

11. Etruscan mirrors: P. Bienkowski, *De speculis Etruscis* (1912), p. 38, fig. 8. *Enciclopedia Italiana*, vol. 14 (1932), p. 758. Greek bronze vessel: *Archäologischer Anzeiger* (1925), pp. 35, 278.

12. Falke-Meyer, *Bronzegeräte des Mittelalters* (1935), p. 41, fig. 243.

13. T. Frimmel, *Von alter und neuer Kunst* (1922), p. 9.

liest Renaissance bronzes in existence, is the work of a Venetian sculptor of the early sixteenth century, perhaps of Tullio Lombardi, to whom the figure has been attributed. The artist, whoever he was, certainly wished to remain anonymous. He cast his statuette without arms in order to sell it as a fragmentary work of classic times. The arms were not broken off, but—as a closer inspection shows—they were left out already in the wax model from which the bronze was cast. The artist made no attempt to imitate the style of ancient bronzes; his work is conceived in the romantic spirit characteristic of Venetian art in the time of Giorgione. His language is—if one may say so—not Latin, but the Venetian dialect of his time.[14]

The so-called Granvella Venus (*Plate* 75) is a much more sophisticated fake; not a poetical emulation of the antique as the Venetian Venus, but a conscious imitation.[15] It is a fragment; already in the sixteenth century the missing feet were replaced in silver. At that time the Venus was one of the treasures of the Granvella Palace in Besançon. The restoration was executed by a local goldsmith as the hallmark on the socle shows. The emperor Rudolph II coveted for many years the collection of the Granvellas. Once he persuaded the owner, François Perrenot, Count of Cantecroix, to sell him Dürer's 'Martyrdom of the Ten Thousand'. The Count, at that time imperial ambassador, had a copy made, which he substituted for the original and sent to the Emperor. The deceit was detected at once and the picture returned together with a letter telling the Count that he should regard his diplomatic mission as concluded.[16] In 1600 the Emperor made new attempts to acquire the best pieces from the collection, this time with full success. The Dürer as well as the 'silver-footed Venus' were among his acquisitions.

The treasures of the Granvella Palace seem to have possessed miraculous powers of regeneration. In 1607, after the Count's

14. L. Courajod, in *Gazette des Beaux-Arts,* vol. 34 (1886), p. 324. L. Planiscig, *Die Bronzeplastiken* (1924), pp. 83 sqq., fig. 149.

15. L. Planiscig, *Die Bronzeplastiken* (1924), p. 66, fig. 114. J. v. Schlosser, *Präludien* (1927), p. 370.

16. P. Levesque, *Mémoires pour servir à l'histoire du cardinal de Granvelle* (1753), vol. 1, p. 190. *Monatshefte für Kunstwissenschaft* (1922), 282.

death, an inventory of his possessions was made.[17] In the case of a classical relief, the so-called 'Bed of Polycletus', we learn that a wax cast was made and kept when the original was sold to the Emperor. But othei works of art, including the Dürer and the Venus appear in the inventory as originals as if they had never left Besançon.

Until 1919 the Granvella Venus was regarded as a work of classical art. The Venus is indeed a rather faithful imitation of Roman bronze statuettes of the first century of our era. Its exact model is now lost, but it must have been similar to the Venus of Grenoble and the 'Venus with the dolphin' in the Bibliothèque Nationale in Paris (No. 248). Even the strange and intricate hairdress is copied from a Roman bronze.[18] Not so classical is the shell in the left hand of Venus, an attribute quite common in Renaissance art, but unusual in Greek and Roman sculpture. In spite of this unclassical trait—there exists, by the way, a replica of the figure without the shell—one might feel tempted to regard our figure as ancient were it not for a number of related statuettes which date without doubt from the Renaissance. A small bronze Venus, likewise in Vienna (No. 84), which is not only similar in style but shows also the same attributes, proves that the Granvella Venus is the work of a North Italian artist of the early sixteenth century.

After Giovanni da Bologna had completed his celebrated statue of Mercury his workshop was teeming with repetitions on a reduced scale which—not to speak of later casts—were dispersed all over the world. Yet it is astonishing to find a torso (*Plate 76*) of this well-known sculpture in a collection of classical art. The identity of Mercury is thinly disguised by the omission of the helmet and by a leather strap descending from the right shoulder of the torso. Under the layer of verdigris covering this fragment the surface is rather uneven. Apparently this is nothing but a faulty cast of Mercury, but instead of returning the metal to the melting-pot as usual, the limbs were broken off and the whole covered with verdigris.[19]

17. A. Castain, 'Monographie du Palais Granvelle', *Mémoires de la Société d'Emulation du Doubs*, ser. 4, vol. 2 (1866), p. 126.

18. Venus from Cyprus: *Pantheon*, vol. 17 (1936), p. 50.

19. L. Planiscig, *Die Bronzeplastiken* (1924), p. 151, fig. 253.

THE EGYPTIAN FASHION

In the course of the seventeenth century a new field was added to the study of antiquity. The art of ancient Egypt was discovered, and this new hobby was taken up eagerly by students and collectors. As Egypt was then a very remote country and no systematic excavations were made before Napoleon's expedition, the objects offered to those interested in Egyptian art and culture were of a rather dubious character. Moreover, ancient Egypt, as it was conceived at the time of its rediscovery, appealed to a general desire for the fantastically incredible and the darkly mysterious, while the study of classical antiquity was a soundly established and thoroughly explored discipline. Consequently early publications on the subject, as for instance the part dealing with Egypt contained in Montfaucon's *Antiquité expliquée*, which appeared in 1719, contain many queer objects and some patent fakes. This became disastrous to the following generation of forgers, who tried to use the plates of this work for their own ends.

A strip of beaten gold, embossed with a strange procession of animal-headed divinities, passed the scrutiny of the eighteenth-century scholar, though he felt doubtful about the alleged provenance of the object from a city wall of Malta.[20] But a couple of bronze reliefs copied after Montfaucon's plate were less fortunate. Landgrave Frederic II of Hesse had the satisfaction of detecting these forgeries, which he had inherited from his predecessor. The forger was clumsy enough to include the case of this precious object, which Montfaucon had reproduced beside the relief, in his spurious copy, so that it appears at the end of the procession, like a large caterpillar.[21]

Copies and variations of Egyptian bronze statuettes were produced in the seventeenth and eighteenth centuries. They are, of course, more deceptive than the forgeries quoted above, but their origin may be recognised, even if they have been endowed with spurious patina, as they betray the style of their period by more than one sign. They may display a smiling face or a revealing

20. B. de Montfaucon, *Antiquité expliquée* (1719), vol. 2/2, pl. 136.
21. R. Hallo, in *Repertorium f. Kunstwissenschaft*, vol. 47, p. 267, fig. 2.

realism in the soft modelling of body and limbs, or some other characteristic strange to genuine Egyptian statuary.[22]

MODERN FORGERIES OF CLASSICAL AND MEDIEVAL BRONZES

A bronze head of a Roman lady gave rise to suspicions by a noticeable disparity in the quality of the modelling. Moreover, the superficial damages of the bust are not due to an accident. As the undisturbed surface of the cast shows, they must have been inflicted on the wax model. K. Kluge, who investigated this case, noticed that the silken net covering the skull is a cast from nature. Almost all of the lady's hair is invisible; such hair as is to be seen in front of her ears and her eyebrows is of the poorest workmanship. Further, he found the modelling of chin, mouth, nose, and ears excellent, while the eyes and throat are hardly modelled at all. Kluge offered a very plausible explanation for these incongruities: on a death-mask neither eyes nor hair nor throat are adequately reproduced, while it does full justice to the more fleshy parts of the face. The very thin lips, shrunk like the lips of a corpse, confirm this explanation.[23]

Equally ingenious was the faker who chose the aquiline type of certain head-shaped Peruvian clay vessels for his version of a Romanesque ewer (*Plate* 77). He changed the hairdress and slightly straightened the receding forehead of his Indian model. He succeeded in conveying a striking impression of grandeur and vividness which he could never hope to match by an invention of his own. The piece was quite a success. It duped two famous collectors before it was found out.[24]

This is not the only example of a faked bronze implement. Spurious inventions—ewers are favourites—give themselves

22. L. Planiscig, *Die Bronzeplastiken* (1924), figs. 300–2. R. Enking, *Der Apis-Altar J. M. Dinglingers* (1939).

23. *Ausonia*, vol. 9 (1919), pp. 122 sqq. K. Kluge, *Die antiken Grossbronzen* (1927), vol. 1, p. 240, fig. 39c.

24. E. Hollaender, *Aeskulap und Venus* (1928), p. 343. Falke-Meyer, *Die Bronzegeräte des Mittelalters* (1935), p. 93, *Fälschungstafel*, fig. f. Cf. W. Lehmann, *The Art of Old Peru* (1924), pl. 73.

76. Mercury. Inspired by Giovanni da Bologna's statue. Bronze. (By courtesy of Kunsthistorisches, Vienna.)

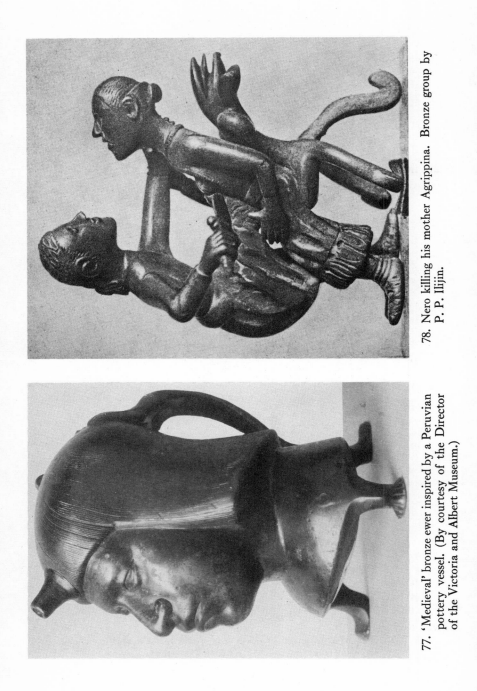

78. Nero killing his mother Agrippina. Bronze group by P. P. Ilijin.

77. 'Medieval' bronze ewer inspired by a Peruvian pottery vessel. (By courtesy of the Director of the Victoria and Albert Museum.)

away by a general tendency to be richer and more imaginative than the comparatively sober originals. Excessive richness of ornament is another sign, for genuine ewers are comparatively plain. I am therefore inclined to believe that criticism uttered with regard to one of the largest and most ornate ewers known, might be justified.[25] This vessel has the shape of a dragon with a man kneeling on its back as handle. Its horizontal body strangely rests on the front paws and on the flattened ends of its wings. There are no hind legs. As on Mohammedan bronzes the whole surface is covered with engraved ornamentation. The design is composed of a few badly drawn motives which are not Romanesque in style.

Gothic figures of bronze and brass have frequently been forged. What has been said here about the style of false Gothic sculptures applies to them as well. But detection is rendered easier by the fact that genuine figures of this kind are very rare. Every specimen turning up unexpectedly should be examined with care before it is accepted. This was, however, omitted when a so-called Dinanderie figure, described as 'Franco-Flemish, around 1400', was exhibited with great pomp with the Castle Rohoncz Collection. Though the exhibition was held at Munich, it was overlooked that this figure was a modern brass replica of the 'Madonna of Alt-Ötting', the most celebrated object of pilgrimage in Bavaria. Copies of this devotional image are found all over Southern Germany. The brass figure, which is over two feet high, is a sample of this pious industry.[26]

A problem arising more frequently than might be expected is that set by the naïve products of crafty but ignorant swindlers. Such things may turn up from the most unexpected quarters of the earth, and being the work of persons unaware of the usual conventions of period and style, they may prove more deceptive than the most elaborate fakes, as they baffle the spectator by their very unexpectedness, instead of trying to convince him by reasonable arguments.

25. Falke-Meyer, *Die Bronzegeräte des Mittelalters* (1935), p. 41, fig. 246. *Sammlung Schloss Rohoncz* (1930), no. 23, pl. 12. R. Berliner in *Belvedere*, vol. 10 (January to June 1931), pp. 25, 182.

26. *Sammlung Schloss Rohoncz* (1930), no. 25, pl. 13. R. Berliner in *Belvedere*, vol. 10 (January to June 1931), p. 23.

Thus much ink was wasted on the work of a crafty locksmith of Bosnia. This man conceived the idea of casting small bronzes for the purpose of selling them to tourists. Before Peter Pezelj Ilijin was found out many papers had been published on the probable date and on the subject of the group shown in *Plate* 78. Depicting the murder of a woman, it was supposed to represent some story from local folklore. What puzzled scholars was the novel combination of characteristics of Romanesque style with local dress, and a certain roughness of make, the whole being covered by what is described as a 'fine green patina'. In the long run the appearance of a replica of the problematic group gave rise to suspicions, and F. Bulic, the Dalmatian archaeologist, found the artist, who enjoyed some fame as a craftsman and a swindler. Peter Ilijin's studies were limited to the Romanesque sculpture at the Cathedral of Trau and in the local museum. He naturally adopted the general appearance of Romanesque sculpture, using, moreover, a motive from the portal at Trau for his group. To the peasant contemporary national costume did not seem incongruous. How far he was from the intention of creating popular Slavonic art is demonstrated by the title he attached to his work: it is not a Slav hero, murdering his unfaithful sweetheart, but Nero killing his mother Agrippina. Another of his creations represents Nero enthroned.[27] It is true that this swindle, dating from the 'eighties of the last century, is old history by now, but nevertheless we should not feel too safe from similar surprises. We have no means of knowing beforehand of what kind of swindle, better adapted to our susceptibilities, we are liable to become victims.

MODERN FORGERIES OF RENAISSANCE BRONZES

It is hard to believe that this smoothly polished statuette of Eve (*Plate* 79) with her strands of pedantically curled hair and her neat apron of fig-leaves, should ever have been endowed with the illustrious name of Benvenuto Cellini. The grinning snake alone would be sufficient proof of the nineteenth-century origin

27. *Wissenschaftliche Mitteilungen aus Bosnien und der Hercegowina,* vol. 2 (1894), pp. 483–95, pls. 6, 7.

of this figure. The extra luscious finish which is characteristic of the decorative bronzes of the Victorian era, is thought by many to be a quality of Cellini's work. Therefore trinkets of similar type appear from time to time under his name. Thus some casts of a coquettishly dancing Eve were believed less than twenty years ago to be works of Cellini. One of them had even been embellished by a pair of large wings screwed on to her shoulders.[28] Figures like these can hardly be called forgeries; they are trinkets typical of the nineteenth century. Out of fashion and banned from the drawing-room, they found a new appreciation as works of the Italian Renaissance. Somewhat better in quality but still unmistakably a nineteenth-century knick-knack, is the doorknocker of gilded copper (*Plate* 80). It is a travesty of Laocoon in a small way: a slim girl is struggling with two lizards, the tails of which have been lengthened and the heads changed to simulate dragons.

Eve (*Plate* 81), dressed in a bathing suit to placate the moral susceptibilities of Puritans, ought never to have been taken seriously. Bode mentioned this rare fake in 1907.[29] It was launched as a work of Andrea Riccio. The gestures are so affected that nobody should be taken in, even without the bathing suit. The aggressive sentimentalism of the couple's glances contrasts strangely with the unwieldiness of their figures.

But there exists another more cunning variety of fakes. Their creators are bent on duping the learned collector, and they occasionally do it with the greatest success. 'Pan Playing the Reed Pipes' at the Ashmolean Museum is one of the masterpieces of Andrea Riccio.[30] It is one of the most delightful creations of the Italian Renaissance. And as used to happen in the golden age, Pan's melody attracted a lovely nymph (*Plate* 82). She is perhaps slightly too heavy for her graceful partner. Her maker preferred to leave the cast in the rough, contenting himself with the most rudimentary chasing, but everybody who knows the Ashmolean Pan will recognise this work at once as Pan's female partner. She is of the same height, and is seated on the same kind of pedestal,

28. *Belvedere,* vol. 10 (January to June 1931), p. 25, pls. 24, 2.

29. W. Bode in *Kunst und Künstler,* vol. 6 (1908), p. 96. H. Tietze in *Metropolitan Museum Studies,* vol. 5 (1934–6), p. 3, fig. 4.

30. L. Planiscig, *Andrea Riccio* (1926), fig. 510.

adorned with shells and garlands. Her feet are disposed in exactly
the same way as those of Pan, the only alteration being that right
and left have been exchanged, to enforce her claim to be his
counterpart. She also holds on her knee the same sort of vase as
does her male prototype. But with her free arm the faker had
some trouble, for Pan holds his pipes in the corresponding hand.
Therefore the lady's arm had to be copied from Riccio's seated
shepherd in the Louvre,[31] but though Riccio's *œuvre* offers a
large number of female models, the forger failed lamentably in
rendering female charm, both of face and body. The body and
arm are lifeless and of poor modelling, the face is heavy, and the
two corkscrew curls are positively inept. Yet the forger was correct in presuming that the wise choice of his prototype would
serve to cover all his shortcomings. His nymph was acquired by
the Kaiser Friedrich Museum of Berlin as a work of Riccio.[32]

CAST MEDALS AND PLAQUETTES OF THE RENAISSANCE

With cast Renaissance medals the task of distinguishing after-
casts from originals is extremely difficult. Only those medals can
really be regarded as originals which have been cast and chased by
the artist who designed them or which come at least from his
studio and were made under his supervision. It is, however, a sad
fact that in many cases we do not know reliable originals of medals,
the best-known specimens being usually regarded as originals until better casts turn up. It results from this that the largest available
number of specimens of a medal should be compared, before
judgment is passed over a piece.

After-casts were made whenever anyone wished to possess a
medal and all collections are filled with casts, accumulated in the
course of four centuries. The reproduction of medals was re-
regarded as a legitimate procedure; in Vienna, in the eighteenth
century for instance, all bronze medals were discarded and replaced

31. L. Planiscig. *Andrea Riccio* (1926), fig. 507.
32. *Jahrbuch der preussischen Kunstsammlungen*, vol. 42 (1921), pp. 1 sqq.
L. Planiscig was the first to recognise the figure as a forgery.

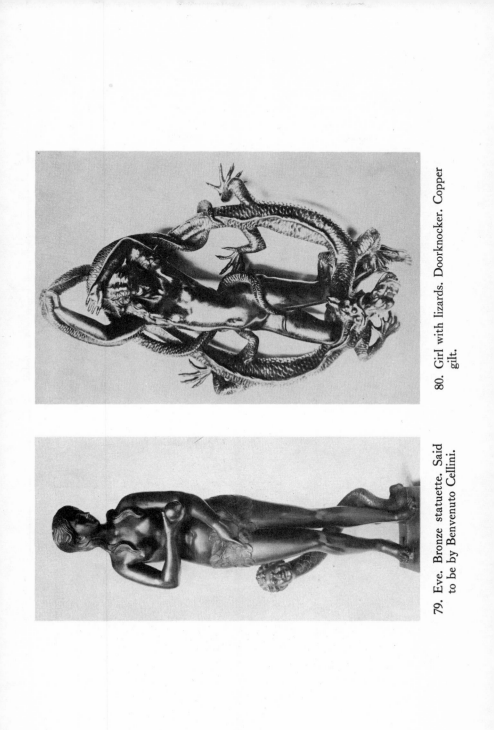

79. Eve. Bronze statuette. Said to be by Benvenuto Cellini.

80. Girl with lizards. Doorknocker. Copper gilt.

81. Adam with Eve dressed in a bathing suit. Bronze group.

82. Nymph. Bronze statuette in the style of Andrea Riccio. Modern forgery.

by after-casts in silver as this nobler metal was alone thought worthy of the Imperial Collections.

Every original was chased and polished after casting, consequently an unworked surface betrays the after-cast. Among the parts of the relief that become most blurred on an after-cast is the lettering. The usual method of distinguishing casts from originals is the examination of the measurements. The size of after-casts is slightly smaller; this is caused by the shrinking of the clay mould when burnt and of the bronze when cooling. Modern forgers are sufficiently inventive to avoid this shrinkage by special methods.[33] A few words should be said of galvanoplastic copies. They are more easily and more frequently made of medals and plaquettes than of statues. If they pretend to be of bronze they may be found out, as the electrolytical process cannot be executed with an alloy. The copper can be found by probing under the bronzed surface.

The first cast medals we know seem to have been invented as false antiques. These incunabula of the craft were purchased by Jean, Duc de Berry, in 1401 and 1402 from two different dealers. Two of them, alleged medals of Augustus and Tiberius, are only known to us from the inventory of the duke's art treasures, but two others described in the inventory have come down to us in various copies. They show Constantine and Heraclius on the obverse and representations symbolical of their rôle as heroes of Christianity on the reverse. Their style is by no means classical, but frankly recalls the art flourishing at the Burgundian court of their time. Nevertheless, we get the impression that the duke bought them as antiques, which he had subsequently duplicated by casts. At any rate the scholars of the sixteenth century accepted them as monuments of antiquity and only in the seventeenth century did doubts begin to be expressed.[34]

Notwithstanding this promising beginning, the achievements of later forgers are comparatively poor. The larger part of what are usually described as faked medals are nothing but restitutions,

33. G. Habich, *Die Medaillen der italienischen Renaissance* (1922), p. 17.

34. J. v. Schlosser in *Jahrbuch der kunsthistorischen Sammlungen*, vol. 18 (1897), pp. 7 sqq. W. v. Bode, in *Archiv für Medaillen und Plakettenkunde*, vol. 3 (1921–2), pp. 1 sqq.

that is posthumous portrait medals, which are often mistaken for contemporary portraits of the persons represented. Apparently the urge to invent forgeries was small, as the existing originals could easily be multiplied without arousing suspicions.

Such fakes as there are fail to be imaginative. A sixteenth-century forger fabricated a Pisanello medal by combining the portraits of Sigismondo Malatesta and Isotta da Rimini.[35] Sigismondo he took from a Pisanello medal and Isotta from a medal by Matteo dei Pasti. Under the blurred reproduction of Isotta's beautiful profile, he inscribed Pisanello's signature. The humanist Paolo Giovio was duped by this medal; he included it in the list of Pisanello's works which he drew up in 1551.

Another combination, likewise based on a Matteo dei Pasti medal, is still less inventive. A sixteenth-century portrait of a man with a beard and a fur-lined coat forms the obverse of a restituted medal in honour of Guglielmo Adelardi, head of the Guelfs in Ferrara in the twelfth century. The design of the reverse, two towers and a gate, has been copied from Matteo dei Pasti's medals of Sigismondo Malatesta. These vestiges of Malatesta's castle apparently float in the void. They are surrounded by the inscription: 'Castrum Guilelmi MCXXX.'[36]

These examples are characteristic of faked medals in general. They are spurious combinations rather than fraudulent inventions.

Wood or stone models for medals as they were usual in Germany in the sixteenth century held a much stronger appeal for forgers than the medals themselves. The neatly carved wooden roundels were always sought after by collectors. In the nineteenth century their number has been greatly augmented by forgeries.

A small stone relief with the portrait of Emperor Maximilian II pretends to be one of these Renaissance models (*Plate* 83).[37] It was the forger's bad luck that the genuine model for this

35. A. Calabi and G. Cornaggia, *Matteo dei Pasti* (1927), pp. 54, 131. The prototypes are illustrated in G. F. Hill, *A Corpus of Italian Medals* (1930), nos. 33, 167, 173.

36. A. Calabi and G. Cornaggia, *Matteo dei Pasti* (1927) pp. 52, 127.

37. G. Habich, *Die deutschen Schaumünzen*, vol. 2 (1934), p. 496, no. 3397, pls. 319, 322. L. Planiscig and E. Kris, *Ausstellung Gefälschte Kunstwerke* (1937), p. 6.

particular medal is still preserved (*Plate* 84). It is a work by Annibale Fontana who, following Italian usage, used coloured wax, while the forger, imagining the model to be by a German artist, used lithographic stone. The execution of the stone model is abominable and the modelling of the very poorest quality. The lion's head which forms the shoulder-piece of the Emperor's cuirass and is visible through the soft folds of his cloak has been completely misunderstood by the forger who rendered it as a misshapen knot of chopped folds.

Medals made as portraits of young people without social standing never would have had the outsize measures some nineteenth-century carver gave to two lovely wooden models he made.[38] He evidently counted on his contemporaries' romantic foible for the young and attractive when he made the portraits of a young man and a young girl. He took the precaution of giving them names of real sixteenth-century families, but inscribed them in letters of typically nineteenth-century cut. 'Anna ein Dochter Benedict Fronleitners Burgers zu Wienn 1533' has strands of hair and pleated sleeves carved in neat parallel lines. Her costume does not belong to the sixteenth century but to the historicising fashion of the nineteenth.

Another forger went in for celebrities. The general style of his model for a medal of René of Anjou is not of the fifteenth but of the sixteenth century.[39] The inscription has, however, the pompous antiquarian character of nineteenth-century lettering: 'Regis Sicelidum effigies est ista Renati.' But the ornament the forger introduced into his border is still worse than the lettering. The profile of a fat young man with woolly curls and a flat hat was supposed to be sufficient to evoke in the spectator the memory of the romantic poet king. The mouldings and border ornaments of a similar wooden model conform still more plainly to a nineteenth-century pattern. It is a double portrait, the boy being represented *en face* and the girl in profile, which is an impossible combination. The object is inscribed 'simul and semper' and one is tempted to

38. G. Habich, *Die deutschen Schaumünzen*, vol. 1 (1929), p. 102, nos. 715, 716, pls. 86, 7; 87, 7.

39. G. Habich, *Die deutschen Schaumünzen*, vol. 1, p. 106, nos. 737, 738, pls. 89, 3; 90, 4.

assume that the forger thought that *simul* and *semper* were the names of the couple. Anyhow the 'Master of René of Anjou' was no master.

For some reason plaquettes, in contrast to medals, did not escape the imaginative grasp of forgers. While it was thought fit to fill the gap in genuine portraiture by miniatures in the case of Joan of Arc, a more lasting material was preferred for Petrarch's Laura. As we have seen, famous women have always been a temptation to fakers. The forger who took a wretched copy of Leone Leoni's medal representing Hippolyta Gonzaga (sixteenth century) and inscribed it in Gothic lettering: 'Laurea Noves relicta Ugone di Sade Franc Petrarc amata', and on the reverse: 'obiit anno MCCCXLVIII', was very naïve, but he was undoubtedly surpassed by the student who published this precious object as a fourteenth-century original and as historical evidence of the problematic existence of Laura.[40]

There exist two authentic portraits of the Doge Francesco Foscari. One is the portrait in profile by Gentile Bellini, the other a marble head with a broken nose, which is a fragment from the destroyed group that crowned the portal to the Palazzo Ducale. As both are conveniently enough assembled in Venice, a Venetian sculptor conceived the idea of combining their evidence in a plaquette cast in honour of his famous compatriot. He used Gentile Bellini's portrait for the composition, and for the shape of the nose missing on the marble, and impressed the deep folds of extreme age visible on the statue into his low relief. This combination he endowed with a background of small circles inscribed in squares, a pattern used by Donatello on his Paduan reliefs. Licudis made a large number of casts from his model, occasionally changing some of the details of his work, and repeatedly exhibited it under his own name. It is easy to imagine his delighted surprise when he was shown an article describing his own work as an exceptionally beautiful original by Donatello, and this by nobody less than by Wilhelm von Bode, the famous expert on Renaissance sculpture, who had moreover backed his judgment by buying the

40. *Annuaire de la Société Française de Numismatique*, vol. 19 (1895), pp. 511 sqq., pl. 5. *Bulletin de la Société Nationale des Antiquaires de France* (1896), p. 77.

plaquette. The piece offered to him was a trial-cast. Licudis hurried to publish a full account of his relief, complete with its prototypes. Bode, however, remained undaunted. He professed the most unshakable conviction in his Donatello as well for reasons of style and artistic quality as on account of the patina, which he declared to be of special rareness and beauty. It is hard to believe that Bode should have been deceived to such a degree by a plaquette which betrays the combination of its two models so plainly and does not conceal the rational touch of the modern artist, which is far removed from Donatello's genius.[41]

Bronze and silver plaquettes reproducing parts of the frieze of a Roman sarcophagus began to circulate in the earlier years of this century and were accepted as sixteenth-century copies from the antique. Doubts as to their authenticity began to arise when it was noticed that the sarcophagus from which the composition was derived was not published earlier than 1719. The discovery of an iron plaquette reproducing the same frieze solved this riddle. It was probably cast in Berlin in the early years of the nineteenth century. Fraudulent later repetitions in silver and bronze tried to pose as sixteenth-century originals.[42]

41. *Jahrbuch der preussischen Kunstsammlungen*, vol. 44 (1923), pp. 53 sqq. *Dedalo*, vol. 4 (1923–4), pp. 393 sqq. *Berliner Museen*, vol. 45 (1924) p. 42.

42. H. Huth in *Münchner Jahrbuch der bildenden Kunst*, N.S., vol. 1 (1924), p. 295. sqq.

83. Forgery of the model for a medal of Maximilian II.

84. The genuine model for the medal of Maximilian II.

85. Modern imitation of an early Chinese bronze vessel. (By courtesy of the Director of the Victoria and Albert Museum.)

86. The Bushell Bowl. (By courtesy of the Director of the Victoria and Albert Museum.)

PART ELEVEN

CHINESE BRONZES

PART ELEVEN

CHINESE BRONZES

By Chinese Bronzes the European collector means bronze vessels dating from a period extending from the end of the second millennium B.C. to about the beginning of our era. Chinese collectors are much more catholic in their outlook. Among native connoisseurs the decorated bronze vessels from the reign of Hsüan Tê (1426–35) enjoy an almost equal fame and are eagerly collected, with the result that the number of forgeries is appallingly large. Moreover, the reign-mark of the third Ming emperor became a kind of trade-mark. It can be found on numerous modern bronzes which pretend in no other way to an early origin.

The early bronzes, i.e. those of the Shang-Yin and Chou dynasties have always been held in great veneration. Since the beginning of our era they were considered to be extremely rare, and in the eleventh century started the long series of archaeological publications dedicated to their study. We do not know when the first forgeries appeared, but in the thirteenth century this industry must have been in full swing as we learn from a contemporary text to which we shall return presently.

Not all the bronzes in pseudo-archaic style are deliberate fakes; on the contrary, the majority are archaising vessels, made without fraudulent intention. This class of bronzes filled the European collections of the nineteenth century, and if any fine ancient pieces were to be found among them, they had slipped in almost by accident. Only since the beginning of this century did we begin to learn something of early Chinese art. Intensive archaeological studies by native and Western scholars, many new finds and the first scientifically organised excavations on Chinese soil, furnished the first solid foundations for the study of this truly monumental art.

In this new light many hitherto admired pieces have lost their halo. A bronze vessel in the shape of a double ram in the Musée Cernuschi was for many years admired as an ancient Chinese bronze.[1] When the double ram of the Eumorfopoulos Collection turned up the difference between ancient and archaistic bronzes became at once clear.[2] Everything has been repeated but no detail has remained unaltered. The scales covering the magnificent rams of the Eumorfopoulos Collection have the lively irregularity of real skin. This is not so in the later version. Here the scales are arrayed between mercilessly straight lines and each scale is exactly like the other. The rams' heads and horns have become angular. They are composed of planes meeting at sharp angles. Even their mouths have been trimmed. Sharp edges were avoided by the makers of ancient bronzes. Down to the smallest detail a curved or at least agreeably irregular outline was achieved. But the silhouette of the Cernuschi vessel has been smoothed to perfect regularity.

It is perhaps no exaggeration to say that such perfect regularity is the main characteristic of modern imitations of ancient Chinese bronzes. The vessel illustrated on *Plate* 85[3] is a fairly literal copy after a piece which was once in the collection of the Emperor Ch'ien Lung. The original is only known from the woodcut illustration in the catalogue of the Imperial Collection.[4] A detailed comparison is thus impossible but even so the imitation is betrayed by its neat and pedantic correctness. Compare with it the slight angularity and the free modelling of genuine Chou bronzes. The fraudulent intention of the copyist becomes clear from the fact that he also copied the dedicatory inscription of his model: 'Po tso i', 'Po had this sacrificial vessel made'.

To the Chinese the ancient bronzes are not only important as works of art but also as venerable historic monuments, on account of their dedicatory inscriptions. The Chinese passion for ancient

1. O. Münsterberg, *Chinesische Kunstgeschichte*, vol. 2 (1912), p. 143, fig. 235. A. J. Koop, *Early Chinese Bronzes* (1924), p. 73, pl. 99.

2. Now in the British Museum. W. P. Yetts, *The Eumorfopoulos Collection*, vol. 1 (1929), p. 54, pls. 8, 9.

3. A. J. Koop, *Early Chinese Bronzes* (1924), p. 44, pl. 10.

4. *Hsi ch'ing ku chin* (1888, facsimile of 1751 ed.), vol. 13, p. 21. Cf. also G. Soulié de Morant, *A History of Chinese Art* (1931), fig. 27.

writing and calligraphy is well known. The inscriptions on the bronzes have always been highly esteemed, studied, collected and forged. The forgers, knowing the weakness of their compatriots, concentrated on inscriptions with historical associations and more or less neglected the artistic aspect of their products.

How quickly our knowledge of early Chinese art has advanced can best be seen from the fact that a bronze, long regarded by Eastern and Western students as one of the most famous of ancient vessels, is today no longer regarded as genuine. It is a tripod *ting* preserved in a Buddhist temple on the Silver Island in the Yangtze-kiang.[5] Its claim to fame is based on its inscription according to which it has been cast by order of a certain Wu Chuan in memory of the graces bestowed upon him by the Son of Heaven; moreover, it has the additional interest of a reference to Nan Chung, known from a poem in the *Book of Odes*. These historical associations fail to compensate for the style of the cauldron. The date of the dedication has been calculated to correspond to 812 B.C. Shape and ornament do not corroborate this date. The silhouette of the cauldron is clumsy and lifeless. The body of the vessel is covered by three rows of scales of complete uniformity which are rounded like roof-tiles. Such a complete lack of imagination is impossible on a genuinely ancient piece, the makers of which shunned the mechanical repetition of a single motif. The cauldron was given to the Silver Island Monastery in 1563; nothing is known of its previous history. Our knowledge of imitations is not sufficiently advanced to decide whether this fake was produced during the T'ang period (618–906) as has been suggested or, as is perhaps more likely, not so long before the cauldron was presented to the monastery.

The so-called Bushell Bowl is a forgery on a particularly ambitious scale (*Plate 86*).[6] This unusually large bronze basin

5. E. A. Voretzsch, in *Hirth Anniversary Volume* (1923), pp. 409 sqq., figs. 1–8. W. P. Yetts, *Chinese Bronzes* (1925), p. 3, pl. 3.

6. S. W. Bushell, *Chinese Art*, vol. 1 (1910), p. 72, figs. 49–50. H. A. Giles, *Adversaria Sinica*, no. 9 (1911), pp. 283 sqq.; no. 10 (1913), pp. 329 sqq. L. C. Hopkins, in *Journal of the R. Asiatic Society* (1912), pp. 439 sqq. B. Schindler, in *Ostasiatische Zeitschrift*, vol. 6 (1918), pp. 224 sqq. P. Pelliot, in *T'oung Pao*, vol. 32 (1936), p. 33.

owes its name to the fact that it was brought to Europe by Stephen
W. Bushell, one of the first European scholars who made a
serious study of Chinese art and archaeology. It is rather unjust
that his name should thus be coupled with a forgery and it would
be better to drop this unfortunate designation. The chief interest
of the basin lies in an enormous inscription which by its verbosity
contradicts the proverbial terse conciseness of Chinese inscriptions. Here again the forger availed himself of the opportunity to
delight his public by a reference to a passage in the classics, this
time to a historical event in the Shu Ching, the *Book of History*.
The date implied is 632 B.C. The vessel itself is rather unworthy of
so interesting an inscription. Its shape is unlike that of any genuine
bronze, foot and handles are out of proportion, and the outline of
the whole is particularly unattractive and heavy. The row of
bosses below the rim is completely foreign to early bronzes. The
motif occurs on Sung pottery and on Ming bronzes; the forger
apparently fell into the wrong style. The flamboyant *t'ao-t'iehs*
look as though they had been stuck on to the vessel's surface.
This feature is never met with on genuine pieces, but is common enough among fakes and imitations as well as among later
bronzes in general. Every ancient bronze was conceived as a
plastic unity. Therefore the relief gives the impression of belonging to the vessel's very body and never looks as if it had been
applied on second thoughts. Although this forgery has been supposed to date from the Sung or Ming period[7] it is fairly obvious
that it is nothing but a nineteenth-century fake. It is now the
fashion to date most of the pseudo-archaic Chinese bronzes into
the Sung period; it must, however, be stressed that this is mere
guesswork. We do not know what early forgeries looked like or
in which way they differed from more modern imitations.

The examination of Chinese bronzes is usually begun with the
patina; but just as with European bronzes its importance is much
overrated. This should not be interpreted as a derogatory
judgment passed lightly on the charm and beauty of patina.
Coatings of malachite and azurite, whether they are polished or
whether their circular crusts are allowed to grow untrimmed on
the surface of bronzes, are the worthiest adornments of a beautiful

7. E. A. Voretzsch, *Altchinesische Bronzen* (1924), p. 41.

piece and have been acknowledged as such from the earliest times. Nobody contests the enhancement brought by red copper-oxide to such a vessel, if the red shines through the green or blue coating in places, or when it appears on the darkened surface of a bronze without verdigris. But all this is no final proof of merit. Ancient bronzes are from two to three thousand years old, and though nobody knows how many scores of years are needed to create the various kinds of coatings in varying circumstances, certainly a much shorter period is sufficient to achieve a satisfactory patina. Given only a few hundred years for its growth, a patina may well be genuine, but not the bronze it covers. And patina was faked at such an early date that we may well shudder at the thought of recognising the fraud after four or five additional centuries have passed over a piece.

The very expert and thorough description of genuine and false patina given by the thirteenth-century scholar Chao Hsi-ku should be as cautionary as it is edifying to read:[8] 'Bronzes which have been lying in the earth for many centuries, acquire a pure blue colour like that of the kingfisher. . . . Here and there the earth has eaten into the metal, forming holes or abrasions, very like the track of a snail. If there are marks of cuttings or boring, the article is a fake. Bronzes which have been lying in water for a long period, will acquire a pure green colour, lustrous like jade. A shorter period will produce the green colour, but not the lustre. As to holes, etc., the same remarks apply as above. It is customary for people nowadays to regard light specimens of these two classes as veritable antiques, ignoring that bronzes which were originally large and thick do not become thus attenuated, but lose only about one-third or one-half of their weight; whereas small or thin bronzes would naturally yield more quickly to the action of earth or water. With regard to cuts from hoes or broken places, where there is no sign of bronze colour, the blue or the green, as the case may be, having penetrated to the very bones of the speci- men; or where possibly there may be in the middle a faint streak of red, like red lead, the article all the same retaining the sound of bronze, such a piece is an antique which has not been immersed in water, but has been passed from collector to collector. The colour

8. Translated by H. A. Giles, *Adversaria Sinica*, no. 9 (1911), pp. 291 sqq.

is that of dark red serge, with red streaks, sometimes in relief, or like the best cinnabar. Placed in a kettle and boiled for a long time in water, the streaks will be still more apparent. Fakes which are worked up with varnish and vermilion are thus easily detected.'

In recent years metallurgists and chemists have investigated the formation and composition of patina.[9] Although science cannot as yet indicate the age of a patinated bronze, even approximately, it does enable us to distinguish organically grown patina from modern substitutes. The old and primitive methods of imitating patina by paint or by powdered malachite in a mixture of wax and resin, can be shown up by a simple chemical test (alcohol) or under the ultra-violet lantern.

We have referred to the Chinese predilection for archaic inscriptions. The fact that an inscription is a forgery need not always condemn the piece on which it appears. In many cases spurious inscriptions have been engraved on genuine pieces in order to augment their price. Here again it is worth while to read Chao Hsi-ku: 'Under the three early dynasties (Hsiah, Shang-Yin, Chou), inscriptions were cast in intaglio, and the script was called *yen nang*, the characters being below the surface of the metal. From the Han dynasty onwards, the inscriptions were either in rilievo, the characters projecting above the surface of the metal, with some intaglio characters among them, or they were incised with tools, as in the case of inscriptions on stone tablets; for it is extremely difficult to cast bronzes with intaglio inscriptions, whereas it is easy to reproduce inscriptions in rilievo, the latter being a sure proof that the bronze in question is not a genuine antique.' The statement that inscriptions were invariably cast with the vessel is important. It is extremely doubtful whether there are any exceptions to this rule. It has been assumed that vessels were occasionally made for stock and that the buyer had the inscription added; proof of this is, however, completely lacking.[10]

Spurious inscriptions on genuine vessels are not infrequent. Often the wording of the inscription is unimpeachable as the

9. H. J. Pleinderleith, 'Technical Notes on Chinese Bronzes with Special Reference to Patina and Incrustation', in *Transactions of the Oriental Ceramic Society* (1938–9), pp. 33 sqq.

10. W. P. Yetts, *The Cull Chinese Bronzes* (1939), p. 4.

forgers, mistrusting their skill, copied genuine models.[11] An interesting inscription of this type has been investigated by Professor Yetts.[12] A bird-shaped bronze vessel shows two inscriptions. The comparatively late date of the vessel contrasted with the early Chou style of the writing. Suspicion having thus been aroused, it was found that the inscription inside the cover was engraved and not cast with the vessel. The inscription in the bottom was an even greater surprise. Apparently the forger found it difficult to use his tools inside the vessel, therefore he engraved the inscription on a metal disc which he inserted as a false bottom. Professor Yetts succeeded in tracking down the genuine inscription which served as model for this forgery.

In other cases inscriptions are found on objects on which one would not expect a Chinese inscription. There exists a type of bronze drum which is usually classified with Chinese bronzes though the early specimens were made in Indo-China by Annamite craftsmen in a distinctly non-Chinese style.[13] The great and widespread favour these drums found is amazing; their production seems to stretch over a period of almost two thousand years and they were distributed over an immensely wide area, covering Indo-China, the Southern provinces of China, Siam, Burma, Java and the Archipelago.

Chinese archaeologists have tried to connect the early drums with the Chinese conquests in the South during the Han dynasty. Chinese inscriptions on some of these drums seem to corroborate this. A drum in the Victoria and Albert Museum, for instance, has an inscription containing a date corresponding to A.D. 199. However, as was pointed out by Professor Pelliot, with regard to their place of origin, it 'does not seem very likely that these drums should in the second century A.D. have been endowed with Chinese inscriptions'.[14] The whole question of the inscriptions needs further

11. Shang Ch'eng-tsu, in *Journal of the North China Branch of the R. Asiatic Society*, vol. 66 (1935), pp. 70 sqq.

12. W. P. Yetts, in *The Burlington Magazine*, vol. 76 (1940), p. 38.

13. V. Goloubew, in *Bulletin de l'École Française d'Extrême-Orient*, vol. 29 (1929), pp. 1 sqq. idem, *L'archéologie du Tonkin* (1937), pp. 8 sqq. R. Heine-Geldern, in *Asia Major*, vol. 8 (1933), pp. 519 sqq.

14. *Bulletin de l'École Française d'Extrême-Orient*, vol. 5 (1905), p. 216.

careful investigation.[15] There is, however, no doubt that drums of this type were produced in China in the last century.[16] It is amusing to observe here a fraud that is the exact opposite of the usual forgeries: the nineteenth-century inscriptions had to be erased in order to pass off these kettle-drums as works of the Han period. The perpetrators of this fraud were, however, rather careless. In two known cases traces of the inscriptions are still distinct enough to allow the date-mark of the reign-period of Tao-Kuang (1821–50) to be deciphered.[17]

15. W. P. Yetts, *The Eumorfopoulos Collection*, vol. 2 (1930), p. 28. P. Pelliot, in *T'oung Pao*, vol. 27 (1930), p. 386. B. Laufer, in *The Burlington Magazine*, vol. 57 (1930), p. 184.

16. B. Laufer, in *The Burlington Magazine*, vol. 57 (1930), pp. 183 sq.

17. F. Heger, *Alte Metalltrommeln aus Südost-Asien* (1902), p. 128, pl. 28.

PART TWELVE

GOLDSMITHS' WORK

PART TWELVE

GOLDSMITHS' WORK

CLASSICAL GOLDSMITHS' WORK AND JEWELLERY

It seems that the Egyptian fashion inspired some extraordinarily early fakes of ancient jewellery. The embossed gold leaf 'from Malta', which we had occasion to mention in another context, must have been produced before 1719, when the engraving after it was published.[1] Its strange procession of monstrous deities belongs to an age for which Egypt was the unexplored land of mysteries and magicians. But when in 1822 Champollion deciphered the hieroglyphs, the Egypt of Cagliostro and of the 'Magic Flute' vanished and its place was taken by the Egypt of immemorial antiquity, the cradle of human civilisation. The forgers kept well abreast of this new development. They went straight back to Menes, the founder of the First Dynasty. The 'Necklace of Menes' in the collection of the Historical Society of New York is one of the more famous pieces of this kind. The name of Menes, impressed with a die on eight oval gold pieces, secured an interest for this object which far exceeds its artistic and metallic value. The 'genuine' appearance of the necklace was attained by incorporating ancient beads of miscellaneous style. 'Three dark-blue glass pendants in the form of corn-flowers or poppy-fruits, a motif and a material characteristic of the time around 1350 B.C., a single well-formed, but injured, barrel-shaped amethyst bead of about the nineteenth century B.C., and two blue glass beads in the form of flattened spheres, of a good period but with surfaces in poor condition, were combined with certain gold parts in a parti-

1. Cf. p. 185.

cularly un-Egyptian and bungling way to mark the centre of the supposed necklace.'[2] This ornament was purchased in 1846, and fabricated not long before in the vicinity of Drury Lane, but the magic name of Egypt's first king carried its poor artistic quality successfully through the nineteenth century.

The beauties of classical and in particular of Etruscan jewellery were rediscovered in the nineteenth century. In the late twenties an Italian nobleman encouraged Fortunato Pio Castellani (1793–1865) to try to revive the techniques of the ancients. And this goldsmith succeeded so perfectly in rediscovering the classical styles and techniques that he created a new style of Italian jewellery. His supreme achievement was the revival of granulation, that is the fabrication of tiny globular grains of gold, which were then soldered to the surface of the jewellery. The peculiar rough surface created by this procedure is one of the principal characteristics of Etruscan goldsmith work. F. P. Castellani,[3] his son Augusto, and several other Italian goldsmiths who followed in their footsteps,[4] not only created a new fashion in jewellery, but were also excellent restorers of genuine pieces, and above all they reached the height of perfection in the copying and imitation of their prototypes. In spite of a certain overdose of regularity and sharpness of outline, it is most difficult to discover shortcomings in the purely ornamental parts; only the human figures and above all the heads and masks appearing on copies and imitations replace classical liveliness by classicist pedantry (*Plate* 87).[5]

Towards the end of the nineteenth century other, much less reputable, manufactures began to spring up beside this very honourable craft. Though they never reached the excellence of

2. C. R. Williams, *Gold and Silver Jewellery* (New York Historical Society, 1924), p. 222, pl. 36. *Journal of the British Archaeological Association*, vol. 11 (1855), p. 72.

3. There is a short biography in Thieme-Becker, *Künstlerlexikon*, vol. 6, p. 143.

4. The most famous is Carlo Giuliano. His sons presented the Victoria and Albert Museum with a small collection of his imitations of classical jewellery. M. H. Spielmann, in *The Magazine of Arts*, N.S., vol. 1 (1903), p. 500.

5. An instructive juxtaposition is to be found in M. Rosenberg, *Geschichte der Goldschmiedekunst, Abt. Granulation* (1918), pp. 4 sqq., figs. 7–10.

the copies and imitations made by the prominent Italian jewellers, some forgers achieved spectacular successes and even more spectacular scandals by their highly imaginative products.

Rouchomowsky of Odessa was as good a goldsmith as his Italian colleagues. But his faculties were exploited by enterprising dealers. Rouchomowsky's embossings are indeed remarkable, and he became world-famous by his masterpiece, which enjoyed the good fortune to be purchased by the Louvre.[6]

The tiara of Saitaphernes has attained popularity due to the commotion it created, not to its artistic qualities (*Plate* 88). It cannot be denied that it only became 'fake No. 1' because those who were responsible for its acquisition were so extraordinarily reluctant to admit the truth about their Greek marvel. Thus the discussion was unduly prolonged and the perfection of the tiara was extolled beyond its merits in order to prove its genuineness. The main reason for the general acceptance of the tiara when it first became known was in reality the complete lack of a precedent for such a forgery, coupled with the confidence its place of provenance inspired. In southern Russia are the sites on which the most beautiful specimens of Greek gold and silver of classical times were found.

The Greek inscription on the tiara refers to its dedication to Saitaphernes by the people of Olbia. For this text the forger drew his inspiration from a genuine inscription of the third century B.C., found in Olbia, one of the Greek settlements of southern Russia. The genuine inscription commemorates the erection of a strong wall around the town of Olbia as a protection against the threats

6. Acquired in 1895. E. v. Stern in *Berliner philologische Wochenschrift*, vol. 17 (1897), pp. 764 sqq. A. Furtwaengler, *Intermezzi* (1896), pp. 81 sqq.; *Neuere Fälschungen* (1899), pp. 31 sqq., figs. 22 sqq. S. Reinach, *Revue archéologique*, ser. 4, vol. 2 (1903), pp. 105 sqq. *Les Arts*, May 1903, pp. 19 sqq. L. Forrer, *Biographical Dictionary of Medallists*, vol. 5 (1912), p. 250. E. H. Minns, *Scythians and Greeks* (1913), p. 461. G. Dittenberger, *Sylloge inscriptionum Graecarum* (3rd ed., 1915), vol. 1, no. 495. Burlington Fine Arts Club, *Catalogue of a Collection of Counterfeits* (1924), no. 185, pl. 40. A. Vayson de Pradenne, *Les Fraudes en archéologie préhistorique* (1932), pp. 519 sqq. H. Tietze, in *Metropolitan Museum Studies*, vol. 5 (1934–6), p. 12, figs. 17–19. Israel Rouchomowsky wrote an interesting autobiography (in Yiddish), *Mein Lebn un mein Arbeit* (Paris, 1928; on the Tiara, see especially pp. 197–208).

of Saitaphernes, a Scythian chief whom the inhabitants had tried to placate with gold without success.

The tiara was sufficiently novel to baffle everybody when it first appeared. But there are some flaws in its appearance which might have attracted notice, even at first sight. The type and expression of the faces can neither be described as Greek nor as Scythian, and the state of preservation is suspiciously perfect. For all essential parts of the relief are intact, while only the unworked space between the figures shows uneven portions, where it has been damaged with a hammer. The discovery of single groups among the outline drawings contained in an illustrated atlas of cultural history published in 1882 ought to have done the rest.[7] But even when Rouchomowsky lifted his incognito and declared the tiara to be his work, he had considerable difficulty in making the authorities believe what he was saying. He pointed out two other pieces he had made, which to judge by their appearance must have had a very elucidating effect. They both show the same technical perfection as the tiara, but a much lesser degree of archaeological correctness. The rhyton or drinking horn, ending in a marine monster, is covered with a profusion of animals, labourers, chariots, pine-trees, and huts. The realism of these embossings and above all the superposition of one figure over the other, which occurs frequently on these reliefs, are anything but classical.[8] The group of two figures, also made of gold, representing Athena and Achilles, could hardly be passed off as an antique, notwithstanding the Greek inscription engraved on its square base. Achilles is screaming and Athena looks as if she were pulling his ear.[9]

Dr. H. Burg has drawn my attention to a hitherto unknown little masterpiece by Rouchomowsky (*Plates* 89, 90). It shows all his qualities without being as hackneyed as the tiara. It is a small gold bottle not much more than seven cm. high and of such minutely fine workmanship that it can only be fully appreciated

7. L. Weisser, *Bilderatlas zur Weltgeschichte* (1882). Cf. H. Tietze, in *Metropolitan Museum Studies*, vol. 5 (1934–6), p. 12.

8. *Les Arts,* May 1903, pp. 19, 21. E. Rocher, *L'Art Décoratif aux Expositions* (1903), pl. 67.

9. *Les Arts,* May 1903, p. 23. E. Rocher, *L'Art Décoratif aux Expositions* (1903), pl. 68.

under the magnifying glass. The ornament on the bottle is laid on in granulation, the figure frieze is embossed in low relief, the contours and inside design being outlined by rows of granules. This technique of outline by granulation occurs on Greek goldsmith-work found in southern Russia.[10] Granulation, used on such a scale, and with such precision, demands infinite skill and patience, as every minute globule of gold has to be fixed separately on to its exact place. The nuptial scenes on the central frieze, with the numerous small cupids in attendance, have been inspired by similar representations on the so-called Kerch vases of the fourth century B.C., found in southern Russia. The woman seated on a couch and the young man standing at her side, with his hand resting on her shoulder, can be seen on a *lekanis* in the Hermitage, an outline drawing of which seems to have inspired Rouchomowsky.[11] The vase on the ground, the goose, and the oval wreath-like shapes held by ladies and cupids obviously derived from the mirrors used at the bridal toilet, are properties common to the Kerch vases. Rouchomowsky produced no slavish copy. He fundamentally altered the facial types, which he drew on definitely archaic lines. In accordance with this he altered the postures of the figures, turning them, almost without exception, into profile, thus avoiding the rich variety of postures of his prototype. Thus the light narrative style of fourth-century Attic art of Rouchomowsky's composition, with its numerous traits of genre and its playful cupids, contrasts with the archaic severity of his design.

The *Sacro Tesoro* swindle is not as famous as the tiara because the objects remained in a private collection.[12] The most extravagant

10. M. Rosenberg, *Granulation* (1915), fig. 124.

11. A. Furtwängler and K. Reichhold, *Griechische Vasenmalerei,* vol. 2 (1909), pl. 68. E. H. Minns, *Scythians and Greeks* (1913), fig. 248. K. Schefold, *Kertscher Vasen* (1930), pl. 13a.

12. G. Rossi, *Commenti sopra suppellettili sacre* (2nd edition, 1890). H. Grisar, *Di un preteso tesoro Cristiano* (1895). H. Grisar, in *Die Religionswissenschaft der Gegenwart* (1927), p. 13. S. Fuchs, *Die langobardischen Goldblattkreuze* (1938), p. 9, note 4. A silver book-cover in Berlin is evidently a product of the same workshop; cf. F. J. Dölger, *Ichthys,* vol. 5 (1938), pp. 193 sqq., and W. Holmqvist, *Kunstprobleme der Merowingerzeit* (1939), p. 63, pl. 17, 2.

of all fraudulent inventions began to appear gradually in 1880. Its immense success was due to its supposed period of origin. For it was bought by the Cavaliere Giancarlo Rossi as an important document of Christianity, dating back to apostolic times. The mere supposition was so entrancing that little heed was taken of the poor quality and the fantastic story of the 'treasure'. Ten embossed book-covers and thirteen crosses, all made of gold or silver, two silver mitres, and numerous other objects, were found by a peasant in what he is said to have recognised as a bishop's tomb. The exact emplacement of this hypothetical vault was never divulged. But it was asserted that body and sarcophagus dissolved as soon as the peasant had set eyes on them. Subsequently the imaginary peasant proceeded to sell the books—manuscripts from the first centuries A.D. which nobody ever saw—to a Franciscan convent, while the covers gradually appeared on the art market of Rome, together with the other objects from the 'tomb'. The peasant and his domain were kept in the dark, though no plausible reason could be given for this secrecy, as the whole treasure remained in Italy and its finder would have been its lawful owner in any case. But nobody seemed to notice this incongruity, and its very mysteriousness helped to increase the value of the treasure. The various periods to which it was ascribed offered little material for comparison, and its iconography was found to be so novel and mysterious that it escaped all comparisons. The copious use of early Christian symbolism incited Cavaliere Rossi, the owner of the majority of the pieces, to mix his dithyrambs on the wonderful quality of his possessions with pious but complicated explanations of their meaning. The result became one of the most unreadable books ever composed in any language. Unfortunately he added illustrations to his text and thus himself showed up the extent of his delusion.

Never before was such utter ineptitude of design, workmanship, and conception combined. The many lambs on the embossings are so clumsily designed that one is tempted to imagine them on little wheels, like children's toys. The 'Lombardic' ornaments which caused much pondering and redating of the treasure are so badly drawn that no period exists that could account for them. But though every single detail is puerile and ridiculous, the fun only really begins if one tries to make out the meaning of the single scenes represented on these objects. One cannot help wondering how anybody managed to deal in earnest with a flat silver tray on which twelve plain beakers are fixed around a centre-piece, supposed to represent a lamb but much more similar to a hen clucking above its brood, the beakers. A cross is stuck into the head of this animal, and another cross composed of two fishes adorns its side, but no number of crosses could make up for its appearance.

The two crossed fishes are only a foretaste of the favourite sym-bol of this treasure, which is filled with fishes to the brim. There is, for instance, a representation of the Last Supper in which the bread and wine is offered by a fish to the grotesque figures sup-posed to be the twelve apostles. The fish waits on them very nicely with the aid of his fins: he holds the bread in front and offers the wine with the other fin behind his back. What could be said in favour of a Crucifix, with two lambs standing on the outstretched arms of Christ? And what about the Ichthys, flattened under the load of a ship, probably meant to represent the Church? But this symbol was not thought to be explicit enough to the pious creator of the 'treasure'. Out of the body of this fish the anchor of hope is growing. Two floating human beings try to clutch it, while two lambs stand on its lower curves. The whole treasure is full of such charming traits, showing the play of a preposterous imagination with Christian symbolism.

PERSIAN SILVER

Practically all the forgeries of Achaemenid (559–331 B.C.) and Sassanian (A.D. 226–641) gold and silver seem to be the work of Eastern craftsmen. Occasionally they are content to copy genuine pieces in their possession which they keep hidden until the copies have been sold. This happened in the case of the find of Persian goldsmiths' work, famous as the Oxus Treasure, which was be-queathed to the British Museum by Sir Augustus Wollaston Franks in 1897. 'Objects of intrinsically less precious material were reproduced in gold, and these counterfeits were first sent to certain collectors for disposal, the originals being temporarily retained. There was much about these objects which struck Sir Augustus Wollaston Franks as suspicious, over and above the fact that some of them were of types which are never found in gold. But not wishing to divert a possibly important source of supply, he determined to purchase at a small percentage above the gold value, and then to await further developments. These were not long delayed, for when once the counterfeits had been sold, the originals were dispatched in their turn. A comparison of the originals with the gold copies at once revealed the difference in quality which had been expected; the imitations had been made with some care, but their modern character was unmistakable. The obvious inferiority of these reproductions did nothing but confirm the genuineness of the originals and of the Treasure as a whole.'[13]

It seems that the same goldsmith who worked in Afghanistan or in the Punjab, produced also a fraudulent copy of a Sassanian silver dish. Its genuine model is now in the British Museum, and was likewise included in the Franks Bequest.[14] It shows Bahram Gur, the famous hunter, who has caught a lion cub and has now to defend himself against the lion and the lioness. A copy of this plate, said to have been found in Peshawar, was acquired for the Imperial Collections of Petersburg. The forger found the complicated technique of the original, a combination of embossing and soldering, too difficult and contented himself with engraving. His copy is quite literal but nevertheless he committed a serious blunder. On the original, the edge of the dish cuts through the hind legs of the attacking lions which are thus only partially represented. The forger engraved the design into the centre of a slightly larger dish but omitted to complete the lion's paws. Thus the great hero is slaying two sadly mutilated animals.

A more imaginative fake was apparently produced at a later date. The initial success of this plate was due to the design of the three animals represented on it. For the lion and the bull he

13. O. M. Dalton, *The Treasure of the Oxus* (1926), p. xvi.

14. Y. I. Smirnov, *Vostochnoe serebro* (1906), p. 6, pl. 26, no. 54 (original), pl. 27, no. 55 (fake). E. Herzfeld, *Archaeologische Mitteilungen aus Iran*, vol. 9 (1938), p. 117, note 1. *Survey of Persian Art*, vol. 1, pp. 728, 750; vol. 4, pl. 231. J. Orbeli and C. Trever, *Orfèvrerie sasanide* (1935), pl. 10.

attacks, as well as the gazelle who flees from the scene of the fight, are beautifully drawn. But some technical details aroused suspicions, which were confirmed when the models for this superior forgery were discovered.[15] They are contained in two fourteenth-century Persian miniatures, which were first published in 1929.[16] They are illustrations to the fables of Bidpai. On one the lion is fighting with the bull, while on the other the swift gazelle escapes from the huntsman, who captures the slow turtle instead. The two motifs were cleverly combined, copied with exactitude and embossed remarkably well, to suggest a style many centuries earlier than their models.

BYZANTINE ENAMELS

A novel and quite convincing style of Byzantine enamels was created in the nineteenth century. The forger who produced them evidently made a very thorough study of genuine enamels. He derived his forgeries mainly from a group of enamels made in Georgia in the eleventh century but he did not neglect Byzantium proper. The plaques from the crown of Constantine Monomachos (1042–50) in Budapest and the Relic of the Cross in Limburg (948–59) were used by him as models for his figures and compositions. He indicated the draped folds enveloping his figures by a thin net of gold lines; the imitation of Georgian enamels is patent, but the forger avoided their angular style. The draperies are covered with a monotonous herring-bone pattern, occasionally interrupted by a spiral.

The imitations of types and faces are fairly efficient, but the pupil placed in the corner of the eye, though usual in medieval Byzantine enamels, never produces there a restless slanting glance, as it does on these modern imitations. The forger avoided iconographical blunders on the whole but once he left out the footstool under the feet of Christ enthroned, an attribute indispensable in Byzantine art. Moreover no medieval artist would have repre-

15. *Burlington Magazine*, vol. 66 (1935), p. 288. H. J. Plenderleith, IIIe Congrès International d'Art et d'Archéologie Iraniens, *Mémoires* (Leningrad, 1939), p. 159, pls. 65–8.

16. A. Sakisian, *La Miniature persane* (1929), pls. 3, 4.

87. Necklace with head of Achelous in Etruscan style. By Carlo Giuliano.
(By courtesy of the Director of the Victoria and Albert Museum.)

88. The Tiara of Saitaphernes. By I. Rouchomowsky.

89. Gold bottle decorated with granulation. By I. Rouchomowsky.

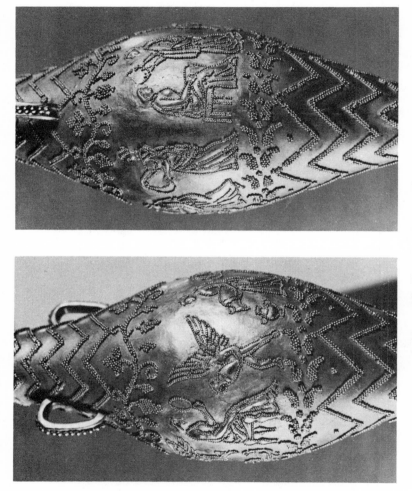

90a and b. Two details from Plate 89.

91. Reliquary of the Holy Thorn. Fourteenth century.
(By courtesy of the Trustees of the British Museum.)

92. Reliquary of the Holy Thorn. Forgery by Weininger.

sented the Madonna accompanied by two saints, whose identity cannot be established by their distinctive attributes.

Notwithstanding all these symptoms, most of these enamels are so well made that they would be completely deceptive but for one circumstance: all the specimens of this style were assembled in one collection and no piece of this kind had been seen before they all were sold to Mr. Botkine. It is hardly conceivable that a modern collector should have held the monopoly of a special style, existing in numerous detached specimens. The conclusion becomes almost inevitable that these fakes were specially made to delude Mr. Botkine, and thus to be insinuated among the genuine enamels of his collection.[17]

These forgeries are even outdone by another spurious Byzantine enamel: a gold plaque with the figure of a dancing girl, one of the best and most deceptive counterfeits ever produced. It was meant to be regarded as a fragment from the Crown of Constantine Monomachos. This crown which we had occasion to mention in connection with the Botkine forgeries, was found in fragments in the 'sixties of the last century and is now in the Budapest Museum. The circumstances of the find are obscure and *a priori* it does not seem unlikely that one of the plaques should have been kept back and sold years afterwards. The forger apparently regarded this as his golden opportunity. As two of the original plaques of the crown represent dancing girls he produced a third dancer. He did this with such mastery of Byzantine technique and style that all the experts were taken in until a Hungarian scholar proved the spuriousness of the plaque which had meanwhile been acquired by the Victoria and Albert Museum.[18] The workmanship of the London plaque is less delicate than that of the crown but this becomes only evident when originals and imitation are compared at close range. The forger was certainly an artist but he was no art historian. Had he known that the dancer swinging a

17. *Collection M. P. Botkine* (1911). Wesendonck, in *Caucasica*, vol. 1 (1924), p. 96. V. Lasareff in *Art Bulletin*, vol. 20 (1938), p. 61, note 172. M. Barany-Oberschall, *The Crown of the Emperor Constantine Monomachos* (1937), p. 89.

18. M. Barany-Oberschall, *The Crown of the Emperor Constantine Monomachos* (1937), p. 86.

veil above her head is a time-honoured motif of classical and medieval art,[19] he would not have placed the veil as a kind of skipping-rope under his dancer's feet. In the original the rinceau of the chased background becomes occasionally almost straight with perpendicular thorns issuing from the main stem but it never becomes a straight line ending in a star as it does near the right hand of the imitation. Moreover the modern origin of the plaque was proved by chemical analysis. The standard of gold of the Budapest panels is 78.5 to 79.3 per cent, while the London plaque is almost pure gold, 99.5 per cent.

MEDIEVAL AND RENAISSANCE GOLDSMITHS' WORK

The desire for the more ornate specimens of medieval and Renaissance goldsmiths' work got so predominant in the nineteenth century that the goldsmiths must have found it difficult to cope with the demand. The simplest way of complying with it was found by the Viennese goldsmith Weininger. Being entrusted, for the purpose of restoring them, with two beautifully elaborate ostensories from the Imperial Treasury of Austria, he copied them both and returned these copies in place of the originals, which he subsequently sold. The swindle was not discovered at once by the officials in charge of the treasure and could not be obvious to those who bought the originals, as the Treasury was not accessible to the public. Thus the pinnacled ostensory became the lawful property of the Germanic Museum of Nuremberg, while the enamelled Reliquary of the Holy Thorn (*Plates* 91, 92) found a permanent home in the British Museum.[20]

Weininger was a skilful goldsmith and the general appearance of his copy is so correct that an unsuspecting person might well accept it as the original. The first thing to be noticed on closer examination is the difference in size and quality of the pearls and jewels forming part of the two reliquaries. The beautifully regular pearls of the original are matched in the copy by irregular ones of

19. Cf. L. A. Mayer, in *Iraq*, vol. 6 (1939), p. 101.

20. J. Destrée in *The Connoisseur*, vol. 79 (1927), pp. 138 sqq. J. Evans, in *The Burlington Magazine*, vol. 78 (1941), p. 196.

inferior quality, and the shapes and sizes of all the stones are different. Though he was scrupulous tc copy the general design of his model, Weininger allowed himself some characteristic deviations in the rendering of its multiple details. He modernised the architecture of the castle forming the base by widening its windows and added crosses to its buttresses. A churchyard, on which the resuscitated rise from their graves, appears above the castle. Here Weininger was disturbed by the smooth surface of the green enamelled mounds; he preferred to cover them with vine leaves. Similar neo-Gothic foliage was substituted for the original ornament surrounding the capsule of the reliquary. The modernisation of the faces and figures also becomes apparent if compared with the original. For some obscure reason Christ got the features of God the Father. What is perhaps most obvious is the modernisation of the script on the scroll. The technical efficiency of this imitation is remarkable. The goldsmiths' work as well as the masterly application of translucent enamel, should be a warning to everybody who is inclined to think that the celebrated craftsmanship of past ages cannot be matched by modern forgers. There were no boundaries to the achievements of nineteenth-century goldsmiths, and there is hardly a type of object, within the range of their craft, at which they did not try their hand.

Of course, Weininger's practice of selling the originals is less common than the sale of copies. Publications with plates illustrating famous collections of goldsmiths' work were frequently used as prototypes. Thus a sixteenth-century ewer with mother of pearl inlay, in the Grüne Gewölbe of Dresden, was copied in silver, to appear in a great exhibition of old goldsmiths' work. But the fine and extravagant design of the original was badly blunted in the copy. Clumsy bosses were substituted for the mother of pearl quadrangles and the same clumsy pattern was substituted for the delicate grotesques of the foot.[21]

One of the most prominent of a few distinct groups of modern goldsmiths' work 'in style' are the 'Marcy fakes', called after their enterprising propagator, L. Marcy.[22] He endowed the objects he sold with enchanting provenances from Spanish castles, cathedrals,

21. M. Rosenberg in *Kunstgewerbeblatt*, N.F., vol. 3 (1892), p. 59.
22. O. v. Falke in *Belvedere*, vol. 1 (1922), pp. 8 sqq., figs. 1–14.

and convents. They actually show some of the characteristics of Spanish goldsmithwork. Lecterns and turreted incense burners belonged to the favourite objects of this workshop, which also excelled in figures, mostly Madonnas, made of silver as well as of ivory.[23] These may be recognised by their too engaging expression and their exaggeratedly affected deportment. Though not badly designed, many of the ornamental motifs appearing in this group betray their modern origin. But the most outstanding characteristic of the Marcy style is an indomitable predilection for motifs derived from architecture. Pinnacles, turrets, gateways, and windows, often assembled to whole façades or castles, appear almost on every single one of these forgeries. Cylindrical turrets with pointed tops are a special feature. Neither the lecterns nor the Madonnas have been spared these adornments, which were evidently thought to be the last word in Gothic craftsmanship, discovered in castles in Spain. A silver purse mount, included in the Burlington Fine Arts Club Exhibition of Fakes,[24] is a striking example of this style. It represents a complete Gothic castle, such as neo-Gothic fantasy might well imagine.

Head-shaped reliquaries shared the universal popularity enjoyed in the nineteenth century by busts in general. But their costly material raised them above the average of antique busts. Though forged male heads of costly material occur occasionally, the tender sex was generally preferred. The reliquary in *Plate* 93 illustrates how the late Gothic predilection for rich detail was overdone by the nineteenth-century imitators. The rich pattern of the dress is quite out of style, the realistic modelling of the face contrasts strangely with the stylised rendering of the hair and with the wide open eyes, meant to give the face a 'primitive' stare. It would be difficult to ascertain what style and country is aimed at, were it not for a very similar bust which was in the former Spitzer Collection and showed the hallmark of Saragossa.[25]

The young lady (*Plate* 94) with the fine Burgundian headdress outshines the reliquary bust by her greater elegance. The

23. See above, p. 170. Cf. *The Burlington Magazine*, vol. 87 (1945), p. 255.
24. No. 201, pl. 40.
25. *La Collection Spitzer* (1890), vol. 1, 'Orfèvrerie religieuse', nos. 102, 103, pls. 19, 20.

93. Reliquary bust. Silver.

94. Head of a lady. Silver and ivory.

95. Silver basin with 'Pelican in her Piety'. Nineteenth-century forgery. (By courtesy of Bibliothek Warburg, Hamburg.)

96. Lion-shaped ewer. Sixteenth century. Lüneburg.

head-dress can be lifted off like a lid, and without it she looks much like a china doll who has lost her wig.[26] But with the head-dress on she looks trim enough with her ivory face and pearl earrings and with her diminutive shoulders, supported by eight open-mouthed lions. Genuine busts of this type never existed.

The allegory of the pelican 'in her piety', who is said to have pecked her breast to nourish her young with her own blood, is one of the favourite symbols of Christian art. Little was known of the actual appearance of the pelican which was represented as a long-necked bird of prey. Such a fantastic bird is represented on a decorative piece of German silver, made in Ulm in 1583.[27] The bird is biting its breast and silver wire symbolises the blood streaming into the beaks of its offspring. This effective group was copied as a centre-piece for a large Gothic basin (*Plate 95*). A realistic nest was substituted for the ornamental basis of its model. The four lions supporting the base are copied from a sixteenth-century ewer in the Lüneburg Treasure (*Plate 96*).[28]

All the pieces enumerated up to now look sober and modest if compared with the extravagantly luxurious goldsmiths' work owned by Baron Karl Rothschild of Frankfurt. In the 'seventies of the last century he began to assemble a collection of sumptuous pieces of medieval and Renaissance goldsmithwork. The baron was lucky enough to acquire the famous Merkel goblet by Wenzel Jamnitzer, but apart from this ornate and richly enamelled table decoration it was difficult to find objects up to his exacting standards without plundering one of the royal treasures of Europe. The dealers found a simpler way of satisfying him. They supplied him with copies and variations of genuine pieces and with many luxurious neo-Gothic and neo-Renaissance inventions.

Some of the richest pieces of the collection were like the Pelican-basin (*Plate 95*) derived from the silver treasure belonging

26. *The G. A. Hearn Collection of Carved Ivories* (1908), no. 153, pl. 175. A similar bust is in the depot of the Vienna Museum (repr. *Kunst und Kunsthandwerk*, vol. 7, 1904, p. 184), a third one is in an American collection (*Gazette des Beaux-Arts*, ser. 6, vol. 29, 1946, p. 320).

27. E. Kris, *Goldschmiedearbeiten* (1932), p. 42, pl. 45.

28. M. Rosenberg, *Der Goldschmiede Merkzeichen*, 3rd ed., vol. 2 (1923), pl. 64. *Eretz-Israel*, vol. 7 (1964), p. 55*.

to the German town of Lüneburg. Since then this treasure has become more generally known, as it got to the Schlossmuseum of Berlin, but in the 'sixties of the nineteenth century comparatively few people had yet seen it in the town hall of Lüneburg. A drinking-horn made of an elephant's tooth is one of the outstanding pieces of this treasure. It is adorned with gilded silver, richly engraved and embossed, and carries the date 1486. Two elephants carry this ceremonial vessel on top of the pinnacled castles placed on their backs. This is an obvious allusion to the elephant's tooth, but the Rothschild horn is carried by 'dragons and castles', which is, to say the least, a novel combination. The dragons look rather dangerous and somewhat Chinese, while their castles are reminiscent of a neo-Gothic façade. Like Weininger, when he copied the Reliquary of the Thorn, the goldsmith who made this horn could not refrain from endowing its architectural parts with many large windows, instead of the few narrow slits of the original. The decoration of the horn itself was considerably enriched, and two little figures were included to give the whole added interest.[29]

A 'hunting bowl' from the Rothschild Collection is a worthy counterpart to the ivory horn. The inside of this bowl is decorated with a rich frieze with hunting scenes, and its centre is crowned by a hill carrying Saint Hubert and the stag. It is difficult to explain why this bowl should rest on four pinnacled feet on which the four Fathers of the Church are sitting. This becomes clearer if one compares the bowl with the Lüneburg treasure. Here the Holy Fathers carry one bowl, while Saint Hubert crowns another.[30] Pieces like this give a fair idea of the heavily pinnacled silver treasures that were let loose on a world full of enthusiasm for the Gothic revival.

Renaissance work was almost as coveted as Gothic pieces. Here the marked predilection of the nineteenth century for ornamental objects devoid of any meaning or purpose becomes more evident than anywhere else.

29. F. Luthmer, *Der Schatz des Freiherrn K. v. Rothschild* (1883), vol. 1, pl. 1; vol. 2, pl. 7. O. v. Falke in *Belvedere*, vol. 5 (1924), 'Forum', p. 2.

30. F. Luthmer, *Der Schatz des Freiherrn K. v. Rothschild*, vol. 2, pls. 4, 5. O. v. Falke in *Belvedere*, vol. 5 (1924), p. 2.

The Elephant (*Plate* 97) with a turreted castle on his enamelled saddle and a base adorned by four cylindrical turrets resting on bowl-shaped enamelled feet, purports to be one of those automata which were the delight of the late Renaissance. Its maker was apparently so sure of the success of his mechanical toy that he thought it superfluous to bother about late Renaissance style and ornamentation.

Severity and 'functionalism' of design were not among the virtues of Renaissance goldsmiths; but in spite of their exuberance they never produced anything as absurd as the spherical tazza with cover reproduced on *Plate* 98.[31] For no particular reason the three lion's claws on which the vessel rests have been fastened to a second enamelled base with globular feet.

The jug (*Plate* 99) gives a fair idea of what the nineteenth century saw in the richly decorated and bejewelled works of Renaissance goldsmiths. The Pegasus with the trumpeting lady on his back is no counterpart to similar enamelled marvels of the Renaissance. Some of the embossings on the surface of the jug, and particularly the ornamentation of its foot, very much resemble genuine pieces. But the flat vine-leaves and palmettes unmistakably betray its nineteenth-century origin.

After all this one is inclined to think that the forgers are exclusively occupied with the more sumptuous kind of goldsmiths' work. But some of them found time to reproduce numerous pieces of early domestic plate. Though such silver is of much plainer appearance than the exuberant masterpieces of Gothic and Renaissance craftsmanship, it would be wrong to suppose that it is much easier to forge. Quite the contrary, their very richness tends to divert the spectator from technical and stylistic details that should be revealing, while those who really love and study old plate know its subtle nuances so intimately that they are alive to slight differences and seemingly negligible shortcomings. Moreover, domestic silver ought to be hallmarked, even if it is of an early date. Though hallmarks and makers' marks are freely forged, old goldsmiths' marks are quite an intricate science and the forgers luckily often select impossible combinations. Thus a large-scale forger of

31. A similar piece is in the Victoria and Albert Museum (309–1878), where it is catalogued as 'French. Late 18th or early 19th century'.

early German silver mixed up hallmarks and goldsmith marks belonging to different places and different periods. The same goldsmith committed the mistake of introducing copies of drawings from the 'Hausbuch' among the copies of prints with which he engraved his cups and goblets. The 'Hausbuch' remained inaccessible till its drawings were published in the nineteenth century. Apart from anachronisms occurring in the choice of ornamental motifs, this Munich forger committed a mistake common to most counterfeits of old plate—he made his ornaments rather too rich and applied them too densely. The desire to make the most of his fraud carried him away. But in any case no connoisseur should be deceived by a casket with engravings the prototypes of which are a hundred years older than the goldsmith whose mark is impressed on the object, while the ornamentation points to a date between the two.[32]

In England hallmarks have been compulsory from the fourteenth century onwards. Apart from spurious trade marks on porcelain the falsification of hallmarks is the only art forgery which is punished under the criminal law. False English hallmarks are frequently produced abroad, but some forgers try to find a way out of the impasse by using an indistinct or copied silversmith's mark, without an official mark, as only the forgery of the latter is prosecuted by the King's Proctor. Others cut out the hallmarks from less alluring genuine pieces, to fix them on their own works, as may be seen on the bottoms of two gravy-boats in the collection of forgeries and imitations at the Victoria and Albert Museum.

This instructive collection of forgeries also contains an embossed dish with a London hallmark for 1797–8 (*Plate* 100). It seems to be the work of some continental forger who never saw any genuine English silver of the period. He copied—clumsily enough—the main figures of the 'Wedding Feast' by David Teniers in Munich and added a strange border of trees framing landscape cartouches, clearly betraying their nineteenth-century origin.[33]

32. Engravings after Schäuffelein (d. 1539 or 1540), mark of Th. Haesel of Augsburg (born 1595) and ornament of about 1570. O. v. Falke in *Belvedere*, vol. 5 (1924), 'Forum', p. 5, fig. 13.

33. Victoria and Albert Museum: 810–1890. For Teniers' picture see E. Hanfstaengl, *Meisterwerke der Älteren Pinakothek* (1922), p. 191.

97. Automaton in Late Renaissance style. By S. Weininger.

98. Tazza with cover. By S. Weininger.

99. Jug. Embossed silver. By S. Weininger.

100. Embossed silver dish with false London hallmark for 1797–98. (Victoria and Albert Museum.)

101. Silver jug. London hallmark for 1758–59. The spout and embossing were added in the 19th century. (Victoria and Albert Museum.)

102. Silver two-handled cup. London hallmark for 1777–78. The gadrooning and roped band were added in the 19th century. (Victoria and Albert Museum.)

Modern embossings inflicted on plain old plate are not infrequent. The style of these ornaments and the way in which they are displayed on the vessel is characteristic of the taste of the average forger. The jug (*Plate* 101) has been overloaded with fruit and flowers which could, if anything, date only from the seventeenth century. But the marks of the jug are of 1758–9.[34]

The two-handled cup (*Plate* 102) was embossed with a view to making it resemble a certain type of genuine vessel. It was a simple piece. On silver vessels made in the late seventeenth and early eighteenth centuries cartouches with inscriptions or monograms sometimes interrupt the gadrooning, while their tops appear as if they had been slipped under a roped band. The same scheme was tried on the unsymmetrical decorative cartouche of this cup, a typical motif of Rococo decoration which contrasts sharply with the candid moulding above which is half a century earlier in style.[35]

This brings us to the question of pasticcios and extensive restorations. As gold and silver objects usually consist of several parts, exchanges and additions may be made without attracting too much notice. M. Rosenberg observed that a Renaissance cup which appeared in the Budapest exhibition of goldsmiths' work in 1884 and was acquired in the following year by Baron Karl Rothschild, had undergone certain changes since it had been photographed for the Budapest publication. What appeared in the Rothschild Collection was a revised edition, enriched by various details. Several enamelled coats of arms, a miniature colonnade, and other items have been incorporated into an already very rich object, doubtlessly with the intention of making it more worthy of the collector who acquired it.[36]

In other cases whole objects were composed of miscellaneous parts. Thus a Gothic reliquary was composed of the most heterogeneous pieces. Apparently the restorer made use of all fragments

34. Victoria and Albert Museum: 844–1890.

35. Victoria and Albert Museum: M. 320–1923. C. Oman, *English Domestic Silver* (1947), p. 207, fig. 101.

36. M. Rosenberg, *Der Goldschmiede Merkzeichen* (3rd edition, 1922), vol. 1, no. 1388a, pls. 28, 29.

he could find. The foot of the reliquary dates from the later four-teenth century. It supports a rather dubious receptacle for relics which is composed of old and new parts, and crowned by a very fine silver-gilt statuette of Saint Augustine which dates from the thirteenth century and seems originally to have been the decora-tion of a pastoral staff. The whole object was arranged for an Imperial collector in the early nineteenth century, and only a few years ago Dr. Kris, in his capacity as keeper of goldsmiths' work in the Museum of Vienna, succeeded in freeing Saint Augustine from his undesirable residence on top of this reliquary.[37]

37. E. Kris, *Goldschmiedearbeiten* (1932), p. 1, pls. 2, 3. For forgeries of Teutonic jewellery from the Migration Period, see below, p. 338.

PART THIRTEEN

POTTERY AND PORCELAIN

PART THIRTEEN

POTTERY AND PORCELAIN

GREEK AND ROMAN POTTERY

With Greek pottery the part played by outright fakes is negligible compared with the harm done by over-zealous restorations. These restorations can be so skilfully done that it is often a very delicate task to distinguish the new and ancient portions. The spirit test helps to show up the paint on restorations and under the quartz lamp the restored patches shine out with all the clearness that may be desired. It shows the edges of the reassembled fragments and the extent of the repainting covering them, and such parts as have been re-placed by clay or plaster stand out with a different fluorescence from the genuine portions of the vessel.

Our understanding of Greek vase-painting has made such pro-gress in recent years that older forgeries have no chance to pass undetected. In the late eighteenth and early nineteenth centuries Greek vases were appreciated for their subject matter only. Forgers had to produce some startling subject and could afford to neglect the artistic side. This was done by the painter who deco-rated a genuine Greek amphora with the happy reunion of Eros and Psyche, a vase which got eventually into the Vatican Col-lection. The abominably painted picture shows Eros and Psyche on a couch waiting for a jar of wine which is being served by a second Eros. The forger wanted to be on the safe side, and copied the scene from an engraved stone; it was his bad luck that the stone he chose was a forgery.[1] In spite of all this the vase found an

1. *Archaeologische Zeitung,* vol. 27 (1869), pp. 19, 116. S. Reinach, *Répertoire des vases,* vol. 1 (1899), p. 405.

admirer, because it confirmed a literary theory then widely held. To the adherents of this theory Apuleius' fairy tale of Amor and Psyche was not a creation of the Hellenistic age, but an old Indo-European myth. An early vase with this subject was therefore warmly welcomed as a proof that the story had already been current in Plato's time.

This was an actual forgery. In other cases the forged vase never existed in reality, but only on paper. This type of swindle is quite frequent with classical inscriptions, but seldom met with with works of art, although the portrait of Prince Rhodocanakis (see above, p. 71) belongs to this category. In 1809 a Sicilian with the name of Scrofani supplied the French archaeologist Aubin-Louis Millin with three drawings allegedly copied from a Greek vase found in Aulis and now said to be in a private collection. Millin published these drawings which are indeed remarkable: one shows the half-figure of a boy emerging from a kind of rockery, while in the sky above a *caduceus*, a winged snake and the mysterious letters *Aga* appear; the second shows a group of gesticulating women on a stage, while the last shows a cow walking out of an amphitheatre. These puzzling pictures caused a number of learned interpretations, and the stage-scene was used to illustrate the Athenian 'Theatre of Dionysos' in a well-known reference-book of classical geography.[2]

Though more or less considerable restorations were bestowed on many Greek vases of every known type, Attic white lekythoi appear to be the favourites of the forgers. One of the reasons for this predilection is that the spontaneity and freshness of their drawings come much closer to modern artistic ideals than the precise draughtsmanship of red-figure vases. Though numerous examples have been excavated, most of the white lekythoi are in a sad state of preservation. The powdery white slip covering the body of these vessels flakes off easily, and of the figures, which were drawn with light strokes of the brush on this delicate ground, frequently nothing is left but some minor traces. These all too frequent damages are rendered worse by fraudulent attempts to replace the lost designs. The forgers never succeed in matching

2. Millin, *Peintures de vases* (1808), ed. S. Reinach (1891), p. 73. W. Smith, *Dictionary of Greek and Roman Geography*, vol. 1 (1854), p. 285.

the grace and beauty and above all the inimitable mastery of draughtsmanship common to genuine lekythoi. Moreover, the world of Greek life and Greek religion is usually a closed book to the forger, and superficial knowledge is apt to produce strange results. Where the forger tries to follow classical models another pitfall threatens him, namely anachronisms. A characteristic example is a white lekythos where the scanty remains of the original design provoked a far-reaching restoration.[3] The scene is of a common type: a tombstone, a dead youth, and a woman bringing offerings to the tomb. The woman is very remarkable. She is nude except for the legs which are covered by a *himation* girded round the hips in a way which looks familiar. The artist was obviously inspired by the drapery of the Venus of Milo or perhaps by the similar Venus of Capua, and forgot that the attire of the Goddess of Love would have been thought most unsuitable for an Athenian lady of the fifth century B.C.

Even small fragments are being forged. A couple of tiny sherds, each with the head of a woman, prove that the modern artist is very far removed from the spirit of Greek design. The glance of the eyes and the drooping inner wrinkle of the mouth give an unmistakably modern expression to the faces.[4]

Roman terra-cotta lamps are so common that only pieces of unusual shape or with interesting decoration in relief are coveted by collectors. An unusually large collection of lamps in which almost every piece could claim to be of special interest was assembled by the Italian antiquary Giovanni Battista Passeri (1694–1780). Part of his collection is now in the museum at Pesaro. Passeri proudly published his treasures in three luxurious and learned volumes which were long regarded as the standard work on the subject. About fifty years ago some of the inscriptions on his lamps aroused suspicion and a close investigation revealed the fact that the Passeri Collection was one of the greatest assem-

---

3. *Monuments Piot*, vol. 22 (1916), pls. 4–5 (reprinted in *Recueil Pottier*, 1937, p. 539). J. D. Beazley, *Attic White Lekythoi* (1938), p. 7, note 1. C. Picard, in *Revue Archéologique*, 6th ser., vol. 14 (1939), p. 106.

4. *Corpus Vasorum Antiquorum*, United States of America, Providence, fasc. 1 (1933), pl. 25, 6 and 7. J. D. Beazley, in *The Journal of Hellenic Studies*, vol. 53 (1933), p. 311.

blages of fakes ever brought together: every single one of the
more ambitious pieces is false. Among them is a curious lamp in
the shape of a bull's head, richly decorated. Its story is not
devoid of interest. An earlier archaeologist speaking of bull-
shaped lamps advanced the theory that they were dedicated to
Artemis *taurobolos*. The well-read forger confirmed this theory
by producing a lamp on which the horns of the bull are inscribed
APΘEM(IΔI) IEPOC—'Dedicated to Artemis'. The joy was
so great that everybody seems to have overlooked the faulty
spelling of the name of the goddess. The story has an epilogue: a
famous modern archaeologist had the brilliant idea that the first
word of the inscription should be read backwards (Methra), thus
proving the lamp to be dedicated to Mithras. This revelation
was regarded as renewed proof of the genuineness of the lamp.
It is a pity that the forger did not live to enjoy this display of
ingenuity.[5]

More recent but conceived in a similar spirit is the forgery of an
early Christian lamp in the shape of a fish. On one flank this fish
shows the monogram of Christ and on the other a cross. Thus it is
characterised as a symbol of Christ.[6] Perhaps thinking of the old
proverb 'Big fishes eat little ones', the forger put a small fish in the
big one's mouth and left it to the purchaser to discover the deeper
meaning of this new symbolism. By some process of muddled
thinking an archaeologist managed to explain the voracious fish
as an illustration of the Gospel verse 'I will make you to become
fishers of men'. The object sold extremely well; quite a number of
museums acquired a specimen; the Berlin Museum, always
ambitious, purchased two.

In 1901 the British Museum was presented with a remarkable
bowl which was quickly to become famous as the 'Constantine

5. J. B. Passeri, *Lucernae fictiles Musei Passerii* (1739), pl. 99. E. Dressler,
in *Roemische Mitteilungen*, vol. 7 (1892), p. 147. F. Cumont, *Textes et monuments* (1896), vol. 2, p. 410. S. Loeschcke, *Lampen aus Vindonissa* (1919),
p. 109.

6. *Amtliche Berichte aus den Koenigl. Kunstsammlungen*, vol. 35 (1913–14),
p. 35, fig. 17, p. 259. F. J. Doelger, *Ichthys*, vol. 5 (1937), pp. 158 sqq. Cf.
also W. de Grüneisen, *Art chrétien primitif du Haut et du Bas Moyen Age*,
pl. 3.

Bowl'.[7] The bowl is of buff ware covered with a vitreous glaze. Incised in the paste is the figure of Christ enthroned and two portrait medallions. An inscription 'VAL. COSTANTINUS PIUS FELIX AUGUSTUS CUM FLAV(ia) MAX(ima) FAUST(a)' identifies the portraits as Constantine the Great and his wife Fausta who died shortly before 330.[8] The bowl would therefore have to be anterior to this date. A work of Christian art, dating from the very years when Christianity became the state religion of the Roman Empire, is a remarkable historical monument. Moreover all accepted theories on the development of early Christian art were upset by the figure of Christ. In the first centuries Christ was represented as an idealised youth of divine beauty, and only later was the type of the bearded majestical Christ evolved. The Constantine bowl would thus be the earliest known representation of the bearded Christ with the cruciform nimbus. This amazing bowl has yet other attractions. To-day the design is visible in faint traces. When the bowl first appeared on the art market, the interior was plain white and the design became visible by a simple but effective conjuring trick. It just had to be filled with water. Its first owner was Count Tyszkiewicz to whom it had been offered by a Roman dealer. 'Not recognising the class of ceramic art, or the period to which it could be assigned (the interior was then white), and besides not collecting vases other than Greek, he declined making the purchase. A few weeks afterwards the dealer returned in a state of excitement and again produced the bowl; this time, however, with the figure of Christ and the inscription plainly visible. The worthy man asserted that thinking the object might look all the better for washing, he put the bowl in warm water and presently, to his great astonishment, beheld the apparition of the image of Christ becoming visible on the inside of the vessel. It is unnecessary to say that there was no hesitation on this

7. H. Wallis, *Egyptian Ceramic Art, Typical Examples of the Art of the Egyptian Potter* (1900), p. 28, pl. 12. J. Strzygowski, in *Byzantinische Zeitschrift*, vol. 10 (1901), p. 734. W. R. Lethaby, in *The Cambridge Medieval History*, vol. 1 (1911), p. 607. A. Lane, in *Transactions of the Oriental Ceramic Society*, 1937–8, p. 33.

8. For the date of Fausta's death see J. B. Bury in his edition of Gibbon's *Decline and Fall*, vol. 2 (1929), p. 586.

occasion as to the purchase, it was bought there and then.' The decoration of a vessel with lines incised in the paste and subsequently glazed is a technique invented by Chinese potters in the Middle Ages. The Constantine bowl if actually dating from the fourth century, would antedate the Chinese examples.

Because of its many unusual features the genuineness of the bowl was contested soon after it turned up. The first argument raised against it was the spelling of Constantine as Costantinus. This, it was said, must be a slip into the Italian idiom of the faker. But this argument can be disarmed, as *n* before *s* was not pronounced in Latin,[9] and even the spelling Costantinus without the n occurs on inscriptions and papyri dating from the time of Constantine.[10]

But later on an element was introduced into the discussions, which lets it appear not unlikely that 'Costantinus' is after all of Italian origin. A miniature from an eleventh-century Italian Exultet Roll is an almost literal counterpart of the engraving on the Constantine bowl.[11] In the manuscript Christ is represented as the supreme judge. On His outstretched hands the stigmata are visible and to His right and left are circular medallions, intended for the sun and moon. On the Constantine bowl every detail of the figure of Christ reappears, down to the folds of His garments and to the two circular dots on His cheeks. Only the stigmata have been omitted. The male and female profile have been inscribed in the two circles. In an eleventh-century manuscript all the features so astounding on a late antique piece are perfectly natural.

CHINESE CERAMICS[11a]

The formidable extent of the lurking, manifold and almost inescapable dangers waiting to ensnare the collector of Chinese

9. W. M. Lindsay, *The Latin Language* (1894), p. 67.

10. O. M. Dalton, *Catalogue of Early Christian Antiquities* (1901), no. 916 (where the reference to *Ephemeris Epigraphica* should read vol. 5, no. 1099). *Byzantinische Zeitschrift*, vol. 11 (1902), p. 671; vol. 12 (1903), p. 436.

11. J. Wilpert, *Die roemischen Mosaiken und Malereien* (1917), vol. 2, p. 1190; idem, in *L'Arte*, vol. 23 (1920), p. 157. The Exultet Roll is in the Collegiate Church of Mirabella-Eclano near Benevento; M. Avery, *The Exultet Rolls of South Italy* (1936), pl. 60.

11a. On forgeries of early Chinese ceramics, see below, p. 341.

ceramics is so universally acknowledged that I need hardly dwell on it here. More than any other, the Chinese potter's is an art of subtleties, solely destined for the appreciation of the initiated few, who have succeeded in developing by deep devotion and assiduous training what amounts almost to a sixth sense. The general veneration for earlier wares was and is assiduously catered for by skilful potters in China and Japan. This may suffice to account for the predominant number of deceptive imitations.

Inscriptions.

Although date inscriptions are occasionally to be found on earlier ceramics, they only became usual during the reign of the early Ming emperors. Then the inscribing of the name of the dynasty and the period of the ruler during whose reign the piece was made became customary. However, this applies only to wares made for the Imperial Court in particular and for the Chinese market in general. Porcelain made for export often shows only meaningless scribbles in place of the beautifully written inscriptions to be found on high-grade wares. The Chinese potters evidently thought that anything was good enough for those illiterate barbarians of foreigners.

The fakers did not miss a device so simple as the inscribing of a few characters and the number of false *nien hao* is endless. The marks of Hsüan Tê (1426–35) and Ch'eng Hua (1465–87) have become notorious among collectors because of the profusion of false specimens. The success of this simple method luckily is threatened by numerous pitfalls. It is not easy to achieve Chinese characters of convincing perfection, even if the faker is a skilled Chinese craftsman.

A Hung Chih (A.D. 1488–1505) inscription is a good example of such revealingly clumsy characters.[1] To quote but a single one of its shortcomings, the three dots of the radical in Chih have been blurred so as to become a stroke with a single remaining dot. Not only are the characters drawn badly, but their writer also failed to arrange them in a satisfactory way in the double circle in which they are inscribed. A genuine early inscription of good quality

1. Illustrated in E. E. Bluett, *Ming and Ch'ing Porcelains* (1933), pl. 4, no. 6.

inevitably must betray that pleasing manner of spacing which plays such a prominent part in Chinese aesthetics. Of course, the blunders of false inscriptions are often far from plainly visible. Some knowledge of Chinese characters is required to discern the flaws in more efficient fabrications. An experienced eye will hardly be deceived by a painstaking copy after the sure strokes of a masterly hand. On a later copy of the Hsüan Tê reign mark for instance, the top and bottom parts of the Hsüan character have slipped asunder.[2] Such lack of symmetry is the undoing of the faker, even if it is betrayed by a stroke of minor importance.

A connection is often established between false marks of this kind and the excellent copies of early originals made during the seventeenth and eighteenth centuries in the imperial factory. But it seems hardly likely that such pieces should have been inscribed with defective script. There exists, moreover, no proof that such valuable copies, made by imperial order, were ever inscribed with other marks than those corresponding to the actual time of their making. In any case, there still exist a number of most deceptive copies of the highest perfection which are duly emblazoned with the Ch'ing mark. Dealers desirous of augmenting the value of such pieces took great pains to erase these genuine marks. The best way to achieve this is to cover it by a newly made mark or seal, meant to establish the early origin of such a piece.

Sir Percival David describes how he discovered such handling on an exceptionally fine bottle with Ju glaze (*Plate* 103)[3]: 'The vase illustrated in the catalogue of my collection, for instance, was for long believed to be a Sung Ju piece. It was only by an unhappy chance that one bright summer's day in Peking I discovered on its base, under the glaze and cunningly concealed by a later seal which had been cut over it, the Yung-chêng *nien hao* in seal characters. The mark is, in fact, barely legible, and so admirably has this eighteenth-century imitation been fabricated that certain Chinese authorities still refuse to believe that the mark is

2. Illustrated in A. D. Brankston, *Early Ming Wares of Chingtechen*. (1938), p. 24, pl. 11.

3. *Transactions of the Oriental Ceramic Society* (1936–7), p. 52. R. L Hobson, *Catalogue of Chinese Pottery and Porcelain in the Collection of Sir Percival David* (1934), pl. 3.

not of the Sung period.' Thus this bottle, which formerly belonged to the Imperial Collection of Peking, is proved to be one of those masterly copies after Sung made in the eighteenth century.

Something similar has happened to a large vase which is now in a Swedish private collection.[4] It bears an iron-red period mark of Hsüan Tê (1426–35), but the sixteenth-century style of its decoration aroused misgivings, and the mark of Chia Ching (1522–66) was discovered under the forged inscription. The genuine mark is in *an-hua* (carved with a needle point and covered by the glaze) and could therefore be concealed without much difficulty.

Collectors have been puzzled by the fact that the reign marks of early Ming emperors are occasionally to be found on pieces the style of which endeavours by no means to imitate actual Ming porcelain. Vases of the *famille verte* or *famille noire* undoubtedly made during the reign of K'ang Hsi (1662–1722) show the reign mark of Ch'eng Hua (1465–87).[5] By no other means do they pretend to such an early origin, and nobody could ever have regarded them as Ming pieces. An attempt has been made to explain this strange phenomenon by the alleged large-scale faking of inscriptions in the eighteenth century, surmising that the potters ceased to care to what pieces they affixed their fraudulent marks. But a religious taboo was the real reason. During the reign of K'ang Hsi, from 1677 onwards, the potters were forbidden for a time to inscribe the reign-name of the emperor on porcelain, in order that the holy name should not be desecrated by breakages. During this period the space destined for the inscription was either left empty or the potters chose an innocuous text. Occasionally they used the name of one of the emperors of the last dynasty who had played such a prominent part in the history of porcelain.[6]

4. L. Reidemeister, *Ming-Porzellane in schwedischen Sammlungen* (1935), p. 23, pl. 23a.

5. Examples are numerous: one is in the British Museum (R. L. Hobson, *Handbook of the Pottery and Porcelain of the Far East* (1937), fig. 116); another came with the Salting Bequest into the Victoria and Albert Museum (W. B. Honey, in *Artibus Asiae*, vol. 3 (1928–9), p. 166).

6. St. Julien, *Histoire et fabrication de la porcelaine chinoise* (1856), p. xlii. Hsü Chih Hêng (translated by F. Perzynski), in *Burlington Magazine*, vol. 52 (1928), p. 70. R. L. Hobson, *Handbook of the Pottery and Porcelain of the Far East* (1937), pp. 93, 170.

Forged inscriptions are not only affixed to pieces intended to be taken for specimens dating from the most renowned periods of Chinese porcelain manufacture, but may also be found on early Chinese pottery. We may assume that the inscription engraved on the neck of a genuine Han vase was intended to pander to the special delight Chinese connoisseurs draw from pieces with inscriptions. In this particular case the forger was highly successful. The inscription reads: 'Hsiao Wu Temple, Yüan Kuang period, second year, number 15.' This points to 133 B.C. Consequently the vase became famous as a dated piece and was used as the main point of departure for the chronology of Han art. All this happened without regard for the fact that the inscription had been placed on the neck of the vase in a somewhat random fashion, and that it had been cut into the clay not only after the firing but after the glaze had peeled away from the surface. This fact was at first concealed by a waxy substance, purporting to be glaze, which had been smeared into the engraved lines of the inscription. After this had been removed it became clear that the signs had been freshly cut.[7] There is another telling detail in the inscription: the emperor during whose reign the vase is alleged to have been made is styled Hsiao Wu, which is his posthumous name.

The Album of Hsiang Yüan-pien.

If fakes were to be arranged according to the success they have obtained and to the part they have played in the research work of scholars, the album of Hsiang Yüan-pien would occupy one of the very first places. When it first turned up in 1885 it was hailed as the only early illustrated account of Sung and Ming porcelain. By its water-colours Europe was initiated to the charms and secrets of early porcelain, practically unknown before. As a consequence of this the album—or rather its copies, as the original was burned before it had been published—was twice reproduced in sumptuous and costly facsimile editions, the later one of which will always be a source of delight to bibliophiles.[8] Hsiang, the

7. F. S. Kershaw, in *Burlington Magazine*, vol. 24 (1913–14), p. 151.

8. Hsiang Yüan-pien, *Chinese Porcelain* (translated and annotated by S. W. Bushell, Oxford, 1908). Hsiang Yüan-pien, *Noted Porcelains of Successive Dynasties* (Peiping, 1931).

supposed author of this catalogue, was a scholar, artist, and collector who was born in 1525, during the reign of Chia Ching, and died in 1590 in the reign of Wan Li. At a time when the Imperial Collections of Peking were as yet inaccessible such an authenticated description of eighty-seven early specimens of porcelain, complete with coloured illustrations, was of unparalleled value. This was recognised at once by the German ambassador to China, to whom the manuscript was at first offered. He did not go to the length of buying it, but had a copy made clandestinely, a fact which was again exploited by the Chinese painter whom he entrusted with this discreet task. Thus a whole series of slightly differing versions of 'Hsiang's album' exist. It is beyond doubt that some of the objects illustrated in the album represent fine specimens of early porcelain, e.g. the white bowls and stem-cups decorated with red fishes or the incense-burner of Kuan ware which has an almost identical counterpart in the David collection.[9] But decisive arguments against the genuineness of the album have been put forward by Sir Percival David.[10] The following are some of his points.

The main indictment is formed by twenty-four of the watercolours in the album, which the accompanying text designates as illustrations of porcelain originals derived from bronze models illustrated in the famous ancient bronze catalogues. In reality these illustrations of the album are nothing but tracings of the woodcuts from the catalogues, embellished by pleasing colours. Apart from the fact that they are mere tracings, the thickly glazed Sung ware to which they purport to belong never would have lent itself to the rendering of the sharply cut reliefs adorning some of these vessels. These phantom porcelains show some remarkable features. One vessel has even a chain of links for suspension, ceramically impossible but natural enough once the source of the illustration is known. It is copied from a bronze vessel with a suspending chain represented on one of the woodcuts of the *Po ku t'u-lu*

9. R. L. Hobson, *Catalogue of Chinese Pottery and Porcelain in the Collection of Sir Percival David* (1934), pl. 15. *Transactions of the Oriental Ceramic Society* (1933–4), p. 44.

10. *Transactions of the Oriental Ceramic Society* (1933–4), pp. 22 sqq. Cf. also P. Pelliot in *T'oung Pao*, vol. 32 (1936), pp. 15 sqq., 345 sqq.

the famous catalogue of early bronzes compiled in the twelfth century. Pseudo-Hsiang amused himself by describing the chain as 'made so well that there is no difference between it and one made of bronze', adding 'Such handicraft is indeed the work of a supernatural being.'[11]

In the text accompanying his Figure 8 Hsiang greatly extols an ink palette of 'Kuan ware'. He commends its smoothness and tells us under what circumstances he acquired it. In reality he copied this masterpiece from a work on jade that was condemned as a forgery by an Imperial Commission in 1779.[12]

The more serious objects contained in the album have been interspersed with some delightful products of fantasy. These are objects with a profusion of the most fragile details, as for instance 'a whorl of banana-leaves'[13] loosely assembled in the shape of what is supposed to be a wine-vessel, or 'lamps' composed of flowers and stylised birds, resting on the most spindly of stems. No collector ever set eyes on such exquisitely delicate objects. As long as Hsiang's album remained unchallenged severe blame used to be laid on the Chinese servants who were accused of having inadvertently broken such priceless treasures. Looking at the oil-lamp,[14] we wonder whether the stems could carry the weight of either flower or leaf. Certainly a flame lit in the flower would have been acutely dangerous to the leaf immediately above, which is 'to shield the flame from draughts'.

Thus one must resign oneself to the fact that this supposed collection of early porcelain is nothing but a beautiful *fata morgana,* which evaporates on approach. Even the most tantalising specimens it contains, the purple Ting wares,[15] coveted but

11. Fig. 68. *Transactions of the Oriental Ceramic Society* (1933–4), p. 36, fig. 19.

12. *Ku yü t'u-lu* ('Illustrated Account of Ancient Jade'), published 1779 after a manuscript which purports to date from A.D. 1176. Cf. P. Pelliot, in *T'oung Pao,* vol. 22 (1923), p. 365. Sir P. David, *Transactions of the Oriental Ceramic Society* (1933–4), p. 36. R. L. Hobson, *Catalogue of Chinese Pottery and Porcelain in the Collection of Sir Percival David* (1934), p. 177.

13. Fig. 29.

14. Fig. 81. *Transactions of the Oriental Ceramic Society* (1933–4), fig. 46.

15. Figs. 3, 18, 51.

never seen by modern collectors, consist for the larger part of tracings after bronzes, which could be endowed with the valuable hue with very little trouble.

T'ang Figures.

In Europe and America of the present day T'ang tomb figures have become the most popular exponents of Chinese art. The horses, the camels, and the slender ladies, and the colour-effect of the broadly applied green and yellow-flecked glazes, are the first things to be remembered when thinking of early Chinese art. But this fame is of very recent date. The first tomb figures arrived in Europe in 1909 and the first excavations were brought to the notice of a Chinese connoisseur not more than two years earlier. However, we have had occasion to remark how quickly the keen commercial sense of the Chinese is liable to react once they become aware of a growing demand for a new kind of goods.[16] Therefore one is not over-astonished to hear that Professor Yetts visited, as early as 1912, a factory which turned out T'ang ceramics on a large scale, and in quite good quality: 'In 1912 I visited a factory at Peking where along shelves stood hundreds of newly-made figures. Comparison of these with the genuine originals which had served as patterns proved that certain modern replicas may defy detection.'[17] Of course, this successful industry is still flourishing and everybody who takes the trouble of looking around has ample opportunity to see numerous examples of its production.

As in many other fields, casts are rather more dangerous than new inventions. Seeing that a large part of the original tomb figures were nothing but serial products, made from a limited number of moulds, there is no considerable difficulty in multiplying existing shapes by further moulding. The clay as well as the firing can be matched without much difficulty, and if the forgers decide to do without a glaze fakes and originals may be dangerously alike. Of course one might designate such objects rather as reproductions than as outright fakes, but as they are being passed off as originals the difference is of a purely theoretical character.

16. See above, p. 139, the remarks on forgeries of Buddhist sculptures.
17. Preface to C. Hentze, *Chinese Tomb Figures* (1928), p. 7.

Modern T'ang sculptures are either uninspired copies of frequent types or daring and absurd inventions, like some monstrous animals with a broadly grinning human face.[18] The types of which the largest number of imitations have so far appeared are horses and ladies. The ladies often betray themselves by the patent modernism of their expression.[19] An instructive specimen of faked T'ang horses was shown in the Exhibition of Counterfeits at the Burlington Fine Arts Club.[20] Its pedantically detailed modelling contrasts sharply with the sketchy character of the genuine pieces.

T'ang statuettes—genuine and false—arrived in Europe in ever increasing numbers and became a common decoration for the mantelpiece. Soon ambitious collectors asked for something more exquisite. Ancient literary references to tomb equipment (*ming-ch'i*) in precious metal gave a valuable hint, and T'ang figures in silver turned up. They are incompetent copies of the pottery statuettes. The ladies have lost all the charm of the ceramic originals, especially when seen in profile,[21] while the figure of a dog in the same material is the feeble copy of a feeble original.[22]

Sung.

Sung porcelain was rare, highly valued, and arduously sought for in the period immediately following the time when it was made. It is therefore not surprising that its imitation should have become an established habit in the Ming period. The *T'ao Shuo* speaks of a potter who was famous for his imitations of the more costly types of Sung ware:[23] 'In the time of the Ming dynasty there lived in the town of Yi-hsing (prefecture Ch'ang Chou, pro-

18. E. Fuchs, *Tang Plastik* (1924), pl. 10. C. Hentze, in *Artibus Asiae* (1925), p. 315.

19. E. Fuchs, *Tang Plastik* (1924), pl. 42. C. Hentze, in *Artibus Asiae* (1925), p. 315.

20. Catalogue no. 62, pl. 44.

21. *Ostasiatische Zeitschrift*, vol. 15 (1929), pp. 14, 211. P. Pelliot in *T'oung Pao*, vol. 28 (1931), p. 239.

22. *Jahrbuch der asiatischen Kunst*, vol. 2 (1925), p. 26. P. Pelliot, in *T'oung Pao*, vol. 25 (1928), p. 186.

23. Chu Yen, *T'ao Shuo* (1774), Bk. 3, fol. 7, verso. S. W. Bushell, *Description of Chinese Pottery and Porcelain* (1910), p. 64.

vince of Chiang-nan) a man named Ou who made porcelain vessels. These were called "Ou ware". In some of them he copied the crackles of Kê ware, in others the coloured glazes of Kuan and Chün ware.' His works have not been identified so far, but it has been assumed that they had the reddish stoneware body typical of the Yi-hsing pottery and were covered with Sung glazes.[24]

The production of many varieties of Sung wares continued long after the end of the Sung period. Though the distinction of later or earlier origin is of first-rate importance to the collector, such later products can hardly be regarded as imitations, not to speak of fakes. Then there are the delicate masterpieces made in the Imperial factory in the Yung Chêng period (1723–35). The many varieties of copies and imitations of early wares and above all of their glazes which were being made in this period of refined eclecticism, were enumerated by T'ang Ying in 1729.[25] In this list appear all the famous Sung glazes, the Ju ware, excessively rare already then, Kê, Chün, Kuan, and so on. Either pieces from the Imperial Palace or recent excavations were sent to the factory as models for these imitations. Many of them do not attempt to imitate the shapes of their prototypes, but merely copy their glaze. Others have the shape as well as the glaze of their models. These pieces clearly denote that they were made in the period in which the perfection of the potter's technique attained its climax. The rendering of the originals is perfect in every respect, so that a distinction between prototype and copy is hardly possible. Of course, it would be out of place to call these peak achievements of eclecticism forgeries. But nevertheless they are highly deceptive.

Sometimes the pure white porcelain peeping out at the base of such a vessel may give a hint, but in many cases we would be in the dark had not the potters proudly affixed the reign-mark of Yung Chêng to their masterpieces. Of course the imitation of the glazes was not always fully successful, and occasionally a tendency to alter the Sung shapes to trimmer and more fluently curved outlines may be observed. This is the case with two flower-pots, one

24. R. L. Hobson, *Handbook of the Pottery and Porcelain of the Far East* (1937), p. 44.

25. Translated in R. L. Hobson, *The Later Ceramic Wares of China* (1925), pp. 63 sqq. Sir Percival David, in *Transactions of the Oriental Ceramic Society* (1936–7), p. 50.

of Chün ware and the other with the mark of Yung Chêng, both of which belonged to the Eumorfopoulos Collection. Here the eighteenth-century potter apparently thought the shape of his model too heavy for literal imitation.[26]

We have seen the full degree of perfection and deceptiveness of Yung Chêng pieces in the case of Sir Percival David's Ju-glaze bottle (*Plate*103), the late origin of which was still doubted by eminent Chinese connoisseurs even after the Yung Chêng mark had already been discovered (see above, p. 235).

A comparative exhibition modelled on the Ming exhibition of Messrs. Bluett, which would juxtapose genuine Sung porcelain with the various kinds of its imitations, would prove most enlightening and clarify a subject which is still imperfectly known.[26a]

Ming.

European collectors were initiated to early Chinese pottery at a late date. As the late Mr. Eumorfopoulos tells in the preface to the catalogue of his famous collection, Ming wares of the more conspicuous types and mostly of rougher make became known only in the first decade of the twentieth century. T'ang ceramics were first brought to Europe in 1909, Sung wares in the second decade, and the delicate Imperial Ming table porcelain, which has now become the almost exclusive ambition of the collector of Ming, appeared only after 1920. But with the exception of the T'ang ceramics, which only became known when the tombs began to be excavated, all these wares were eagerly collected and cherished in China and Japan. Consequently they were copied and imitated and possibly even intentionally forged, from the sixteenth century onwards. The imitations of the seventeenth and eighteenth centuries have been mentioned because of the problem of inscriptions. Even now, when the Western market has finally been developed, the monopoly of forgeries has not been shifted from the East, as Chinese and Japanese forgers work not only more cheaply but also more efficiently than European potters.

26. Burlington Fine Arts Club, *Catalogue of a Collection of Counterfeits* (1924), no. 80, pl. 43. R. L. Hobson, *The Eumorfopoulos Collection,* vol. 6, pl. 36.

26a. This was written in 1948. Such an exhibition was held in London: *Ju and Kuan wares* (1952). H. M. Garner, in *The Burlington Magazine,* vol. 94 (1952), p. 351.

While at the beginning the Ming wares collected in Europe be-longed for the greater part to the larger, and somewhat coarser vases, flower-pots, etc., which partly originated from provincial factories, nowadays interest has been focused on the Imperial wares of Kingtehchen. The variety of shapes and decoration of the table porcelain made for the Imperial Court is comparatively small, the predominant shapes being plates and bowls, but just these re-current types were the favourites of Eastern collectors from the very beginning, a fact which caused excellent copies to be made that may only be distinguished from their prototypes by the very subtlest of differences.

As has been said above, a number of the most perfect of these copies of bowls and plates bear the K'ang Hsi or the Ch'ien Lung reign-mark. It is generally assumed therefore, that really fine and deceptive copies, either with or without spurious Ming reign-marks, belong to the same period and were also made at the Imperial factory. In some cases the shape and make, and particu-larly the hues of the underglaze blue corroborate a K'ang Hsi or Ch'ien Lung origin, but the general attribution of efficient copies after Ming porcelain to such early and august sources may after all be, at least in part of the cases, a slight euphemism, comparable to the general tendency of attributing all copies of ancient Chinese bronzes to the Sung period.

It would be a grave mistake to assume that copies from the K'ang Hsi period are technically inferior to their Ming prototypes. Quite the contrary, the technique of porcelain-making has been brought to a climax of flawless perfection going beyond the aims of the Ming potters. The minor irregularities of shape, glaze, and colouring which are particularly dear to the true lover of Ming have been banished from the later reproductions.

A. D. Brankston gives an excellent definition of these subtle changes:[27] 'The glaze of the K'ang-Hsi piece is smooth and regular, the body is exactly moulded to shape, and the colour chalk white. The Yung-lo piece carries more of the character of the man who made it. The body undulates slightly, the glaze is thicker in some parts than in others, and is of a solid rich texture. The colour varies in different specimens from cream-white to an icy blue-

27. *Early Ming Wares of Chingtechen* (1938), p. 9.

103.
Bottle with Ju glaze.
Period of Yung-chêng
(1723–35). (By cour-
tesy of Sir Percival
David, Bart.)

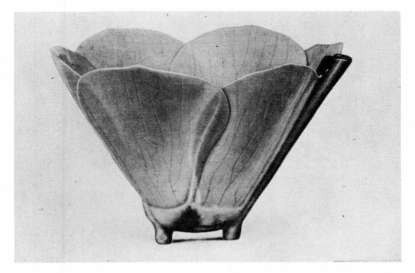

104. Magnolia-shaped wine-cup. Modern Chinese.

105. Majolica dish by Torquato Castellani (1871).

106. Back of the dish shown in Plate 105.

grey tone, according to the firing conditions. Under the foot the glaze where thin is oxydised to a faint golden yellow, while the base of the K'ang-Hsi piece is of a uniform white. The foot-rim of the Ming piece is almost invariably finished with a knife, that is, cut to leave a flat surface, neither wedge-shaped nor rounded. The Ch'ing potters preferred a rounded foot-rim, which appears to have been smoothed with the finger or a brush while the paste was still soft.'

Some years ago Messrs. Bluett conceived the happy idea of organising a loan exhibition where genuine Ming pieces and later copies closely resembling them, were shown together. The results of the exhibition have been laid down in an excellently commented illustrated catalogue.[28]

Plate 104 shows a magnolia-shaped wine-cup which caused some commotion some years ago when it was acclaimed as a Ch'êng Hua (1465–87) piece.[29] The cup consists of six yellow leaves and a straight brown stalk running alongside two of the petals. The whole rests on three short yellow feet. The kinship of this vessel with a K'ang Hsi water-dropper illustrated by R.L. Hobson[30] is evident. The K'ang Hsi magnolia looks like a real flower. The stalk is of realistic design, and as it is a real water-spout it rises above the level of the petals. On the 'Ming' magnolia the stalk is smaller and straighter. It is now neither a real stalk nor a spout. When this yellow magnolia-cup turned up, it was argued that it was of thinner porcelain, and of more delicate workman-ship than the K'ang Hsi specimen, and must therefore date from the golden age of Chinese porcelain. It soon lost its unique posi-tion when an identical piece turned up, and shortly afterwards the modern Chinese factory became known that turned out these clever imitations. It is not without interest to note the source from which the defenders of the magnolia-cup derived their arguments. It is no other than the album of Pseudo-Hsiang, where plate 49 represents what purports to be a magnolia-cup from the period of Ch'êng Hua. This is an elaborate affair, many-coloured and of complicated shape, resting on a knobbly stem which ends in

28. E. E. Bluett, *Ming and Ch'ing Porcelains* (1933).
29. *Ostasiatische Zeitschrift*, vol. 19 (1933), pp. 71 sqq.
30. *The Later Ceramic Wares of China* (1925), pl. 48.

three most fragile but spiky leaves. No cup could ever have stood on such a foot, nor could anybody have drunk out of it without either breaking it or being pricked by its more salient protrusions.[31]

Ch'ing.

European interest for Chinese porcelain was created by the wares of the Ch'ing dynasty (1644–1908), which were not only imported directly after they had been made, but of which large numbers were specially made for this very export trade. There is no need to stress that these porcelains are usually far from being of first-rate quality. While any vessel of Chinese porcelain has been treasured when it reached the West, an event recurring with increasing frequency since the Renaissance, the forming of important collections began only near the end of the seventeenth century. Then the coveted wares were mainly contemporary and such earlier pieces as may occasionally have come along with them slipped in by chance.

To say that Ch'ing wares were faked in Europe from the eighteenth century onwards would be an understatement, as the manufacture of European china is nothing but a protracted attempt at faking Chinese porcelain, with the aim of diverting to European manufactures some of the money spent on imported ware. Though one can hardly regard this as something unlawful, the early history of the imitation of Chinese porcelain, or rather the invention of china in Europe, was accompanied by every symptom consistent with piracy and fraud. The precious secrets of the problematic kaolin mixture were anxiously guarded, in many cases by the simple means of depriving the craftsmen of their liberty, with the frequent result that they escaped to trade their secrets at another court. In the artistic field designs were pirated all over Europe. Yet this chaotic state of things not only led to the flourishing of European china in general, but produced some most deceptive copies of Chinese wares which may occasionally escape recogni-

31. R. L. Hobson (*The Wares of the Ming Dynasty* (1923), p. 78) says on the subject of this cup and of the Chrysanthemum (Hsiang fig. 65): 'These two pieces are absurdities as shown in the Album. Neither of them could be used for drinking and the magnolia cup could not be made to stand up by any natural method.'

tion even nowadays, if they have not been stamped with a European factory mark. A greatly admired group of porcelain peacocks belonging to the Royal Palace in Munich was to be included among the treasures of the great Exhibition of Chinese Art held in Berlin in 1929. At the last moment the caduceus mark was discovered, proving the peacocks to be a product of Meissen.[32]

European fakes of the nineteenth century are usually less delicate of make. The objects chosen by the forgers were naturally those most coveted by the collectors of their time, namely the richly decorated K'ang-Hsi and Ch'ien Lung ware. Powder-blue vases, *famille noire*, and above all *famille rose* were favourites with the china forgers as well as with the collectors. But the imitations hardly reach the standard even of second-rate Chinese originals. The chief fault of the forgers was that they usually failed to enter deeply enough into the peculiar Chinese way of designing. Although many of the prototypes are mere routine work, they are free from the clumsiness and everyday commonness of their European imitations. In the Exhibition of Forgeries organised by the Burlington Fine Arts Club in 1924 a genuine *famille rose* plate was shown along with an European forgery based on it.[33] It shows in the centre a scroll with two cocks, while the rim is decorated with four landscapes alternating with flowers. The forger simplified his task by leaving out the landscape panels. The main and fundamental difference lies, however, in the treatment of the flowers and animals. The Chinese plate is not a great work of art, but only of average quality. But the Chinese craftsman has been trained in the great tradition of Far Eastern art with its penetrating observation of nature. The birds and flowers of the original are painted with the sureness of the brush-stroke which we constantly admire in Chinese and Japanese art. In the European imitation the two cocks show incompetent draughtsmanship and the flowers have become clumsy little bunches of leaves in which stem and petals can no longer be distinguished.

32. A. Hausladen, *Köstlichkeiten aus dem Münchner Residenzmuseum* (1922), p. 92 sq. O. Kümmel, in *Zeitschrift für bildende Kunst*, vol. 62 (1928–9), p. 263.

33. Burlington Fine Arts Club, *Catalogue of a Collection of Counterfeits* (1924), no. 73, pl. 42.

EUROPEAN POTTERY AND PORCELAIN

Majolica.

It is very unlikely that Italian majolica was forged before the nineteenth century.[1] The old technique had gradually died out and made way for the new fashion of porcelain. Such little interest in Italian pottery as existed was mainly caused by a curious legend according to which Raphael himself decorated majolica vases. In the later eighteenth and in the early nineteenth century a few collectors—Goethe among them—bought majolica dishes; it was, however, only about 1850 that majolica became the craze. Collectors put the modest productions of the potter's art on a level with the works of the great Renaissance painters and sculptors, and were willing to pay any price for rare pieces.

Simultaneously serious attempts were made in Italy and elsewhere to revive the lost majolica technique, attempts forming part of the wider movement which tried to reform the applied arts by a return to the old methods of craftsmanship. Outstanding among the Italian potters of the nineteenth century was Torquato Castellani (b. 1846).[2] He was one of the younger members of the famous Castellani family of collectors, art dealers and imitators. His grandfather Fortunato Pio Castellani (1793–1865) rediscovered the forgotten ancient Etruscan technique of granulation (above, p. 209), his father Alessandro, an art dealer, was the owner of a famous collection of majolica which was sold by auction in 1878.

Plate 105 shows one of Torquato Castellani's works. It was certainly not intended as a forgery as it is signed and dated—16th March 1871—on the back (*Plate* 106).[3] In style it corresponds to nineteenth-century paintings showing Quattrocento youths in profile. Enlightened by the circumstantial signature on the back

1. There is one possible exception. A faience dish in the Stuttgart Museum, of German workmanship and dating from the seventeenth century, shows on the back the date 1546. Pazaurek (*Hausmaler,* 1925, p. 66) regarded it as an early forgery of Italian majolica.

2. G. Corona, *La Ceramica* (1885), p. 220.

3. L. Planiscig and E. Kris, *Ausstellung Gefälschte Kunstwerke* (Vienna, 1937), no. 8.

of the dish, one is inclined to think that this young man could never be seriously deceptive. Quite apart from the head, the trellis pattern filling part of the background and the two strange flowers appearing on both sides of the head seem to exclude all error. Yet a vase that was in a famous collection of Italian majolica shows an exact replica of the head, complete with trellis and flowers. Certainly Castellani and his colleagues signed not more than a percentage of their works.

This dish exemplifies a characteristic turn in the collectors' taste. For the older generation the masterpieces of Italian ceramic were the rich mythological compositions of Urbino dishes. This 'Rafaello Ware', as it was called, receded into the background as soon as the vogue for portraits started. We have observed the same fashion in connexion with Quattrocento paintings where the demand for portraits created such a flood of imitations that the genuine examples are now definitely in the minority (see p. 51).

Some comparatively early forgeries show portraits of famous men. Best known of these is a dish in the Musée Cluny at Paris on which the Uffizi portrait of Raphael appears in a slightly embellished version.[4] Such copies of famous paintings are never found on genuine majolica. The majolica painters usually worked from engravings and only rarely did they copy paintings. In these cases they always adapted their prototype to the exigencies of their material and technique. The idea of copying famous pictures on dishes is typical of the porcelain manufactures of the eighteenth and nineteenth centuries. It is an open question whether the Raphael dish—and a similar dish in London (*Plate* 107)—are out and out fakes, or whether somebody used a genuine old dish, scraping off its centre decoration and repainting and refiring it.

It goes without saying that the series of 'beauties', busts of young ladies decorating the inside of dishes made at Deruta and Gubbio, has been augmented in numbers by the modern Italian majolica artists. As early as 1885 an Italian author poked fun at the endless series of Renaissance ladies the beauty of which, if not

4. H. Delange, *Recueil de faiences italiennes* (1869), pl. 73. E. Hannover, *Pottery and Porcelain* (ed. by B. Rackham, vol. 1, 1925), fig. 179. B. Rackham, *Catalogue of Italian Maiolica* (1940), p. 322.

always obvious, was at least guaranteed by the inscriptions on the scrolls—*Maddalena bella, Gentile bella, Camilla bella,* etc.[5]

Albarelli adorned with portraits are a favourite variety of nineteenth-century majolica. One fails to understand why apothecary jars should be decorated with portraits of young men or pretty ladies but the predilection for this type of decoration overruled such reasoning. Occasionally the whole length of an *albarello* of the tall type has been filled with the bust of a lady in profile whose proportions had to be distorted accordingly.[6] On one of these pieces the portrait was combined with a pattern of peacock feathers derived from a prototype dating from the late fifteenth century. However, the lady's profile has been shaded with blue, in a way not practised in the fifteenth century. Moreover the painter did not succeed in outlining the profile with one bold line, as it is done on genuine pieces. There is a blue *pentimento* denoting his first mistaken attempt.

At the beginning of our century collectors suddenly turned their interest towards 'primitive' majolica, that is the Tuscan wares of the fourteenth and early fifteenth century. The charm of their simplicity was now being rediscovered. A large proportion of the originals were, however, fragments brought to light by excavation and the complete vessels had to be made new to order. The originals were not within easy reach of the forgers who had to glean their inspiration from the plates of illustrated publications. An example is a jug formerly in the Beckerath Collection, one of the first assemblages of early majolica.[7] It is rather literally copied from an illustration in an Italian book on majolica but the rich decoration of the prototype has been reduced to the solitary figure of a grotesque animal. It was a grave mistake on the part of the forger to concentrate on this single figure. For the medieval craftsman these fantastic animals belonged to the everyday language of art. The modern imitator had no means of grasping

5. G. Corona, *La Ceramica* (1885), p. 62.

6. Burlington Fine Arts Club, *Catalogue of a Collection of Counterfeits* (1924), no. 157, pl. 48.

7. *Die Majolica-Sammlung A. von Beckerath* (Sale Berlin, Lepke, November 4, 1913), no. 7, pl. 1. F. Argnani, *Le ceramiche e maioliche faentine* (1889), pl. 7, fig. 3. O. v. Falke, *Die Majolikasammlung Pringsheim* (1914), p. 25.

the vigour and liveliness of Gothic animal ornamentation, and painted what these creatures seemed to him to be: a badly drawn and misshapen form.

Palissy and German Stoneware.

In our day, when the simple shapes of Sung porcelain have become the ideals of contemporary pottery, it is perhaps not easy to understand the magic appeal which the overloaded rustic wares of Palissy had on potters and collectors of the nineteenth century. But just that over-abundance of detail which may seem interesting but repulsive to the modern eye was vital to the interior decoration of the last century. Moreover, the individuality of Bernard Palissy, his romantic biography, and the fact that his pottery was his personal invention, made him the ideal of all ambitious French potters. Many of them passed considerable time in experiments—like their sixteenth-century prototype—in the hope of achieving a similar success.[8] This was finally attained by Jean Charles Avisseau (1796–1861). After he had experimented for years, his 'Palissy wares' achieved a fame proportionate to his pains. His imitations of Palissy originals are fairly accurate and deceptive. The distinction between old and new pieces is rendered more difficult by the fact that there are no authenticated wares from Bernard Palissy's own hand and that his works were imitated and multiplied by his immediate followers. A huge decoration piece, at the Musée de la Reine Bérengère of Le Mans, which is crowded with reptiles, amphibious animals, and vegetables, makes it seem likely that J. Ch. Avisseau was rather inclined to overdo the effects derived from his models. This table-centre is an early Avisseau. It bears the signature 'Avisseau à Tours 1845'. Jean Charles Avisseau, his son Édouard, and George Pull were the first imitators, but with the progress of the nineteenth century Palissy was fervently imitated by many potters and factories inside and outside France.

At the same time as Palissy ware, German stoneware came back into fashion. As the nineteenth century advanced a row of stone-

8. See the chapter on the 'Revival of the Art of Faience Painting' in M. L. Solon, *A History and Description of the Old French Faience* (1903), pp. 151 sqq.

ware jugs had to adorn the shelf of every German dresser. The cheaper varieties of these wares are less deceptive than the cheap 'Palissy' pieces. No attempt was made to imitate either the clay or the effects of the exceptionally long period of firing in the kiln, or the salt glaze. Only a general imitation of the shapes and types of decoration was being sought. But apart from this innocuous mass production, there are the products of the skill of a number of individual potters who sought, with a zeal akin to that shown by the followers of Palissy, to revive the ancient craft.[9] Such pieces are ambitious in every respect. They are not copies of genuine wares but free variations, in shape as well as in decoration, and their pretensions are expressed by elaborate, dated inscriptions. There exists, for instance, a colossal jug by one Peter Löwenich of Siegburg (b. 1787, d. 1845) which bears not less than three sixteenth-century dates (1547, 1559, and 1592). As little reason is given for this affluence of dates as for the representation of Jeanne d'Arc, the 'Magden von Orlians' as she is called on the inscription of this jug.[10]

Joan of Arc and her history offer irresistible temptations to the imaginative forger. We had occasion to mention some forged illuminations.[11] But examples can be found in almost every technique. I shall take this opportunity to describe a few examples which, though they take us away from the stoneware, show the strange fancies a favourite subject could beget in the forgers' minds. Of particular charm is an ivory statuette which opens in the style of the *Vierges ouvrantes*,[12] with the difference that Joan's opened body is supported by her sturdy armoured legs. Inside, her martyrdom is represented in relief. Another pleasing invention should not pass unmentioned. During her trial Joan of Arc mentioned an armour which she had dedicated to the Church of Saint Denis. This gift seems to have disappeared at an early date. In the early nineteenth century someone tried to make up for the loss. He adorned the venerable Abbey of Saint Denis with a monumental brass, showing the armour and a couple of axes with an

9. A. Walcher-Molthein, in *Belvedere*, vol. 5 (1924), 'Forum', pp. 37 sqq.

10. *Belvedere*, vol. 5 (1924), 'Forum', p. 38, figs. 1–2.

11. See above, p. 91.

12. See above, p. 168.

explanatory inscription in what he thought to be fifteenth-century French: 'Ce que estait le harnais de Jehanne par elle baille en hommage à monseigneur Saint Denis.' With the passage of time this brass plate became accepted as an authentic and contemporary memorial of Saint Joan, and in the long run it advanced to a national monument, shown to every visitor. This went on till the spell was broken by Mr. Ffoulkes who took the trouble to investigate the origin of this brass.[13] The armour is copied after a Milanese armour of the sixteenth century which had been connected with Joan of Arc at an early date. It is now in the Musée de l'Artillerie at Paris. The models for the two weapons at its side are in the same collection: an English pole-axe of the fifteenth century and a Bohemian axe dating from the seventeenth century.

Porcelain.

In the field of European ceramics of the eighteenth century everything was imitated by everybody, and beginning from the fact that the whole of the European china manufacture is an open attempt at faking Chinese porcelain the whole history of the craft is a series of mutual betrayals of professional secrets and of the wholesale stealing of ideas and inventions. As soon as one factory, be it Meissen, Sèvres, or Wedgwood, produced a novel and successful shape or colour scheme, it was pirated by as many factories as wanted to partake in its success. Small manufactures even copied the marks of renowned factories along with their wares. The state of things created by these quite general practices is so complicated that it can hardly be gone into outside a special history of the craft. Nor did these habits change with the nineteenth century; the imitation of everything, old and new, remained as usual as ever. Thus the delimitations between degrees and qualities of imitations and of deliberate modern forgeries are necessarily blurred.

A point of great importance in the detection of fakes is the paste. This applies in particular to English porcelain of the eigh-

13. *Burlington Magazine,* vol. 16 (1909–10), pp. 141 sqq. C. Buttin, in *Mémoires de la Société Nationale des Antiquaires de France,* 8th series, vol. 2 (1913), pp. 1 sqq.

teenth century which mostly consists of 'soft paste' (not kaolinic) and shows considerable variety. To quote Mr. Rackham: 'The old porcelains were a complicated composition of which the constituents in many cases have been deduced only by analysis, and which it would be virtually impossible to reproduce with exactness. Hence a practised eye and touch can generally tell the difference between the old steatite porcelain of Worcester, for instance, and French fakes which are sometimes apparently of kaolinic hard paste, and always very different.' In *Analysed Specimens of English Porcelain* (1922), Herbert Eccles and Bernard Rackham have published the results of their investigations. Hardly anything on these lines has been done regarding continental porcelain. Here, however, research is far less promising as the true kaolinic porcelain is apparently of far more uniform composition. Regarding English porcelain, the exhaustive paper on 'Reproductions and Fakes of English Eighteenth Century Ceramics' by Wallace Elliot, in Volume 2 of the *Transactions of the English Ceramic Circle* (1939), should be consulted.

In the following I wish to mention a few examples coming under these categories: (1) fraudulent copies, (2) reproductions of their early models, made by still-existing factories, (3) total forgeries.

The frequent occurrence of spurious marks is not surprising. More surprising is the indiscriminate use that has been made of them. Often the style of the porcelain and the factory mark have little in common. Thus a Cleopatra group in early Meissen style bears the mark of the Vienna factory.[14] The figure was copied from one of the groups of Muses modelled in 1745 by Kaendler for Frederick the Great. Kaendler himself described the Muse in a list of his works as 'Melpomene who invented the tragedies, represented as she sits, sinking to the ground and with a dagger in her right hand'.[15] The forger changed the Muse into Cleopatra

14. *Fortrolig Fortegnelse over en Raekke Forfalskninger* (Exhibition Copenhagen, 1915), no. 105, pl. 30.

15. M. A. Pfeiffer, in *Werden und Wirken, ein Festgruss K. W. Hiersemann zugesandt* (1924), p. 282. O. v. Falke, *Katalog C. H. Fischer* (Sale Cologne, 1906), no. 446, pl. 35. E. Zimmermann, *Sammlung C. H. Fischer* (1918), no. 111, pl. 16.

107. Nineteenth-century forgery of an Italian majolica dish. (By courtesy of the Director of the Victoria and Albert Museum.)

108 and 109. Forgery of a Sèvres porcelain vase. English, about 1860.
(By courtesy of the Director of the Victoria and Albert Museum.)

with the snake. Melpomene's theatrical gesture with the dagger apparently suggested to him the idea of suicide.

In some cases the famous old wares are still being turned out in the same factories where they were originally invented. Among the porcelain figures modelled by Kaendler in 1743 is one representing a 'Freemason clad in his apron, with the proper attributes, well dressed, standing on a base, with a ground plan in one hand, by his side a pedestal on which are lying a square, a level, a pair of compasses, a plumb-rule and so forth.'[16] There exists a rare old version of this figure, with a pug dog sitting on the ground in place of the pedestal with the instruments. This dog is supposed to be an allusion to a rival masonic institution, the *Mopsorden*. In the nineteenth century the factory of Meissen produced a new version of the 'Freemason', the main figure being formed from the old mould but the accessories altered to combine both the original versions.[17] The copyist had the curious idea to place the dog on top of the pedestal. This arrangement looks absurd enough, but in order to gain more space the pedestal had to be pushed back so that it overhangs the main base, thus destroying the balance of the group.

The costly porcelain ware of Sèvres has been counterfeited to an even greater extent than Meissen. The imitations from the middle of the nineteenth century clearly indicate the then prevailing taste. What people admired in Sèvres porcelain, and what the forgers copied, were the sumptuous shapes and the rich gaudy colours; what they neglected was the delicate draughtsmanship of the paintings which are as good as the best works of the contemporary miniaturists. A typical example is a vase with *bleu de roi* ground and the Sèvres mark which came to the Victoria and Albert Museum with the Jones Collection, so rich in genuine pieces (*Plates* 108–109).[18] At first sight the vase looks convincing. However, a glance at the paintings reveals that they cannot have been executed in the time of Boucher and Fragonard. 'Amor and

16. *Werden und Wirken, ein Festgruss K. W. Hiersemann zugesandt* (1924), p. 276. E. Zimmermann, *Meissner Porzellan* (1926), fig. 56.

17. O. Pelka, in *Die Weltkunst*, vol. 6 (31 July 1932), p. 3. O. Posner, *Bilder zur Geschichte der Freimaurerei* (1927), p. 111.

18. E. S. Auscher, *A History and Description of French Porcelain* (1905), pl. 22. Victoria and Albert Museum, *Catalogue of the Jones Collection*, vol. 2 (1924), p. 36.

Psyche' clearly reflect the academic art of the nineteenth century in spite of an unsuccessful attempt to give Psyche certain *rococo* airs. As Mr. King has pointed out, the shape of the vase corresponds exactly to one shown at the Great Exhibition of 1862 by the Coalport Factory.[19] There can be no reasonable doubt that the vase of the Jones Collection is likewise a product of Coalport. We learn, moreover, from the historian of this factory that 'very successful copies of the Sèvres and Chelsea have also been at one time or other produced, and on these the marks of those makers have also been copied.'[20] As in so many cases, the borderline between imitation of a past style and forgery is rather indistinct. The same factory produced two similar vases. One was publicly exhibited as the product of Coalport and was awarded a gold medal for the successful imitation of Sèvres; the other, sold as the genuine article, proved how well the imitation had succeeded.

There is one important point which, though usually not coupled with any fraudulent intention, should be mentioned here. This is the repairing of damaged pottery. Many pieces which look complete and undamaged to the naked eye reveal their secrets under the ultra-violet lamp. A piece may have been broken and put together again, the cracks being then concealed by paint. Or it may be a fragment, the missing portions of which were replaced by plaster and painted and varnished to imitate the colouring and glaze of the original fragments. In both cases the ultra-violet lamp will not only show up the cracks and new portions but it will also show to what extent the painting has covered the genuine parts. While the glaze of pottery remains dark, plaster is brilliantly fluorescent, and the colours and varnish shine out in a yellowish hue from the purple ground of the old pieces. These things are clearly visible under the quartz lamp, but they are frequently so well done as to be invisible even on close examination in neutral light.[21]

19. *Art Journal, Catalogue of the International Exhibition* (1862), p. 29. L. Jewitt, *The Ceramic Art of Great Britain* (1883), fig. 617.

20. L. Jewitt, op. cit., p. 174. C. MacKenzie, *The House of Coalport* (1951), pp. 74, 79, 82.

21. J. J. Rorimer, *Ultra-violet Rays and Their Use in the Examination of Works of Art* (1931), pp. 31 sqq. M. Pease, in *The Metropolitan Museum of Art Bulletin*, vol. 16 (1957–58), pp. 236–240 (an instructive example of the use of ultra-violet light and radiography).

PART FOURTEEN

GLASS

PART FOURTEEN

GLASS

LATE ANTIQUE GILDED GLASS

The antique technique of gilded glass consists of gold leaf spread over an even surface. Designs are incised into this with a needle by erasing the gold and letting the glass shine through. The picture so obtained is covered by a layer of colourless glass. This technique was in particularly high favour with the early Christians. Many of the original pieces formed the bottoms of glass vessels, of which, however, they alone have been preserved in most cases, and frequently only in a more or less fragmentary condition.

They began to be sought after when the catacombs were being excavated on a larger scale, and as early as 1759 one of the founders of modern archaeology, Comte de Caylus, had occasion to say:[1] 'This technique [of gilded glass] has been re-invented at Rome, only a few years ago. I had the opportunity of examining some specimens which are very well done: one has utilised this device to dupe foreigners, but the man in possession of this little secret died without publishing it.'

When early Christian gilded glasses began to be studied systematically in the nineteenth century, Caylus' vague reference to forgeries caused a minor panic among scholars. Perfectly genuine glasses came thus to be suspected and in particular some masterly portraits of a quality high above the average production were for a long time regarded as eighteenth-century imitations. Only in comparatively recent times have they been restored to their rightful place in the history of Roman art.[2]

1. *Recueil d'antiquités*, vol. 3 (1759), p. 195.
2. C. Albizzati, in *Roemische Mitteilungen*, vol. 29 (1914), pp. 240 sqq.

There are, however, some real forgeries. Two faked glass medallions have been tentatively connected with the forger 'who died without revealing the secret' which, incidentally, was no secret at all in the time of Caylus, for the technique was used in Bohemia for the *Zwischengoldgläser*, tumblers, on which designs in gold or silver leaf are enclosed between two layers of glass.[3] The Metropolitan Museum now preserves the two glass medallions in question as examples of forged gilded glass.[4] It is not quite certain whether they are really eighteenth-century forgeries or perhaps of more recent make. They are rather different from each other. One shows the bust of a king who looks as if he had come straight out of a pantomime, accompanied by a second bust which seems to be floating in the air. The design is extremely naive and does not aim at the imitation of any particular style. The forger of the second glass had some vague idea that early Christian art was rigid and hieratic. He can hardly be blamed for excessive naturalism. The figures on his medallion—two bearded men with two boys in front—are stiff as mummies and their wide open eyes stare glassily at the spectator. The monogram of Christ appears in the centre but it is hardly recognisable, as one half of the X has been omitted.

Though ridiculous in themselves these attempts to match the style of early Christian art look genuine enough if compared with a group of painted glasses said to have been found in the catacombs of Rome. Their maker avoided the intricate and difficult technique of engraving on gold leaf. He was content to paint with gold and enamel colours, a technique never found on genuine pieces. He was not concerned with early Christian style or subject matter but chose his motifs at random. In spite of all their shortcomings these glasses have deceived some collectors and will probably do so in future.

ISLAMIC ENAMELLED GLASS

Islamic enamelled glass lamps were copied with high accuracy and without fraudulent purpose by Joseph Brocard, a skilful

3. R. Schmidt, *Das Glas* (1922), p. 365. W. B. Honey, in *The Connoisseur*, vol. 92 (1933), p. 379.

4. *The Art Bulletin*, vol. 9 (1926–7), p. 353, figs. 5, 6.

French glass-maker. He worked around the sixties and seventies of the last century. Signed pieces by him are being preserved, for instance, in the British Museum, in the Musée Arabe of Cairo, and in the Oesterreichisches Museum of Vienna.[5] However, be it that Brocard did not sign all the vessels he made or that the signatures later disappeared, a number of his lamps have become mixed up almost inextricably with the originals. His copies are of such minute exactitude that it is understandable if a certain uneasiness prevails among students of Islamic glass. Brocard's copies have, moreover, never been properly studied and compared with their prototypes. During the lifetime of their maker they were much admired and collected, but to-day they share the fate of all the imitations produced by the retrospective movement and are relegated to the cellars of the great museums.

Some years ago an enamelled glass lamp turned up; according to its inscription it had been made for an unnamed child of Nâṣir al-dîn Muḥammad, son of Arghun al-Nâṣirî, Viceroy of Egypt (died in 1330 or 1331). In spite of a certain sober regularity, this lamp looked highly convincing at first sight, but two eminent Islamic scholars recognised its modern origin.[6] The imitator's task was twofold: he had to produce a lamp of convincing shape and decoration and, at the same time, he had to provide a suitable inscription. He avoided copying an existing lamp and preferred to combine motifs taken from the rather limited range of ornaments used on the genuine pieces. The crucial problem was, however, the inscription. Here the dangers of an error—philological, historical or calligraphic—were too numerous, therefore he preferred to make a literal copy of an existing inscription and gave himself away by his faithful reproduction of all the individual

5. B. Bucher, *Die Glassammlung des K. K. Osterreichisches Museums* (1888), pp. 31, 52. C. J. Lamm, *Mittelalterliche Gläser und Steinschnittarbeiten* (1930), index, p. 547. L. Rosenthal, *La verrerie française depuis cinquante ans* (1927), p. 8, pl. 2.

6. P. Ravaisse, *Une lampe sépulcrale en verre émaillé* (1931). Reviews by L. A. Mayer (*Journal of the Palestine Oriental Society*, vol. 13 (1933), p. 115), and G. Wiet (*Syria*, vol. 14 (1933), pp. 203 sqq.). A lamp by Brocard in the Musée Céramique at Sèvres shows an identical inscription (E. Bayard, *L'art de reconnaître les fraudes* (1914), p. 197, fig. 84).

peculiarities of his model. Thus he repeated the curious division of the word *walad* and copied a word written vertically by a whim of the calligrapher. Moreover, he included a blazon with a cup in his decoration, which he probably regarded as a fitting ornament as it frequently occurs on Islamic lamps. But as it does not appear on the other lamps dedicated by Arghun's grandson, it cannot have been his coat of arms. This lamp is said to have been discovered in the loft of a French château where it lay buried underneath a heap of onions.

STAINED GLASS

Stained glass is not only fragile, but also subject to the vicissitudes of climate and season, to which the outside of glass windows is inevitably exposed. Decay and breakages necessitate periodical repairs, including re-leading and the replacement of broken or ruined portions. The admiring spectator rarely is aware how much of what he sees on a cathedral window is not a masterpiece of medieval art but is actually due to later or even to recent repairs.

From the very beginning these patchings had to conform more strictly to their genuine surroundings than restorations of any other kind. But though it is hard work to distinguish anything clearly on a church window in its original position, such repairs as were carried out in periods when glass-painting was still a live art are betrayed by some trait proper to the style of their time. Principally, later glass is fundamentally different from the medieval metal, and the higher degree of its translucency often betrays its presence, even at first sight.

It is considerably more difficult to distinguish medieval stained glass from modern panels or windows made of 'antique glass' specially fabricated for the purpose of matching early glass-paintings. But still more dangerous than this technical mimicry is the retrospective approach to medieval art engendered by the Gothic Revival. The congenial restorations of the nineteenth century put many riddles to the student of French cathedral sculpture, but to the student of French cathedral windows they become baffling. For medieval glass-painting observed more fixed rules and was considerably more restricted in its means of expression than medieval sculpture. Hence it is not only easier to master its language correctly, but the danger of slips into modernism is considerably diminished.

Viollet-le-Duc, the architect and archaeologist, who played such a leading part in the Gothic Revival of France, felt justifiably proud of the restorations of cathedral glass carried out under his supervision: 'Everybody knows of the attempts made during the last thirty years to give new splendour to the art of glass-painting. Our glass-makers have occasionally produced excellent pasticcios. They have succeeded in completing old windows with such perfect imitations that one is unable to distinguish their restorations from the ancient parts. It follows from this that they have gained ample knowledge of the making of stained glass, regarding as well the technique as the artistic qualities required for this kind of painting. Among these "facsimiles" the following deserve to be quoted as the most remarkable examples: the panels for the restoration of the windows in the Sainte-Chapelle, executed by Messrs. Lusson and Steinheil, those of the twelfth-century windows at Saint-Denis, made by M. A. Gérente, the restoration of the stained glass of Bourges and Le Mans, done by M. Coffetier.'[7]

What was the pride of Viollet-le-Duc mars our pleasure in medieval glass, and the more so as we are justified in assuming that the laudable skill of these worthy glass-makers was not applied exclusively to restorations. But however deceptive such imitations may be when we look at the dazzling colours of the translucent window-panes, there exists after all a safer means to distinguish old and new. This is the corrosion of old glass, which covers the outside of most stained-glass windows with a kind of iridescent film. There are circumstances which may prevent corrosion but such cases are rare, and its absence is always a good reason for suspicion. Sometimes, however, the surface of genuine old glass has been cleaned, thus removing the patina.

The effects of natural corrosion are varied. They cause constant surprises to the scientist. This is mainly due to three reasons: the composition of the glass is by no means uniform, nor is the degree to which the colours have been fired, and thirdly the atmos-

7. *Dictionaire raisonné de l'architecture*, vol. 9 (1868), p. 384.

spheric influences work differently in every single case, according to the climate of the place and the location of the window. The reasons for corrosion are the influence of air, weather, and, in a minor degree, of micro-organisms. It is a gradual destruction of the surface of the glass, which becomes uneven and pitted. There are no simple rules by which this process can be defined.[8] This is unlucky for the connoisseur, but it is also fortunate, for up to now forgers have not succeeded in devising an effective substitute for centuries of exposure. The scars obtained by the application of hydro-fluoric acid are highly characteristic and can be distinguished from natural corrosion if the glass is examined under the microscope.[9] Attempts at imitating the holes of corrosion by sprinkling dark enamel colour with a brush on the back of the glass, are described by J. A. Knowles.[10] This sounds reminiscent of Joni's recipe for producing spurious fly-spots for his panels (above, p. 30). But, as a matter of fact, one should be able to distinguish colour spots, which would stand out, if ever so slightly, in relief, from holes in the glass.

The problem of the Tree of Jesse window in the Abbey Church of Saint-Denis is a classical example of the value of corrosion for the distinguishing of new and old portions on a medieval window. This window, which is one of the most famous specimens of early stained glass, was seriously damaged in the Revolution. But parts of it were saved and brought to Paris. After the Restoration they were returned to the abbey, to become in 1848 the objects, or rather the victims, of one of the masterly resettings praised by Viollet-le-Duc. Since then varying views have been put forward regarding the proportion of old and new parts in this Tree of Jesse, but nobody seemed to be able to decide which parts were the work of the twelfth century and which had been added in the nineteenth. It has been said that the restoration of Henri Gérente was so skilfully done that one could not recognise which parts were new, but only quite recently a scholar bent on investigating this case conceived the excellent idea of

8. On the subject of corrosion see M. Drake, *A History of English Glass-painting* (1912), pp. 155 sqq.

9. M. Drake, *A History of English Glass-painting* (1912), pl. 30, fig. 6.

10. *Journal of the Royal Society of Arts*, vol. 72 (1923–4), pp. 47 sqq.

examining the window from the outside.[11] Here the corroded old
glass stands out unmistakably from the dull surface of the new
parts. Four of the central panels and a few small fragments stand
out clearly from the rest of the window. They are covered by a
greyish coating, probably consisting of dissolved lime. This coating shows different hues, according to the colouring of the single
pieces of glass, and thus allows the design to be distinguished
while the rest of the outside of the window is completely uniform
and does not give any hint as to its decoration. The four panels
thus singled out coincide exactly with a description of the remains
of the old window, written in 1844, before the restoration had
been begun. Christ and three figures of kings are mentioned, the
Virgin having been mistaken for a king. Even the missing heads
mentioned in the manuscript which have, of course, since been
restored by Gérente, can be recognised from the outside. Everything else is new, including the portrait of the donor, Abbot Suger.
The puzzling perfection with which the style of the originals has
been matched is explained by the fact that the painters used the
Tree of Jesse at Chartres as their model.

So far the puzzles set by the achievements of the virtuous restorer. The greater part of forged stained glass consists of fraudulent copies which give, of course, the smallest amount of trouble
to the forger and offer the minimum danger of lapses. But even
here pitfalls may be lurking. For instance, in Austria in the
seventies knowledge of the fundamental rules of medieval glass-
painting was less established than in contemporary France. On
account of its historical interest a fourteenth-century glass panel
in a country church, representing Duke Albrecht of Hapsburg
with his two wives, was fraudulently copied. But the forger inadvertently changed the narrow helmet worn by his model into a
kind of royal night-cap, so as to be able to show more of the face.
This face he shaded carefully and realistically, though shading
did not become usual till a somewhat later date. He repeated the
same mistake all over his panel and rendered it still more conspicuous by the tiled floor, which is drawn in perspective, another
blatant anachronism. Minor deficiencies of the script and the coats

11. A. Watson, *The Early Iconography of the Tree of Jesse* (1934), p. 112,
pls. 24, 25. L. Grodecki, in *Bulletin monumental*, vol. 110 (1952), pp. 51–62.

of arms become negligible beside such blunders. Yet for quite a time the museum which acquired 'Duke Albrecht of Hapsburg' took just as little notice of these shortcomings as the forger.[12]

In the sixteenth century small glass panels painted in brown tones were a usual feature of the decoration of windows in private houses. Now the vogue of these panels, the most outstanding variety of which are Swiss and Flemish roundels, has almost passed. As they belong to the less costly class of antiques and the time when they were being forged most extensively was not over-critical, most of these fakes are rather carelessly done and their style clearly betrays the time of their origin. A large part of them is frankly romanticist. One of them shows a slim *landsknecht*, in an elegant but unhistorical uniform, who graciously leans on his standard, casting a fiery glance from under a cap that has been tilted at a rakish angle. Certainly this beau ranges among the more ingratiating subjects. He stands alone in the centre of a wide space of clear glass, in which two cracks have been picturesquely arranged so that they rather enhance than damage the impression created by the design.[13] The whole appearance of this hero is typical of a medievalism we had occasion to see in pictures and drawings made in the same period.[14]

VENETIAN GLASS

The average products of the glass-blower may be of the highest technical quality and admirably characteristic of their respective periods in style and design; they have, however, been designed for mass production, and, whatever their refinements, they can be adequately reproduced by skilled technicians. Thus beautiful but typical glasswares have been imitated with almost absolute per-fection, so that it becomes unusually difficult to distinguish the genuine from the spurious. There is only one guiding light of consolation. It is the forger's habitual predilection for rare and ambitious pieces. By trying to equal or even to surpass the peak

12. F. Kieslinger in *Belvedere*, vol. 6 (1924), 'Forum', pp. 1 sqq., figs. 3, 4.
13. J. A. Knowles in *The Connoisseur*, vol. 69 (1924), p. 206.
14. See above, p. 40 and p. 101.

achievements of the old craft, the forgers are liable to blunder and thus give themselves away.

A large Venetian glass dish (*Plate* 110) decorated in gold and oil colours on the under side may be taken as such an attempt. This most ornate of all techniques of the glass-houses of Murano was in use during a comparatively short period, around the middle of the sixteenth century. It was practised as a rule on large dishes which can have been used only as ornamental pieces, as the painting, not being fired, is apt to come off when handled. Specimens of this kind are rare and the temptation to augment their number led to the creation of the dish illustrated here. The forger followed the traditions established by his prototypes by dividing the bottom of his dish into medallions, surrounding a centre. Further, he followed the habit of Renaissance craftsmen, by using different prints as models for his representations. Some of these are in style, as for instance the centre, which is a copy of part of Marcantonio Raimondi's 'Quos ego', or the figure of a seated woman to the left of the top which is taken out of the 'Judgement of Paris' by the same engraver.[15] But with others he was definitely less fortunate. Above all, the lady running with windblown garments and an elongated cornucopia in her left hand is a bad but unmistakable derivation from the famous Botticellian type of the running girl. No craftsman of the High Renaissance would have thought of including such an unfashionable figure in his work. The four busts in the medallions on the rim of the dish represent more lapses into pernicious Quattrocentism, and the two naked women are more modern than anything else.

15. Bartsch nos. 245 and 352. M. Pittaluga, *L'Incisione Italiana nel Cinquecento* (1930), figs. 86, 89. The shepherd blowing a horn is copied from Benedetto Montagna's engraving, Bartsch no. 27, the *spinario* from the niello Dutuit 481.

PART FIFTEEN

FURNITURE

PART FIFTEEN

FURNITURE

Among the many things that have been written about faked furniture a book-review by Mr. A. J. Penty published in the *Architectural Review* has struck me as the most elucidating. It contains a delightful account of the author's own experiences in the antique fakers' trade, which I have pleasure in reproducing here, with the kind permission of the editor.[1]

'In the early days of my career I spent a year or so in the employ of a firm of antique fakers. It was an accident of circumstances that got me there, but it was great fun and I decided to stay for the experience. The firm I was with faked furniture. But they did not belong to the order of super-fakers who pry upon collectors and literally live by fraud. They were merely the ordinary respectable fakers who give the public what they want, and value for money. True, they sold as old, pieces of furniture that were really new, but I am of the opinion that generally speaking the public wanted to be deceived. They had come to the conclusion that to furnish with antiques was "the thing" and they were only too ready to accept anything as old on a salesman's responsibility.

'My experience of the antique trade was not in this country, but in New York. I was employed as a designer. Why should a firm of antique fakers employ designers? For two reasons. The first is that the models were not generally available to copy from, but only photographs, often very small ones taken from the illustrated papers. The designer took these photographs, improvised the details, and prepared working drawings; and only a designer familiar with the styles could do this. The other reason is peculiar to America. Designers were needed to adapt the old

1. Vol. 67, (1930), pp. 33–6.

styles to American ideas of accommodation. The accommodation of old English furniture is different from that of American furniture. In consequence, if the average American were shown a piece of genuine Chippendale, he would not buy it because it would not give the accommodation he demands. But he has read in the papers that Chippendale furniture is *the* thing and he demands Chippendale. To overcome this difficulty Chippendale has to be re-designed to adapt it to American ideas of accommodation. Sometimes this makes exceptional demands on the ingenuity of the designer, as, for instance, when he is required to design a Chippendale table with a centre leg, no precedent for which exists. For in America dining tables are mostly round. This kind of design was known among us as "Chipplewhite"—one of the firm's clients having one day asked to see specimens of that distinctive style.

'In this establishment there was no separate drawing-office. The designers worked in one of the showrooms on an upper floor. The shoppers who came in every day little suspected that the drawings upon which we were engaged would in due course make their appearance as furniture in rooms two or three hundred years old. Yet such was the case, and at times even the elect were deceived. On one occasion a Queen Anne cabinet made its appearance in the showroom. It was, within the limits of the style, an original design, and it was so skilfully faked that the manager was deceived, mistaking it for a genuine antique, and called on one of the designers to admire it, when to his amusement the designer told him he had designed it himself. (The antique trade is full of amusement, and it is recommended as a vocation for anyone who finds life rather dull.) In the showroom in which we worked lengths of oak panelling occupied the wall space. They were supposed to be parts of panelled rooms that were stored away in the warehouse, though as a matter of fact the remaining pieces did not exist. Clients who desired oak-panelled rooms were shown these specimens. When anyone of them expressed an admiration for a particular piece the salesman would address himself to one of my colleagues. "Wilkinson," he would say, "how many feet have we got of such and such a panelling?" Wilkinson would refer to a book he kept in a drawer and discover it had not been entered up, and then he would make his way to the telephone. "Is that the store-house?" he would ask. "How many feet of panelling 37d have you got?" After waiting a moment he would inform the salesman in the presence of the client that there were seventy-eight feet of it. And when the client had gone, we all joined in a good laugh.

'This ruse was very effective. When a client took the bait, the dimensions of the room were secured and a design prepared show-ing how the panelling could be adapted to fit the room. This, of course, always involved piecing out of the "old work" by a piece "faked to match", and care was taken that the "match" was not too good. Fortunately for this procedure clients rarely asked to see the remainder of the panelling which was supposed to be in stock. When they did, one excuse after another was trumped up until sufficient time elapsed for it to be made. On one occasion when a client was very insistent, the salesman had to feign illness and actually had to keep away from business until the room was made.'

Though Mr. Penty relates his personal experiences only, the antique factory he describes is by no means unique and the picture he gives of a certain kind of trade is highly characteristic, and not only for antique furniture made in the U.S.A. Hunting for old panelling to fit rooms of given measurements amounts to an almost open invitation to the faker, and one should not blame him if he is only too ready to respond to it.

The blending of artistic qualities and adaptability to the de-mands of a modern household applies to furniture alone among all kinds of antiques. It is responsible for the huge demand. This is being satisfied by the furniture makers of the whole world on a corresponding scale. From conscientious copies of fine genuine pieces to fantastic but alluring inventions 'in style', from more or less extensive restorations to the deliberate use of less valuable old pieces for forgeries, everything is being done to conduct this trade successfully.

These facts are an open secret, and though the most obvious conclusions from them are sometimes disregarded, they frequently give rise to exaggerated apprehension. But in reality the faker in-tent on producing pieces apt to stand the test of a serious examina-tion has no easy time. His primary preoccupation is invariably the

110. Glass dish painted in oil colours and gold. Imitation of Venetian Renaissance work.

111. Cupboard in Gothic style. German forgery of *c.* 1870. (By courtesy of the Germanisches Nationalmuseum, Nürnberg.)

choice of suitable materials, and here already his difficulties begin. All forgers of antique furniture are unanimous in stating that successful faking can hardly be done without genuinely old wood. Thus a modern French collection of recipes for the fabrication of faked furniture has to admit that specially prepared and artificially aged wood can never equal old wood, as no amount of faking can rival the effects of real age and genuine patina.[2] Consequently the forger is above all obliged to provide himself with old wood. Old furniture of little value serves this purpose best. But the large-scale factories of antique furniture have to cover their needs by the purchase of the beams and floor boards of demolished houses.

Owing to the predominant part they play in the minds of most purchasers of antique furniture, the forger must above all concentrate on endowing his fabrications with worm-holes. If genuine, these worm-holes are the results of the burrowing of grubs inside the wood. They devour it, leaving irregular channels filled with wood-dust in their wake. These burrows are concealed inside the wood. All that becomes visible on the surface if the decay of the wood has not reached a fatal degree, are the circular holes bored by the beetles which make their exit from the wood after emerging from the pupal stage.[3] In order to secure for his works the results of these activities of the furniture beetle the faker is constrained to use worm-eaten wood. Where he has to cut or saw it the burrows become visible, thus betraying him, as no craftsman of the old times would have dreamed of using faulty or damaged wood. But to-day this trait has been given such wide publicity by all writings dealing with the faking of furniture or with its detection, that the forgers are at least as well cautioned against the dangers of open burrows as the collectors. They are therefore careful to conceal all traces with the exception of the round exit-holes. This may be achieved either by the concealment of the open burrows in places hidden from prying eyes or by pasting them over with some suitable substance.

Though many and amusing theories have been put forward on the subject of artificial worm-holes, their successful imitation has

2. *Trucs et Procédés par un groupe de practiciens* (1929), Préface par A. Goumain, p. 72.

3. Charles J. Gahan and F. Laing, *Furniture Beetles* (1932).

so far not been achieved. The celebrated story of the shot-gun used for riddling the wood with holes, though much repeated, may be discarded as fantastical. The circular exit-holes may be imitated with a drill, but the forger cannot obtain the same effect as the grub (see also p. 300). Though it has probably been attempted, the systematic breeding of the death-watch beetle with grubs trained to feed on faked furniture has so far remained a wishful dream of furniture fakers.

It seems advisable not to attach too great importance to the simple devices by which it is generally said to be possible unfailingly to recognise false from true. The fakers are at least as alert to these signs as the collector who is anxious to avoid forgeries. If anybody feels over-confident in these hints on technique, construction, and damages, he should not omit to study the memoirs of M. André Mailfert.[4] They were written after the author had retired from a large factory of French period furniture, to the foundation and development of which he had up to then devoted his life. Though almost all those who bought furniture in his establishment were perfectly aware of its true origin, M. Mailfert was just as well aware that they did not re-sell his products as imitations. It is hardly to be expected that somebody who found such inexhaustible zest in inventing all kinds of *trucs* should all of a sudden indulge in confessions of complete sincerity. The anecdotes in which his book abounds are, to say the least, tinged with the author's humorous fantasy, and so are the exaggeratedly scientific details he gives on some technical points, like the many grades of dust collected by him for the appropriate soiling of furniture. But though the products of M. Mailfert's factory did not actually attain the places in prominent collections he claims for them, the fact remains that the large-scale production of 'antique' furniture has been taking place there for many years, and probably still continues. Nor is his the only factory of this kind. The book of recipes mentioned above is written for a wide circle of craftsmen. Moreover, there exists another little book of

4. *Au pays des antiquaires, Confidence d'un 'maquilleur' professionel* (1935). Mailfert's imitations of ancient furniture are dealt with in two illustrated articles by H. Huth in *Kunst und Künstler*, vol. 28 (1930), pp. 105 sqq., and in *Apollo*, vol. 23 (1936), pp. 200 sqq. Le Corbusier, *L'art décoratif d'aujourd'hui* (1925), pp. 58–61.

memoirs which strikes a middle course between the *Trucs et procédés* and the *Pays des antiquaires*.[5] But it is entirely devoid of the ingratiating sense of humour of the latter. In their technical conclusions all three are practically unanimous, though M. Mailfert naturally seems to be the most up to date.

A frequently recommended and seemingly simple means for the detection of forgeries consists of the examination of the runners or bottoms of drawers, which must show signs of genuine wear if the piece is antique. But alas, M. Mailfert describes with visible relish how a man may comfortably earn his wages by sitting on a stool and opening and closing each drawer of a chest a number of times sufficient to achieve the work of generations in a single day.

Hand-made and machine-made screws are another characteristic frequently employed to distinguish true from false. Machine-made screws are, of course, apt to betray the modern origin of the piece of furniture in which they are found, but it is now quite a time since the fakers have become aware of this and are consequently careful to use screws turned by hand, at least for the more valuable types of period furniture.

Then there are those countless little details cunningly devised to evoke an old-time atmosphere. Most prominent among these small characteristics of age and wear are the fly-spots. Nasty disfigurement though they are, they enjoy considerable prestige among collectors. M. Mailfert professes to go much further in the detailed imitation of the numerous grades of fly-dirt than Signor Joni. Though his classification of fly-spots appears to be an amusing hoax, he doubtless knew well how to satisfy his clients by sufficient and deceptive imitations of the activities of flies.

The impression of indubitable antiquity is enforced by many other quaint additions to spurious pieces. Dust and grime are skilfully rubbed into those places where they may be expected to gather in reality. Ink-spots are very appropriate on and inside writing cabinets. Suitable objects are forgotten in the drawers. One may find there curls or letters, an old playing card or a grimy visiting card, the latter two varieties always being genuinely antique. The completely finished piece is stained, battered and

5. Ariste Per, *Vingt ans de truquage dans le meuble ancien* (1925).

broken, and then perfunctorily repaired, in order to suggest un-skilled modern work on a piece of fine antique craftsmanship. Mailfert loved in particular to paste a number of faded tickets on to his products which bear fictitious inventory numbers and other similar enhancements. Other characteristics are the faked signa-tures meant to imitate those frequently used by the *ébénistes*. Mailfert is very proud of his imitation of them, but in reality he failed, as he used to compose his signatures of single letters in-stead of the composite name-stamps employed by the old masters. However, this error has been pointed out some time ago and will probably be avoided by his followers.

Apart from the artificial ageing and the signs of wear fabricated with such wicked skill by the fakers it should not be overlooked that signs of genuine wear and damages are bound to appear once an imitation or fake has become second-hand. For many imitations and forgeries may by now have attained an age sufficient to obliterate all signs of recent make.

The intimate knowledge of the making of old furniture and the skill and relish with which M. Mailfert imitated technique and damages down to the smallest details, tend to show that the im-portance of technicalities for the distinction between genuine and faked furniture should not be exaggerated. The forger frequently is at the same time a restorer of antique furniture and his oppor-tunities for examining its make by taking it apart and reassembling it afford an intimate knowledge of all technical details. His short-comings may much more often be revealed by his failure to match the style. As M. Mailfert repeatedly asserts, he is particularly proud of producing no copies, but variations of genuine models. The modern versions of a style differ perceptibly from this style itself and their shapes and still more often their decora-tion betray their modernity.

GOTHIC FURNITURE

Another and perhaps the gravest danger incurred by the faker are his attempts to outdo his genuine prototypes not only in exuberance but also in all the characteristics of their specific style. Perhaps the best examples for this peril are afforded by a group of pieces of neo-Gothic furniture made on the Continent. A number of portentous looking Gothic cupboards were fabricated at Cologne around the seventies of the last century, and these pieces got into most of the great Continental collections of the time.[6] Like the decorative masterpieces of Gothic goldsmiths' work made for the Baron Rothschild[7] they are overloaded with sculptures and ornaments of every description, and like these super-fakes they betray in every single detail of their design the Gothic Revival. This movement represents the most complete attempt of turning the clock back that was ever made. But though every artist and every craftsman was conscientiously trained in the rules of the Gothic style, and though throughout the whole century countless Gothic churches were built and innumerable houses and churches furnished with 'Gothic' furniture of every description, all these works look to our eyes much more 'nineteenth century' than 'Gothic'.

The date of origin of these Gothic cupboards is not only betrayed by the style of the figures adorning them but above all by the carved ornaments and by a certain mixture of playfulness and pedantry pervading their whole make-up. Though the group of forged pieces that will be described here was only made in the 'seventies, the restoring and copying of Gothic furniture began at a somewhat earlier date. Adalbert Stifter, the Austrian writer who was also a member of the Imperial Commission for the Preservation of Ancient Monuments, devoted a large part of one of his novels, written around the middle of the last century, to a Utopia of rich collectors of old local furniture in Gothic and Renaissance style, who maintained a private workshop for its restoration and re-setting as well as for the fabrication of new specimens in the old style. Their work as restorers as well as imitators is described in detail, and at the same time the persuasion is expressed that sufficient knowledge enables the modern craftsman to recreate the antique pieces he admires.[8]

6. O. v. Falke, *Deutsche Möbel des Mittelalters* (1924), p. xxxi. A sideboard in similar style was acquired for the Victoria and Albert Museum in 1863; cf. F. G. Roe, in *The Connoisseur* (June 1946), p. 98, fig. 5.

7. See p. 221.

8. *Der Nachsommer* (1857).

The cupboard on which the Cologne workshop of the seventies seems to have based its decorative scheme, comes from the collection of Alexandre Du Sommerard, the founder of the Musée Cluny, who died in 1842. This early sixteenth-century oak dresser has side panels of somewhat later date, a modern bottom and most intricate neo-Gothic iron fittings.[9] There can be no doubt that craftsmen able to produce such ironwork and woodwork produced also complete specimens of Gothic furniture.

This oak dresser has the Virgin of the Annunciation carved on one of its top doors and the Angel on the other. This arrangement is repeated on several of the dressers and cupboards made in the Cologne workshop.[10] But rich though the decoration of the Musée Cluny dresser is, it was not deemed sufficient by its German imitators. They hardly ever left a single panel of their cupboards without ornamentation and indulged in what may almost be described as an orgy of figured decoration. On one of these cupboards all four doors and both drawers have been adorned by figures or scenes in bold relief and two additional figures have been placed in niches (*Plate* 111).[11] As these carvings —some of which are old—differ considerably in style, the whole piece looks more like a museum of late Gothic sculpture than like a cupboard. The stylistic vagaries of the Cologne fakers occasionally went so far as to include into their German Gothic furniture a figure unmistakably derived from Italian art, like a statue of Saint Francis placed in the central niche of one of their cupboards.[12]

The iconography of these cupboards is occasionally more amusing than correct. On the piece boasting the Italian Saint Francis, for instance, not less than three coats of arms are to be seen, which is rather too much to make clear for whom it was made. Still more amusing is a dresser on the door of which an

9. E. Haraucourt, *Musée des Thermes et de l'Hôtel de Cluny, Catalogue des Bois Sculptés et Meubles* (1925), no. 511, pl. 23.

10. J. v. Falke, *Mittelalterliches Holzmobiliar* (1894), pl. 12, 2. F. Luthmer, *Deutsche Möbel* (1902), figs. 60 and 61.

11. A. Roeper and H. Boesch, *Möbel aller Stilarten* (1896), pl. 2. *Mitteilungen aus dem Germanischen Nationalmuseum* (1905), p. 72, pl. 4.

12. J. v. Falke, *Mittelalterliches Holzmobiliar* (1894), pl. 12, 2.

angel holds a pot-shaped helmet above the head of a kneeling knight with a rosary.[13] Above the lock is the monogram of Christ and below it the date 1483. The Gothic four has been disfigured so as almost to look like the eight at its side, a calligraphic slip which might be taken for a spontaneous burst of honesty from its maker. In other cases some ornamental motifs have been badly misunderstood by the fakers. One of the smaller cupboards, for instance, has a Madonna carved on the top central door.[14] Three linen-fold panels form the lower portion of this piece. The linen-fold of the central panel is interrupted by a quatrefoil filled with the monogram of the Virgin. Such an interruption is contrary to the very essence of linen-fold ornament. The coquettish forged ironwork adorning these pieces is fully as quaint as the carving. It should, however, be noted that the carving of the pieces of this rather numerous group is remarkably well done.

'Um Ein Tausend Acht Hundert und achtzig und acht Bin wieder ich zu Stande gebracht Durch Meisters Ruf und Zeichen erwacht Hat sein Blick mir geholfen aus Nacht.' ('In one thousand eight hundred and eighty and eight I have been put together again awakened by master's call and sign, his glance has helped me to emerge from the night.') This inscription may be read in florid Gothic lettering along the top of a large Gothic cupboard which certainly needed more than the master's magical sign to be put up, though some of its panels are probably old. The remarkable thing about this piece is not only the pride expressed by its maker but his strange idea of putting five panels from a Calvary as pinnacles on top of his work. Though apparently genuine, these look decidedly out of place in the position assigned to them.[15]

Elaborate faking and patching and the large percentage of spurious pieces naturally tended to create exaggerated misgivings regarding richly decorated Gothic furniture. This was the fate of the famous *coffre Gérente* in the Musée Cluny, a particularly elaborate oak chest in the style of the fourteenth century. The whole

13. J. v. Falke, *Mittelalterliches Holzmobiliar* (1894), pl. 16, 2.

14. J. v. Falke, *Mittelalterliches Holzmobiliar* (1894), pl. 15, 2.

15. Vienna, Österreichisches Museum für Kunst und Industrie, *Katalog der Special-Ausstellung mittelalterlichen Hausraths* (1893), no. 560. J. v. Falke, *Mittelalterliches Holzmobiliar* (1894), pl. 14.

chest is covered with carvings. On the front are twelve figures of knights with their coats of arms, on the right side a group of knights on horseback, on the left an oak tree with an erotic allegory, and on the back groups of jugglers, while the lid shows twelve scenes in quatrefoils surrounded by ornament. Originally in the Gérente Collection, since 1869 in the Musée Cluny, the chest was held for many years to be one of the most interesting pieces of medieval furniture that have survived. Paul Gsell, the chronicler of the table-talk of Anatole France, narrates how startled everybody was when Edmund Haraucourt, Director of the Musée de Cluny, told them one day: 'Recently I experienced the greatest and most tiresome surprise. You know well our celebrated fourteenth-century coffer, so much praised in all the art manuals?'

Anatole France: 'Certainly.'

Haraucourt: 'It's a forgery.'

And as he told them how he had made this unfortunate discovery, Haraucourt entreated the company: 'But for Heaven's sake, Messieurs, be discreet. For this coffer is the glory of our museum. It is so celebrated that I could not make up my mind to deprive the public of it.'[16]

However, the secret was not kept, and in the official catalogue of the Museum the coffer was described as 'composed of two distinct parts, one dating from the fourteenth, the other from the nineteenth century'; only the lid and the left side panel were regarded as ancient.[17] Meanwhile an American scholar identified the two chivalrous scenes. The twelve knights on the front and the heathen warriors galloping towards them on the right side represent the defence of a pass against the Saracens, an episode from the third Crusade, told in a French poem of the late thirteenth century, the *Pas Saladin*.[18] Now the question arose: could any modern forger have known this obscure poem, which, up to 1915,

16. P. Gsell, *Anatole France and his Circle* (1922), p. 23.

17. E. Haraucourt, *Musée des Thermes et de l'Hôtel de Cluny, Catalogue des Bois Sculptés et Meubles* (1925), no. 457, pl. 12. A. Feulner, *Kunstgeschichte des Möbels* (3rd edition, 1930), fig. 56.

18. R. S. Loomis, 'Richard Coeur de Lion and the Pas Saladin', in *Publications of the Modern Language Association of America*, vol. 30 (1915), pp. 523 sqq., fig. 9.

remained unknown to all the medievalists who studied the *coffre Gérente?* Thus M. A. Lambert was prompted to examine the chest. His minute investigation, a model of its kind, led to its complete rehabilitation.[19] It is indubitably genuine, apart from four of the twelve quatrefoils of the lid and numerous minor and, for the most part, insignificant patches. M. Lambert found that the oak lining of the chest, though vigorously cleaned, was uniform and old. All restorations of the carvings were fitted in very cunningly and effectively aged by beating the wood with wire brushes. M. Lambert could detect them only by the absence of all remains of a coat of white paint which had covered the chest before it was restored. On all the genuine parts of the chest vestiges of this paint could still be discovered under the uniform coating of brown wax. Some of the patchings on the lid are so placed as to suggest that at least a number of them were not made for the sake of repairs only, but rather to mitigate the indecency of some of the love-scenes represented. Perhaps the missing portion of the lid was removed for similar reasons.

These restorations, which are very skilful and deceptive, were made before Viollet-le-Duc examined the coffer in the Gérente Collection in the fifties of the nineteenth century. He, the great restorer, was deceived by its restored portions. In his *Dictionnaire du Mobilier Français* (I, p. 28) he included a drawing of one of the modern quatrefoils and another of the ornamental iron fittings which are also modern. M. Lambert had the satisfaction of discovering the source of the iron lock and mounts. It is an exact copy of the ironwork on a small box, likewise in the Gérente Collection. Viollet-le-Duc reproduced it in the same volume as the *coffre Gérente* (*Dictionnaire* I, p. 82), without noticing the identical shape of the fittings.

RENAISSANCE FURNITURE

Italian cassoni came into fashion at a somewhat later date than Gothic furniture. Their vogue did not begin before the last de-

---

19. A. Lambert, 'Le Coffre du Pas Saladin est-il authentique?' in *Revue archéologique*, 5th series, vol. 33 (1931), pp. 275 sqq.

cades of the nineteenth century. But from all we know of the Quattrocentist workshops of nineteenth-century Italy, they must have begun faking cassoni as soon as these began to attract the notice of collectors.

The example I shall describe here is not a cassone, but only a *cofanetto*, but it may help to draw attention at least to one type of faked cassoni. This small coffer shows rich mouldings, a vaulted lid, and profuse gesso decorations.[20] The front panel shows a relief copy of the central group from Pinturicchio's fresco in the Libreria of Sienna, representing the betrothal of Emperor Frederick III to Eleonora of Portugal. This composition has been adorned on either side by a group of graceful youths and each of the noble consorts is accompanied by a small dog. On the back of this coffer is a dedicatory inscription with the date 1457. Pinturicchio's fresco was not begun before 1503. Apart from this there are patent modernisms in the rendering of the figures. Not only the clever choice of the nuptial scene points to the Siennese origin of this forgery. The shape of the *cofanetto* is derived from a coffer destined for the seals of the governors of Sienna which was made in 1373.[21] This Gothic coffer shows a moulded lid of almost identical shape, and gilded gesso decorations which inspired the author of the marriage coffer.

It is not unlikely that I. F. Joni himself may have been the author of this ingenious pasticcio. He mentions as a matter of course that he made *cofanetti* on a large scale, and owns on another occasion to having borrowed a motif from Pinturicchio's frescoes —namely the portrait of Alberto Aringhieri in the Duomo of Sienna, of which he painted a copy on an old panel.[22] But from what Joni says it may be gathered that the fabrication of such coffers was rather general in Sienna at the critical time.[23] The gesso technique applied on this *cofanetto* was also used for the decoration of full-sized cassoni. Marriage scenes, as well as festive

20. *Mitteilungen des Gewerbe-Museums zu Bremen*, vol. 18 (1903), p. 66, pl. 9.

21. C. Ricci, *Il Palazzo Pubblico di Siena* (1904), fig. 134. P. Schubring, *Cassoni* (1915), No. 40, pl. 7.

22. Joni, *Memorie*, pp. 170, 179, 184; *Affairs*, pp. 204, 217, 223 sqq.

23. Joni, *Memorie*, p. 116; *Affairs*, p. 137.

processions, are enacted on them by persons in picturesque cos-
tumes derived from genuine pieces.

Carved and painted Italian picture-frames are another type of
ornate woodwork of the Renaissance that is being collected. Some
of these frames surrounded looking-glasses, but a large proportion of them were separated in the last century from the pictures
for which they had been made, to be replaced by the heavily
gilded cornices of which every self-respecting collection had
adopted a uniform design. Meanwhile the antique frames were
picked up by amateurs of antique craftsmanship, and flourishing
manufactures turning out many specimens grew up in Italy and
particularly at Sienna. Such frames appear to have belonged to the
stock-in-trade of Giovacchino's shop, in which Joni started his
career, and we are justified in supposing that his was not the only
firm to embark on that line.[24]

Many of these counterfeits not only imitate the more ornate of
the genuine specimens, they even try to outshine them by the
florid profusion of their decorations. The frames are often betrayed by some detail plainly belonging, not to the Renaissance,
but to the revival of the nineteenth century. Thus a rich Siennese
mirror frame in sixteenth-century style is betrayed by the shape
of a vase and by the realistically carved bird perching on it, which
is rather out of place among the fantastic animals of the more
authentic-looking parts of the carving.[25] But even better than by
such details, the eye is able to assess the merits of the piece by the
equilibrium of body and ornament. While even the richest
genuine Renaissance frames look solidly compact and harmonious,
their imitations are top-heavy, the forgers having concentrated
exclusively on the decoration.

At present the standardised designs of the heavy nineteenth-
century frames have fallen into disgrace. Public and private collections are therefore looking for old frames which might be
fitted on to their treasures. But in most cases 'antique' frames are
made to measure, not only in the appropriate style, but with every
imaginable sign of age and wear. This is done without any deceit-
ful intention, simply for the reason that these faded frames are

24. Joni, *Memorie,* p. 116.
25. E. Bock, *Florentinische und Venezianische Bilderrahmen* (1902), p. 81.

now considered most suitable for setting off old pictures. For reasons of price and expeditiousness painting is usually preferred to carving in the decoration of the products of this modern industry.

Not before the nineties did English furniture of the Tudor and early Stuart period become the centre of widespread interest. But as in many other fields, it appears that the major attempts at counterfeiting lie rather in the earlier than in the later part of its vogue. Nowadays the field has been so well explored that important pieces turning up unexpectedly and without reliable pedigree are apt to arouse suspicion, however great their merits seem to be. In the nineties it was appreciably easier to put over a fraud.

A court cupboard with the portrait of a lady on its central door belongs to a series of forgeries of which a large number were gradually sold to a collector who was told that these pieces were the heirloom of an impoverished North-country family. The furniture was supposed to have been made by the carpenters of the family during the reign of James I. The late Mr. P. Macquoid discovered the fraud and consequently the collection was returned to the 'carpenters of the reign of James I'. However, an illustration of the court cupboard can still be seen. In the accompanying text the large portrait bust of a lady is said to be 'probably that of the owner of the cabinet, which may have been made for her wedding. It is very well executed, especially as regards the dress and ruff'. As a matter of fact the execution of the costume is too detailed to inspire confidence. It does not imitate the carvings of its supposed period, but its paintings. Still more fanciful is the inscription carved in outsize letters on the centre of the cornice. Its very obtrusiveness would render it suspicious; but the forger's idea of sandwiching the date ('A. 1603 D.') was distinctly unlucky. The worm-like, S-shaped ornaments covering the rest of the cupboard are as much out of style as the portrait and the inscription (*Plate* 112).[26]

It seems that dates are an enhancement of genuine old furniture. Thus a fine armchair of the early seventeenth century was dis-

26. F. S. Robinson, *English Furniture* (1905), pp. 83 sq., pl. 38. P. Macquoid in *Journal of the Royal Institute of British Architects,* vol. 13 (1905–6), pp. 205, 214 sq.

figured in the nineteenth century by a painted inscription containing the alluring date 1625. But the words 'sursum corda' inscribed above are rather unlikely on the back of a chair, and the coat of arms below it was granted only in 1709 to the family whose name the chair bears. Moreover, the style of the lettering is typically modern Gothic.[27]

Even in forgeries of recent date the correct handling of the wood is more easily attained by the faker than an equal degree of correctness in the choice of the decorative motifs. The ageing of the wood and the study of the old techniques of construction form the foundation of the forger's education, but as it is more often than not his habit to create 'in period style' rather than to copy genuine specimens, he is apt to blunder in the choice of the decoration. These blunders need not always be quite as bad as the realistically carved woman sprawling on the front panel of a boxchair purporting to date from the end of the sixteenth century. It has rightly been pointed out that 'women writhing upon the floor' did not belong to the stock of motifs of the English carpenter of the Tudor period.[28]

EIGHTEENTH-CENTURY FURNITURE

The earliest imitations of French eighteenth-century furniture on record were made in Russia only very little later than the originals. When in 1800 Elizabeth Vigée-Lebrun visited Moscow she saw in the palace of Prince Bezborodko furniture by Daguerre bought in Paris in the first years of the French Revolution. 'When I went to see him he showed me rooms full of furniture, bought in Paris from the workshops of the famous upholsterer Daguerre. Most of this furniture had been imitated by his serfs, and it was impossible to distinguish between copy and original.'[29]

27. Victoria and Albert Museum, *Catalogue of English Furniture*, vol. 2 (1930), no. 516, pl. 7.

28. H. Cescinsky, *The Gentle Art of Faking Furniture* (1931), pl. 44. Cf. also the review by R. Edwards in *The Burlington Magazine*, vol. 60 (1932), p. 218.

29. E. Vigée-Lebrun, *Memoirs* (1904), p. 151. D. Roche, *Le mobilier français en Russie* (1913), vol. 2, p. 9.

Unfortunately it is not possible to identify these Russian copies. The contents of the Bezborodko Palace have been dispersed; some of its treasures are now in the Wallace Collection but we do not know what became of the genuine and the spurious Daguerre furniture.

When, after a period of comparative neglect, eighteenth-century furniture became again the fashion, interest was at first concentrated on the two *ébénistes* who had always been popular, Boulle and Riesener. A characteristic illustration of Riesener's fame is provided by a commode in the Wallace Collection.[30] It bears the spurious and misspelt signature RIESNER, is of German workmanship and dates from about 1800. This commode was for a considerable time regarded as a work by Riesener. From such modest beginnings the path leads to the flourishing modern industry which we had occasion to mention in connection with the activities of Mailfert (see above, p. 272 and *Plate* 113).

Far more ambitious than any of the cabinets produced by Mailfert and his colleagues, and one of the most successful forgeries ever perpetrated, is the ornamental cabinet said to have been presented by the Emperor Charles VI to Prince Eugène of Savoy after the latter had won the Battle of Peterwardein against the Turks (1716).

The cabinet, heavy with silver, tortoiseshell and marble inlay, is of rare luxury.[31] It turned up at an antique dealer's in Munich, the dealer vouching for its august provenance which he said he was bound on his honour not to disclose. It was at first boosted in U.S.A., but was acquired by an Austrian collector, who humbly presented it to his Emperor and received a knighthood as reward for so magnificent a gift. Though its spuriousness was detected at a much earlier date, the cupboard of Prince Eugène could not be denounced as a forgery before the abolition of the Austrian monarchy (*Plate* 114).

The front and sides of the cabinet are of pear-wood, polished

30. D. S. MacColl, in *The Burlington Magazine*, vol. 45 (1924), p. 113. H. Huth, *Abraham und David Roentgen* (1928), p. 72, pl. 111.

31. *Jahrbuch der Kunsthistorischen Sammlungen*, vol. 26 (1906–7), pp. 313 sqq. E. Leisching, in *Kunst und Kunsthandwerk*, vol. 24 (1921), p. 74. *Kunsthistorisches Museum, Ausstellung Gefälschte Kunstwerke*, Vienna (1936), no. 26.

black. The interior is of soft wood and poor workmanship and has partly been stained black to disguise this fact. Only the central portion of the interior has been richly decorated with gilding and mirrors and with a drawing representing the Battle of Peterwardein. On the outside the cupboard is a rather heavy array of niches built up in two stories and crowned by gables with volutes. The niches are crammed with silver statuary representing allegories of a type more usual in the nineteenth than in the eighteenth century. Characteristic of the choice of subjects is 'Merchant Shipping', a woman bent under the load of a heavily rigged vessel. The central niche carries, of course, what purports to be a portrait bust of Prince Eugène of Savoy, but the head is devoid of either personality or resemblance.

The historic pretensions raised on behalf of the cabinet could not stand up to examination. It could not be overlooked that there was not a single allusion among all the eloquent imagery of the piece to its having been an imperial gift to a victorious commander. But apart from the fact that particularly the silver sculptures are cleverly done, the whole cabinet with its rich array of columns, pilasters, and niches, where hardly an inch of the surface has been left unadorned, corresponds admirably to the neo-baroque style of the later nineteenth century. This elaborate edifice resembles most closely the buildings of the Vienna Ringstrasse, which were erected not long before the cabinet was made.

The history of the cabinet of Prince Eugène would be incomplete without any mention of a similar cabinet, purporting to commemorate the routing of the Turks before Vienna in 1683. This piece turned up at a Vienna dealer's in the very year of the donation of the Peterwardein cabinet. Its provenance was likewise a secret, and it had a relief of Prince Eugène in its interior. However, this second piece was never published and disappeared again into complete obscurity.

As the styles of furniture developed since the late seventeenth century are the only ones that can actually be adapted to modern ways of life, the largest proportion of fakes and imitations is provided in these styles. But though every one of them has a marked character of its own, the furniture of this period became in general more simple, and consequently its characteristics grew more refined and subtle, and the same is naturally the case with the characteristics distinguishing fakes and originals.

The forgers endeavoured to augment the numbers of the more usual types of furniture, with occasional lapses due to their conceivable desire to supply rare and particularly coveted pieces in numbers equalling the demand for them. But they had to avoid the fabrication of exact reproductions of well-known pieces which would have been too easily traceable. Therefore they had to produce altered variations of their models, a proceeding that frequently proves pernicious, as it is just these small modern inventions which are apt to give away the forgery. Frequently these deviations of the imitations from the originals are simply due to the faker's failure to understand the actual meaning of the decorative motifs he wished to reproduce.

Such subtle misunderstandings can be noticed on a faked George II settee that was copied from a plate in P. Macquoid's *History of English Furniture*.[32] Almost all the details of the original have been reproduced by the faker, though with varying luck. He was fairly successful with the back of this settee, but the ornamentation of the top rail looks in the copy decidedly *Art Nouveau*. He was equally unfortunate in the shaping of the supports of the arms. Their curves are much too exuberant for this rather reticent style. Most characteristic of this fake is the ornamentation of the pendants between the legs. It is thin and of indefinite design, with a kind of open cartouche in the centre, and corresponds to no known style. It bears no resemblance whatever to the carved pendants adorning the model settee. This can be explained by the text Macquoid devoted to his plate. For here these pendants are described as rather too solid in shape, and the carving as being coarse. Therefore the forger did his best to improve on the genuine eighteenth-century carving.

32. R. W. Symonds, in *Old Furniture*, vol. 2 (1927), p. 156, fig. 5 (a paper published for the second time in *Arts and Decoration*, vol. 49 (January, 1939), p. 16). The statement that 'no genuine piece of such an elaborate and bad design has survived' needs modification. For the original see P. Macquoid, *A History of English Furniture: The Age of Mahogany* (1906), p. 127, fig. 108. P. Macquoid and R. Edwards, *The Dictionary of English Furniture*, vol. 3 (1927), p. 93, fig. 28.

112. Cupboard dated 1603. Forgery.

114. Detail from the Cabinet of Prince Eugène of Savoy.

113. Chest of drawers. By A. Mailfert.

115. Tapestry with the figures of the Emperor Frederick III and Pope Pius II. (The two figures copied from the woodcut shown in Plate 116.)

116. The Emperor Frederick III and Pope Pius II. Woodcut from Hartmann Schedel's *Nuremberg Chronicle* (1493).

PART SIXTEEN

TAPESTRIES

PART SIXTEEN

TAPESTRIES

In the sixteenth century Brussels gradually became the world centre of tapestry manufacture. The trade-mark of the Brussels weavers, a B or BB (Brussels, Brabant) and a red shield, was regarded as a guarantee of perfect workmanship. It was freely copied, especially in Antwerp. After a prolonged litigation of which the documents have been preserved, the weavers of Antwerp agreed in 1619 to abstain henceforward from using the trade-mark of Brussels on their work. But other manufacturing centres persisted in their use of the Brussels mark. A Dutch weaver of Schoonhoven used it in 1631 but to allay the pangs of his conscience he declared that on his work BB stood for 'Bon, bon'.[1]

More than other works of art tapestries are liable to become the victims of decay. They are attacked by moths and dampness, some of the threads employed were not sufficiently resistant, and careless use caused much damage to the delicate fabrics. Old restorations were made rather inconsiderately. Frequently damaged portions were simply cut off and discarded, discoloured portions were touched up with paint, mending usually was of the rougher kind, and fragments from different tapestries were frequently patched together whether they fitted or not. It is not very long since faithful restorations and imitations of tapestries were first attempted. But nowadays these can be executed most skilfully, and the restorer or imitator has also learned to avoid modern materials like aniline dyes or cotton threads.

Restorations of old tapestry are usually visible on the back, and may be thoroughly investigated with the help of the ultra-violet lamp, as the new threads show a fluorescence different from the

1. J. Denuce, *Antwerpener Teppichkunst* (1936), pp. xxxi, 57.

old ones, thus rendering 'invisible' repairs clearly visible. This method has not been sufficiently exploited up to now, though it seems to be a particularly promising branch of the scientific investigation of works of art.[2]

The manufacture of tapestry is very costly, and therefore forgeries, though by no means non-existent, are comparatively rare, and among them 'fragments' prevail, owing to their small dimensions. The work of the forger of tapestries is also open to all the stylistic and iconographic pitfalls that threaten the fakers of paintings.

A good illustration of this is a Gothic tapestry of modern origin, said to have been found in a 'crypt of a church in Spain'[3] (*Plate* 115). The floral ornament of the border, the flowers overgrowing the edge of the paved floor, the three niches framed by thin Gothic columns and arches, the brocade background of these niches, as well as the *mille fleurs* decoration above them, are all in the best tradition of the early sixteenth century. Though they do not belong to any of the usual types of tapestry design, the figures are no doubt genuinely late Gothic. The only hitch is the source from which they have been derived. Before this was discovered the scene represented on the tapestry caused much speculation. It was at first thought to represent the coronation of Frederick III as Emperor of the Holy Roman Empire. While the pope seated at his side is described on the scroll as Aeneas Sylvius, who became pope as Pius II, Frederick was crowned by Nicholas V. More difficulties were created by the two Electors appearing at the sides. Their escutcheons do not correspond to the titles inscribed on the scrolls above their heads. The Margrave of Brandenburg on the left (*Marchio brandē*) is represented with the arms of the Duchy of Saxony, and the Elector Palatine on the right has a coat of arms which has no connection whatever with the Palatinate and does not correspond to the arms of any German sovereign.

All these problems were solved when it was discovered that the

2. J. J. Rorimer, *Ultra-violet Rays and their Use in the Examination of Works of Art* (1931), p. 38.

3. *The Burlington Magazine,* vol. 12 (1907–8), pp. 100 sqq., 164 sqq. *Art in America,* vol. 5 (1917), pp. 182, 251. G. E. Pazaurek, *Gläser der Empire- und Biedermeierzeit* (1923), p. 244, note 2.

whole tapestry was a combination of two woodcuts from Hart-mann Schedel's *Nuremberg Chronicle*[4] (*Plate* 116). The centre of the tapestry is a most literal copy of the central group of one wood-cut, the only difference being that the pillars of the canopy rising behind the two princes have been omitted, while its brocade pattern has been spread over the background of all three niches. The Electors have been copied from another woodcut, represent-ing among other subjects the seven Electors. But the forger com-mitted the mistake of copying the Margrave of Brandenburg with the coat of arms belonging to his neighbour the Duke of Saxony, a blunder that would surely have been avoided by a contemporary copyist of Wolgemut's woodcut. Moreover he was unaware of the sin he committed by inverting the coat of arms which shows now the bend sinister, the sign of illegitimacy. The fault may lie with the tapestry-weaver who reversed the design, but it is somehow reminiscent of the left-handed painter whom Tristram Shandy's father employed with the same deplorable result. The reason why the Elector Palatine bears an imaginary escutcheon instead of his proper arms, remains obscure.

In German and Swiss tapestries the Gothic tradition remained alive right to the beginning of the seventeenth century. As col-lectors tend to neglect these products of a retardatory style, the temptation to pass them off as early pieces is great. This is what happened to the Swiss tapestry shown in *Plate* 117. Its subject is King Solomon solving the riddles of the Queen of Sheba. She asks him which of the two flowers in her hand is real and which artificial, and which of the two children dressed alike is a girl. Wise King Solomon at once finds the answers: the real flower is the one on which the bee has alighted (a bee-hive appears in the back-ground) and the girl is the child who gathers the apples into her skirt. The tapestry is now dated 1511, a date incompatible with the costume which is typical of the fashions worn all over Europe in the Elizabethan age. A glance at the detail shows what has happened (*Plate* 118): the six in 1611 was clumsily altered into a five.[5]

4. Printed 1493 (fol. 267v, 184r). Cf. A. Schramm, *Der Bilderschmuck der Frühdrucke*, vol. 17 (1934), pls. 231, 266.

5. This was discovered by Dr. Betty Kurth, to whom I wish to express my warmest thanks for this, the previous and the following example. Cf. also

117. The Riddles of the Queen of Sheba. Tapestry with the spurious
date 1511.

118. Detail from Plate 117.
The date 1611 has been
altered to 1511.

119. Esther, Ahasuerus and Haman. Tapestry, dated 1559.

120. A later photograph of the tapestry shown in Plate 119 (detail). The date has meanwhile been changed to 1509.

A tapestry with the story of Esther (*Plates* 119–120) suffered the same fate.[6] It now shows the date 1509, which, though too early, is not as impossible as 1511 on the 'Queen of Sheba' tapestry. The rejuvenation was less radical and the reward of this moderation is a more plausible date. However, the forger must have been unaware of a piece of incriminating evidence: a photograph taken some years earlier which shows the tapestry in its original state with the date 1559.

Altered dates may occur on oriental carpets as well as on European tapestries. A Turkish prayer rug of the so-called Ladik type shows now the date 1110 of the Hegira (A.D. 1698–9). It was obtained by the same kind of manipulation. It is on record that the carpet was originally dated 1210 (A.D. 1795–6). The alteration was simple but not very clever as carpets of this type were not made before the middle of the eighteenth century.[7]

H. Goebel, *Wandteppiche*, vol. 3, 1 (1933), p. 183, fig. 151b. B. Kurth, 'The Riddles of the Queen of Sheba in Swiss and Alsatian Tapestries', in *The Connoisseur*, vol. 106 (1940), p. 236.

6. H. Goebel, *Wandteppiche*, vol. 3, 1 (1933), p. 184.

7. W. Grote-Hasenbalg, *Der Orientteppich* (1922), vol. 1, p. 79. *Metropolitan Museum Studies*, vol. 1 (1928–9), p. 110, fig. 13.

PART SEVENTEEN

BOOKBINDINGS

PART SEVENTEEN

BOOKBINDINGS

Old bookbindings are generally treated with much less respect than the products of other crafts. Bindings are frequently transferred from one book to another, and neither far-reaching restorations nor new bindings in style are considered in themselves a dishonesty. We do not propose to deal here with these alterations and imitations, but only with some groups of intentional forgeries, which are important because they were turned out in large numbers.

The manufacture of sixteenth-century bindings of illustrious provenance, which assumed considerable dimensions in the second half of the nineteenth century, was initiated by L. Hagué, or Hacquet, a Belgian bookbinder, who worked in Paris as well as in French provincial towns, and also in London and Brussels.[1] An Italian team consisting of an amateur and a craftsman called Vittorio Villa, was at work in Bologna, and later on in Milan.[2] Villa once wanted to take a whole case of Grolier, Maiolus, and Henry II bindings to France but came up against the Italian law forbidding the export of valuable works of art, whereupon he candidly told the official that the bindings were all his own work. He died in 1892.

Though both of them also embarked on complete forgeries, they frequently chose the simpler way of embellishing old bindings by the impression of ornamental tools and by the imprints of famous bibliophiles.

1. A. Claudin, in *Bulletin du bibliophile et du bibliothécaire*, 1891, pp. 513 sqq. C. Davenport in *The Library*, N.S., vol. 2 (1901), pp. 389, sqq. G. A. Bogeng, *Streifzüge*, vol. 1, (1915), pp. 182–187. *The Times Literary Supplement* (1941), pp. 488, 502.
2. A. Claudin, in *Bulletin du bibliophile et du bibliothécaire*, 1891, p. 519. G. Fumagalli in *La Bibliofilia*, vol. 4 (1902–3), p. 313.

Such changes were executed with varying luck. Occasionally the fraud may be evident at first sight, for instance if devices and owners' inscriptions have been inserted in rather unlikely places.

The spine of a fine binding belongs to this class.[3] Its covers were designed by Geofroy Tory. The circles on the back alternately contain the initial *F* and the emblem of the salamander, both surmounted by crowns. This design does not fit in with Tory's rich ornament, nor does it seem likely that a royal binding would carry the emblems of François I on the spine only.

The ample and frequently careless use of royal initials, coats of arms, and emblems is characteristic for this group of fakes. The letters were printed wherever any free space was available between the original ornaments. Sometimes the letters are even printed across the original fillets, as happened on a François I binding 'made in Bologna'.[4]

The plain fillets were also disregarded when a sixteenth-century binding of mediocre quality was transformed into a book from the library of Maiolus (*Plate*121).[5] The original binding was simple and of rough make. As the book contains prayers addressed to the Virgin, a panel stamp representing the Madonna with the Child on a crescent forms the centre of both covers. The border originally consisted only of two silver bands outlined in gold, the inner one being accompanied by plain fillets. The forger filled the free space with a copy of the interlacing on the cover of a Maiolus binding.[6] In the process of copying, the elegant outlines of the

3. G. Brunet, *La Reliure ancienne et moderne* (1878), pl. 73. 176 *Historic and Artistic Bookbindings . . . selected from the Library of Robert Hoe* (1895), pl. 25. Cf. E. P. Goldschmidt, *Gothic and Renaissance Bookbindings* (1928), p. 246 note.

4. H. Harisse, 'Falsifications bolognaises' in *Bulletin du bibliophile et du bibliothécaire* (1902), p. 440, fig.

5. W. H. J. Weale, *Bookbindings and Rubbings of Bindings in the National Art Library* (1894), vol. 2, p. 61, no. 253.

6. For the genuine binding cf. G. D. Hobson, *Maioli, Canevari, and Others* (1926), no. 80. 176 *Historic and Artistic Bookbindings . . . selected from the Library of Robert Hoe* (1895), pl. 20 This binding was formerly in the Libri Collection (Libri sale, 25–7–1862, lot 557). Thus it is probable that the binding in the Victoria and Albert Museum is the work of Hagué who was Libri's bookbinder. G. D. Hobson, *Maioli, Canevari, and Others* (1926), no. 88 (Turin, Museo Civico) shows the same pattern as our plate 91, only the figure of the Virgin is different.

original pattern became clumsy shapes, an impression which is intensified by the crimson and green colouring. The edges of the design encroach on the fillets of the original ornament. The faulty gilding and colouring poses unsuccessfully as agedness. The border has been filled by a foliated ornament which fails to match the style of the interlacing in the centre. It covers the plain fillets of the ill-treated original, which are distinctly visible beneath its imprint. At the bottom of the upper cover, part of the silver band has been erased to give place to the owner's inscription, *Tho. Maioli et amicorum*. This adds the final touch to this concoction, for the book of prayers was published in 1577, which is late for a genuine Maiolus. The bindings bearing his name were executed between 1550 and 1566, and Thomas Mahieu, secretary to Catherine de Medici, is last heard of in 1572.[7]

In all these re-tooled and sophisticated bindings a certain discrepancy between the old and the new parts was unavoidable. Only in completely new bindings could Hagué give rein to his imagination. French royal bindings were his special favourites. Henri II and his bibliophile mistress Diane de Poitiers were posthumously presented with a large library in sumptuous bindings.

In November 1897 Sotheby's announced the sale of 'A remarkable collection of books in magnificent modern bindings, formed by an amateur (recently deceased)'.

Poor amateur! His 'magnificent modern bindings' broke his heart. He had, it appears, collected and cherished for years the 110 bindings contained in this catalogue, accepting with complete trust every famous initial and every inscription they bore. But alas, what had been sold to him were 110 brand new masterpieces by L. Hagué. He acquired them as objects of great value at proportionate prices, and would have lived happily ever after had he not had the unfortunate idea of sending the lot to the auction room. The auctioneers could not help being suspicious, and the verdict of the experts, to whom they referred for judgment, was disastrous. This verdict was the owner's death warrant. His heirs proceeded with the sale, for which the catalogue prepared with love and care by the collector was used. His passionately tender descriptions of the bindings reveal the full measure of the

7. G. D. Hobson, *Maioli, Canevari, and Others* (1926), p. 60.

122. Bookbinding with the initials of Henri II and Diane de Poitiers. Forgery by L. Hagué.

121. 16th-century bookbinding. The central medallion is genuine; the ornamentation and inscription were added in the 19th century. (Victoria and Albert Museum.)

123. Bookbinding in French Renaissance style. Forgery by L. Hagué. (By courtesy of the Director of the Victoria and Albert Museum.)

cruelty of his deception. Only one word from the title-page of this document had to be altered: from 'old' the 'magnificent bindings' became 'modern'.

Their very magnificence, combined with their untarnished brilliance, ought to have rendered these bindings suspicious. For this particular customer Hagué invariably chose the richest interlaced patterns and the most florid ornaments. Sometimes he produced specimens more ornate than any genuine piece, like the elegant binding (*Plate* 122) which is decorated with an enormous H (for Henri II) of scroll-work, the transversal bar of which encloses the French royal coat of arms. Above and below the H appears the double D intertwined by crescents, the monogram and emblem of Diane de Poitiers. The gilded floral ornaments on the binding are a characteristic example of the neo-Renaissance style of the late nineteenth century.[8]

Henri II and Diane de Poitiers hold the record but there are several popes and French kings. Grolier and Maiolus also play a prominent part among the pearls of this collection. One of the Maiolus bindings covers a manuscript 'Officium Beatae Virginis Mariae' which with the two similar books mentioned above makes one wonder whether the famous Maiolus Library was quite as full of prayer-books as that.

Not all of Hagué's bindings show the same exuberance. The Henri II binding (*Plate* 123) follows genuine models quite closely, but it was an unfortunate idea to pass it off as a book from the Royal Library. The crowned H's are squeezed into the very corners, outside the ornament, in a place where no binder of the Renaissance would have put the royal initials. It seems that Hagué did not always work with the perfect technique he employed for his best customer. This binding is of comparatively poor workmanship. The crowns on top of the H's came out very blurred. Some of Hagué's tools were too sharp and have left cuts in the leather. The gilding was so poorly done that it is already coming off in places.[9]

The most pretentious fake of a royal binding ever made was

8. Sale Sotheby, 11 November 1897, no. 47.
9. Victoria and Albert Museum, A.M. 989–1897.

sold in 1911 with the Hoe Collection.[10] It was then attributed to
Nicolas Eve, the *relieur ordinaire du roy Henri III*. It is a red
morocco binding decorated on both covers with a full-length
portrait of King Henri III. The portrait is done in mosaic of
coloured leather with the exception of the flesh parts—face and
hands—which were painted on vellum and pasted on. Needless
to say that this curious technique was never used on genuine old
bindings. The portrait is framed by a profusion of royal initials
(no less than 44 times repeated) and fleurs-de-lys.

The most successful of all spurious bindings were the painted
Siennese book-covers. There is one thing genuine about them:
they were actually made in Sienna. The artist who evolved his own
version of primitive Siennese bookbindings was F. J. Joni.[11] He
devoted himself to their manufacture until the more remunerative
task of painting primitive Siennese pictures began to take up too
much of his time. In his autobiography Joni himself informs his
readers of the various stages of his invention.[12] An agent who
used to sell the products of the workshop once pointed out to
Joni's boss that a small water-colour would look lovely in the
centre of a period binding which he described rather vaguely as a
wooden tablet with the miniature in the centre and some ornament
on two sides of it. As a suitable centre piece for such a book-cover
he indicated the photograph of a miniature by Liberale da Verona
representing the 'Labourers in the Vineyard'.

Joni describes how he set to work. He gathered inspiration
from some photographs of illuminated manuscripts and prepared
the tablet with gesso ornaments. These he gilded and then painted
the rest. We know this bookbinding: it was sold with the Cavalieri
collection at Milan in 1914 and is illustrated on plate 22 of the sale
catalogue. A very similar binding is shown on plate 3 of the Hoe
publication, where it is described as a Venetian bookbinding en-

10. Reproduced in colours: 176 *Historic and Artistic Bookbindings* . . .
selected from the Library of Robert Hoe (New York, 1895), pl. 59. Hoe sale,
New York, 24 April 1911, no. 327, reproduced as frontispiece of the sale
catalogue; cf. E. P. Goldschmidt, *Gothic and Renaissance Bookbindings* (1928),
p. 73.

11. See above, p. 29.

12. Joni, *Affairs*, p. 127; *Memorie*, p. 108.

closing an early edition of Politian. Joni copied here with minute exactitude the picture of Aeolus, also in the Cathedral Library of Sienna, and likewise painted by Liberale da Verona.[13] Only one other wooden binding of this medallion type is known to me.[14] The miniature in the centre represents an old man at whose feet a youth is kneeling. In the centre of the back cover is a coat of arms.

Later on Joni came across a pamphlet describing the painted covers of the accounts-registers of the treasury at Sienna.[15] On some of his bindings he covered the background with gold foil, adorned by a punch-work pattern. On this background he invariably painted the figure of some saint. Another book-cover illustrated in the Hoe publication has only a single coat of arms on the back cover.[16] Later on Joni made more ample use of the descriptions in the pamphlet and adorned the boards of his back covers with a profusion of coats of arms. To these he sometimes added inscriptions, similar to those from the real 'Biccherna' and 'Gabella' bindings, as he had seen them quoted in the pamphlet. When he ventured on the fabrication of a fifteenth-century cover for the accounts of the tax-office (Gabella), he mixed up the strict order of precedence by putting the 'camerlengho' at the end, instead of the beginning. This achievement he proudly reproduced in the Italian version of his autobiography.[17] A similar cover purports to have adorned an inventory of the cathedral treasure of Sienna.[18] Here Joni mixed up the various institutions of his home town. The official presiding over the cathedral works was called *operaio*, but Joni promoted him to the rank of camarlingo. Only a single official is mentioned, but Joni did not refrain from introducing twelve coats of arms. These errors did not save Joni from persecution, as somebody thought that such a cover, which was displayed in the window of a shop, might have been stolen from the

13. For the original see: A. Venturi, *Storia dell'arte italiana*, vol. 7/4 (1915), fig. 515.

14. *Catalogue de la Bibliothèque de S. E. D. Paolo Borghese*, vol. 1 (1892) p. 673, no. 4538, pl. 1.

15. L. Mussini in *L'Art*, 3rd year, vol. 2, p. 225 sqq.

16. 176 *Historic and Artistic Bookbindings . . . selected from the Library of Robert Hoe* (New York, 1895), pl. 2.

17. Joni, *Memorie*, p. 132.

18. J. Brinckmann in *Kunstgewerbeblatt*, N.S., vol. 14 (1903), p. 229.

Duomo.[19] On another binding he filled the tablet forming the back cover with thirteen coats of arms in gesso relief, without any inscription.[20] Joni himself published reproductions of two of his works;[21] notwithstanding this a Joni front cover was published as an old Siennese original two years after the appearance of his book.[22]

Joni himself gives a description of his technique: 'At first I used knitting-needles of various sizes for the worm-holes, pushing them in and drawing them out with the aid of pincers, in order to keep the holes intact. Later I invented a new system, for which I used a small borer. The bronze bosses at the corners of the covers I made look old by bathing them in ammonia, and for the small iron plates which served as clasps in the centre I used iodine, which gave them just the right degree of rustiness'[23]

From Joni's first experiments in the craft to his later achievements, all his book-covers, which are numerous, can be recognised by their uniform characteristics. But beyond this the fact must be borne in mind that nothing like these painted wooden bindings ever existed before Joni, neither in Sienna nor anywhere else. The original wooden covers of the Biccherna and Gabella, between which the accounts of each term were kept, are thick wooden boards.[24] The top cover was primed and inscribed with the names of the officials who were responsible for the contents. It was further decorated by the arms of these officials, and by a picture representing either the camarlingo counting the money or some religious subject. The whole is never arranged in the way of sixteenth-century book-covers, with border, centre-piece, etc., but the inscription fills about one-half of the board and the painting the other. These covers were single boards, not bindings backed with leather, like Joni's. Joni, who was proud never to have gone to look at the originals, made a fanciful but successful invention.

19. Joni, *Memorie*, pp. 143–5; *Affairs*, pp. 171–3.
20. Schaefer in *Mitteilungen des Gewerbemuseums zu Bremen*, vol. 17 (1902), pl. 9.
21. Joni, *Memorie*, pp. 98, 110, 132.
22. *Zeitschrift für Bücherfreunde*, 3rd series, vol. 2 (1933), p. 112 and pl.
23. Joni, *Memorie*, p. 116; *Affairs*, pp. 137 sqq.
24. E. Carli, *Le tavolette di Biccherna* (1950).

PART EIGHTEEN

FAKES WITHOUT MODELS

PART EIGHTEEN

FAKES WITHOUT MODELS

It is generally assumed that forgers only set to work where the demand exceeds the supply. But it seems that some fakers proceed like clever businessmen who know how to create a demand for objects unheard of before. Armed with remarkable gifts of imagination, they produce whole classes of antiquities in styles of their own and invent historic and prehistoric civilisations as a suitable background for their creations. These fakers may well be described as past masters of the art of faking, for their works are free of the blemish of imitation, as they invent origin, purpose, and style alike.

L'AGE DE LA CORNE

The Horn Age might almost be described as a logical postulate.[1] Its inventor based it on sound reasoning. He thought: before the Bronze Age began, man lived through the Stone Age. What did he do before he began to use flints? Evidently he must have used implements made of horn and bones. This conclusion is eminently reasonable, only the fact that human evolution omitted this important phase may be regarded as a minor drawback. Anyhow, it was not too difficult to provide what prehistoric man had failed to produce. Bogus excavations on the sites of the lake dwellings of Switzerland yielded ample material for the establishment of the Horn Age. But the Horn Age people had not only

1. N. Roger, in *L'Illustration*, 10 March 1928, pp. 235 sqq. A. Vayson de Pradenne, *Les fraudes en archéologie préhistorique* (1932), pp. 210 sqq., pls. 11–13.

left their tools about the place, they also had artistic ambitions
They covered their tools with nice, regular ornaments on an
elegantly polished ground. In contrast to their grandsons, the
men of the Stone Age, they even mastered the art of writing.

Every day new and startling finds were produced. At first they
found quite a good market, though most of the experts were
suspicious from the very beginning. But after a time the im-
pudence of the promoters of the Horn Age outgrew the boundaries
of their prehistoric speciality. They were no longer content to
carve deer antlers but faked a letter advocating the purchase of
one of their works. It was addressed to the director of the Museum
of Neuchatel and purported to come from the keeper of prehistoric antiquities of the museum, then temporarily absent. The
faked signature brought the matter before a court of law and the
depositions of the workers engaged on the excavations left no
doubt about the peaceful industry engaged in the fabrication of
the *Age de la corne*. Thus its fate was sealed.

MOABITICA

The discovery of an inscription of Mesha, King of Moab (II
Kings iii. 4) in 1869 called the attention of wide circles to the
Moabites. This inspired Selim, an icon-painter of Jerusalem, to
invent the art of the Moabites. He concentrated on pottery, and
especially on clay figures. In spite of their coarseness they show
distinct features, sometimes belonging to Turks with the fez,
sometimes they wear beards after the fashion of Frenchmen *à
la Napoléon III*. For some unknown reason most of these objects
are adorned by seven dots. Inscriptions are profuse, but they are
all completely meaningless.

Clermont-Ganneau and other scholars did not hesitate to de-
nounce these impudent forgeries as soon as they became acquainted with them.[2] But they had undeserved and highly remunerative
success in other quarters, and these quarters being the Prussian

2. C. Clermont-Ganneau, *Les fraudes archéologiques en Palestine* (1885),
pp. 103 sqq. A. Vayson de Pradenne, *Les fraudes en archéologie préhistorique*
(1932), pp. 452 sqq. A. S. Yahuda, in *Jewish Quarterly Review*, vol. 35 (1944),
pp. 139 sqq.

State Collections, the question of their authenticity became a political issue. As many as 1,700 specimens of 'Moabite' culture had been rashly acquired for the Museum of Berlin, and the newly founded German Empire regarded this purchase as the first stage of its programme of cultural activity in the Near East. German scholars and politicians went to every length to safeguard the authenticity of the 'Moabitica', which became for some time a patriotic question. At long last Theodor Mommsen, the famous historian, saved the dignity of German scholars by admitting the error before the forum of the Prussian Diet. Thereupon the 1,700 pieces of clay were buried in the depths of a museum depot and the 'Corpus Inscriptionum Moabiticarum' never got beyond its prospectus.

THE HERCULES SARCOPHAGUS FROM TARRAGONA

The Hercules sarcophagus from Tarragona is one of the most childish and absurd forgeries ever made.[3] One might regard it as a local hoax, were it not for its enormous success. Serious scholars were taken in, so that as recently as 1930, fifty years after its alleged discovery, an eminent archaeologist felt compelled to read a paper to his academy, demonstrating the modern origin of the sarcophagus.

According to an ancient tradition, *sicuti Afri putant* as Sallust says, Hercules is said to have died on Spanish soil. Pomponius Mela, who was himself a Spaniard, relates how the temple in Gades was considered holy because it contained the grave of Hercules Aegyptius.[4] In 1850 Don Buenaventura Hernandez Sanahuja had the good luck of finding near his native Tarragona the sarcophagus which contained the mummy of the Egyptian Hercules (Fig. 2-4). The sarcophagus is supposed to have been broken into pieces when dug up by ignorant workmen so that only some

3. J. von Minutoli, *Altes und Neues aus Spanien* (1854), vol. 2, pp. 153 sqq. P. Paris, in *Revue archéologique*, 5th ser., vol. 14 (1921), pp. 146 sqq. M. von Boehn, *Spanien* (1924), p. 14. P. Wolters, *Sitzungsberichte der Bayer. Akademie der Wissenschaften* (1930), fasc. 6.

4. Sallust, *Jug.* 18. Mela 3, 6.

FIGURE 2.

marble plaques remained, covered with pictorial decorations in a kind of inlay technique. The scenes very appropriately refer to Egypt and Spain with Hercules as the connecting link. The main scene (Fig. 2) shows a subject of particular interest for Spain: Hercules opening the Straits of Gibraltar. With outstretched arms and hands he separates two mountains, the Pillars of Hercules, so that the waters of the Atlantic may flow into the Mediterranean. The colonisation of Spain by immigrants from Egypt is shown to the right and left. To the left the colonists are seen as they leave their African home, clearly characterised by a crocodile, a camel and a palm-tree, while to the right the savage aboriginals are trying to ward off the invaders who are approaching Spain on foot and in barges. In the upper register, beneath an inscription of hieroglyphs and Iberian characters, both meaningless scribbles, we see the monthly occupations. Here Hernandez' interpretation is particularly elucidating. He starts on the left with January: worshipping the Apis; February: the flooding of the Nile Valley (with a small crocodile); March: the fertilised soil dries; April: sowing; May: planting; June: hay-making; July: reaping; August harvest of fruit; September: vintage; October: rest (in a double bunk); November: frost; December: sacrifice. Hernandez continues: 'On the bottom right we see the tunny fisheries which are so rich on the Spanish coast near Malaga.' Rather more obscure in its meaning is an enchanting fragment showing an elephant-headed god who lifts up a mummy with his trunk and shares a boat with an owl (Fig. 3).

An Egyptian sarcophagus of Hercules was too much, even for the most credulous minds, and outside Spain the plaques were from the first rejected as forgeries. But soon a new chapter in the

FIGURE 3.

history of this fake began. The success denied to the sarcophagus as a whole came to one of its fragments. It shows a man and a woman under palm-trees (Fig. 4). The connection of this fragment with the sarcophagus was soon forgotten and it began to lead a life of its own. The symbols connecting the mouths and bodies of the two figures challenged the ingenuity of various interpreters. One scholar went so far as to discover on this plaque the earliest representation of spermatozoa, thus proving that the microscope was known in ancient Egypt. Another even saw 'the vital protoplasms' lying between the two figures, the painter of which seems to have anticipated so many discoveries of modern science. This painter knew, it appears, all about the origin of life, and managed to express in pictorial form that 'all terrestrial life—of plants and animals—is due to the union at the beginning of the universe of the two principles of heat and moisture'. The Egyptian theory had been dropped and the plaque was regarded as Phoenician, an art far less well known. Here it was accepted as 'The origin of Life from the connubium of Baal and Tanait, the supreme Phoenician gods'.[4a]

4a. *American Journal of Archaeology* vol. 20 (1916). p. 210.

FIGURE 4.

SARDINIAN IDOLS

Like most of the forgeries discussed in this chapter the Sardinian idols combine extremely barbaric workmanship with an
intriguing symbolism inviting interpretation. This combination
proved invariably successful and had the additional advantage of
requiring no artistic talent. The Sardinian idols were intended to
augment the number of genuine statuettes from the Iron Age
of Sardinia representing warriors and other human figures,
executed in a most primitive style.

Our knowledge of Sardinian antiquities goes back to the
writings of the Italian general Alberto de la Marmora (1789–1863),
who devoted his life to the exploration of Sardinia. Already in
1840 La Marmora complained that the prices of these bronze
figures were rising as some collectors had lately become interested
in them.[5] By then the forgers had been active for more than ten

5. A. de la Marmora, *Voyage en Sardaigne*, (second edition, 1840), vol. 2,
pp. 171 sqq., atlas pls. 17–31. E. Pais, in *Atti della R. Accademia dei Lincei,*

years and La Marmora was their chief victim. These figures (*Plate* 124) could be made in large quantities as their makers did not waste time on modelling or anatomical studies. Although no two figures are exactly alike, the series as a whole is monotonous. Their maker apparently thought that pagan idols were devils: therefore he produced an endless series of devils, mostly armed with pitchforks. The horns on their heads are another becoming attribute which resembles the horned helmets of the genuine statuettes of warriors. The abundance of snakes and of heads gives these figures their peculiar character. Some have two heads, one above the other, and even from the shoulders of some diminutive heads sprout forth. Occasionally we find mysterious looking but meaningless inscriptions. A redeeming feature in all this repulsiveness and absurdity are the tiny baby devils which some of the figures carry in their arms (*Plate* 124, left).

By and by doubts in the antiquity of these idols began to be heard and the forgers saw their flourishing business in danger. With great cunning they fabricated a manuscript which purported to be the note-book kept between September 1496 and March 1498 by Michele Gili, notary of Cagliari.[6] Gili, a keen student of antiquities, had the good luck of meeting Giovanni Virde, a local savant of Sassari who, in spite of his age—he was seventy— provided Gili with sketches and descriptions of numerous idols of the devil type. These sketches adorn the note-book. La Marmora took the bait and acquired this precious manuscript containing the proof of the genuineness of his figures. He and his contemporaries went on searching the mythologies of East and West for comparable monstrosities. Among the parallels La Marmora found were the idols of the Obotrites, which show indeed some

(Serie 3), *Memorie della classe di scienze morali*, etc., vol. 7 (1880–1), pp. 366 sqq. (on p. 374 a list of the spurious pieces in La Marmora's atlas). G. Perrot and C. Chipiez, *Histoire de l'art dans l'antiquité*, vol. 4 (1887), p. 9, fig. 3. C. Albizzati, in *Enciclopedia Italiana*, vol. 14 (1932), p. 757. H. Tietze, in *Metropolitan Museum Studies*, vol. 5 (1934–36), p. 3, fig. 3. The Sardinian idols are discussed and reproduced as genuine by W. Kirfel, *Die dreiköpfige Gottheit* (1948), p. 143.

6. A. de la Marmora, in *Memorie della Reale Accademia delle Scienze di Torino*, 2nd ser., vol. 14 (1854). *Corpus Inscriptionum Latinarum*, vol. 14, p. 781.

resemblance, and which are likewise forgeries.[7] In the eighteenth century someone felt the urge to create the art of the Obotrites, a Slavonic tribe which inhabited Mecklenburg before the German conquest. Unlike the Sardinian figures and the rather similar Baphomets (see below), the idols of the Obotrites do not need any learned explanation. Each god has his name neatly engraved on his back.

BAPHOMETS

Looking up 'Baphomet' in the *Encyclopedia Britannica*, we learn that a Baphomet is 'the imaginary symbol or idol which the Knights Templars were accused of worshipping in their secret rites, in which they were supposed to have revived the impurities of the Gnostic Ophites'. The first part of this definition is historically correct. In the infamous process against the Knights Templars in 1306 one of the incriminations was that they had adored a heathen idol called Baphomet, a name which, as we now know, is nothing but a corruption of Mahomet. The belief that the Templars revived the 'impurities of the Gnostics', is a late echo of a once famous book by the Viennese orientalist Josef Hammer-Purgstall, *Mysterium Baphometis revelatum*, published in 1818, a book unique for its combination of erudition and absurdity.[8] Hammer-Purgstall firmly believed in the guilt of the Knights Templars, in their blasphemous and obscene rites, their ritual murders and all the other accusations. One day while look-

7. A. G. Masch and D. Wogen, *Die gottesdienstlichen Alterthuemer der Obotriten, aus dem Tempel zu Rhetra* (1771). C. Levezow, in *Abhandlungen der Königl. Akademie der Wissenschaften zu Berlin*, 1834 (published 1836), pp. 143 sqq. M. Vasmer, 'B. Kopitars Briefwechsel mit Jakob Grimm', *Abhandlungen der Preussischen Akademie der Wissenschaften* (1937), p. 143. G. Oesten, in *Zeitschrift für Ethnologie*, vol. 38 (1906), p. 1014. V. Jagic, *Entsiklopediya Slavyanskoi Filologii*, vol. 3 (1911), pp. 9 sqq. C. Schuchhardt, *Arkona, Rethra, Vineta* (2nd ed., 1926), p. 40. L. Leger, *Les anciennes civilisations slaves* (1921), p. 123. The curious idea to inscribe the idols with their names was suggested by a passage in the Chronicle of Thietmar of Merseburg where the *dii singulis nominibus insculptis* in the Slavonic Sanctuary are mentioned (ed. Holtzmann, p. 302, 15).

8. Published in *Fundgruben des Orients*, vol. 6.

ing at some quaint figures in the Imperial Collections of Vienna, where they were regarded as Tibetan idols, he recognised in a flash the Baphomets which had been worshipped by the unfortunate Templars (*Plate* 125, 126).

These small stone figures are of varied but invariably queer shape. Some of them are androgyne, all of them are dreadfully ugly, and of the coarsest workmanship. They are covered with symbols, as the sun, the moon, flames, a T-shaped cross, and some others. In addition to these they bear inscriptions in Greek, Latin, and Arabic characters, none of which, however, make any sense, although scholars have read into them whatever they wanted them to say.

Hammer-Purgstall's 'Revelation' did not remain unchallenged. The Knights Templars, now accused for the second time, found gallant defenders, and the Baphomets went again in search of an author. The prehistoric artists of Sardinia (see above, p. 307), the medieval alchemists, the Ismaelites and Druses, were in turn credited with their authorship.[9] Nowadays the Baphomets are regarded as forgeries dating from the time of the Gothic Revival, during which the Knights Templars became a favourite subject of literature. Their connection with the Templars, however, does not go back beyond 1818, while a figure of this type was illustrated as early as 1755. The first person to discuss a Baphomet was at a loss what to think of it. In a letter to the editor of the *Gentleman's Magazine*[10] 'Palaeophilus' asked the 'Learned in the Orien-

9. S. Assemanni, *Catalogo de' codici mss. orientali della Biblioteca Naniana* (1787), p. 111. *Collezione di tutte le antichità che si conservano nel Museo Naniano di Venezia* (1815), fig. 396. F. M. von Nell, *Baphomet* (1820), declared the figures to be alchemistic symbols. T. J. A. P. Mignard, *Monographie du coffret de M. le Duc de Blacas* (1852); *Suite de la monographie* (1853). E. Pfeiffer, in *Zeitschrift für Kulturgeschichte,* vol. 4 (1897), pp. 385 sqq. E. Babelon, in *La Grande Encyclopédie,* vol. 5, p. 307. Héron de Villefosse, in *Bulletin de la Société Nationale des Antiquaires de France* (1900), pp. 305 sqq. S. Reinach, 'Bas-reliefs enigmatiques', in *Revue africaine,* vol. 52 (1908), pp. 155 sqq. J. v. Schlosser, *Kunst- und Wunderkammern* (1908), p. 113, fig. 94. S. Reinach, *Cultes, mythes et religions,* vol. 4 (1912), p. 252. H. Tietze, in *Metropolitan Museum Studies,* vol. 5 (1934–6), p. 1, fig. 1. L. Planiscig and E. Kris, *Ausstellung Gefälschte Kunstwerke* (1937), p. 12.

10. Vol. 25, p. 104.

124. Sardinian idols.

125. Baphomets.

126. Baphomets.

127. Lead badges by Billy and Charley of London.

tal Languages and Antiquities' for an explanation of his figure, as neither the Society of Antiquaries nor the 'Marocco Ambassador and his attendants' were able to satisfy his curiosity. About its provenance the inquirer knew only that it had been 'presented to an English gentleman by a Greek patriarch at Smyrna, near thirty years ago'. Whereupon another correspondent of the *Gentleman's Magazine* sought an explanation for the monster in the myth of Isis and Osiris.[11] The Comte de Caylus, a famous and learned connoisseur, was more cautious. In his *Recueil d'Anti-quités* (1761)[12] he reproduced a figure which was said to have been brought to Europe by a missionary, 'qui disoit l'avoir trouvée en Asie', but Caylus thought that it reminded him of some recent forgeries of German origin. He concludes: 'J'avoue que je ne comprens rien à cette figure.'

MOZARABIC MANUSCRIPTS ON LEATHER

At the sale of Guglielmo Libri's collection of manuscripts, lovers of rarities were given an opportunity to buy a 'Mozarabic letter', which, as Libri himself put it, 'must be considered among the most extraordinary manuscripts still existing'. This letter was indeed extraordinary: 'written on nearly a square piece of skin on both sides, having the ground coloured a light green, with numerous small spots of different colours, intended no doubt for ornament. The borders are ornamented with rude drawings in brown, that at the bottom exhibiting a representation of a battle between blacks fighting with bows, arrows, etc., and bearing African features. This piece of leather bears evidence of having been hung up for some purpose or other.'

Libri asserted that this masterpiece was written in the seventh century, and even pretended to have understood its text. Less ingenious persons are likely to be puzzled by the first word (or is it a sentence?): 'Moxerelabulabnostraprigeniseiuspatermateram-

11. Ibid., p. 164.

12. Vol. 4, p. 51, pl. 17. Cf. Winckelmann, *Geschichte der Kunst des Alterthums,* 1. Teil, 2. Cap., 2: Abschnitt (1764; ed. J. Lessing, 1870), p. 65, where two such figures are mentioned as idols of the Druses.

bulareaoceanus.' The illustrations are worthy of this farrago and their resemblance to the paintings of the Hercules Sarcophagus is striking. It would be wrong to call this piece of leathern effrontery unique; Libri had two more skins of the same kind.[13]

BILLY AND CHARLEY

Medieval leaden pilgrims' badges belong to the commoner type of finds. Many of them were dug up from the bed of the Thames. This inspired two workmen from the East End, who set to to cast such badges themselves. The idea of these pioneers was almost immediately taken up by William Smith and Charles Eaton, who gained immortality as 'Billy and Charley'. They started a large-scale production of leaden badges sometime around 1857.[14] Billy and Charley had a somewhat childish conception of the Middle Ages. Their imagination was apparently brimful of kings and knights in armour. They surrounded these figures with meaningless inscriptions, adding dates, with a preference for the eleventh century, but always using Arabic numerals (*Plate* 127). These articles were produced by the thousand, and though they were soon denounced as forgeries, the demand appears to have remained satisfactory and fresh supplies seem to have been fabricated at a more recent date.[15] They are still on sale, sometimes as 'Billies and Charleys', sometimes as antiquities, and sometimes as 'quaint old curios'.

13. *Monuments inedits . . . du Cabinet de Guillaume Libri* (1862), pl. D. Catalogue Libri sale, Sotheby, 1 June 1864, no. 48, pl. 13. *Biblioteca Lindesiana, List of MSS. . . . exhibited at Haigh Hall* (1898), nos. 54–6. M. R. James, *A Descriptive Catalogue of the Latin MSS. in the John Rylands Library* (1921), p. xii.

14. G. Clinch, in *The Burlington Gazette*, vol. 1 (1903), pp. 157 sqq. J. Hilton, in *Archaeological Journal*, vol. 63 (1906), pp. 244 sqq. Burlington Fine Arts Club, *Catalogue of a Collection of Counterfeits* (1924), pl. 40. T. Borenius, *Medieval Pilgrim's Badges* (1930), pp. 24 sqq., pl. 9. *Catalogue Lanna Collection* (Sale Lepke, Berlin, 21 March 1911), no. 1275, pl. 98. C. C. Oman, *Apollo*, vol. 48 (1948), p. 95.

15. T. Sheppard, *Forgeries and Counterfeit Antiquities*, Hull Museum Publications, no. 54 (1908), p. 9.

THESSALIAN ANTIQUITIES

Billy and Charley had a follower in more recent times who supplied the collectors of two continents with 'Thessalian antiquities'.[16] He shared the pair's partiality for lead, though his models were also obtainable—at a higher price—in bronze, and he worked in a rather similar childishly primitive style. His only new features were the stylised animals pandering to the predilection for the Scythian 'Animal Style' which became fashionable among art collectors in the early 'twenties. Some of the Thessalian animals were copied after genuine pieces found in Poland and Russia, a plaque with an interlaced band imitates a typical Lombard ornament, but the majority of the figures are pure products of fantasy, combining the primitive with the abstruse as do all the forgeries discussed in this chapter.

16. *Arethuse,* vol. 2 (1925), pp. 60, 142, pls. 12–14; vol. 6 (1929), p. xxxii. *Ars Asiatica,* vol. 7 (1925), pl. 60, nos. 755 and 757; review in *Artibus Asiae* (1927), p. 147. *Art and Archaeology,* vol. 20 (1925), p. 130. J. Werner, *Slawische Bronzefiguren aus Nordgriechenland* (1952). C. Cecchelli, in *Memorie storiche forogiulesi,* vol. 40 (1952–53), pp. 189–204, and vol. 41 (1954–55), pp. 185–187.

PART NINETEEN

CONCLUSION

PART NINETEEN

CONCLUSION

This book is intended as a discussion of forgeries and not as a treatise on the psychology and aesthetics of faking, a subject which has been dealt with in a stimulating paper by Hans Tietze.[1] Neither does it attempt to explain the mind of the forger. The study of forgeries and the study of forgers have much in common but they are not identical. It is frequently assumed that there is a forger behind every fake; but in reality the part of the forger is considerably smaller, especially if we regard as a forger anyone who produces a fraudulent imitation *e nihilo*. Most fakes were once modest and insignificant works of art that have been changed into interesting and saleable objects, wrecks and fragments built up into something new or copies and casts transformed into originals.

However, these remarks are not meant to give credit to the often repeated story of the innocent forger, dished up every time one of the great forgers has been found out. The artist who spends his life creating works of art in the style of a bygone epoch and remains immaculately unaware of the fact that wicked dealers may sell his creations as antiques, is a myth. Bastianini, Dossena and all the others who declared themselves to be innocent victims of the dealers, were very careful to endow their works with dirt, cracks and other outward signs of age. The legend of the innocent forger is usually combined with that other legend of the genius whose

1. H. Tietze, 'The Psychology and Aesthetics of Forgery in Art', in *Metropolitan Museum Studies*, vol. 5 (1934–6), pp. 1 sqq.; see also *Zeitschrift für Aesthetik und allgemeine Kunstwissenschaft*, vol. 27 (1933), pp. 209 sqq.

masterpieces were so spurned and neglected that he was forced to sell them under the name of some famous artist of the past. The neglect of living art is the saddest and most depressing chapter in the annals of art collecting, and the value attached to everything old has certainly always been a strong incentive to the forger. It is, however, a fact that the genius is a most uncommon sight in the ranks of the forgers. There were great artists like Michelangelo, Luca Giordano and, maybe, Pieter Brueghel who occasionally tried their hands at forgery. No Michelangelo, not even a Luca Giordano can be found among the professional forgers. The reason is obvious: the stronger the personality of an artist and the more individual his artistic language, the less adept he is in the art of mimicry which every forgery demands. There are exceptions, or rather, artistic affinities like that between Brueghel and Bosch, or between Michelangelo and classical sculpture. On the other hand, Luca Giordano made a poor job of his Dürer imitation. His baroque and decorative talent had nothing in common with Dürer's art. There have always been minor artists who could express themselves well enough in the idiom of a bygone age and some of them succumbed to the temptations of forgery. One may quote, for example, Georg Schweigger in the seventeenth century, who could evoke to perfection the sculptural style of the time of Dürer or—to cite more recent cases—Bastianini's Quattrocento sculptures or Pallas y Puig's Hispano-Moresque ivories. There are also such able craftsmen as Castellani or Rouchomowsky whose technical skill was in no way inferior to that of the ancients.

But even the most adaptable talent, the most perfect imitator, has his own personality, however slight it may be, he has his own distinctive inflection and, above all, he is a child of his own time. Every forgery will—unconsciously—show symptoms of the style of the epoch which produced it. Contemporaries may not discern it but, seen from a distance, the signs of the true period of origin gradually become apparent. Friedländer once said that the life of a forgery does not outlast thirty years, in other words its own generation. This must not be taken literally. There are, for instance, numbers of bronzes and engraved stones, which have so far yielded no answer to the question 'Classical or Renaissance?' It is, however, a truism that we are particularly sensitive to the idiosyncrasies of the generation of our fathers. Our interpretation of the past constantly undergoes changes or, as Friedländer puts it: 'Since every epoch acquires fresh eyes, Donatello in 1930 looks different from what he did in 1870. That which is worthy of imitation appears different to each generation. Hence, whoever in 1870 successfully produced works by Donatello, will find his performance no longer passing muster with the experts in 1930. We laugh at the mistakes of our fathers, as our descendants will laugh at us.'[2]

The marks by which we may recognise a forgery can be grouped in three classes (1) technical, (2) archaeological, and (3) stylistic. The importance of technical symptoms is often overrated. A case like that of the figure presumed to date from the Bronze Age but made with an iron tool, is rare. Usually the forger is a technical expert well conversant with the methods of ancient craftsmanship. There are few technical processes the secret of which has been lost and there are no unprocurable materials. The main technical difficulty of the forger is the successful imitation of the patina and of the signs of decay. Over archaeological 'evidence' the forger is more liable to blunder. Such details as subject matter, especially of religious art, the correct representation of dress or armour, the palaeography and language of inscriptions, abound in pitfalls. Technical and archaeological errors are often sufficient in themselves to condemn a forgery and they have the additional advantage that they can be demonstrated with scientific exactitude, without involving the subjective element necessarily implicit in every artistic judgment. Nevertheless they are outside the aesthetic sphere proper. Style must always remain the essential criterion.

It has always been taken for granted that forgeries are made for material gain. However, this assumption may lead into various errors. The cheap price at which a work of art was bought is usually put forward as a proof of its authenticity. 'Nobody', it is said, 'would produce a forgery for so little money.' But cheapness may have other reasons. Once a fake has been recognised for what it is , it is worthless. It disappears into the lower and less reputable strata of the art market or lands up in the junk shop, waiting there for the day when it will be rediscovered. The bargain price may

2. M. J. Friedländer, *On Art and Connoisseurship* (1942), pp. 259 sqq.

also be due to the slave wages for which the copyist frequently works.

Ambition has certainly always been a strong incentive to the forger. The reasoning 'if my work is mistaken for a Rembrandt, I am as good as Rembrandt' is illogical because it confuses original creation with imitation, but it remains the motive of many forgeries. Delight in a hoax is another not infrequent motive. I remember an old friend of mine, an Austrian amateur painter, who modelled some clay lions and buried them among the ruins of a castle in Carinthia. Year after year he looked forward to the moment when his lions would be found and exhibited in the local museum. He did not live to see the fulfilment of his wish, but one day the lions may come to light to puzzle some archaeologist of the future. Patriotism also plays an important part among the incentives to forgery. The rival claims of the Italian local savants of the eighteenth century were often supported by *ad hoc* fabricated proofs. With the romantic movement, when every nation took a new pride in the monuments of its past, the desire increased to produce what could not be found but did exist once, or might have existed. Hanka, the forger of the early Czech manuscripts, once sighed: 'Utinam habeamus etiamsi suspecta et falsa'.

Whenever the question of forgeries is discussed, someone will ask: 'Why all this fuss about forgeries? If some millionaire wants to invest his money in something of which he is completely ignorant, that is his own affair. And if a crank derives pleasure from his collected fakes better still, for he does not feel he has wasted his money.' Most art lovers will surely agree. However, all forgeries are potentially dangerous. The crank who acquired some two thousand indifferent paintings and drawings as works of Corot collected his treasures for his private enjoyment. But when, after his death, this accumulated rubbish was dispersed as Corot's work, our whole conception of the great artist was called in question. We had to ask: 'Was it only at some rare moments that Corot was a great painter? Was it possible that his main output consisted of trash and cheap imitations of his own masterpieces?' The 'pure text' is more than a preoccupation of philologists. A great artist, whether a Shakespeare, Michelangelo or Corot, is entitled to have his *œuvre* purged of unwelcome additions.

The objection might be made that so many forgeries are successful and seem to fulfil the function of the originals. What is the
secret of their success? Before we attempt to give an answer to
this question, we should distinguish carefully between forgeries
and art forgeries. The majority of fakes have none or only very
slight artistic pretensions. They are collected as rarities, for the
sake of their subject matter or simply as monuments of the past,
and their artistic qualities are purely incidental. As to art forgeries
proper, it has repeatedly been said that the secret of their success
is the unconscious blending of modern features with an ancient
foundation.

The artistic language of the past has—like any dead language—
to be learned and studied. The forgery is a kind of short-cut, it
translates the ancient work of art into present-day language and
serves the same purpose as translations and modernisations in
literature. This seems to be indeed the secret of many forgeries.
However, the re-interpretation of ancient art in the light of the
present day is no distinctive feature of forgeries. It is characteristic
of even the most objective reproductions. It is the fate of the art of
the past to be perpetually adapted to the taste of the moment. We
see the artist in our setting instead of in his own. Only by an
attempt at historical understanding can we hope to reverse the
process and to transfer ourselves into *Dichters Lande.*

It has been suggested, not ironically but seriously, that forgeries ought to be encouraged. A genuine Van Gogh will always
be the privilege of a few. A flourishing industry would bring his
pictures within the range of everybody. This suggestion was made
by a well-known writer on art. The obvious reply is that legitimate copies and reproductions exist for this very purpose. They
replace the original as far as the power of the copyist or of the
mechanical reproductive process go. But of its ultimate inner-
most qualities the original creation keeps its secret. From a moral
and legal point of view, forgeries form a category by themselves,
but otherwise they have much in common with reproductions
and copies, in that they approach the original without reaching it.

It is a sign of the power of a great work of art that it can be
plundered, plagiarised, copied and imitated and that all the derivatives will to some degree live through the virtue of the original.

Even in the worst translation something of a great poem survives; the most amateurish performance of a great play or work of music does not destroy all its beauties. In the same way an outstanding work of figurative art always transmits something of its greatness to its derivatives. Workshop pieces, copies, reproductions, imitations, forgeries, they will all shine in a reflected light and may blind our judgment.

Disappointing in their own works, forgers often excel as imitators, for they have the best of both worlds. Stealing the virtue of the ancients, they adapt their gains to the taste of their contemporaries, and, like Aesop's wren, who was carried up on the eagle's shoulders, they fly ahead when the flight is over.

APPENDIX

An Early Dürer Forgery.

The numerous forgeries of Dürer's works dating from the seventeenth century have been mentioned above (page 33). A typical example is the 'Head of Saint Paul' in the Gallery at Bamberg (*Plate* 128).[1] It is an oil painting on parchment. Dürer occasionally used parchment for his paintings, and the choice of this uncommon ground was intended to impart an extra touch of authenticity to this work. The forger used a safe method of producing a convincing 'Dürer head': he copied Dürer's portrait of Hieronymus Holzschuher (now at Berlin; *Plate* 129), but disguised Holzschuher by transforming him into a saint. The Saint Paul in another of Dürer's works, the so-called 'Four Apostles' (now at Munich) provided the model for this saint's long beard and hair.

The author of the 'Head of Saint Paul' is apparently Johann Georg Fischer (1580–1643), a man who specialised in such pastiches. Out of three authentic self-portraits of Dürer he concocted a fourth, spurious one (now at Aschaffenburg).[2] Every detail in his paintings had to be a quotation from one of Dürer's genuine works.

1. *Katalog der Historischen Ausstellung der Stadt Nürnberg* (1906), p. 339. F. Dörnhöffer, in *Repertorium für Kunstwissenschaft*, vol. 29 (1906), pp. 444.

2. H. Kehrer, *Dürers Selbstbildnisse* (1934), p. 73. A similar concoction is Fischer's 'Christ Carrying the Cross' (Erlangen) with figures from various works by Dürer, even from the Prayerbook of the Emperor Maximilian. F. Haack, *Funde und Vermutungen zu Dürer* (1916), p. 88, pls. 22–24.

Dutch Forgers of the Eighteenth Century.

The writings of the Dutch essayist Justus van Essen (1734) give a vivid picture of the malpractices prevailing in the Dutch art trade of his time.[3] False pedigrees for pictures, originals replaced by copies, and the forgery of the signatures of artists, are described as very common practices. However, van Essen does not mention another widespread technique, namely the embellishing of pictures. The Dutch paintings from the beginning of the seventeenth century, with their simple compositions and subdued or monochromatic colour schemes, were particularly vulnerable to this practice.

The Museum in Vienna has possessed since 1796 a landscape which used to be exhibited as the joint work of Jan van Goyen and Philips Wouwerman, as it showed the monograms of both artists (*Plate* 130). The landscape shows clearly the style of Van Goyen, but the staffage in the foreground—horses, cows, sheep and a dog—on the other hand, are in the style of Wouwerman. In 1923, Hofstede de Groot found the animals 'not good enough' for Wouwerman, but it was only during a recent cleaning that these figures disappeared and Van Goyen's original composition emerged (*Plate* 131.)[4]

The staffage which had deceived spectators for more than one hundred and fifty years was probably the work of Robert Griffier, who seems to have specialised in this kind of forgery. Johann van Gool, writing in 1751 says of him: 'I have seen paintings by Ruysdael into which this Griffier had inserted figures and horses which he copied so cleverly and deceptively after Wouwerman that eminent connoisseurs believed them to be originals by that master and even bought them'.[5]

Gradually the forgers of Dutch paintings of this type died out. The last one was no real person but the hero of Balzac's story *Pierre Grassor* (1839). Pierre Grassor painted pictures in the Dutch style for an art dealer, and at first was unaware that they

3. Van Essen's writings on this subject have been translated into German by A. Bredius, in *Kunstchronik*, N. F., vol. 24 (1913), p. 185.

4. L. von Baldass, in *Belvedere*, vol. 13 (1938–43), p. 173.

5. *De nieuwe schouburg*, vol. 2 (1751), p. 141.

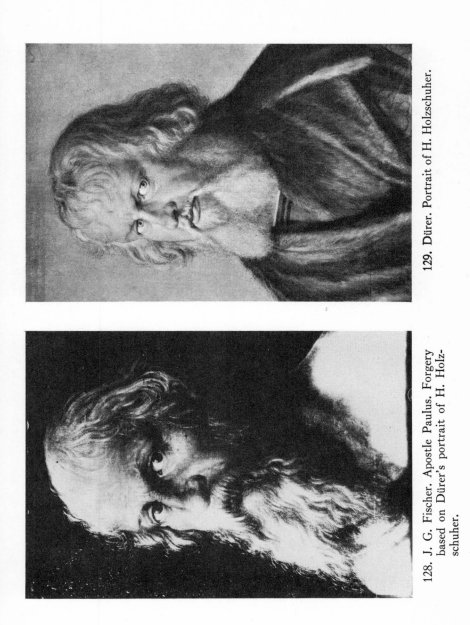

128. J. G. Fischer. Apostle Paulus. Forgery based on Dürer's portrait of H. Holzschuher.

129. Dürer. Portrait of H. Holzschuher.

130. Landscape by Jan van Goyen. The figures in the style of Wouwerman were fraudulently added. (By courtesy of Kunstverlag Wolfrum.)

131. The painting shown in Plate 130 restored to its original state.

133. Turkey. Forgery of a medieval fresco. Schleswig.

132. Madonna. Forgery of a medieval fresco. Lübeck.

were sold as originals. Later, when he visited the house of his future father-in-law, he was surprised to see that about half the old masters in the collection were his own works: 'il était Rubens, Paul Potter, Mieris, Metsu, Gérard Dou!... Il était à lui seul vingt grands maîtres!' ... The young sinner became a paragon of all virtues. He replaced the forgeries in the collection of his father-in-law by true masterpieces, gave up the forging of pictures, and became a fashionable society painter. 'Le Musée de Versailles n'a pas pu se dispenser de commander une Bataille à un si excellent citoyen'.

In the nineteenth century there was no longer room for forgers of Potter, Mieris and Metsu. Their places were taken by those who specialised in spurious Vermeers and Frans Halses.

Forgeries of German Medieval Frescoes.

In Germany the discovery of medieval wall paintings is always celebrated as a major event. They are invariably admired, whether or not they have artistic merit.

In 1942, incendiary bombs fell on the Gothic Marienkirche at Lübeck and destroyed part of the building. The heat caused by the fire had an unexpected result. Thick layers of whitewash peeled off the walls of the nave and revealed underneath fragments of Gothic wall paintings. In July, 1948, the work of restoration of the church was begun, and in the summer of 1950 it was decided to search for similar paintings in the choir, where hitherto none had been found. On September 2, 1951, the reopening of the church was celebrated with great pomp. The aspect of the Marienkirche had changed completely: rows of Saints of gigantic size, ornaments and fabulous beasts covered the walls of the choir (dating from the thirteenth century) and of the nave (fourteenth century). Nowhere else in Germany could be found a cycle of medieval frescoes of such magnitude; moreover, these were remarkably well preserved.[6] Postage stamps with reproductions of some of the frescoes were issued to celebrate the event. Everybody praised and fêted Dietrich Fey, the restorer who had rescued and preserved these treasures for posterity.

6. H. A. Gräbke, *Die Wandmalereien der Marienkirche zu Lübeck* (1951).

This lavish praise embittered Fey's assistant, Lothar Malskat, the man who had done all the actual work. Nobody mentioned his name. He decided to speak up, although not at once. In May, 1952, he caused a world sensation by declaring publicly that the frescoes in the choir were his own work. All the twenty-one figures of saints, each one about ten feet high, were painted by him alone. They were not restorations, nor even over-zealous restorations, but forgeries. Of the original Gothic frescoes nothing had been found but insignificant traces of the sandals or of the bare feet of a few of the saints. The illustrations in a popular book on medieval painting which Fey had given him for this purpose provided Malskat with models.

That was not all. Malskat revealed that, in the service of Fey, for years he had been producing paintings and drawings in the style of old and modern masters, especially of the French Impressionists, which Fey had been selling as originals. Malskat sent this information to the public prosecutor, and on October 9 Fey was duly arrested and his house searched. The forgeries which were found there and confiscated consisted of seven paintings in the style of Rousseau, Vlaminck, Chagall and others, and twenty-one drawings in the style of Degas, Matisse, Beckmann, Barlach and others.

This incident made certain people recall that in 1948 Fey had been accused of forgery. At Bremen he had sold paintings and drawings by Cézanne, Gauguin, Matisse, Rodin, Corinth, Kokoschka and others, which turned out to be fakes. Fey had spent only two days under arrest; he declared that he had inherited the works of art from his father and had been unaware of their spurious character, and so the case against him was dropped.

The ecclesiastical authorities of Lübeck who had allowed the restorers to work without any control or inspection tried hard to prevent a public scandal, but by then it was too late. The art historians had to admit that they had been deceived by Malskat's forged frescoes in the choir, but found some comfort in the fact that there were still frescoes in the nave which were genuine works from the fourteenth century. Now Malskat disappointed them by declaring that even these were, for the most part, his own creations.

A commission of experts met on October 20 and confirmed Malskat's claims.[7]

Fey was provisionally set free on January 9, 1953, but Malskat, who had incriminated himself to spite his former employer, was arrested on the twenty-third of the same month. The affair ended two years later, in January 1955, when Lothar Malskat was sentenced to eighteen months imprisonment, and Dietrich Fey to twenty months. Both were forbidden to practise as church restorers for three years.

Apart from their poor quality, the frescoes are not at all bad as imitations of Gothic paintings. Malskat had found an easy formula: S-shaped figures, long flowing lines for the garments, a long curve for the nose and one eyebrow, short curves for the other eyebrow, eyes, and mouth, and the figure was perfect. The Madonna reproduced here (*Plate* 132) is not entirely Malskat's invention; he merely transformed an old but very damaged Madonna into the linear style of the fourteenth century.[8] The original fresco was not distinct enough to show that the Christ Child was stroking the cheeks of his mother, as is often the case in medieval paintings. Malskat misunderstood the gesture and rendered it as a kind of Hitler salute given with the left hand.

Before Malskat's revelations art historians had studied and discussed the wall paintings in detail. They pointed out Byzantine and French influences, discussed the relation of the frescoes to illuminated manuscripts, tried to trace the literary sources of the iconography, and were able to distinguish the 'hand' of the leading master from the parts executed by his helpers. It was even suggested that one of the heads might be a self-portrait of the medieval master.

It is gratifying to find among so much misspent ingenuity one correct observation, namely the close relation in style between the paintings at Lübeck and the frescoes in the cloister of the cathedral of Schleswig. 'They seem to be an anticipation (*Vorstufe*) of the

7. The report was published in *Kunstchronik*, vol. 5 (1952), pp. 324–326, 331. *Die Marienkirche zu Lübeck und die Denkmalpflege* [papers by various authors, reprinted from *Deutsche Kunst und Denkmalpflege* (1955)].

8. The fresco in its pitiable state before restoration is reproduced in *Die Marienkirche zu Lübeck und die Denkmalpflege* (1955), p. 3.

style of the frescoes at Schleswig', wrote one author.[9] The wall paintings at Schleswig really are similar in style to those at Lübeck, but they are also earlier, since they were painted by Fey and Malskat in 1937.

These paintings in the cloister at Schleswig are a different type of forgery. Here, paintings were already in existence, but they had been so extensively restored in the years 1888–91 that they no longer counted as works of medieval art. The world wanted to see the frescoes in their original state, and Fey and Malskat obediently painted 'frescoes in their original state'. It was 1937, and then even medieval frescoes had to conform to the new spirit.[10] As Malskat later said: 'I had to paint the Apostles as long-headed Vikings because one did not want Eastern round-heads'.[11] Then Himmler came and took the wall paintings under his protection.

Malskat also made an inadvertent contribution to the 'cultural–historical sensation' which kept German scholars busy for years, the *'Schleswiger Truthahnbilder'*, or the pictures of turkeys at Schleswig.[12] One of the frescoes at Schleswig shows 'Herod and the Murder of the Innocents' and beneath it—also in the style of the thirteenth century—a frieze of eight medallions with turkeys (*Plate* 133). In due course it was pointed out that the turkey is an American bird and was unknown in Europe before the sixteenth century. How could it have been known in Schleswig in the thirteenth century? The answer was very simple: long before Columbus the Vikings had reached America. Nothing was hitherto known about Viking journeys to America in the thirteenth century, but it could easily be assumed that they had continued their expeditions through the centuries. Moreover, they might well have taken live turkeys into their boats, thus providing themselves with fresh meat for the long journey home. Not all

9. Gräbke, *op. cit.*, p. xvi.

10. A Stange, *Der Schleswiger Dom und seine Wandmalereien* (1940). F. H. Hamkens, *Die Sinnbilder im Schleswiger Dom. Zwischen Heidentum und christlicher Welt* (1942).

11. Interview with Malskat, *Hamburger Abendblatt*, January 24–25, 1953.

12. R. Hennig, 'Die Schleswiger Truthahnbilder aus dem 13. Jahrhundert', in *Archiv für Kulturgeschichte*, vol. 31 (1943), pp. 328–342.

the turkeys were eaten; a few were brought alive to Schleswig, where they were much admired and depicted on the walls of the cloisters.

There was great rejoicing about this discovery which proved that regular trade relations between America and Northern Germany already existed in the thirteenth century. There were, however, a few discordant voices, and among them that of the painter August Olbers, the man who had restored the frescoes in the late nineteenth century. He declared that he had painted the much discussed turkeys. Inasmuch as no traces of the original frieze below the 'Murder of the Innocents' had been preserved, he painted four foxes and four turkeys as animals which would symbolise the character of Herod. Olbers' testimony was brushed aside with scorn. Who would trust the memory of a very old man? Had not Fey declared that the turkeys—which in the meantime had multiplied from four to eight—were undoubtedly painted in the thirteenth century?

Han van Meegeren.

In May, 1945, soon after the liberation of Holland, the Dutch painter Han van Meegeren had to face a serious indictment. He was accused of collaborating with the Nazis during the German occupation, and especially of having sold to Goering a national treasure, a painting by Vermeer representing 'Saint Mary Magdalen Washing Christ's Feet'.

In July of the same year Han van Meegeren made a sensational confession: the painting sold to Goering was a forgery perpetrated by Van Meegeren himself. Moreover, he added, proudly, he had faked paintings by Frans Hals and Pieter de Hoogh, and no less than five Vermeers, among them the 'Supper at Emmaus' which in 1937 had been acquired for an enormous sum for the Boymans Museum at Rotterdam (*Plate* 134).

Van Meegeren's self-accusation created a world sensation. The Pieter de Hoogh and Frans Hals pictures were small fry and most of the Vermeers were unknown to the art world, but the 'Supper at Emmaus' had immediately after its discovery become world-famous. At first Van Meegeren's revelations met with general incredulity. Who would believe a self-styled forger? Van

Meegeren was asked to prove that he was able to paint pictures of such high quality. Under police supervision he agreed to paint another Vermeer, a 'Jesus in the Temple'.

Van Meegeren's confession cleared him from the accusation of collaboration with the enemy, but now he had to face a new charge: getting money under false pretences, especially by selling pictures with false signatures. Disgusted, he left the 'Jesus in the Temple' unfinished; it lacks all signs of artificial ageing.

Meanwhile, a group of technical experts and art historians investigated the 'Vermeers' and other paintings. After ten months of hard work, applying the latest methods of spectrography and microchemical analysis, they came to the unanimous conclusion that Van Meegeren had spoken the truth. The paintings were undeniably his work.

While the art world was arguing whether Van Meegeren was a feeble imitator or a genius who could paint as well as Vermeer, the trial took place. It lasted from October 29 to November 12, 1947. Van Meegeren declared that the forgeries were his vengeance on a hostile world. 'Now I have proved that I am a gifted artist, and that the art critics had misjudged me and hindered me in my profession. These very same critics praised my works in the style of the seventeenth century, and believed them to be by a master of the rank of Jan Vermeer'. He congratulated the technical experts on the clever way they had reconstructed his technical methods. 'In the future the forging of pictures will be impossible', was his ironical comment. He added that he found the writings of the monograms of Vermeer and De Hoogh the most troublesome part of his task. The trial ended with Van Meegeren's condemnation to one year in prison. A few weeks after the sentencing, on December 30, 1947, he died from a heart attack.

Van Meegeren's biography is without any particular interest. He was born in 1889 at Deventer, and studied first architecture, then painting. He was moderately successful, but did not achieve real fame. Books on modern Dutch art, and the usual reference books did not include his name.[13] Of his paintings and drawings,

13. The large literature on the forgeries of Han van Meegeren is mostly of an ephemeral character. An excellent and well-illustrated report on the

134. 'The Supper at Emmaus'. Imitation of Vermeer by H. van Meegeren. (By courtesy of A. C. L., Brussels.)

135. 'The Last Supper'. Imitation of Vermeer by H. van Meegeren.
(By courtesy of A. C. L., Brussels.)

only those which are free imitations of Dutch seventeenth-century masters show talent and technical skill; his religious and symbolical compositions are repulsive.

To think that such a tenth-rate artist should have been able to paint the 'Supper at Emmaus' which was hailed as Vermeer's greatest achievement. When it turned up suddenly in 1937, the general chorus of enthusiasm was not broken by a single dissenting opinion. If anyone had any doubts, he kept them to himself. In the extensive literature on the painting there was not a single word of doubt concerning the attribution to Vermeer, let alone concerning the authenticity of the painting.

The technical experts and restorers were deceived along with everyone else. Van Meegeren knew that they would start by examining the hardness of the paint. The paint layer of his Vermeer was very hard and resisted alcohol to a remarkable degree. He avoided the usual method of forgers, a thin layer of glue, as by then too well known;[14] instead of the traditional drying oils he used an artificial phenolic resin which in a short period of time imparted to the surface of the painting an exceptional hardness. He painted on top of genuine old paintings, as forgers usually do. The old canvasses provided cracks which could be made visible on the new surface, and by rolling the finished picture around a stick more cracks could be produced. This simple method is as old as the seventeenth century, but still seems to be efficient.[15] The cracks were filled with ink to imitate the dirt which is always present in them and makes them visible to the eye.

Van Meegeren had taken into account the possibility of a

---

scientific examination was published by P. B. Coremans, *Van Meegeren's Faked Vermeers and De Hooghs* (1949). A masterly profile of the artist Van Meegeren was given by C. L. Ragghianti in *Sele-Arte*, vol. 3, no. 17 (1955), pp. 56–67. Many important details are contained in newspaper articles which are not easily accessible to the student. I have quoted from the report on the trial in the *Nieuwe Rotterdamse Courant*, October 29, 1947. The attempts to rehabilitate two of the paintings have been well summarised by A. Chastel in *Le Monde*, March 5, 1955.

14. See above, p. 27.
15. See above, p. 37.

chemical analysis of the colours, and was careful to employ only pigments which were known in Vermeer's lifetime. At the trial the experts triumphantly pointed out that the ultramarine that Van Meegeren used had been adulterated: spectrography revealed that it contained a very small admixture of cobalt blue, a colour first produced in the nineteenth century. This proved the modern origin of the painting, but only after Van Meegeren had declared himself to be the painter of the 'Supper at Emmaus'.

The painting made an overwhelming impression when it was first shown to the public. Perhaps this immediate appeal should have been a warning. F. J. Mather had written in a different context: 'A blatant and insistent charm is the essential characteristic of every successful forgery. . . . The false object excited me more, had more 'kick', than any authentic masterpiece ever has. The masterpiece does not, in the vigorous parlance of modern youth, 'knock you dead'. It keeps a certain aloofness, waits in dignity upon your recognition and understanding'.[16] But nobody remembered this warning.

The chord of ultramarine and yellow, the dominant colours of the painting, is truly conceived in the spirit of Vermeer. The still life on the table—bread, a glass and a jug set against the white linen—is *bonne peinture* in the best Dutch tradition. The hands in the centre of the composition are most expressive, especially Christ's blessing hand which seems to sink slowly down, as if in resignation.

And the faces—but here we have to mention how the attitude toward Vermeer's work changed toward the turn of the century. For the Impressionists, Vermeer was the revolutionary painter of the 'View of Delft'; it was this picture which made the Mauritshuis at The Hague a place of pilgrimage for the painters of the nineteenth century. For the twentieth century, Vermeer was no longer an open-air painter. Now he was admired for his quiet figures in interiors, those reticent human beings whose immovable, mask-like faces refuse to communicate their inner thoughts by vulgar mimicry. Van Meegeren knew the ideals of the modern public, the 'arte non eloquente'. Not surprisingly, somebody found in

16. 'Art and authenticity', *Atlantic Monthly*, vol. 143, no. 3 (1929), p. 316.

the 'Supper at Emmaus' 'the classical restraint of a Piero della Francesca'.[17]

Han Van Meegeren achieved what the official church art of the twentieth century was unable to achieve. He painted the only religious picture of our time which was able to move modern men. In its 'quietism' it differed even from Rembrandt's religious paintings; there was no trace of the supernatural or miraculous. It showed a deeply human, an 'inner' religion—in short, the religious ideal of the twentieth century.

And how well the new Vermeer fitted into art history! Every art historian had learned at school that Vermeer's style derived ultimately from Caravaggio. Now a lucky discovery provided the final proof. The new painting was based on Caravaggio's 'Disciples at Emmaus'. By using Caravaggio's composition as the basis for his own, Van Meegeren cleverly avoided what has proved to be the stumbling block for every modern artist—the task of *composing* a painting in the way the old masters did it. Van Meegeren's other religious paintings show how he failed utterly when he lacked this support.

The 'Supper at Emmaus' is certainly the highest achievement of Han Van Meegeren's artistic career. A face, radiant, looking down under half-closed eyelids, mask-like but full of inner pain, had haunted him throughout his life. It appears as the head of a woman in several of the symbolist paintings he painted in his younger years and under his own name. But here, as the head of Christ, it is transformed into art because he borrowed Vermeer's modelling and colour scheme.

For once in his life Van Meegeren had become a creator; impotent in the idiom of his own day, he was able to create in the language of a master of the past. But he succeeded only once. He belonged to the long line of artists who had only a single creative moment in their lives, like the poets who are known for one poem, like the musicians who are remembered for a single melody.

All the other Vermeers he painted look like parodies of the 'Supper at Emmaus'. In his most ambitious work, the 'Last Supper', he had to plagiarise himself (*Plate* 135). The difference between the 'Supper at Emmaus' and the other Vermeer imitations

17. *The Art News*, April 9, 1938.

is immense. They were accepted as originals, and one was even acquired for the Rijksmuseum at Amsterdam, but this was during the war, when newly found paintings were at once stored in places of safety and a wider public was unable to judge them. One wonders what the verdict would have been if the world had had an opportunity to view this ever-increasing flood of new Vermeers. It has been said that the all too ready acceptance of the paintings induced Van Meegeren to bestow less care on them; actually, they are as carefully painted as the Emmaus picture, but his creative moment had passed.

After Van Meegeren's death an attempt was made to steal his title to fame. Daniel George van Beuningen, the wealthy Dutch collector who had acquired the 'Last Supper' for an enormous sum for his own collection and had contributed generously to enable the Boymans Museum to acquire the 'Supper at Emmaus' set out to prove that these two pictures were after all genuine works of Vermeer. A well-organised propaganda campaign attempted to discredit the results of the trial. This was not easy, particularly in the case of the 'Last Supper'. The X-ray photograph had shown that this picture was painted on top of an old canvas with a hunting scene. By accident a photograph of the painting in its original state turned up—it was a work by A. Hondius—and, moreover, the art dealer in whose possession the painting had been, could produce the bill which showed that Van Meegeren had purchased it in May, 1940. The only way out was to declare that all the evidence, including the photograph and the bill, had been faked by the technical expert at the time of the trial.

Poor Van Meegeren. He had been so proud of his achievements, and now someone wanted to rob him of his laurels. He had already paid a heavy penalty for announcing to a shocked world that he was the creator of the admired paintings. He might easily have kept the secret and admitted only the one forgery which had been sold to Goering. Van Meegeren was very vain and all through his life he strove after fame. He achieved it late in life, and then only in disguise, but he will always be remembered as the creator of one of the very few forgeries which can count as a work of art in its own right.

The Female Heads from Centuripe.

The latest and at the same time the most ambitious addition to the number of pseudoantique paintings is a series of female heads and half-figures painted on terra-cotta roundels. They turned up in 1939, but a few male portraits had come to light a few years earlier. One of them had found its way into the Museum of Historic Art at Princeton. All of them were rumoured to have been found somewhere at Centuripe in Sicily, but the exact spot and date of their discovery remains a secret. They were believed to be Hellenistic works from the third century B.C.

The series of seven female beauties proved irresistible. A wealthy Italian acquired them for a considerable sum and presented them to Mussolini. Il Duce gave them to the Museo Nazionale at Naples, whose incomparable collection of ancient paintings lacked just one thing—female portraits from Centuripe. The heads adorned the Museum for exactly two days. Then war broke out and the seven ladies were stored in a place of safety. Meanwhile one could admire them in the plates of a luxurious publication which met with an enthusiastic reception.[18]

Our illustration (*Plate* 136) shows one of the lovelies. The beauty of her face is beyond dispute. One might argue about her shoulder, but luckily the painter has made provision for various tastes. Some might prefer her tall right side, others her shorter left shoulder. And should someone find the melodious line of her upper lip too much like a moustache, then let his eyes rest on her enchantingly small lower lip. Who could resist the charm of such lips? Certainly not the archaeologist who wrote that one might almost think to be in front of a modern work of art, were it not for those lips, 'lips which have so much in common with Sicilian coins'.

An Italian proverb says: 'Beauty without virtue does not last for long.' After the end of the war the seven beauties did not come back to their museum. A rumour was current that they had perished from mould. Perhaps their disappearance was caused by the two spirited attacks on their authenticity by Carlo Albizzati,

18. G. E. Rizzo, *Ritratti di età ellenistica* (1940).

the first of which was published in 1942, when it took great moral courage to deny the genuineness of Mussolini's gift.[19] Now, although they are probably no longer in existence, it may still be worth-while to mention them, because in archaeological literature they are still very much alive.[20]

Early Forgeries of Classical Sculptures.

Our collections of classical sculptures still contain many works which were produced in the Renaissance period. The relief with 'Medea and the daughters of Pelias' in the Berlin Museum (*Plate* 137) has been doubted more than once, but appears as genuine in the latest catalogue of the Museum.[21]

It was already in existence in the sixteenth century, as can be seen from a drawing after it in the sketchbook of Giovannantonio Dosio.[22] The relief goes back to an outstanding Greek work from the fifth century B.C., which is known to us from a poorly preserved but undoubtedly antique copy in the Museo Lateranese at Rome (*Plate* 138). It was this relief in the Lateran which the forger of the Berlin relief copied.

Archaeologists seem to be reluctant to admit that the cold, stiff, almost neoclassical workmanship of the Berlin relief could be found in the first half of the sixteenth century. In fact, Renaissance artists showed a predilection for this style, and were particularly successful when they imitated it. One need only refer to the bronze statuettes of Antico or the forgeries of Roman coins which were produced at Padua in the sixteenth century. As the forger of the marble relief had to copy a rather damaged model, he got many details wrong, but not wrong enough to open the eyes of some eminent archaeologists. He failed to recognise the dagger

19. C. Albizzati, in *Athenaeum*, n.s. xx (1942), pp. 62 sqq.; n.s. xxvi (1948), pp. 237 sqq.

20. W. H. Gross, in *Convivium Konrat Ziegler zum 70. Geburtstag* (1954), p. 66.

21. E. Löwy, in *Bullettino della Commissione Archeologica Comunale di Roma*, vol. 25 (1897). C. Blümel, *Römische Kopien griechischer Skulpturen* (1931), p. 46.

22. C. Huelsen, *Das Skizzenbuch des G. Dosio* (1933), pl. 53.

136. Spurious Hellenistic portrait, said to be from Centuripe.

137. Medea and the daughters of Pelias. Sixteenth century. Berlin.

138. Medea and the daughters of Pelias. Ancient. Rome.

139. Maenad. Neo-Attic relief. Venice.

140. Maenad. Sixteenth-century imitation. Venice.

141. Forgery of an eagle-shaped Germanic fibula.

142. Chinese neolithic vase with geometrical decoration. The human and animal figures are fraudulent additions.

in the hand of the woman to the right, and rendered it as a branch, and he left out the scabbard which seemed meaningless to him. He was unable to distinguish between the chiton and the himation of the woman in the centre, and completely misunderstood the bronze tripod on which the kettle is resting.

The Museo Archeologico at Venice possesses two beautiful marble bases of triangular shape with relief decoration. Both come from the Grimani collection and were regarded as ancient already in the sixteenth century.[23] A comparison of the two reliefs, which at first sight look remarkably alike, is very instructive. *Plate* 139 is the Neo-Attic copy of a Greek relief from the end of the fifth century B.C. Typical is the delicate and sensitive rendering of the human body, and, in sharp contrast to it, the ornamental play of the crisp, ridge-like folds of the drapery.

Nothing of that kind can be found in the other relief (*Plate* 140), which must be a fraudulent copy dating from the first half of the sixteenth century. Fraudulent, because it has been damaged on purpose. The technique is quite different. The Greek artist used the drill for the deeply cut folds of the drapery. The Renaissance artist was used to the chisel, which necessitated a different technique. Where he did use the drill, as in the heads of Ammon and the sphinxes, the effect achieved is curiously regular and pedantic. It is also interesting to compare the typically Greek profile of the maenad on one relief and the angle formed by forehead and nose on the other.

Etruscan Terra-Cotta Figures.

Etruscan statues of large size are rare, but as every economist knows, demand creates supply. Two terra-cotta warriors, one life-size, the other larger than life (2.44 m.), together with the head of a third one were acquired for the Metropolitan Museum of Art of New York between 1915 and 1921. They combine

23. Arndt-Amelung, *Einzelaufnahmen*, no. 2469–2474. H. Egger, *Codex Escurialensis* (1906), p. 98. C. Huelsen, *Il libro di Giuliano da Sangallo* (1910), p. 45. L. Curtius, *Pentheus* (1929), p. 17, n. 2. C. Anti, *Il Regio Museo Archeologico nel Palazzo Reale di Venezia* (1930), pp. 30 and 138.

motifs taken from Greek as well as from Etruscan bronze statuettes.[24]

One day a sister statue to the famous Etruscan Apollo from Veii (in the Museo di Villa Giulia, Rome) turned up. The newly discovered figure represented—very appropriately—Diana. Actually, this statue is a forgery. Alceo Dossena modelled it as an archaic Greek figure with a smiling face, but later, after his 'Greek' statues had become discredited and Etruscan art had become more fashionable, someone decided to change the Greek smile into a serious Etruscan face. The metamorphosis was so successful that the statue was acquired for the City Art Museum of St. Louis.[25]

Teutonic Jewellery From the Migration Period.

The forgeries of Teutonic jewellery reflect the history and migrations of the Germanic tribes. Forgers working in the homeland itself are impartial and pay equal attention to the various tribes; the Italian forgers concentrate on the Ostrogoths and Lombards; whereas their Spanish colleagues produce works of the Visigoths exclusively.

Since the greatest demand is for the beautiful large eagle-shaped fibulae of gold inlaid with garnets, forgers have been particularly active in that field.

The Third Reich brought about an enormous interest in Germanic antiquities, and it was a particular stroke of good luck when a gorgeous eagle-shaped fibula turned up in 1936 (*Plate* 141). It was reported to have been discovered at Königsberg in Moravia, and thus it became a suitable tribute from the Sudetenland to the Third Reich. It was acquired for an enormous sum for the Germanisches Nationalmuseum at Nürnberg. Soon after its

24. A. W. Byvanck, *De Kunst der Oudheid*, vol. 2 (1949), p. 456. D. F. de Ruyt, in *L'Antiquité Classique*, vol 19 (1950), p. 266. R. Bianchi Bandinelli, *Storicità dell'arte classica* (1950), p. 120. D. von Bothmer and J. V. Noble, *An enquiry into the forgery of the Etruscan terra-cotta warriors* (1961).

25. W. Lusetti, *Alceo Dossena scultore* (1955), pls. 7–9. P. Cellini, *Paragone*, vol. 7, no. 81 (1956), pp. 54–58. R. Herbig, *Bulletin of the City Art Museum of St. Louis*, vol. 43 (1958), pp. 22 sqq. L. Banti, *Studi etruschi*, vol. 26 (1958), pp. 237–241.

acquisition, Hans Zeiss and other archaeologists declared it a forgery. A thorough investigation yielded some surprising results. Under one of the inlaid stones was found a bristle from a toothbrush, and although in those days the ancient Germans were being credited with many achievements, no one claimed that they had used toothbrushes. Moreover, the modern origin of the fibula could be proven by the fact that it consisted, at least in part, of chemically pure gold. The Museum won the ensuing lawsuit, and in December, 1940, Herbert Marwitz, the dealer who had sold the eagle to the Museum, was convicted of fraud and condemned to five years imprisonment. From this moment the fibula became a political issue. At the instigation of the party, the Reichsamt für Vorgeschichte declared the fibula to be genuine, and got together a number of German and foreign experts who were willing to testify to its authenticity. In 1949, by sheer accident, the workshop was discovered which for a number of years had provided Marwitz with Teutonic jewellery; but by then Marwitz had reacquired most of the objects that had been confiscated at the time of his trial, and had left Germany in order to sell his wares abroad.[26]

When, in 1939, the Burlington Fine Arts Club in London held an exhibition of 'Art in the Dark Ages in Europe', its main attraction was the 'treasure from a Lombard chieftain's grave'. The great museums of Ireland, Scandinavia, and Hungary had lent to the exhibition some of their most precious possessions, all of which were eclipsed by the Lombard treasure. It was notable not only because it was immaculately preserved, but also because it was almost entirely of pure gold. The few parts that were not solid gold, such as a helmet with ornamental bands, a sword and two daggers, were at least decorated with gold. The outstanding piece was a golden collar with a relief in the centre: a king seated on a throne surrounded by warriors and Victories, one of which

26. H. Kühn, in *Ipek*, vol. 15/16 (1941–42), pp. 267–268. M. Alagro, in *Archivo Español de Arqueología* (1942), p. 174. 90. *Jahresbericht des German-ischen Nationalmuseums* (1944), p. 5. G. Lill, in *Germania*, vol. 28 (1944–50), pp. 54–62 (the best account of the Marwitz forgeries). On Marwitz' forgeries of gold vessels from the Bronze Age, see R. Hachmann, in *Germania*, vol. 36 (1958), pp. 436–446.

carries a standard with the inscription 'VICTVRIA'. The entire scene, including the inscription with its Barbaric misspelling, is copied from the well-known relief of King Agilulf, now at Florence. This coincidence did not remain unnoticed, but the conclusion which was drawn from it was that the new treasure must have come from the tomb of King Agilulf. Later, however, the realization that numerous details corresponded to well-known Lombard objects, aroused some suspicion, and the treasure disappeared from sight for a number of years.

In 1949 it was again taken from the vaults of the bank where it had been kept in expectation of a buyer, and exhibited for the second time. By now it had become a dazzling sight, rather like the treasure in Aladdin's cave. The number of objects had increased enormously. There were now no less than four crowns and about a dozen swords, daggers and knives. The word 'VICTVRIA', a kind of Wagnerian *leitmotif*, could now be read on a golden cross, and, repeated several times, on a drinking horn.

The enthusiastic description of the incomplete treasure in the catalogue of the Burlington Club of 1930 had provided a few useful hints as to its true identity. The author had said that the treasure was as important as the one found in the seventeenth century in the tomb of the Franconian King Childeric. In 1949 the similarity between the two treasures became even more striking. The treasure of Childeric contained many golden bees; the Lombard treasure in its second, enlarged edition boasted of six large and eight small bees of gold. The author of the exhibition catalogue of 1930 had surmised that the treasure came from the tomb of King Agilulf; now there was irrefutable proof in the shape of a crown with the inscription: 'REX ITAL TOTIVS GRAT DI GLORIA ACILVLF'.[27] And in addition there was the sword of Agilulf's wife Theodolinda with her portrait and the identifying inscription: 'THEODELENDA REC GLORIOSIS-SEMA'.[28]

27. The inscription is copied from the one of the crown at Monza.

28. *Catalogue of an exhibition of art in the Dark ages in Europe* (1930), pp. 99–107. *Pantheon* 6 (1930), pp. 326–328, 4 figs. S. Fuchs, *Die langobardischen Goldblattkreuze* (1938), p. 10 n. W. von Stoker and H. Zeiss, in *Germania*, vol. 24 (1940), p. 272.

Early Chinese Ceramics.

The painted pottery of neolithic China became known around 1920 as the result of excavations. Since then many of these vessels have migrated to European and American collections. Some forgers felt dissatisfied with the characteristic severe geometrical decoration, and tried to enliven the vessels by adding human figures and animals (*Plate* 142). The human figures look 'rather childish, but lack the spontaneity of genuine children's drawings. The horse which can be seen in the panel on the left is much better drawn, but is an animal which was still unknown in neolithic China.

The latest addition to Chinese art is the Hui-hsien pottery. The name is derived from a place where this pottery is reported to have been found under more than mysterious circumstances. Most of the objects are covered with a shiny black lacquer coating which gives them an appearance not unlike Greek painted vases. They would be roughly contemporary with these vases if the date usually proposed for the Hui-hsien pottery—the fifth century B.C.—could be accepted. A certain amount of the Hui-hsien ware consists of faithful reproductions of miscellaneous bronze objects, among them some mirrors in Han style. However, what most enchanted European and American collectors were not these copies of bronzes but human figures of very stylised geometrical shapes. They correspond in all essentials to the ideals of Western sculpture in the post-Picasso epoch.[29]

29. G. Ecke, in *Artibus Asiae*, vol. 15 (1952), pp. 305–323. *Far Eastern Ceramic Bulletin*, vol. 6, no. 1 (1954) (special number). E. von Erdberg-Consten, in *Oriens Extremus*, vol. 2 (1955), pp. 1–11.

INDEX

A CATALOGUE OF SELECTED DOVER BOOKS
IN ALL FIELDS OF INTEREST

A CATALOGUE OF SELECTED DOVER BOOKS
IN ALL FIELDS OF INTEREST

WHAT IS SCIENCE?, *N. Campbell*
The role of experiment and measurement, the function of mathematics, the
nature of scientific laws, the difference between laws and theories, the limita-
tions of science, and many similarly provocative topics are treated clearly and
without technicalities by an eminent scientist. "Still an excellent introduction
to scientific philosophy," H. Margenau in *Physics Today.* "A first-rate primer
. . . deserves a wide audience," *Scientific American.* 192pp. 5⅜ x 8.
Paperbound $1.25

THE NATURE OF LIGHT AND COLOUR IN THE OPEN AIR, *M. Minnaert*
Why are shadows sometimes blue, sometimes green, or other colors depending
on the light and surroundings? What causes mirages? Why do multiple suns
and moons appear in the sky? Professor Minnaert explains these unusual
phenomena and hundreds of others in simple, easy-to-understand terms based
on optical laws and the properties of light and color. No mathematics is
required but artists, scientists, students, and everyone fascinated by these
"tricks" of nature will find thousands of useful and amazing pieces of information. Hundreds of observational experiments are suggested which require no
special equipment. 200 illustrations; 42 photos. xvi + 362pp. 5⅜ x 8.
Paperbound $2.00

THE STRANGE STORY OF THE QUANTUM, AN ACCOUNT FOR THE GENERAL
READER OF THE GROWTH OF IDEAS UNDERLYING OUR PRESENT ATOMIC
KNOWLEDGE, *B. Hoffmann*
Presents lucidly and expertly, with barest amount of mathematics, the problems and theories which led to modern quantum physics. Dr. Hoffmann begins
with the closing years of the 19th century, when certain trifling discrepancies
were noticed, and with illuminating analogies and examples takes you through
the brilliant concepts of Planck, Einstein, Pauli, Broglie, Bohr, Schroedinger,
Heisenberg, Dirac, Sommerfeld, Feynman, etc. This edition includes a new,
long postscript carrying the story through 1958. "Of the books attempting an
account of the history and contents of our modern atomic physics which have
come to my attention, this is the best," H. Margenau, Yale University, in
American Journal of Physics. 32 tables and line illustrations. Index. 275pp.
5⅜ x 8.
Paperbound $1.75

GREAT IDEAS OF MODERN MATHEMATICS: THEIR NATURE AND USE,
Jagjit Singh
Reader with only high school math will understand main mathematical ideas
of modern physics, astronomy, genetics, psychology, evolution, etc. better than
many who use them as tools, but comprehend little of their basic structure.
Author uses his wide knowledge of non-mathematical fields in brilliant ex-
position of differential equations, matrices, group theory, logic, statistics,
problems of mathematical foundations, imaginary numbers, vectors, etc.
Original publication. 2 appendixes. 2 indexes. 65 ills. 322pp. 5⅜ x 8.
Paperbound $2.00

THE MUSIC OF THE SPHERES: THE MATERIAL UNIVERSE — FROM ATOM TO QUASAR, SIMPLY EXPLAINED, *Guy Murchie*
Vast compendium of fact, modern concept and theory, observed and calculated data, historical background guides intelligent layman through the material universe. Brilliant exposition of earth's construction, explanations for moon's craters, atmospheric components of Venus and Mars (with data from recent fly-by's), sun spots, sequences of star birth and death, neighboring galaxies, contributions of Galileo, Tycho Brahe, Kepler, etc.; and (Vol. 2) construction of the atom (describing newly discovered sigma and xi subatomic particles), theories of sound, color and light, space and time, including relativity theory, quantum theory, wave theory, probability theory, work of Newton, Maxwell, Faraday, Einstein, de Broglie, etc. "Best presentation yet offered to the intelligent general reader," *Saturday Review*. Revised (1967). Index. 319 illustrations by the author. Total of xx + 644pp. 5⅜ x 8½.
Vol. 1 Paperbound $2.00, Vol. 2 Paperbound $2.00,
The set $4.00

FOUR LECTURES ON RELATIVITY AND SPACE, *Charles Proteus Steinmetz*
Lecture series, given by great mathematician and electrical engineer, generally considered one of the best popular-level expositions of special and general relativity theories and related questions. Steinmetz translates complex mathematical reasoning into language accessible to laymen through analogy, example and comparison. Among topics covered are relativity of motion, location, time; of mass; acceleration; 4-dimensional time-space; geometry of the gravitational field; curvature and bending of space; non-Euclidean geometry. Index. 40 illustrations. x + 142pp. 5⅜ x 8½. Paperbound $1.35

HOW TO KNOW THE WILD FLOWERS, *Mrs. William Starr Dana*
Classic nature book that has introduced thousands to wonders of American wild flowers. Color-season principle of organization is easy to use, even by those with no botanical training, and the genial, refreshing discussions of history, folklore, uses of over 1,000 native and escape flowers, foliage plants are informative as well as fun to read. Over 170 full-page plates, collected from several editions, may be colored in to make permanent records of finds. Revised to conform with 1950 edition of Gray's Manual of Botany. xlii + 438pp. 5⅜ x 8½. Paperbound $2.00

MANUAL OF THE TREES OF NORTH AMERICA, *Charles Sprague Sargent*
Still unsurpassed as most comprehensive, reliable study of North American tree characteristics, precise locations and distribution. By dean of American dendrologists. Every tree native to U.S., Canada, Alaska; 185 genera, 717 species, described in detail—leaves, flowers, fruit, winterbuds, bark, wood, growth habits, etc. plus discussion of varieties and local variants, immaturity variations. Over 100 keys, including unusual 11-page analytical key to genera, aid in identification. 783 clear illustrations of flowers, fruit, leaves. An unmatched permanent reference work for all nature lovers. Second enlarged (1926) edition. Synopsis of families. Analytical key to genera. Glossary of technical terms. Index. 783 illustrations, 1 map. Total of 982pp. 5⅜ x 8.
Vol. 1 Paperbound $2.25, Vol. 2 Paperbound $2.25,
The set $4.50

IT'S FUN TO MAKE THINGS FROM SCRAP MATERIALS,
Evelyn Glantz Hershoff
What use are empty spools, tin cans, bottle tops? What can be made from
rubber bands, clothes pins, paper clips, and buttons? This book provides
simply worded instructions and large diagrams showing you how to make
cookie cutters, toy trucks, paper turkeys, Halloween masks, telephone sets,
aprons, linoleum block- and spatter prints — in all 399 projects! Many are easy
enough for young children to figure out for themselves; some challenging
enough to entertain adults; all are remarkably ingenious ways to make things
from materials that cost pennies or less! Formerly "Scrap Fun for Everyone."
Index. 214 illustrations. 373pp. 5⅜ x 8½.   Paperbound $1.50

SYMBOLIC LOGIC and THE GAME OF LOGIC, *Lewis Carroll*
"Symbolic Logic" is not concerned with modern symbolic logic, but is instead
a collection of over 380 problems posed with charm and imagination, using
the syllogism and a fascinating diagrammatic method of drawing conclusions.
In "The Game of Logic" Carroll's whimsical imagination devises a logical game
played with 2 diagrams and counters (included) to manipulate hundreds of
tricky syllogisms. The final section, "Hit or Miss" is a lagniappe of 101 additional puzzles in the delightful Carroll manner. Until this reprint edition,
both of these books were rarities costing up to $15 each. Symbolic Logic:
Index. xxxi + 199pp. The Game of Logic: 96pp. 2 vols. bound as one. 5⅜ x 8.
                                                            Paperbound $2.00

MATHEMATICAL PUZZLES OF SAM LOYD, PART I
selected and edited by M. Gardner
Choice puzzles by the greatest American puzzle creator and innovator. Selected
from his famous collection, "Cyclopedia of Puzzles," they retain the unique
style and historical flavor of the originals. There are posers based on arithmetic,
algebra, probability, game theory, route tracing, topology, counter and sliding
block, operations research, geometrical dissection. Includes the famous "14-15"
puzzle which was a national craze, and his "Horse of a Different Color" which
sold millions of copies. 117 of his most ingenious puzzles in all. 120 line
drawings and diagrams. Solutions. Selected references. xx + 167pp. 5⅜ x 8.
                                                            Paperbound $1.00

STRING FIGURES AND HOW TO MAKE THEM, *Caroline Furness Jayne*
107 string figures plus variations selected from the best primitive and modern
examples developed by Navajo, Apache, pygmies of Africa, Eskimo, in Europe,
Australia, China, etc. The most readily understandable, easy-to-follow book in
English on perennially popular recreation. Crystal-clear exposition; step-by-
step diagrams. Everyone from kindergarten children to adults looking for
unusual diversion will be endlessly amused. Index. Bibliography. Introduction
by A. C. Haddon. 17 full-page plates, 960 illustrations. xxiii + 401pp. 5⅜ x 8½.
                                                            Paperbound $2.00

PAPER FOLDING FOR BEGINNERS, *W. D. Murray and F. J. Rigney*
A delightful introduction to the varied and entertaining Japanese art of
origami (paper folding), with a full, crystal-clear text that anticipates every
difficulty; over 275 clearly labeled diagrams of all important stages in creation.
You get results at each stage, since complex figures are logically developed
from simpler ones. 43 different pieces are explained: sailboats, frogs, roosters,
etc. 6 photographic plates. 279 diagrams. 95pp. 5⅝ x 8⅜. Paperbound $1.00

PRINCIPLES OF ART HISTORY,
H. Wölfflin

Analyzing such terms as "baroque," "classic," "neoclassic," "primitive," "picturesque," and 164 different works by artists like Botticelli, van Cleve, Dürer, Hobbema, Holbein, Hals, Rembrandt, Titian, Brueghel, Vermeer, and many others, the author establishes the classifications of art history and style on a firm, concrete basis. This classic of art criticism shows what really occurred between the 14th-century primitives and the sophistication of the 18th century in terms of basic attitudes and philosophies. "A remarkable lesson in the art of seeing," *Sat. Rev. of Literature*. Translated from the 7th German edition. 150 illustrations. 254pp. 6⅛ x 9¼. Paperbound $2.00

PRIMITIVE ART,
Franz Boas

This authoritative and exhaustive work by a great American anthropologist covers the entire gamut of primitive art. Pottery, leatherwork, metal work, stone work, wood, basketry, are treated in detail. Theories of primitive art, historical depth in art history, technical virtuosity, unconscious levels of patterning, symbolism, styles, literature, music, dance, etc. A must book for the interested layman, the anthropologist, artist, handicrafter (hundreds of unusual motifs), and the historian. Over 900 illustrations (50 ceramic vessels, 12 totem poles, etc.). 376pp. 5⅜ x 8. Paperbound $2.25

THE GENTLEMAN AND CABINET MAKER'S DIRECTOR,
Thomas Chippendale

A reprint of the 1762 catalogue of furniture designs that went on to influence generations of English and Colonial and Early Republic American furniture makers. The 200 plates, most of them full-page sized, show Chippendale's designs for French (Louis XV), Gothic, and Chinese-manner chairs, sofas, canopy and dome beds, cornices, chamber organs, cabinets, shaving tables, commodes, picture frames, frets, candle stands, chimney pieces, decorations, etc. The drawings are all elegant and highly detailed; many include construction diagrams and elevations. A supplement of 24 photographs shows surviving pieces of original and Chippendale-style pieces of furniture. Brief biography of Chippendale by N. I. Bienenstock, editor of *Furniture World*. Reproduced from the 1762 edition. 200 plates, plus 19 photographic plates. vi + 249pp. 9⅛ x 12¼. Paperbound $3.50

AMERICAN ANTIQUE FURNITURE: A BOOK FOR AMATEURS,
Edgar G. Miller, Jr.

Standard introduction and practical guide to identification of valuable American antique furniture. 2115 illustrations, mostly photographs taken by the author in 148 private homes, are arranged in chronological order in extensive chapters on chairs, sofas, chests, desks, bedsteads, mirrors, tables, clocks, and other articles. Focus is on furniture accessible to the collector, including simpler pieces and a larger than usual coverage of Empire style. Introductory chapters identify structural elements, characteristics of various styles, how to avoid fakes, etc. "We are frequently asked to name some book on American furniture that will meet the requirements of the novice collector, the beginning dealer, and . . . the general public. . . . We believe Mr. Miller's two volumes more completely satisfy this specification than any other work," *Antiques*. Appendix. Index. Total of vi + 1106pp. 7⅞ x 10¾.
Two volume set, paperbound $7.50

THE BAD CHILD'S BOOK OF BEASTS, MORE BEASTS FOR WORSE CHILDREN, and A MORAL ALPHABET, *H. Belloc*
Hardly and anthology of humorous verse has appeared in the last 50 years without at least a couple of these famous nonsense verses. But one must see the entire volumes — with all the delightful original illustrations by Sir Basil Blackwood — to appreciate fully Belloc's charming and witty verses that play so subacidly on the platitudes of life and morals that beset his day — and ours. A great humor classic. Three books in one. Total of 157pp. 5⅜ x 8.
Paperbound $1.00

THE DEVIL'S DICTIONARY, *Ambrose Bierce*
Sardonic and irreverent barbs puncturing the pomposities and absurdities of American politics, business, religion, literature, and arts, by the country's greatest satirist in the classic tradition. Epigrammatic as Shaw, piercing as Swift, American as Mark Twain, Will Rogers, and Fred Allen, Bierce will always remain the favorite of a small coterie of enthusiasts, and of writers and speakers whom he supplies with "some of the most gorgeous witticisms of the English language" (H. L. Mencken). Over 1000 entries in alphabetical order. 144pp. 5⅜ x 8.
Paperbound $1.00

THE COMPLETE NONSENSE OF EDWARD LEAR.
This is the only complete edition of this master of gentle madness available at a popular price. *A Book of Nonsense, Nonsense Songs, More Nonsense Songs and Stories* in their entirety with all the old favorites that have delighted children and adults for years. The Dong With A Luminous Nose, The Jumblies, The Owl and the Pussycat, and hundreds of other bits of wonderful nonsense. 214 limericks, 3 sets of Nonsense Botany, 5 Nonsense Alphabets, 546 drawings by Lear himself, and much more. 320pp. 5⅜ x 8.
Paperbound $1.00

THE WIT AND HUMOR OF OSCAR WILDE, *ed. by Alvin Redman*
Wilde at his most brilliant, in 1000 epigrams exposing weaknesses and hypocrisies of "civilized" society. Divided into 49 categories—sin, wealth, women, America, etc.—to aid writers, speakers. Includes excerpts from his trials, books, plays, criticism. Formerly "The Epigrams of Oscar Wilde." Introduction by Vyvyan Holland, Wilde's only living son. Introductory essay by editor. 260pp. 5⅜ x 8.
Paperbound $1.00

A CHILD'S PRIMER OF NATURAL HISTORY, *Oliver Herford*
Scarcely an anthology of whimsy and humor has appeared in the last 50 years without a contribution from Oliver Herford. Yet the works from which these examples are drawn have been almost impossible to obtain! Here at last are Herford's improbable definitions of a menagerie of familiar and weird animals, each verse illustrated by the author's own drawings. 24 drawings in 2 colors; 24 additional drawings. vii + 95pp. 6½ x 6.
Paperbound $1.00

THE BROWNIES: THEIR BOOK, *Palmer Cox*
The book that made the Brownies a household word. Generations of readers have enjoyed the antics, predicaments and adventures of these jovial sprites, who emerge from the forest at night to play or to come to the aid of a deserving human. Delightful illustrations by the author decorate nearly every page. 24 short verse tales with 266 illustrations. 155pp. 6⅝ x 9¼.
Paperbound $1.50

CATALOGUE OF DOVER BOOKS

THE PRINCIPLES OF PSYCHOLOGY,
William James
The full long-course, unabridged, of one of the great classics of Western literature and science. Wonderfully lucid descriptions of human mental activity, the stream of thought, consciousness, time perception, memory, imagination, emotions, reason, abnormal phenomena, and similar topics. Original contributions are integrated with the work of such men as Berkeley, Binet, Mills, Darwin, Hume, Kant, Royce, Schopenhauer, Spinoza, Locke, Descartes, Galton, Wundt, Lotze, Herbart, Fechner, and scores of others. All contrasting interpretations of mental phenomena are examined in detail—introspective analysis, philosophical interpretation, and experimental research. "A classic," *Journal of Consulting Psychology.* "The main lines are as valid as ever," *Psychoanalytical Quarterly.* "Standard reading . . . a classic of interpretation," *Psychiatric Quarterly.* 94 illustrations. 1408pp. 5⅜ x 8.
Vol. 1 Paperbound $2.50, Vol. 2 Paperbound $2.50,
The set $5.00

VISUAL ILLUSIONS: THEIR CAUSES, CHARACTERISTICS AND APPLICATIONS,
M. Luckiesh
"Seeing is deceiving," asserts the author of this introduction to virtually every type of optical illusion known. The text both describes and explains the principles involved in color illusions, figure-ground, distance illusions, etc. 100 photographs, drawings and diagrams prove how easy it is to fool the sense: circles that aren't round, parallel lines that seem to bend, stationary figures that seem to move as you stare at them — illustration after illustration strains our credulity at what we see. Fascinating book from many points of view, from applications for artists, in camouflage, etc. to the psychology of vision. New introduction by William Ittleson, Dept. of Psychology, Queens College. Index. Bibliography. xxi + 252pp. 5⅜ x 8½. Paperbound $1.50

FADS AND FALLACIES IN THE NAME OF SCIENCE,
Martin Gardner
This is the standard account of various cults, quack systems, and delusions which have masqueraded as science: hollow earth fanatics. Reich and orgone sex energy, dianetics, Atlantis, multiple moons, Forteanism, flying saucers, medical fallacies like iridiagnosis, zone therapy, etc. A new chapter has been added on Bridey Murphy, psionics, and other recent manifestations in this field. This is a fair, reasoned appraisal of eccentric theory which provides excellent inoculation against cleverly masked nonsense. "Should be read by everyone, scientist and non-scientist alike," R. T. Birge, Prof. Emeritus of Physics, Univ. of California; Former President, American Physical Society. Index. x + 365pp. 5⅜ x 8. Paperbound $1.85

ILLUSIONS AND DELUSIONS OF THE SUPERNATURAL AND THE OCCULT,
D. H. Rawcliffe
Holds up to rational examination hundreds of persistent delusions including crystal gazing, automatic writing, table turning, mediumistic trances, mental healing, stigmata, lycanthropy, live burial, the Indian Rope Trick, spiritualism, dowsing, telepathy, clairvoyance, ghosts, ESP, etc. The author explains and exposes the mental and physical deceptions involved, making this not only an exposé of supernatural phenomena, but a valuable exposition of characteristic types of abnormal psychology. Originally titled "The Psychology of the Occult." 14 illustrations. Index. 551pp. 5⅜ x 8. Paperbound $2.25

FAIRY TALE COLLECTIONS, *edited by Andrew Lang*
Andrew Lang's fairy tale collections make up the richest shelf-full of traditional children's stories anywhere available. Lang supervised the translation of stories from all over the world—familiar European tales collected by Grimm, animal stories from Negro Africa, myths of primitive Australia, stories from Russia, Hungary, Iceland, Japan, and many other countries. Lang's selection of translations are unusually high; many authorities consider that the most familiar tales find their best versions in these volumes. All collections are richly decorated and illustrated by H. J. Ford and other artists.

THE BLUE FAIRY BOOK. 37 stories. 138 illustrations. ix + 390pp. 5⅜ x 8½.
Paperbound $1.50

THE GREEN FAIRY BOOK. 42 stories. 100 illustrations. xiii + 366pp. 5⅜ x 8½.
Paperbound $1.50

THE BROWN FAIRY BOOK. 32 stories. 50 illustrations, 8 in color. xii + 350pp. 5⅜ x 8½.
Paperbound $1.50

THE BEST TALES OF HOFFMANN, *edited by E. F. Bleiler*
10 stories by E. T. A. Hoffmann, one of the greatest of all writers of fantasy. The tales include "The Golden Flower Pot," "Automata," "A New Year's Eve Adventure," "Nutcracker and the King of Mice," "Sand-Man," and others. Vigorous characterizations of highly eccentric personalities, remarkably imaginative situations, and intensely fast pacing has made these tales popular all over the world for 150 years. Editor's introduction. 7 drawings by Hoffmann. xxxiii + 419pp. 5⅜ x 8½.
Paperbound $2.00

GHOST AND HORROR STORIES OF AMBROSE BIERCE,
edited by E. F. Bleiler
Morbid, eerie, horrifying tales of possessed poets, shabby aristocrats, revived corpses, and haunted malefactors. Widely acknowledged as the best of their kind between Poe and the moderns, reflecting their author's inner torment and bitter view of life. Includes "Damned Thing," "The Middle Toe of the Right Foot," "The Eyes of the Panther," "Visions of the Night," "Moxon's Master," and over a dozen others. Editor's introduction. xxii + 199pp. 5⅜ x 8½.
Paperbound $1.25

THREE GOTHIC NOVELS, *edited by E. F. Bleiler*
Originators of the still popular Gothic novel form, influential in ushering in early 19th-century Romanticism. Horace Walpole's *Castle of Otranto*, William Beckford's *Vathek*, John Polidori's *The Vampyre*, and a *Fragment* by Lord Byron are enjoyable as exciting reading or as documents in the history of English literature. Editor's introduction. xi + 291pp. 5⅜ x 8½.
Paperbound $2.00

BEST GHOST STORIES OF LEFANU, *edited by E. F. Bleiler*
Though admired by such critics as V. S. Pritchett, Charles Dickens and Henry James, ghost stories by the Irish novelist Joseph Sheridan LeFanu have never become as widely known as his detective fiction. About half of the 16 stories in this collection have never before been available in America. Collection includes "Carmilla" (perhaps the best vampire story ever written), "The Haunted Baronet," "The Fortunes of Sir Robert Ardagh," and the classic "Green Tea." Editor's introduction. 7 contemporary illustrations. Portrait of LeFanu. xii + 467pp. 5⅜ x 8.
Paperbound $2.00

CATALOGUE OF DOVER BOOKS

EASY-TO-DO ENTERTAINMENTS AND DIVERSIONS WITH COINS, CARDS, STRING, PAPER AND MATCHES, *R. M. Abraham*
Over 300 tricks, games and puzzles will provide young readers with absorbing fun. Sections on card games; paper-folding; tricks with coins, matches and pieces of string; games for the agile; toy-making from common household objects; mathematical recreations; and 50 miscellaneous pastimes. Anyone in charge of groups of youngsters, including hard-pressed parents, and in need of suggestions on how to keep children sensibly amused and quietly content will find this book indispensable. Clear, simple text, copious number of delightful line drawings and illustrative diagrams. Originally titled "Winter Nights' Entertainments." Introduction by Lord Baden Powell. 329 illustrations. v + 186pp. 5⅜ x 8½.   Paperbound $1.00

AN INTRODUCTION TO CHESS MOVES AND TACTICS SIMPLY EXPLAINED, *Leonard Barden*
Beginner's introduction to the royal game. Names, possible moves of the pieces, definitions of essential terms, how games are won, etc. explained in 30-odd pages. With this background you'll be able to sit right down and play. Balance of book teaches strategy — openings, middle game, typical endgame play, and suggestions for improving your game. A sample game is fully analyzed. True middle-level introduction, teaching you all the essentials without oversimplifying or losing you in a maze of detail. 58 figures. 102pp. 5⅜ x 8½.   Paperbound $1.00

LASKER'S MANUAL OF CHESS, *Dr. Emanuel Lasker*
Probably the greatest chess player of modern times, Dr. Emanuel Lasker held the world championship 28 years, independent of passing schools or fashions. This unmatched study of the game, chiefly for intermediate to skilled players, analyzes basic methods, combinations, position play, the aesthetics of chess, dozens of different openings, etc., with constant reference to great modern games. Contains a brilliant exposition of Steinitz's important theories. Introduction by Fred Reinfeld. Tables of Lasker's tournament record. 3 indices. 308 diagrams. 1 photograph. xxx + 349pp. 5⅜ x 8.   Paperbound $2.25

COMBINATIONS: THE HEART OF CHESS, *Irving Chernev*
Step-by-step from simple combinations to complex, this book, by a well-known chess writer, shows you the intricacies of pins, counter-pins, knight forks, and smothered mates. Other chapters show alternate lines of play to those taken in actual championship games; boomerang combinations; classic examples of brilliant combination play by Nimzovich, Rubinstein, Tarrasch, Botvinnik, Alekhine and Capablanca. Index. 356 diagrams. ix + 245pp. 5⅜ x 8½.   Paperbound $1.85

HOW TO SOLVE CHESS PROBLEMS, *K. S. Howard*
Full of practical suggestions for the fan or the beginner — who knows only the moves of the chessmen. Contains preliminary section and 58 two-move, 46 three-move, and 8 four-move problems composed by 27 outstanding American problem creators in the last 30 years. Explanation of all terms and exhaustive index. "Just what is wanted for the student," Brian Harley. 112 problems, solutions. vi + 171pp. 5⅜ x 8.   Paperbound $1.35

SOCIAL THOUGHT FROM LORE TO SCIENCE,
H. E. Barnes and H. Becker
An immense survey of sociological thought and ways of viewing, studying, planning, and reforming society from earliest times to the present. Includes thought on society of preliterate peoples, ancient non-Western cultures, and every great movement in Europe, America, and modern Japan. Analyzes hundreds of great thinkers: Plato, Augustine, Bodin, Vico, Montesquieu, Herder, Comte, Marx, etc. Weighs the contributions of utopians, sophists, fascists and communists; economists, jurists, philosophers, ecclesiastics, and every 19th and 20th century school of scientific sociology, anthropology, and social psychology throughout the world. Combines topical, chronological, and regional approaches, treating the evolution of social thought as a process rather than as a series of mere topics. "Impressive accuracy, competence, and discrimination . . . easily the best single survey," *Nation*. Thoroughly revised, with new material up to 1960. 2 indexes. Over 2200 bibliographical notes. Three volume set. Total of 1586pp. 5⅜ x 8.
Vol. 1 Paperbound $2.75, Vol. 2 Paperbound $2.75, Vol. 3 Paperbound $2.50
The set $8.00

A HISTORY OF HISTORICAL WRITING, *Harry Elmer Barnes*
Virtually the only adequate survey of the whole course of historical writing in a single volume. Surveys developments from the beginnings of historiography in the ancient Near East and the Classical World, up through the Cold War. Covers major historians in detail, shows interrelationship with cultural background, makes clear individual contributions, evaluates and estimates importance; also enormously rich upon minor authors and thinkers who are usually passed over. Packed with scholarship and learning, clear, easily written. Indispensable to every student of history. Revised and enlarged up to 1961. Index and bibliography. xv + 442pp. 5⅜ x 8½. Paperbound $2.50

JOHANN SEBASTIAN BACH, *Philipp Spitta*
The complete and unabridged text of the definitive study of Bach. Written some 70 years ago, it is still unsurpassed for its coverage of nearly all aspects of Bach's life and work. There could hardly be a finer non-technical introduction to Bach's music than the detailed, lucid analyses which Spitta provides for hundreds of individual pieces. 26 solid pages are devoted to the B minor mass, for example, and 30 pages to the glorious St. Matthew Passion. This monumental set also includes a major analysis of the music of the 18th century: Buxtehude, Pachelbel, etc. "Unchallenged as the last word on one of the supreme geniuses of music," John Barkham, *Saturday Review Syndicate*. Total of 1819pp. Heavy cloth binding. 5⅜ x 8.
Two volume set, clothbound $13.50

BEETHOVEN AND HIS NINE SYMPHONIES, *George Grove*
In this modern middle-level classic of musicology Grove not only analyzes all nine of Beethoven's symphonies very thoroughly in terms of their musical structure, but also discusses the circumstances under which they were written, Beethoven's stylistic development, and much other background material. This is an extremely rich book, yet very easily followed; it is highly recommended to anyone seriously interested in music. Over 250 musical passages. Index. viii + 407pp. 5⅜ x 8. Paperbound $2.00

THREE SCIENCE FICTION NOVELS,
John Taine
Acknowledged by many as the best SF writer of the 1920's, Taine (under the name Eric Temple Bell) was also a Professor of Mathematics of considerable renown. Reprinted here are *The Time Stream*, generally considered Taine's best, *The Greatest Game*, a biological-fiction novel, and *The Purple Sapphire*, involving a supercivilization of the past. Taine's stories tie fantastic narratives to frameworks of original and logical scientific concepts. Speculation is often profound on such questions as the nature of time, concept of entropy, cyclical universes, etc. 4 contemporary illustrations. v + 532pp. 5⅜ x 8⅜.
Paperbound $2.00

SEVEN SCIENCE FICTION NOVELS,
H. G. Wells
Full unabridged texts of 7 science-fiction novels of the master. Ranging from biology, physics, chemistry, astronomy, to sociology and other studies, Mr. Wells extrapolates whole worlds of strange and intriguing character. "One will have to go far to match this for entertainment, excitement, and sheer pleasure . . ."*New York Times*. Contents: The Time Machine, The Island of Dr. Moreau, The First Men in the Moon, The Invisible Man, The War of the Worlds, The Food of the Gods, In The Days of the Comet. 1015pp. 5⅜ x 8.
Clothbound $5.00

28 SCIENCE FICTION STORIES OF H. G. WELLS.
Two full, unabridged novels, *Men Like Gods* and *Star Begotten*, plus 26 short stories by the master science-fiction writer of all time! Stories of space, time, invention, exploration, futuristic adventure. Partial contents: *The Country of the Blind, In the Abyss, The Crystal Egg, The Man Who Could Work Miracles, A Story of Days to Come, The Empire of the Ants, The Magic Shop, The Valley of the Spiders, A Story of the Stone Age, Under the Knife, Sea Raiders,* etc. An indispensable collection for the library of anyone interested in science fiction adventure. 928pp. 5⅜ x 8.
Clothbound $4.50

THREE MARTIAN NOVELS,
Edgar Rice Burroughs
Complete, unabridged reprinting, in one volume, of Thuvia, Maid of Mars; Chessmen of Mars; The Master Mind of Mars. Hours of science-fiction adventure by a modern master storyteller. Reset in large clear type for easy reading. 16 illustrations by J. Allen St. John. vi + 490pp. 5⅜ x 8½.
Paperbound $1.85

AN INTELLECTUAL AND CULTURAL HISTORY OF THE WESTERN WORLD,
Harry Elmer Barnes
Monumental 3-volume survey of intellectual development of Europe from primitive cultures to the present day. Every significant product of human intellect traced through history: art, literature, mathematics, physical sciences, medicine, music, technology, social sciences, religions, jurisprudence, education, etc. Presentation is lucid and specific, analyzing in detail specific discoveries, theories, literary works, and so on. Revised (1965) by recognized scholars in specialized fields under the direction of Prof. Barnes. Revised bibliography. Indexes. 24 illustrations. Total of xxix + 1318pp.
Vol. 1 Paperbound $2.00, Vol. 2 Paperbound $2.00, Vol. 3 Paperbound $2.00,
The set $6.00

HEAR ME TALKIN' TO YA, *edited by Nat Shapiro and Nat Hentoff*
In their own words, Louis Armstrong, King Oliver, Fletcher Henderson, Bunk
Johnson, Bix Beiderbecke, Billy Holiday, Fats Waller, Jelly Roll Morton,
Duke Ellington, and many others comment on the origins of jazz in New
Orleans and its growth in Chicago's South Side, Kansas City's jam sessions,
Depression Harlem, and the modernism of the West Coast schools. Taken
from taped conversations, letters, magazine articles, other first-hand sources.
Editors' introduction. xvi + 429pp. 5⅜ x 8½.   Paperbound $2.00

THE JOURNAL OF HENRY D. THOREAU
A 25-year record by the great American observer and critic, as complete a
record of a great man's inner life as is anywhere available. Thoreau's Journals
served him as raw material for his formal pieces, as a place where he could
develop his ideas, as an outlet for his interests in wild life and plants, in
writing as an art, in classics of literature, Walt Whitman and other contemporaries, in politics, slavery, individual's relation to the State, etc. The
Journals present a portrait of a remarkable man, and are an observant social
history. Unabridged republication of 1906 edition, Bradford Torrey and
Francis H. Allen, editors. Illustrations. Total of 1888pp. 8⅜ x 12¼.
                              Two volume set, clothbound $25.00

A SHAKESPEARIAN GRAMMAR, *E. A. Abbott*
Basic reference to Shakespeare and his contemporaries, explaining through
thousands of quotations from Shakespeare, Jonson, Beaumont and Fletcher,
North's *Plutarch* and other sources the grammatical usage differing from the
modern. First published in 1870 and written by a scholar who spent much of
his life isolating principles of Elizabethan language, the book is unlikely ever
to be superseded. Indexes. xxiv + 511pp. 5⅜ x 8½.   Paperbound $2.75

FOLK-LORE OF SHAKESPEARE, *T. F. Thistelton Dyer*
Classic study, drawing from Shakespeare a large body of references to supernatural beliefs, terminology of falconry and hunting, games and sports, good
luck charms, marriage customs, folk medicines, superstitions about plants,
animals, birds, argot of the underworld, sexual slang of London, proverbs,
drinking customs, weather lore, and much else. From full compilation comes
a mirror of the 17th-century popular mind. Index. ix + 526pp. 5⅜ x 8½.
                                            Paperbound $2.50

THE NEW VARIORUM SHAKESPEARE, *edited by H. H. Furness*
By far the richest editions of the plays ever produced in any country or
language. Each volume contains complete text (usually First Folio) of the
play, all variants in Quarto and other Folio texts, editorial changes by every
major editor to Furness's own time (1900), footnotes to obscure references or
language, extensive quotes from literature of Shakespearian criticism, essays
on plot sources (often reprinting sources in full), and much more.

HAMLET, *edited by H. H. Furness*
Total of xxvi + 905pp. 5⅜ x 8½.   Two volume set, paperbound $4.75

TWELFTH NIGHT, *edited by H. H. Furness*
Index. xxii + 434pp. 5⅜ x 8½.   Paperbound $2.25

CATALOGUE OF DOVER BOOKS

La Boheme by Giacomo Puccini,
translated and introduced by Ellen H. Bleiler
Complete handbook for the operagoer, with everything needed for full enjoyment except the musical score itself. Complete Italian libretto, with new, modern English line-by-line translation—the only libretto printing all repeats; biography of Puccini; the librettists; background to the opera, Murger's La Boheme, etc.; circumstances of composition and performances; plot summary; and pictorial section of 73 illustrations showing Puccini, famous singers and performances, etc. Large clear type for easy reading. 124pp. 5⅜ x 8½.
Paperbound $1.00

Antonio Stradivari: His Life and Work (1644-1737),
W. Henry Hill, Arthur F. Hill, and Alfred E. Hill
Still the only book that really delves into life and art of the incomparable Italian craftsman, maker of the finest musical instruments in the world today. The authors, expert violin-makers themselves, discuss Stradivari's ancestry, his construction and finishing techniques, distinguished characteristics of many of his instruments and their locations. Included, too, is story of introduction of his instruments into France, England, first revelation of their supreme merit, and information on his labels, number of instruments made, prices, mystery of ingredients of his varnish, tone of pre-1684 Stradivari violin and changes between 1684 and 1690. An extremely interesting, informative account for all music lovers, from craftsman to concert-goer. Republication of original (1902) edition. New introduction by Sydney Beck, Head of Rare Book and Manuscript Collections, Music Division, New York Public Library. Analytical index by Rembert Wurlitzer. Appendixes. 68 illustrations. 30 full-page plates. 4 in color. xxvi + 315pp. 5⅜ x 8½.
Paperbound $2.25

Musical Autographs from Monteverdi to Hindemith,
Emanuel Winternitz
For beauty, for intrinsic interest, for perspective on the composer's personality, for subtleties of phrasing, shading, emphasis indicated in the autograph but suppressed in the printed score, the mss. of musical composition are fascinating documents which repay close study in many different ways. This 2-volume work reprints facsimiles of mss. by virtually every major composer, and many minor figures—196 examples in all. A full text points out what can be learned from mss., analyzes each sample. Index. Bibliography. 18 figures. 196 plates. Total of 170pp. of text. 7⅞ x 10¾.
Vol. 1 Paperbound $2.00, Vol. 2 Paperbound $2.00,
The set $4.00

J. S. Bach,
Albert Schweitzer
One of the few great full-length studies of Bach's life and work, and the study upon which Schweitzer's renown as a musicologist rests. On first appearance (1911), revolutionized Bach performance. The only writer on Bach to be musicologist, performing musician, and student of history, theology and philosophy, Schweitzer contributes particularly full sections on history of German Protestant church music, theories on motivic pictorial representations in vocal music, and practical suggestions for performance. Translated by Ernest Newman. Indexes. 5 illustrations. 650 musical examples. Total of xix + 928pp. 5⅜ x 8½.
Vol. 1 Paperbound $2.00, Vol. 2 Paperbound $2.00,
The set $4.00

THE METHODS OF ETHICS, *Henry Sidgwick*
Propounding no organized system of its own, study subjects every major methodological approach to ethics to rigorous, objective analysis. Study discusses and relates ethical thought of Plato, Aristotle, Bentham, Clarke, Butler, Hobbes, Hume, Mill, Spencer, Kant, and dozens of others. Sidgwick retains conclusions from each system which follow from ethical premises, rejecting the faulty. Considered by many in the field to be among the most important treatises on ethical philosophy. Appendix. Index. xlvii + 528pp. 5⅜ x 8½.
Paperbound $2.50

TEUTONIC MYTHOLOGY, *Jakob Grimm*
A milestone in Western culture; the work which established on a modern basis the study of history of religions and comparative religions. 4-volume work assembles and interprets everything available on religious and folkloristic beliefs of Germanic people (including Scandinavians, Anglo-Saxons, etc.). Assembling material from such sources as Tacitus, surviving Old Norse and Icelandic texts, archeological remains, folktales, surviving superstitions, comparative traditions, linguistic analysis, etc. Grimm explores pagan deities, heroes, folklore of nature, religious practices, and every other area of pagan German belief. To this day, the unrivaled, definitive, exhaustive study. Translated by J. S. Stallybrass from 4th (1883) German edition. Indexes. Total of lxxvii + 1887pp. 5⅜ x 8½.   Four volume set, paperbound $10.00

THE I CHING, *translated by James Legge*
Called "The Book of Changes" in English, this is one of the Five Classics edited by Confucius, basic and central to Chinese thought. Explains perhaps the most complex system of divination known, founded on the theory that all things happening at any one time have characteristic features which can be isolated and related. Significant in Oriental studies, in history of religions and philosophy, and also to Jungian psychoanalysis and other areas of modern European thought. Index. Appendixes. 6 plates. xxi + 448pp. 5⅜ x 8½.
Paperbound $2.75

HISTORY OF ANCIENT PHILOSOPHY, *W. Windelband*
One of the clearest, most accurate comprehensive surveys of Greek and Roman philosophy. Discusses ancient philosophy in general, intellectual life in Greece in the 7th and 6th centuries B.C., Thales, Anaximander, Anaximenes, Heraclitus, the Eleatics, Empedocles, Anaxagoras, Leucippus, the Pythagoreans, the Sophists, Socrates, Democritus (20 pages), Plato (50 pages), Aristotle (70 pages), the Peripatetics, Stoics, Epicureans, Sceptics, Neo-platonists, Christian Apologists, etc. 2nd German edition translated by H. E. Cushman. xv + 393pp. 5⅜ x 8.   Paperbound $2.25

THE PALACE OF PLEASURE, *William Painter*
Elizabethan versions of Italian and French novels from *The Decameron*, Cinthio, Straparola, Queen Margaret of Navarre, and other continental sources — the very work that provided Shakespeare and dozens of his contemporaries with many of their plots and sub-plots and, therefore, justly considered one of the most influential books in all English literature. It is also a book that any reader will still enjoy. Total of cviii + 1,224pp.
Three volume set, Paperbound $6.75

THE WONDERFUL WIZARD OF OZ, *L. F. Baum*
All the original W. W. Denslow illustrations in full color—as much a part of "The Wizard" as Tenniel's drawings are of "Alice in Wonderland." "The Wizard" is still America's best-loved fairy tale, in which, as the author expresses it, "The wonderment and joy are retained and the heartaches and nightmares left out." Now today's young readers can enjoy every word and wonderful picture of the original book. New introduction by Martin Gardner. A Baum bibliography. 23 full-page color plates. viii + 268pp. 5⅜ x 8.
Paperbound $1.50

THE MARVELOUS LAND OF OZ, *L. F. Baum*
This is the equally enchanting sequel to the "Wizard," continuing the adventures of the Scarecrow and the Tin Woodman. The hero this time is a little boy named Tip, and all the delightful Oz magic is still present. This is the Oz book with the Animated Saw-Horse, the Woggle-Bug, and Jack Pumpkinhead. All the original John R. Neill illustrations, 10 in full color. 287pp. 5⅜ x 8.
Paperbound $1.50

ALICE'S ADVENTURES UNDER GROUND, *Lewis Carroll*
The original *Alice in Wonderland*, hand-lettered and illustrated by Carroll himself, and originally presented as a Christmas gift to a child-friend. Adults as well as children will enjoy this charming volume, reproduced faithfully in this Dover edition. While the story is essentially the same, there are slight changes, and Carroll's spritely drawings present an intriguing alternative to the famous Tenniel illustrations. One of the most popular books in Dover's catalogue. Introduction by Martin Gardner. 38 illustrations. 128pp. 5⅜ x 8½.
Paperbound $1.00

THE NURSERY "ALICE," *Lewis Carroll*
While most of us consider *Alice in Wonderland* a story for children of all ages, Carroll himself felt it was beyond younger children. He therefore provided this simplified version, illustrated with the famous Tenniel drawings enlarged and colored in delicate tints, for children aged "from Nought to Five." Dover's edition of this now rare classic is a faithful copy of the 1889 printing, including 20 illustrations by Tenniel, and front and back covers reproduced in full color. Introduction by Martin Gardner. xxiii + 67pp. 6⅛ x 9¼.
Paperbound $1.50

THE STORY OF KING ARTHUR AND HIS KNIGHTS, *Howard Pyle*
A fast-paced, exciting retelling of the best known Arthurian legends for young readers by one of America's best story tellers and illustrators. The sword Excalibur, wooing of Guinevere, Merlin and his downfall, adventures of Sir Pellias and Gawaine, and others. The pen and ink illustrations are vividly imagined and wonderfully drawn. 41 illustrations. xviii + 313pp. 6⅛ x 9¼.
Paperbound $1.50

Prices subject to change without notice.

Available at your book dealer or write for free catalogue to Dept. Adsci, Dover Publications, Inc., 180 Varick St., N.Y., N.Y. 10014. Dover publishes more than 150 books each year on science, elementary and advanced mathematics, biology, music, art, literary history, social sciences and other areas.